GUNPOWDER & EMBERS

BAEN BOOKS by JOHN RINGO

LAST JUDGEMENT'S FIRE
(WITH KACEY EZELL AND CHRISTOPHER L. SMITH)
Gunpowder and Embers
Smoke and the Water (forthcoming)

BLACK TIDE RISING
Under a Graveyard Sky
To Sail a Darkling Sea
Islands of Rage and Hope
Strands of Sorrow

The Valley of Shadows
(with Mike Massa)
River of Night
(with Mike Massa)

Black Tide Rising
(edited with Gary Poole)
Voices from the Fall
(edited with Gary Poole)

MONSTER HUNTER MEMOIRS
(WITH LARRY CORREIA)
Monster Hunter Memoirs: Grunge
Monster Hunter Memoirs: Sinners
Monster Hunter Memoirs: Saints

TROY RISING
Live Free or Die
Citadel
The Hot Gate

LEGACY OF THE ALDENATA
A Hymn Before Battle
Gust Front
When the Devil Dances
Hell's Faire
The Hero (with Michael Z. Williamson)
Cally's War (with Julie Cochrane)
Watch on the Rhine (with
Tom Kratman)

Sister Time (with Julie Cochrane)
Yellow Eyes (with Tom Kratman)
Honor of the Clan
(with Julie Cochrane)
Eye of the Storm

COUNCIL WARS
There Will Be Dragons
Emerald Sea
Against the Tide
East of the Sun, West of the Moon

INTO THE LOOKING GLASS
Into the Looking Glass
Vorpal Blade (with Travis S. Taylor)
Manxome Foe (with Travis S. Taylor)
Claws that Catch (with Travis S. Taylor)

EMPIRE OF MAN
(WITH DAVID WEBER)
March Upcountry and
March to the Sea
(collected in *Empire of Man*)
March to the Stars and *We Few*
(collected in *Throne of Stars*)

SPECIAL CIRCUMSTANCES
Princess of Wands
Queen of Wands

PALADIN OF SHADOWS
Ghost
Kildar
Choosers of the Slain
Unto the Breach
A Deeper Blue

Tiger by the Tail
(with Ryan Sear)

STANDALONE TITLES
The Last Centurion
Citizens (edited
with Brian M. Thomsen)
Von Neumann's War
(with Travis S. Taylor)
The Road to Damascus
(with Linda Evans)

To purchase any of these titles in e-book form,
please go to www.baen.com.

GUNPOWDER & EMBERS

JOHN RINGO
KACEY EZELL
CHRISTOPHER L. SMITH

Gᴜɴᴘᴏᴡᴅᴇʀ & Eᴍʙᴇʀs

This is a work of fiction. All the characters and events portrayed in this book are fictional, and any resemblance to real people or incidents is purely coincidental.

A Baen Books Original

Baen Publishing Enterprises
P.O. Box 1403
Riverdale, NY 10471
www.baen.com

ISBN: 978-1-9821-2428-1

Cover art by Dave Seeley

First printing, January 2020

Distributed by Simon & Schuster
1230 Avenue of the Americas
New York, NY 10020

Library of Congress Cataloging-in-Publication Data

Names: Ringo, John, 1963– author. | Ezell, Kacey, author. | Smith,
    Christopher L. (Christopher Lee), 1975– author.
Title: Gunpowder and embers / John Ringo, Kacey Ezell, Christopher L. Smith.
Description: Riverdale, NY : Baen, 2020. | Series: Last judgement's fire
Identifiers: LCCN 2019041770 | ISBN 9781982124281 (hardcover)
Subjects: GSAFD: Science fiction. | Fantasy fiction.
Classification: LCC PS3568.I577 G86 2020 | DDC 813/.54—dc23
LC record available at https://lccn.loc.gov/2019041770

Pages by Joy Freeman (www.pagesbyjoy.com)
Printed in the United States of America
10 9 8 7 6 5 4 3 2 1

As always
For Captain Tamara Long, USAF
Born: May 12, 1979
Died: March 23, 2003, Afghanistan
You fly with the angels now.

For EZ, the hero of my story
and coolest guy I'll ever meet.
And for my mom, LeEllen McCartney,
who taught me to love dragons. —kc

For Sandra K. Smith

February 27, 1947–October 31, 2018

Thanks for being my biggest fan, Mom.
I finally wrote one you could read
without covering your eyes.

PROLOGUE

ARIEL FELT EXCITEMENT SKITTER ALONG HER NERVES AS HER mother smoothed her hair back with trembling fingers.

"So beautiful," her mother whispered in her roughened, wasted voice. "Your hair like queensilk, so soft and full. Dark like your eyes, like the finest warrior's chitin."

"Thank you, mother," Ariel said. Despite the illogic of emotions, something warm and joyous curled within her breast at her mother's words. For once, the older woman was noticing Ariel—really paying attention to *her*. Normally, she was far too busy fighting to complete her tasks and win her spot in the larvae chamber. Which was a good thing. The colony needed the full efforts of Ariel's mother and all of the other acolytes in order to thrive.

And full effort it was, Ariel thought. The number of Holy Warriors, workers, and drones had grown considerably recently. The demand for power, and therefore acolyte labor, had increased exponentially.

Ariel herself had begun working shortly after she could walk. Her mother had taught her to read, and then she'd been shown to the turbine chamber, to assist the acolytes there. She'd started by cleaning and fetching things for the adults, and as her body and mind had developed, she'd taken over responsibility for the upkeep and maintenance of the all-important turbines. The turbines produced the electricity that fed the colony. Without power, there would be no nest, and the Queen would deny them her Blessings and protection, and the colony would die. Any who escaped would be reduced to grubbing in the dirt like the unbelievers. She'd been taught that this could not be allowed to happen, so as the older acolytes had faded away, Ariel had naturally stepped into their roles. This was the order of things.

Only the hardest, most successful workers were allowed into the bliss of the larvae chamber. The others (which all too frequently included both of Ariel's parents; they were growing too frail to be truly useful) were left to suffer the tremors and pains of being left wanting.

Not today, though. Today, Ariel's mother would not only be there in the chamber, she would have a prime position from which to receive the Child's Blessing. In fact, the only person better placed than Ariel's mother would be Ariel herself. For today was Ariel's First Blessing. She had come of age and could finally, at sixteen years old, take her place as an adult working for the good of the colony.

"I am ready," Ariel said, smoothing her hands down the front of her smocklike garment. Though not nearly as fine as queensilk, the adult tunic was far smoother and better fitting than anything she'd been allowed to wear as a juvenile. It had been made from true silk, spun by specialized workers who had emerged from metamorphoses with a specialized gland on their forelegs. Only useful adults wore true silk. Juvenile humans made do with cast-offs and whatever they could scrounge from plant fibers.

That same silk lined the tunnel they followed toward the heart of the colony, dimming the lights shining at distant intervals along the top of the walls. All around them, faces peered out of doorways and alcoves. Hungry, longing looks creased the countenances of those other acolytes following their progress. Some called out to Ariel's mother. Some, mostly children she knew, or had taught, watched with wide eyes. Some merely fell in behind Ariel, hoping to be allowed to be part of the ceremony. Ariel didn't know if they'd be successful or not. She'd never seen a Child's Blessing before.

As they neared the chamber, the compound eyes of the Holy Warriors began to replace the hollowed, hungry stare of human acolytes. As was proper, Ariel dropped her gaze to the floor and concentrated on following her mother through the twisting, silk-lined tunnels. The sound of mandibles clicking behind her made Ariel very glad that her mother had been thorough anointing Ariel's new clothing. Without the proper scent, the Holy Warriors wouldn't recognize her as an acolyte and they would attack to protect the colony. Especially this deep, near the precious Children and the Almighty Queen.

Soon, they came to the massive double doors leading to the chamber. Ariel had been told that they'd once closed completely, sealing off the chamber from the rest of the world. Over the decades since the Arrival, however, layers of silk had wedged them open until they stood silent—immobile sentinels marking the entrance to the holiest of holies. The heart of the nest. The chamber.

It was very dim inside. The only light came from a few ancient fixtures that some acolyte or another had rigged up by running lines of the precious queensilk to them. Like in the hallway outside, these fixtures hung high on the walls, shrouded in layers of the conductive silk. Diffused light left the room in a kind of perpetual twilight.

At least to human eyes. The holy ones had other ways of sensing, ones that didn't rely upon the presence of light.

One of the Holy Warriors came forward and inspected Ariel, her six feet surprisingly soft and quick for an animal stretching over four meters in length. Like the tiny ants she resembled, the warrior had a long, lean body encased in a tough exoskeleton with the overwhelmingly large mandibles of her warrior caste. These mandibles opened and closed as she moved, allowing Ariel to glimpse the jagged, cutting edges that lined each meter-long appendage. The warrior stood so close that Ariel imagined she could see her antennae quiver as she tasted the air around Ariel, testing for the proper anointing chemicals. After a breathless moment, the warrior dipped her head and stepped to the side, allowing Ariel to pass.

"Follow the Holy Warrior," Ariel's mother murmured, her voice threaded through with equal parts reverence and excitement. Ariel steeled her own nerves and obeyed, keeping her eyes on the fur-covered chitin of her guide's posterior. With every step onto the increasingly thick silk, the analytical part of Ariel's mind whispered that her steps would be noticed and transmitted as a series of vibrations to every warrior present...and to the

Almighty Queen herself. Perhaps for the first time, she would know of Ariel's existence.

The thought was both frightening and exhilarating.

Finally, the tunnel emptied out into an open area, a three-dimensional obloid bubble within the sea of queensilk. Very little light penetrated here, just enough for Ariel to make out the outline of her guide and to see that the walls forming the obloid were pocked with alcoves, some small, some larger. Her steps must have slowed, because her guide turned around and clicked her oversized mandibles in a warning. Ariel jumped. The Holy Warrior's message was clear: Follow instructions or be destroyed. They would brook no disobedience here in this holiest of places. Ariel swallowed hard and followed closer, mentally berating herself for her inattention.

The bubble was large enough that the top ceiling and both side walls curved away into darkness as they made their way directly across from the entrance. Once the opposite wall came into view, Ariel could see that her guide was leading her to one of the smallest alcoves, just a meter or so off the center path that they'd taken.

"A small one, that is good," Ariel's mother breathed, making Ariel jump again. She'd quite forgotten her mother's presence during this unnerving journey. "The larger ones give much more of a powerful Blessing. It might be too much for you for your first time."

Ariel nodded and once again noticed the bit of longing she'd heard in her mother's voice. She'd always sounded thus. And finally Ariel would learn why.

The Holy Warrior stood aside and Ariel's mother murmured that this was Ariel's signal to approach the alcove.

Within, lit only by the faintest of light filtering through from somewhere, lay the Child. White and helpless, she lay nestled in the silk alcove, wriggling and opening her mouth. Ariel's mother made a cooing sound.

"Is she not beautiful?" Ariel's mother whispered as she placed her own hand on the back of Ariel's neck. "She is perfect for your first time. Now, simply put forth your hand to call down her blessing upon you."

Ariel gulped and reached forward, fingers trembling. With her mind a riot of cautions and self-doubt, she brushed her fingertips against the invisibly fine hairs covering the Child's white, soft chitin.

Pleasure exploded within her body, roaring up from her loins to engulf each of her senses in an overload of joy. Every nerve ending lit up in incandescent revelry. Her ears rang with the melody of gladness. Her lips tasted of pure indulgence. The scent of bliss engulfed her, threatening to drown her in such happiness that she'd never breathe again. All of it closed around her, leaving her gasping in the darkness as delectation overwhelmed her mind.

William Schilling, Baron of Ironhelm, stared intently at the messenger before him.

"Nothing? Nothing at all?" Schilling said, scowling.

"No, milord, no news from your man in the Hive," the messenger said, carefully keeping his gaze on the floor. "His handler waited an extra week. It's unusual, to say the least."

"Highly." Schilling steepled his fingers before his chin. "It's possible our friend ran afoul of the Queen, or found himself in the belly of one of her soldiers. Unfortunate, if that's the case."

"Yes, milord."

"Thank you. You may go."

The messenger bowed, turned, and quickly took his leave. Schilling allowed himself a tight smile—displays of fear in his presence, no matter how small or trivial, never failed to please him.

"Lady Moore," he said, turning to the beautiful young woman next to him, "What are your thoughts on this matter?"

"As you said, my lord. It would be unfortunate if something had happened to . . . what was his name, again?"

"Called himself Gunslinger, for some reason," Schilling said.

"Ah, yes, rather silly, I thought."

"Allowing for a few personality quirks in reliable assets tends to get better results, I've found," he said. "At least until those assets become less than reliable. Speaking of which, how is my pet dragon?"

She was good at controlling her emotions, but he caught the anger in her eyes at the words.

"Quetzalith is fine, my lord." Her words were clipped, her voice even. "In fact, if my lord pleases, I'd like to take him out to hunt this afternoon."

"By all means, my dear," he said. "One more thing before you go, however. Gunslinger's last message mentioned a Gant population growth, and his suspicions that the Queen has matured. I need verification, and I only trust the cultists so far. Having honest information flowing my direction is imperative. Whom would you recommend?"

She thought about her answer for some moments, her tanned brow furrowing in concentration.

"Hopkins, I believe would be a good choice, my lord," she said, finally. "He's unobtrusive, easygoing, and very observant. Also literate."

"Excellent. Thank you my dear."

He nodded in return to her curtsey, and admired her figure as she strode toward the door. Beautiful, intelligent, and loyal. He congratulated himself, again, for his fantastic taste.

The loss of his informant was a setback, for sure, but one that could be overcome. It had taken almost thirty years of diligent planning and work, but things were coming together nicely.

His rail system, integral to bringing the recovering—but still largely separated—population back together again, was steadily becoming more efficient. Goods, information, and money were being moved through the Territories more rapidly than they had since the Gants came, and with that, his influence.

That influence was key, more so than the land that came quietly with it. He was destined to unify this fractured country, and God help any that stood in his way.

CHAPTER ONE

CHUCK GORDON PUMPED THE HANDLE ONE MORE TIME, SLOWLY, as the water neared the top of his bucket. He rubbed his eyes as dawn broke over the farm, the sun sending streaks of pink through the twilight.

"Hurry up with that water, son," Pa said, his voice carrying over the yard. "You know how your Ma is about gettin' her coffee started."

"Yes, sir." Chuck's breath steamed in front of him as he grabbed the full bucket and started for the house. Pa opened the stockyard's gate. The flock of thirsty goats made a beeline for the crick, crying out and butting each other as they ran.

His younger sister was already in the kitchen, sorting the stuff she'd need to start breakfast. Chuck carefully wiped his boots off on the mat near the door, knowing she would throw a fit if he muddied up her clean kitchen floor first thing in the morning.

"Mornin' Ellie," he said, placing the bucket near the hot stove. "Need anything else?"

"Morning," she said through a yawn. "Eggs, and that big bag of flour."

Chuck nodded, and with a grunt, heaved the sack closer to the stove, as Ellie built up the fire. He stepped through the door, almost running into Pa.

"Easy there, pardner," Pa said, smiling. "I got the eggs already. I need you to check the fence line."

"But Pa, I ain't even eaten yet," Chuck said. His stomach growled loudly, emphasizing his complaint.

"Don't you worry, I'll have Ellie fry you up some eggs while you get ready. There's some bread leftover from yesterday, you can eat as you ride." He raised his voice, "Ellie! Get Chuck a lunch ready, he's got to head out!"

"Aw, Pa, that means I got to make more bread for us," Ellie whined. "Why can't I ride out, and Chuck make breakfast?"

"Now, young lady, you still have a year or two before you can go out on your own, you know that," Pa said, gently. "'Sides, you remember the last time Chuck cooked?"

Ellie's giggle came from behind him.

"It wasn't that bad," Chuck muttered. "I only burned one batch of biscuits."

"Yeah, and the others made great bricks, son." Pa clapped him on the shoulder. "Now go get ready."

"Yes, sir."

Sunlight filtered through the gaps in the barn walls, painting bright streaks on the floor. It was still hard to see, though, so Chuck lit the oil lantern by the door, taking it with him to Millie's stall.

"Hey girl," he said, hanging the lamp above the door. "How's my sweet girl today? You ready for a little exercise?"

The chestnut roan nickered, thumping Chuck's chest with her nose as he patted her withers.

"Okay, girl," he said with a chuckle. He pulled the lump of sugar from his shirt pocket and let her take it from his hand. "I can't hide nothing from you, can I?"

A few minutes later, he led Millie out of the barn. Pa met him, holding a small satchel, a canteen, and Chuck's weapons.

"All right, boy, here's your vittles and your iron. Sorry about breakfast, but my trick knee is acting up, and I don't want you stuck out there if weather hits later."

Chuck nodded, took the food and gear, then mounted up.

Chuck rode slowly along the fence line, keeping one eye on the rails, one on the sky. The afternoon sun cast long shadows behind him, combining the silhouettes of his body and Millie's into a monstrous shape. He noted, not for the first time, how much it resembled the giant insects he watched for. They were close enough to the mountains that the threat of dragons kept the giant ants—Gants in local parlance—away most of the time, but the clouds rolling in over the mesa to the northeast showed indication of becoming a nasty electrical storm. That much tasty voltage sometimes proved too much of a temptation, and could bring packs of the nasty, horse-sized insects boiling out of their underground nests.

"Riding the lightning," Pa would say with a chuckle, though the joke was always lost on Chuck. He'd asked, once, what made it so funny.

"Honestly, nothing funny about it, son," Pa'd said. "Used to be how we'd get rid of the troublemakers. Now, it brings 'em."

Pa hadn't explained more, that time. Chuck let it go, filing it away into "Pa's sense of humor" along with "Pull my finger" and calling Ma "Crazy Squaw."

Fence seems okay, he thought. *Might should head back to the house before it gets too late.* On the one hand, he wasn't quite done with his patrol. On the other, Millie was getting jumpy, rolling her eyes and flicking her ears nervously.

"Easy, girl," Chuck said, patting her neck. "We'll be done here before that storm gets close. Ain't nothing to worry about."

As if God wanted to prove him a liar, a sharp scream cut through the thick air somewhere ahead, just beyond a slight rise. Millie shot him a look.

"Yeah, I know, you told me," he said, kicking her into a light trot. "No need to go barreling into trouble, though. Like Pa says, 'If it's there, it'll find you fast enough.'"

Chuck pulled his Marlin rifle from its saddle boot, working the lever action and disengaging the safety.

"Probably just some coyotes, Millie. Nothin' we ain't dealt with before."

Another scream, louder than the first, put paid to that notion. What—or who—ever was up ahead, it wasn't a coyote.

They topped the ridge at a third scream, the source now in plain view: Two men on horseback, dingy gray robes flapping behind them, bore down on a third lying at the bottom of the rise. A large and apparently dead roan lay atop the man, leaving only his arms and one leg free. He raised the Marlin to his shoulder, aiming just above the rider's heads. No point in picking sides before he knew what was going on.

A shot rang out before he could squeeze the trigger. The trapped man below him took aim again, firing at the others. Chuck couldn't tell if he'd hit them but it had definitely gotten their attention. They pulled up short, pointing in his direction as another round kicked up dust next to them, before turning and riding off.

Chuck lowered the rifle, watching the pair retreat as he walked Millie down the grassy knoll toward the stranger. The man turned at the sound of hooves, twisting awkwardly as he tried to bring Chuck into his sights. Without urging, Millie snorted and sidestepped, almost disdainfully moving out of the man's sight picture as Chuck raised the rifle's muzzle. The man dropped his pistol, obviously exhausted.

"A Samaritan, as he traveled, came where the man was," Pa's words rang in his ears as he approached. "And when he saw him, he took pity on him."

Chuck dismounted and approached the man, careful to keep his movements slow and nonthreatening. He made a show of easing the hammer on the Marlin down to half-cock and flicking the safety on before sliding the rifle back into the sheath and removing his canteen.

"Here you go, sir," he said, kneeling next to the man. "You need to drink."

He held the man's head up slightly as he tipped the canteen, stopping only when the stranger started coughing. Chuck rolled him over on his side as much as he could. Pink foam sprayed from the man's lips, disappearing into the low scrub grass under him.

"I'll do what I can for you, sir," Chuck said, as the coughing fit subsided, "but I ain't as good as Ma at patchin' people up. Can you ride?"

"I don't think," the man said, weakly, before another round of coughing cut him off. He shook his head "no."

Chuck rocked back on his heels, thinking hard. Like Ma said, he was pretty strong, "for a skinny cuss," but wasn't sure if it would be enough to lift the dead animal. He had to try, though, at least to help make the stranger more comfortable for the short term. He nodded sharply and stood up, planting his boots at shoulder width before hunkering down again.

"All right, sir, I'm going to try and lift him off you as long as I can. You think you can slide out when I do?" At the man's weak nod, Chuck said, "Okay, on three. One, two...THREE."

Chuck heaved, throwing everything he had into his legs. Grunting at the effort, he watched as the dead horse moved, two inches, four...

Agonizingly slowly, the stranger slid his leg out from under the saddle. Chuck let go, breath exploding from his lungs. The carcass landed with a low thud.

The smell of gunpowder wasn't as strong as it had been when he'd first approached. A sickly-sweet smell assaulted Chuck's nose as he turned back to the stranger—it took everything he had to not gag. The man had been shot several times—one low in the gut, just below the waistline. Another bullet had torn into his shoulder, still another in the leg that had been trapped under the horse.

The animal itself didn't appear to be injured, just dead. The thick lather on its flanks and withers indicated it had been ridden hard for days. It just done gave out, as far as he could tell.

Another coughing fit and Chuck raised the canteen. The man shook his head, motioning for him to come closer. He fumbled at his neck, trying to pull something out from under his shirt. Chuck looped a finger through the thin beaded chain, carefully easing whatever was attached to it into the fading light. The formerly light breeze stiffened, ruffling the hair protruding from his hat. Next to a pair of dog tags, hung what looked like a key.

Weird looking, Chuck thought. The end was round, with teeth set at random intervals both inside and out. Greenish-black tarnish covered most of it, as though it hadn't been well cared for for a long time. *Don't look like it fits any door I ever seen.*

The stranger gasped, eyes wide as he grabbed for Chuck's shirt with his right hand. With his left, he grabbed for Chuck's hand and wrapped it around the strange key he wore. Chuck felt the edges of the metal digging into the flesh of his hand.

"Gordon.... Coulee..." he said, his breath carrying the same smell as his belly. "Coulee! Say it!"

The dog tags had read "Morgan, A." Chuck shrugged mentally—he wasn't going to argue with a dying man.

"Yes, sir. Gordon Coulee. My name's Chuck Gordon. It's nice to meet you, sir."

The stranger smiled, pink film covering his teeth.

"Good... Good boy." One hand released Chuck's shirt to pat him on the shoulder before falling to his side. "Gordon."

Chuck had read the phrase "his last breath rattled out of his lungs" in Pa's old books but had always thought it was just a fancy way of saying "died." It was a bit of a surprise to hear it for himself.

"PA!" Chuck cried, feet thudding up the worn dirt path to his family's farmhouse.

"Gol'dangit, Chuck! I just mopped!" His fifteen-year-old sister Ellie glared daggers at him from the other side of the kitchen as the screen door slammed behind him.

"Pa!" Chuck called again. "I need you!"

"He's out in the barn, idiot!" Ellie screeched. With tanned skin, a lean build, and hair and eyes dark as sin, Ellie took after their mother in both looks and volume. "Get those muddy boots out of here afore I pull what little brains you got out them jug ears!"

"Sorry, Ellie," Chuck said, squashing a pang of guilt as he turned on his heel. *I'll make it up to her later,* he thought.

He pushed back outside and ran full tilt for the barn. When he reached the open doors, he slowed, his chest heaving from the run.

"Pa?" he called out, quietly, so not to startle the horses. They'd be liable to kick holes in their stalls if they got spooked and then Pa would take it out of his hide.

"What's up, son?" Pa said, his deep, soothing voice coming from the darkness to Chuck's left. Chuck turned, relief flooding through him, to see his father sitting on a stool, cleaning tack.

"Pa, I gotta show you something. Someone."

"Someone's here?"

"Yes. Well, not exactly. He's dead. He was bad hurt when I found him. Being chased by cultists, I think. Anyway, he's down in the creek."

"Cultists?" Pa said, frowning. His big hands stilled and he carefully set the bridle he'd been cleaning aside. He stood and reached for the big rifle he always kept nearby.

"They're gone. Rode off when they saw me. But they'd already shot Coulee and his horse had fallen on him. I got him out but I think it was too late."

"All right, son, let's go take a look," Pa said, plunking his old hat down on his head.

"Also, sir, he had this thing. Seemed to think it was real

important..." Chuck held out the key-like object he'd removed from the stranger's ball-chain necklace. Pa squinted at it in the dark and then his eyes went wide as he strode forward to pluck it from Chuck's hand.

"Gunslinger," Pa said breathlessly, then he headed out of the barn at a run, leaving Chuck to follow as best he could.

Chuck had swapped horses so poor Millie could get a rest. Instead, he sat atop Ma's spirited mare and Pa rode his usual gelding. Chuck led the way in the fading light as the storm ahead continued to build. By the time they'd reached the cut where the dead man lay, fat raindrops had started to patter down around them.

As they approached the body, Pa suddenly let out a long, low string of curses and sat back, stopping his gelding in his tracks. Chuck followed suit, watching from horseback as his father dismounted to examine the unfortunate body.

It was hard to see in the dimness but Pa's face looked unusually grim, even more so than Chuck would have expected upon finding a corpse on their land.

"Gunslinger," Pa said softly. "I thought you were dead a long time ago."

"You know him, Pa?"

"Used to. Did he say anything?"

"Just told me his name was Gordon Coulee. And he tried to pull out his necklace. I thought it was just dog tags like yours but he had that weird key-looking thing on there."

Pa Gordon paused, then turned in his crouch and looked over his shoulder at his son.

"He said his name was what?"

"Gordon Coulee."

"You had it this whole time, you sonofabitch," Pa breathed, turning back to the body. Then he did something that Chuck never would have expected.

He laughed.

"Pa, something's not quite right," Chuck said, pointing at the body. "When I left him, he was on his back and his clothes weren't all mussed up."

The stranger's corpse lay on its side, shirt pulled open and pants at his knees.

"I think them fellers may have come back after I left."

The crack of a rifle shot in the distance echoed off the hills around them.

"Shit. Help me, son," Pa ordered, slipping his hands under Gunslinger's shoulders. Without hesitation, Chuck got his feet.

Another rifle shot rang out, causing Chuck to duck his head instinctively as they fought to lift the dead weight across Pa's gelding. They got the man situated, Pa keeping watch while Chuck mounted. Then he swung himself into the saddle and the pair of them took off, riding hell-for-leather back home.

They topped the rise, only to come face-to-face with the pair of cultists. Pa swore again, kicking his horse forward, slamming into the man closest to him. The big gelding hardly slowed as the cultist disappeared under its hooves. Chuck followed Pa's lead but his moment's hesitation gave his target just enough time to dodge out of the way. Chuck drew his Marlin as he pulled Ma's mare around, firing before the horse stopped moving. The cultist stumbled backwards as the back of his head exploded outward. Chuck watched his body crumple to the ground.

It was curious. He'd never shot a man before. He would have expected to feel something more.

"Chuck!" Pa barked.

Chuck blinked and refocused his eyes on Pa's pale, rain-wet face. Overhead, lightning cracked across the sky.

"Those weren't the ones shooting, we gotta get home!"

"Yes, sir!" Chuck answered through the deafening boom of thunder. He kicked the mare into a run once again.

More flashes of lightning illuminated their wild ride home. The rain stung Chuck's face as they hurtled through the wet darkness. Some of the odd detachment that had dogged him since he'd shot the cultist started to melt away, leaving a cold fear in its wake. His mother and his sister were home, vulnerable. If the cultists attacked them...

The sound of more gunshots rang out amid the booms of thunder as Chuck and Pa crested the rise leading to the farmstead. Chuck could feel the mare's sides heaving as she ran. Another bolt of lightning illuminated a terrifying scene. Around twenty cultists spread out around the farmhouse. He watched as two broke off, heading toward the barn.

Pa, guns blazing and cussing a blue streak, bore down on

the man inside the pen. Bullets whizz-cracked by Chuck's head as he steered the mare with his knees. Well trained, she reacted quickly, dodging to the left as Chuck twisted to draw a bead on the next closest man. Betrayed by the rough ground, his mare caught a hoof as he pulled the trigger. The bullet that should have ended the cultist just missed, plowing into the ground behind him. The cultist turned, raising his rifle just as Ellie opened fire from the side window. He dropped before Chuck could fire again.

"Quit steppin' on my 'maters, dammit!" Ma's voice rang out, followed by several shots. The man in her garden went down, weakly trying to crawl away. He stopped after the next gunshot.

"Chuck!" Pa said from his left. His old man had made it to the side of the cabin, hunkering down behind the woodpile. "Get down here, boy! I'll cover you!"

Chuck realized he was silhouetted against the clouds, the occasional lightning streaks making him an easy target. He kicked the mare, aiming her toward Pa's hiding spot. His father discouraged any would-be marksmen with a few well-placed bullets from his rifle.

Chuck didn't wait for the mare to stop before dismounting and joining the older man. "Pa, I got an idea. I can see everything from behind the chimney."

At his father's nod, Chuck duck-walked to the rear of the cabin, checked to make sure the backyard was clear and climbed quickly onto the roof of the cabin, staying low. He took up a firing position behind the large brick chimney, reloaded the Marlin with shells from his belt and took a deep breath before surveying the yard in front of him.

Cult members had spread out around the area, mostly sticking to what little hard cover they had. The low rock wall of the well hid one, the water trough in the large goat pen covered another. Two lay dead in the pen, cut down by Pa on his initial attack. The two that had made for the barn were still there, he guessed, either hiding inside, or getting into position in the loft.

Need to keep an eye out for them. Movement near Ma's small tool shed caught his eye. Three of the intruders huddled together, sparing the occasional glance around the corner or firing blind with pistols. Just beyond them, concealed in the slightly taller grass the goats hadn't eaten yet, Chuck caught sight of four men. His elevated position gave him an advantage—Ma, Pa and Ellie wouldn't be able to see them from their positions.

Gonna haveta get those fellers first. Anyone else that starts shootin' at me should get everyone else's attention.

Six bullets, range at about a hundred yards each. Nearest target first, save the furthest for last. Deep breath, work the lever action.

Chuck leaned out, bringing the Marlin to bear and firing smoothly, lining up his next shot as soon as he'd chambered a round. He ducked back behind the chimney after his fourth shot, just ahead of a volley from the intruders. Chips of brick stung his cheek as he reloaded. Gunfire from below put a stop to any retaliatory fire from the cultists, giving him a chance to take another peek around the corner.

Seven cultists lay dead or, at the very least, unconscious. The four in the grass were mostly dead, each one lying face down, the back of their skulls blown to craters. His family had taken out three of the remaining attackers—one of the men behind the shed and the man behind the well both lay unmoving in the mud. Trough guy was down but not necessarily out, doubled over clutching his belly.

Bullets cracked into the chimney. Chuck spun to his left, taking a bead on the hen house, just as a cultist's head came above the roof line. He fired, winging the far man before he could fire, then shifted the barrel of the Marlin to the approaching threat and removing it. A thump and cursing, followed shortly after as the body fell.

"Fox in the henhouse!" Two quick volleys sounded from below him. No more movement from that direction. "Nice work, Ma!"

He took a chance on another look out at the yard. The previously bold cultists seemed to be rethinking their decision to attack the farm, if the lack of shooting or movement was any indication. By his count, there were eight men still close to the house and two in the barn. One of the men appeared in the hayloft.

"Prepare, brothers, our Bliss awaits us!" he said, a flash of lightning making him easy to see. "They will fall to our overwhelming numbers! The moment of our victory is at ha—"

A round neatly snapped his head back before the body fell into the darkness.

"I got plenty more!" Ma shouted from below him. "Y'all just keep coming and I'll give 'em to ya one at a time!"

Chuck reloaded, noting that he had six shells left on his belt. He moved fast, staying low while working his way back to the edge of the roof, keeping watch for any attackers. There was still one behind the coop and another on the side of the house who needed to be dealt with.

He hit the ground, immediately slapping his back to the wall, head swiveling left and right looking for threats. The coast clear for the time being, he sidled toward the corner.

A cultist lay under the mostly decapitated corpse of his compatriot, struggling to move the dead weight from his chest. A sharp strike with the butt of the Marlin put him to sleep. As he turned toward the coop, he caught the click of a hammer cocking.

Chuck dropped before he could think. He rolled, snapped the Marlin to his shoulder, and pulled the trigger as the sights lined up. Two shots sounded as one and the cultist's bullet whistled as it flew over his head. Another shot from the Marlin put the cultist down for good.

The remaining invaders made a break for it, zigzagging as they ran. Chuck hesitated, conflicting thoughts racing through his head. Shooting a man in the back was wrong but, these men had tried to kill him and his family...

Two shots from his right dropped the running cultists before he could make a decision.

"That'll teach ya, ya lousy bastards!" Ma screamed obscenities punctuated with rifle fire. As the bodies twitched with each round, the barn door flew open. The last cultist rode out on Ellie's roan gelding, using the horse as cover. Chuck raised his rifle.

"Come on. Just need a clear shot..." he whispered. The man showed more brains than his friends, staying low until he was over the ridge. "Dangit!"

He turned his attention back to the unconscious man near the wall just as Pa rounded the corner.

"All clear on my side," Pa said. "How 'bout you?"

"Yessir, all clear," he said, then noticed the blood on Pa's shirt. "Pa! You got hit!"

"This?" Pa said, trying to hide his wince with a grin. "Nothin' but a love tap, kid. Now what have we here?"

Pa hunkered down next to the cultist, careful to keep enough distance in case the man tried something, before slapping him on the cheek. The man's eyes snapped open at the second strike.

"Easy there, 'migo," Pa said, the steel in his eyes belying his friendly words. "You got about three shakes to tell me what you're doin' here and why I shouldn't send you off to meet your friends."

"We will return, nonbeliever," the cultist said, smiling tensely, eyes bright with zeal. "Your family will fall to our knives for the Master's progeny."

"That so?" Any inkling of compassion in Pa's face fell away. "Don't seem to be in much position to be makin' threats."

"I will join my brothers and receive my final Bliss but not by your hand..." The man closed his eyes as his body began to twitch.

"Where did you come from?" Pa said. When there was no answer, he rolled the corpse from the now still cultist. "Dammit."

Blood flowed into the ground from the cultist's thigh, the small knife he'd used still in his hand. The man's body gave one more spasm before he stopped breathing.

"Ain't gettin' much from him now." Pa spit, motioning to Chuck. "Let's go check on your Ma."

As if in answer, rifle fire came from the front of the house. Pa gave a small grin and approached the corner.

"Belinda! They're gone! Stop shooting!"

"I'll quit shootin' when I'm damn good and ready to quit shootin'!"

"Fine, but don't blow my damn head off when I walk in!" Pa said, opening the door.

"Don't tempt me!"

Chuck tossed another shovelful of dirt on the hastily dug grave. After all the energy and excitement of the battle had worn off—and coupled with the last few hours of backbreaking labor—his arms felt like lumps of lead. Shallow as it was, the pit near the compost heap was wide, the cultist's bodies were stiff and hard to move and the bags of lime were heavy. Still, the job had to be done, otherwise the livestock would be at more risk from anything sniffing around for a free meal. Last thing they needed, on top of the damage to the ranch, would be losing stock or horses to a hungry predator.

"Let's go get cleaned up, son," Pa said, sounding as tired as Chuck felt. "I need to have your Ma look at this shoulder again... and we need to talk."

"About what, sir?"

"Things. But later. Let's get back and get cleaned up first."

"Getting cleaned up" meant a bath in the frigid creek behind the house, after stripping off the bloodstained clothing he was wearing. He dropped these in a pile of debris to be burned, since he didn't really want to wear them again. Ma had trained him not to let good clothes go to waste...but with the mingled blood of the cultists and the acrid scent of burnt powder, he'd be willing to take her irate words. He had other clothes.

As it was, Chuck returned to the farmhouse blue-lipped from the icy water and wrapped in a horse blanket that had been hanging on the drying line. The warmth the waterlogged wool gave him was worth the complaints from his muscles. His Ma greeted him with semi-sober eyes and jerked her head at her daughter. Without a single smart remark, Ellie got up and got him a bowl of chili from the pot simmering on the stove.

"Thanks, sis," Chuck said as he sat in the chair. He was suddenly too hungry to even think about going upstairs to dress.

For a few moments, Chuck ate in relative silence while his mother tended to Pa's wounds. Ellie fussed about the kitchen, an unfocused flurry of activity. She'd start putting things to rights in one spot, notice something else on the other side of the room, concentrate on that until the next distraction came along and repeat the whole process. He finished mopping the last of the chili out of his bowl with a hunk of cornbread, watching her go back to where she'd started for the second time. Pa cursed softly as whatever Ma was doing hit a tender spot.

"Son," he said, shifting uncomfortably in the chair. "You know this changes things."

"I'll say!" Ellie burst out, her voice sounding high and hysterical. "We've never been bothered by cultists before, now we've killed twenty of them on our own land! What were they doing here? Will they come back? Why did they have to be so young?"

To Chuck's astonishment, his acid-tongued sister burst into tears.

Chuck got up from the table and wrapped his arms and the horse blanket around her. She leaned into his chest and sobbed, deep wracking sounds that shook her whole body. Her tears fell hot onto his skin.

"Ellie," he said softly.

"I killed him, Chuck." She turned her face up to his, red-rimmed eyes streaming. "He couldn't have been much older than me but I k-k-kill..."

She trailed off into a soft but high-pitched wail, fists weakly hammering his chest. Chuck looked around in panic.

"Give her to me," Ma said. She'd left Pa sitting in the chair and come over to where her children stood before the wood stove. Chuck tried to let go of his sister but she clung to him with talonlike fingers as she continued to make those horrific sounds.

Ma swore, then reared back and cracked her hand across Ellie's face. Ellie blinked, the awful blankness leaving her eyes and her cries faltered and stilled.

"You're okay, sweet girl," Ma said then, her rough voice gentle. "You're alive and you're okay. Your Pa and brother are safe. You're safe. No need for such carryings on. Come lay down now like a good girl and rest."

She took Ellie's arm and gently but firmly disentangled her daughter from Chuck, then steered her through the curtain back to the bedrooms at the back of the farmhouse. As the curtain fell closed behind them, Chuck turned to look at his father.

"She'll be fine, son," Pa said. "Happens like that sometimes, first time you kill a man. Ellie's young yet but she'll be all right. How are you?"

"Beat. A bit shaky. But I think I'm all right."

"Good. Because like I was saying, things have changed. This ain't over."

"You think they'll come back? More, I mean? Come looking for their friends?" Chuck could feel his eyes widen at the thought.

"I do," Pa said, nodding. "But not for their friends. They'll come looking for this."

He held up the dead man's dog tags and the strangely shaped object that hung with them.

"You know what this is, boy?"

"No, sir."

"It's a key, son. It might just be the key to our salvation. It was lost a long time ago but it looks like ol' Gunslinger found it."

"Gunslinger...you mean Mr. Coulee?"

"No, son. Gordon Coulee was never his name. He was trying to tell you something else. Gordon is me. He was bringing this key to me. Because I'm one of few men in the world who knows how to make this thing work." He reached into his shirt, drawing out a necklace almost exactly like Gunslinger's.

Chuck could make out his Pa's name, and the letters USA under them.

"Is Coulee one too, sir? One of them that knows?"

Pa shook his head, looking silently at the key for a moment before answering.

"Coulee isn't a person. Coulee is a place. Grand Coulee Hydroelectric Plant. It's where I last saw Gunslinger. It's where we thought we lost this."

"What's a hydroelectric plant?"

Pa shook his head slightly, blowing out a deep breath.

"Can't go into detail right now, but it's where we used to make electricity, before the Gants came. Me, Gunslinger, and others were supposed to blow it up, taking the megahive with it. We failed."

Pa, as far as Chuck knew, had never lied to him. But still—making lightning? It didn't sound believable. Pa looked dead serious, though, his eyes lacking the sparkle they'd have when he was joking.

"Son, I need you to return it to its rightful owners."

"Who owns it?"

"The United States of America. Or what's left of them, anyway. You've got to take this to the Bunker."

"Me?" Chuck asked, his voice breaking. "Why me, sir? Why not you?"

"I'm old, Chuck. As the Good Book says, there comes a time when the man hands his son the sword. This is a key but it's a sword as well. Besides, I've your mother and sister to care for. I expect we'll be traveling a bit, trying to pull the cultists and bugs off your trail."

"Pa, that's suicide!"

"Hell, boy, I'm old but I ain't *that* old," Pa said with a chuckle. "I got a few tricks up my sleeve. We'll lead 'em on a merry chase, while you take this where it needs to go."

"I thought the Bunker was a myth?" Chuck said, feeling as if the entire world were spinning upside down and he couldn't quite seem to keep up.

"It's real, all right. Just not too many people know where it is. I'm one."

"All right," Chuck said, taking a deep breath. "When do I leave?"

"Now."

"NOW?"

"Well, soon, at least. Put some clothes on. Say goodbye to your Ma, first, but yeah. It's time, son. You're as ready as I can make you. Destiny's come a-calling. Time for you to go out and meet it."

Ma insisted he stay the night at home. In this case, "insisted" meant a mean right hook, cursing in several languages, and a carving knife. With some fast talking and a lot of kisses, Pa'd managed to get her calmed down—eventually. The upshot was that Chuck would head out early the next morning.

"Now look here, Belinda," Pa said, while Chuck hugged his sister goodbye. "I need to get the boy on his way. Few favors to call in over in town. I'll meet up with you at the spot."

Ma nodded once before grabbing Chuck again in a fierce embrace.

"You come back to me, boy. You hear?"

"Yes, ma'am. Right after I get done. I promise."

"Good boy."

"All right, Bel, turn him loose," Pa said, gently pulling Chuck away and turning him toward Millie. "Time ain't on our side. You and Ellie get moving, too. I'll see you in a few hours."

Ma pressed her fingertips to her lips, then took a deep breath and her daughter's hand. The two of them turned and went back into the house. Chuck watched them go, then swung up into place on Millie and followed his father out to the road that lead to town.

"What about the farm?" Chuck asked after a few silent, uncomfortable moments.

"It'll be taken care of," Pa said. "I have a thought or two about that. That's why we buried those bodies. Someday, you might need a place to come back to."

"Where will you go, Pa?"

"Better if you don't know that, boy."

"Yes sir," Chuck said, soberly. "But, how will I find you again?"

"You get to the Bunker. I'll send word to you there."

They rode in silence for a few minutes after that. After the previous night's storm, the air felt clean and light, the sun shining down upon them like a blessing. Chuck breathed in the scents of sage and red dirt, feeling it would be awhile before he came home to the desert.

As he rode, Chuck occasionally reached up to touch the key he wore on Gunslinger's chain, guts churning with excitement and fear. On the one hand, he was leaving home for an adventure like the ones he'd read about. On the other, armed men had attacked his home and shot his Pa. Even made his baby sister cry. *That* part had never been in any of the old books.

The sun climbed higher into the sky as they approached the town of Rawlins. Pa had told him once that, back before the war, Rawlins had been just a dot on the map in the middle of nowhere. In that respect, not much had changed. The most traffic that Rawlins got was the infrequent mail stage that came north out of Ogden. Nominally, Rawlins and the surrounding area were considered part of Deseret. For the most part, though, the families that settled that far north preferred no allegiance other than to themselves and sometimes their neighbors. This close to the Bug Zone, not much else mattered. Ogden sure as hell wasn't sending armies to keep them safe. Families like Chuck's were forced to do it on their own.

Well, on their own with the help of the small, tightly knit fortified communities that had sprung up here and there. Gant nests were still a problem, particularly in the old cities that had become deathtraps during the invasion. People banded together for mutual aid and support... and firepower. In case the Gants got hungry.

It wasn't terribly uncommon to see a Gant warrior scout out on whatever business they conducted. That was why a man carried a rifle and rode a fast horse. Though even sometimes that wasn't enough. Warrior scouts could sometimes outpace a thoroughbred.

Mostly, though, they ignored humans unless directly confronted. Of greater concern were the strange human cultists that worshipped the giant insects as gods. But cultists generally stuck pretty close to the nests. It was rare to see them out this far into the hinterlands. Even more rare that they'd attack a homestead. In fact, he'd never heard of it happening before.

Scavengers were a bigger worry, most times. The long periods of time spent in poisoned territories had a tendency to drive them crazy. Stories of homes ransacked weren't uncommon. Worse were the cooking fires with blackened human bones nearby.

Up ahead, Pa reined his horse to a stop, interrupting Chuck's musings. He followed suit, waiting silently for his father to speak. Bullet Gordon took a deep breath, squinted at him, then shrugged and dismounted.

"We're about a mile outside of the town walls," Pa said. "Before we get there, I want to give you two more things."

He reached into a saddlebag and pulled out what looked like an old, faded sheet of paper, folded several times into itself.

"This ain't much," He said, unfolding it about halfway, angling it so Chuck could see better. Blue, red and black lines, some solid, some dotted, crisscrossed the page, intersecting at dots with names. Pa had made some alterations over the years, it seemed, drawing in heavy borders and shading certain areas. His handwritten notes covered the paper, labeling territories and various dangers. The places marked HERE THERE BE DRAGONS and GANT COUNTRY grabbed Chuck's attention. "But it was hard to come by before the bugs came and even harder after.

"It's a map, son, a good one. Made back when we could draw them as accurate as possible." He pointed to Laramie. "We're about here, more or less. Where you're going is..."

Pa opened up more of the map before pointing to Washington D.C.

"...about here. A little farther west, actually, near Lost River. Got it?" At Chuck's nod, he continued. "Don't mark the spot, understand? Just in case someone gets hold of the map. Keep it in your head."

"Yes, sir."

"Now, I ain't sayin' to go there but this would be a good place to stock up," he said, pointing to a dot labeled Pittsburgh. "If you do find yourself there, Liberty Bridge will put you on the right path."

Chuck nodded.

"Good, now the last thing."

Chuck watched as his father flipped up the leather flap covering his rifle's sleeve. Pa had made the saddle sheath himself. He'd had to, because finding something big enough to carry around a fifty-caliber rifle was difficult.

"You remember how to fire her, son?" Pa asked as he held the rifle out. Chuck accepted it with two hands, then held it as Pa went back to unstrap the custom sheath from the rest of his tack.

"Yes, sir, but won't you need Fat Lady?"

"Possible but it's likely you'll need her more. Now, it's hard to find rounds for her these days. Might be a cache at the Bunker, or one they know of, but you might just have to reload, so save your brass when you can."

"Yes, sir."

"You know how to fix the saddle sheath on your gear?"

"Yes, sir."

"Do it now, boy. We ain't got all day."

Chuck dismounted and did as he was told. When he was finished, Pa gave him a respectable-sized pouch full of rounds to stash in his saddlebag and around his person. Then he checked to see that Fat Lady was as discreet as she was going to be and pulled himself back into the saddle.

Pa gave a grunt of satisfaction, turned and rode on. As he followed his father, Chuck tried not to think about what it meant that Pa had just given Fat Lady to him. Either he didn't expect to survive what was coming next, or he thought Chuck would need a helluva lot of firepower in order for *him* to survive.

"Mornin', Gordon," Sheriff John McLaughlin said, glancing up from his paper. As Chuck and Pa walked in, the dark skin of his face showed suspicion. "How're y'all doing today?"

"Sheriff," Pa said, nodding as he stopped a few feet in front of the lawman. He waited, silently, until the lawman sighed.

"All right, I see you mean business," Sherriff McLaughlin said, folding the paper and placing it on the desk in front of him. "How can I help you?"

"I need some things from your brother-in-law's store and I need it on credit."

"You know ol' Gabe is a skinflint. He ain't going to take credit."

"Not from me, maybe but from you he will," Pa said, giving Sheriff McLaughlin the smile Chuck recognized as his crafty one. "And I know you, as a good Christian, wouldn't refuse to help a neighbor in need, right?"

"Well now, see here, Gordon, I'd love to help you—really I would—but I can't just barge in and demand that he give you wares with no guarantee of payment!" He held up his hands to stop Pa's argument. "I'm not saying you'd skip out or nothing like that but let's be reasonable."

"How's your boy doing? He's what, about two years younger than Chuck here, ain't he? I seem to recall a certain wet-behind-the-ears deputy a while back that came to me for help..."

"Dammit, I knew that would come up," Sheriff McLaughlin said, heaving himself to his feet and leaning forward as though his bulk would give his indignation more weight. Chuck found himself involuntarily stepping back from the barrel-chested man. "Soon as you walked in, I thought 'Here we go.' Ten years I been waiting for the other shoe to drop."

"Them Rumfelt boys had you by the short and curlies, if I remember it right. How did you say it? 'I can't bring a posse, or they'll kill him.'" Pa stopped, the smile dropping from his face. "I need your help, John, and I need to collect on that favor. I'll never ask another one. I wouldn't be here if weren't serious."

Sheriff McLaughlin's face showed mixed emotions. After several seconds of silence, he finally sighed heavily, shaking his head.

"Fine. What do you need?"

Pa smiled, reaching into his vest.

"I have a little list..."

"There ya go, Mr. Gordon. I checked the list—it looks like we got everything you need." Gabe tightened the last strap holding the bags to the saddle and wiped a trickle of sweat from his forehead. "Shouldn't need anything 'til after you get to...where was it?"

"Barstow. Thank you kindly," Pa said shaking Gabe's hand. He reached into his shirt pocket and turned to the sheriff. "I know I said I'd never ask another favor but I need one more."

McLaughlin's face clouded over, until he saw what Pa held in his hand.

"It's the deed to my place. I can't take most of the stock and I'll need someone to watch over it while I'm gone. If you and yours could stay out there 'til I get back, I'd be mighty appreciative. It's got good water and about a hundred head of goats. Anything you can make off half that herd is yours to keep." He threw a pointed look at the sheriff's waist. "Heather's a good cook, ain't she? The garden'll need tending but there's fresh 'maters ready to pick and other such."

"I don't know what to say, Gordon."

"Just say you'll do it, so's I ain't gotta worry about it while I'm gone."

"I will," McLaughlin said, taking the deed from Pa. He shook his hand. "Don't worry about nothing, Gordon. We'll keep it in good shape for you."

"Much obliged, John," Pa said as he swung into his saddle. "Be seein' you."

Chuck mounted Millie and followed Pa out of town, riding in silence. He lost track of how many times he started to say something and thought better of it, before starting the process over again a few seconds later. Before he could get the nerve to say something, Pa stopped.

"All right, we're far enough out of town now," he said as he dismounted, motioning that Chuck should as well. "I got to say some things and I want you to just listen."

Chuck nodded.

"This is where we part ways, son. From here out you're on your own. Been thinkin' about this day for a long while, now, and I'm confident I've done everything I could to prepare you for this. Trained you, taught you, tempered you. Short of naming you 'Sue,' I can't think of any more I could'a done."

Chuck opened his mouth but the hitch in his throat stopped him short. Pa smiled.

"You don't need to say nothin'." The older man grabbed him in a rough hug. "I'm proud of you, boy, and I know you'll do us proud."

Chuck hugged his father back, mixed emotions of fear, excitement and confusion washing through him. Pa had never acted like this before and it scared him. Still, he couldn't help feeling that this was his chance to do something in the world.

Just as it seemed he'd be overwhelmed, Pa clapped him on the shoulder.

"I love ya, boy, don't ever forget that," he said, breaking away with a firm but gentle shove. "Now get on that nag and get goin'."

"Yessir."

Chuck watched Pa ride away without a backward glance. Not that he would have expected one. He'd done what he could and now Pa would focus on his next set of tasks.

Time for Chuck to do the same.

"C'mon, Millie," he said, clucking his tongue at the mare. Millie tossed her head and turned obediently down the road leading out of the small, dusty town.

It was a five-day trip to Laramie. Chuck followed I-80, riding alongside the crumbling stone ribbon. Pa had told him it had been an "interstate highway" before the war, some kind of big road people had driven on in "automobiles."

He'd seen a few of those around town, rusting metal skeletons picked over for anything useful, or stripped of all but the bare frames, pulled by horses. He never could figure how they were more useful than a good wagon.

Nowadays, there wasn't much left but a wide scar in the landscape and piles of a crumbling substance his pa called "ass fault." Off to the side, where he occasionally spat a stream of tobacco juice, Chuck could see where years of stagecoach and wagon wheels had cut ruts into the dirt and weeds alongside the old road bed. They had to circumnavigate the most torn up parts. Millie picked her way through the rubble without concern.

On that first night, Chuck figured out one of the reasons why Pa had told him to take the old road. Besides being the most direct route, it was also relatively well traveled, as such things went. The morning had been well advanced by the time he'd left Rawlins, so sunset saw him approaching the crossing of the North Platte River.

Millie nickered as they walked up to the two bridges that crossed the thin stream of water. Like the road, the bridges were crumbling and neglected but someone had at least made an effort to patch them, using what looked like old railroad ties. The result wasn't pretty but would at least get them over the river without having to touch the water. You never knew what the river could wash down, so it was always better safe than sorry. Lots of folk had gotten sick from drinking or bathing in unfiltered water. Bad sick, not just a case of the trots.

All that aside, the river crossing seemed like a perfect place to make camp.

Clearly, he wasn't the only one who thought so. As Millie clopped across, Chuck could see a few groups clustered around unshielded campfires. One or two faces turned his way. He politely touched the brim of his hat in greeting, shifting to make sure they saw his Marlin. No reason to let anyone think he might be easy picking.

He found a good spot. Not too far from the river, somewhat sheltered by some scrubby sage. While the sun painted the western sky in orange and red, Chuck set himself up a modest, comfortable camp. He rolled out his bedroll, used some stones to construct a small fire ring and started up a cheerful little blaze. While the tinder snapped under the heat of the infant fire, he found himself smiling, despite everything. He'd always liked to camp out.

"Nice fire you got there, mister."

The high, timid voice came out of the gloom near the sage. Chuck looked up to see a girl walking toward him. She wasn't tall but seemed young, maybe his own age.

Lightish-colored hair tumbled down over her shoulder. She walked with a sway to her hips that kept catching his attention, no matter how gentlemanlike he tried to be.

"Thank you. Welcome to join me," Chuck said. "I ain't got much but I got enough to share," he added, noticing the hollows under her cheeks.

"I'll make it worth your while," she said, her voice quivering just slightly. "I ain't no charity case." The firelight played over her face and he couldn't quite miss how she bit her lower lip. Nor how her hands trembled.

"Hospitality ain't charity," Chuck said softly. "What's your name, ma'am?"

"Jill. And don't call me 'ma'am.' I ain't no lady," she said with a toss of her hair. He supposed she was trying to look flippant but it just ended up making her look scared.

"To me you are, Ms. Jill," Chuck said. "I would be honored if you would share my fire and my meal."

Jill pressed her lips together tightly, her eyes big and dark as she studied him. Then, her shoulders slumped in grateful defeat, she nodded.

"Thank you," she whispered. "I shouldn't...but thank you just the same."

Chuck nodded and turned to rummage in his saddlebags for his trail rations. He had some jerky and some of Ma's dried onions and such. They'd make a good stew. He and Jill could share and it would stretch his single ration into plenty of food for both of them.

"Can I help?" she asked a moment later. Chuck glanced up at her and then shook his head.

"No, ma'am," he said, cursing the way he sounded stiff. "I've got this under control. You look a mite tired. It will be my pleasure to cook for you tonight and let you take your ease."

She laughed then, a short, bitter sound devoid of any humor. It sounded like the laugh of an old woman, weary from life's cruelties. It definitely shouldn't have come from someone his own age. And pretty to boot. Though maybe, he thought, that was the problem right there.

He glanced up at her, noticing that she'd moved closer to the fire, pulling a threadbare shawl-thing around her shoulders. Without saying anything, he threw another log on, causing a fountain of sparks to erupt up alongside the twisting smoke. Jill jumped back and then gave him another of those sad little smiles and held her hands out to the building blaze. He gave her a nod in return and then busied himself with cooking.

Once he had the water boiling, Chuck went back to his pack and removed a blanket from his bedroll. He didn't say anything, because he didn't want to trip over his own tongue, but he draped this blanket over Jill's shoulders. She startled at his touch and then wrapped it around herself gratefully. She bit her lip and looked as if she might cry. He looked quickly away.

Tears had never been something that Chuck handled well. In a kind of panic, he seized on whatever came to mind to try and distract her.

"Uh, do you, uh, live around here?"

"Just there," she said, pointing back into the gloom.

"With your family?"

"Ain't got none," she replied, with a bit of a harsh laugh. "It's just me and Pete and the other girls."

"Pete's your man?" he asked. It wouldn't do to be poaching. "He's welcome to join us for dinner."

"Pete's my pimp," she said baldly. "He'll probably come 'round later, to make sure you're treating me right."

"I, uh," Chuck fumbled. "Oh. I didn't know."

Jill's face drained of color and her eyes got wide and panicky.

"Oh, shit. You didn't? You thought? Oh hell. I'm so sorry. I'll go. He's gonna kill me for wasting all this time and you're the only one without a family..."

"No," Chuck said quickly. "You don't have to go. I just, was surprised, is all."

"Pete won't let me stay if it's not business, mister."

"I'll pay you," Chuck said quickly. "Same as if we...you know. Stay, have a good meal. Sleep safely for a night." The way she flinched when he moved suddenly had him guessing that most nights she didn't get that guarantee.

"You mean it, mister?" she asked, her eyes still wary.

"Yes, ma'am."

And in the morning, he promised himself, he'd take her away from all of this. He could buy more supplies in Laramie, get her a horse. He'd rescue her from whatever it was that haunted her big, dark eyes.

They ate quickly, sitting close together. Afterwards, they curled up in Chuck's bedroll together. It was a tight fit, especially with the addition of Chuck's weapons. He knew better than to leave them unattended.

Despite the awkwardness of having to behave like a gentleman with the warm weight of a lovely woman pressed close, Chuck succumbed to sleep with relative ease. First day out and already this had been quite the adventure.

When Chuck woke, Jill was gone. So were his saddlebags, which held most of his food and cooking supplies, some ammo and a little bit of his money. Most of that he'd stashed on his person, according to Pa's instructions. She'd left him the horse, his tack and a note of thanks for being such a nice boy.

He looked around for a minute or two but this area was too well traveled for him to track her and he had no idea which direction she'd gone.

"Gol-DANGIT! Idiot!"

Millie glanced up at his outburst, slowly chewing the mouthful of grass she'd cropped.

"Yeah, I know, Millie. I fell for it."

Kicking a few good-sized rocks helped get the mad out but did little to get him on his way. He'd better get a move on and break camp if he was going to make it to Laramie on what he had left. He'd have to forage along the way as it was.

As he was getting ready to ride out, he oh-so-casually approached one of the families camped nearer to the bridge.

"Ah, pardon me, sir. You didn't happen to see a young lady leaving this morning, did you? Possibly with a gentleman that she didn't look to pleased to be with?" Chuck asked the father.

The man huffed a snort of laughter and looked at Chuck with pitying eyes.

"You mean Big-Eyed Jill McTavish? That girl sitting at your fire last night? She ain't got no man, son. Thought you knew.

She plies her trade up and down I-80, earning a buck on her back or with a scam. Did she get you for more than her price?"

Something crumpled within Chuck's chest and he suddenly found it hard to breathe. The man's knowing smirk made Chuck want to bury his fist in the man's round face but that wasn't right. The man hadn't done nothing 'cept let Chuck be hung with his own rope.

"Afraid so, sir," Chuck said tightly. "I appreciate the information."

The man laughed again, then reached out and clapped Chuck's shoulder companionably. He was a rather large man, so Chuck fought not to stagger under the force of the blow.

"Well, live and learn, young man. Live and learn. Best of luck to ya. Watch out for them girls down Laramie way. They'll scam circles around our Jill."

"Yes, sir," Chuck said as he mounted Millie. He touched the brim of his hat as he'd been taught and then kicked the mare into a gallop away toward the east.

CHAPTER TWO

"C'MON, GARMAN! IT'S LIKE YOU'RE NOT EVEN TRYING."

Garman looked up at his sparring partner from his position on the ground, gasping, trying desperately to form the words of an insult. He scowled as Ronen, his self-satisfied smirk just visible in the predawn twilight, reached out a hand to help him up.

"You...are...an...ass..."

"No such thing as a fair fight, brother. You gotta be ready for anything out in the real world."

Garman took the hand weakly, letting the Journeyman pull him into a sitting position. Only then did he turn his head up, letting his friend see his wicked grin.

"Oh shi—"

Too late.

Garman twisted, using his legs to snare the other man's, throwing his weight into the move. Ronen smacked the ground next to him, breath exploding from his lungs.

"That's...more...like...it..."

"Your mistake was not finishing me," Garman said, tapping him on the temple. "You're dead now."

"That won't happen again," Ronen said, rolling onto his side slowly. "Wish I'd seen that grin of yours sooner."

They both stood, squared up, only to be stopped by the bell for morning call to quarters. The rematch would have to wait.

"Oh, great," Ronen said, rolling his eyes and heaving a sigh.

33

"Nothing like sitting around for a few hours pretending to study small unit tactics and logistics."

"It's important. Otherwise, why would we be learning it?"

"Is it? I mean, look around, man. We don't go out en masse to take on the forces of evil, do we?"

"But we need to be prepared—"

His friend cut him off with a slash of his hand.

"For what? Waves of relentless enemies? Hordes of barbarians, crashing upon the gates?"

"Well, no, not right now."

"Exactly. Nothing. We're preparing for the possibility of something happening sometime, maybe. How many of the Masters have seen any fighting, at all? Four? Five? Less than ten, for sure, and even then it was before we were born." He stopped, gesturing around the windswept grass of their practice area. "Even the Journeymen have to go farther and farther out to find a Gant to make Master and then what? Go recruiting, walk the Earth settling minor disputes between locals, find a chapterhouse to teach at? Does that sound like the best use of our skills? Mediator? Teacher? Nursemaid?"

"We never know what will happen, Ro," Garman said, sighing. "Just because there's peace now doesn't mean there will be in the future." They'd had this argument before and would likely have it again. He began to walk back toward the main buildings that formed their chapterhouse. A small breeze wafted the smell of cooking meat in his direction, causing his stomach to rumble in anticipation.

"We should be proactive, not reactive," Ronen said, falling into step beside Garman. "Why not get in on the ground floor before anything serious starts? Think about it, we get involved with local police forces and militias, go out and take care of the trouble while it's small and manageable, rather than after it blows up? We know what to look for, where the weak spots are and who would cause trouble. If we got them out of the way in the beginning, we could have peace and order. And, we'd be calling the shots."

"You don't think people would have an issue with us telling them what to do?"

"Well, yeah, at first but we just apply the same lessons and techniques we use here but on a larger scale. Discipline, you know? Haze them until they fall in line."

"And if that doesn't work?" Garman asked, stepping onto the cracked concrete apron that fronted the chapterhouse's main hall.

The ancient metal building with its semicircular roof had been repaired over and over again, until it had a distinctive patchwork appearance. It was the least uniform thing about the chapterhouse, and Garman appreciated the small irony there.

"Then we ask them to relocate somewhere else. But here's the kicker—if we get every place on the same page, there's nowhere else to go! Any trouble makers would have to follow the rules, or take their chances with the Gantists or dragons. Nothing like the fear of certain death to keep people in line." Ronen grinned. "And, the more aggressively resistant ones? They just disappear quietly one night."

"Please tell me you haven't gone to Master Munn with this," Garman said, shaking his head. Ronen was always saying strange things, mostly just to get a reaction. But the hair on the back of Garman's neck started to rise anyway.

"I tried to, actually. Kind of a recon thing, you know, feel him out."

"And?"

"'We don't pick sides, Adept, we keep the peace. We prepare for the greater threat—the Gants,' and 'Windfist seek not adventure and excitement,'" Ronen said, mockingly. He spat. "Typical rearward thinking."

"Where, pray tell, did you get these ideas? No one around here talks like that?"

Ronen sheepishly glanced around the yard.

"Met a girl in town a few months back on liberty," he said, leaning closer. "Had an interesting chat about how things were going in the world. Get to spend some time with her whenever I go into town."

"Oh, I get it now," Garman said, grinning. "I take it she has a thing for the strong, ambitious type?"

Ronen's smile spread across his face as fast as the flush. Garman cupped his hands in front of his chest.

"And *big* plans for the future, too, I'll bet," he said, chuckling.

"Something like that."

"But you haven't had a pass in weeks."

"Well, let's just say that I know how to come and go as I please, when I please, if I really feel the need to do so."

"You sneak out?"

"Shh . . . not so loud, man. It's not something I want to broadcast to every brother in the chapterhouse. But yeah, I can get out of here without anyone knowing."

Garman thought about it. Town was a few klicks away and the Adepts could easily cover it at a run in less than an hour. Figure thirty minutes run time with no pack, a couple of hours in town, Ronen could easily make it back before reveille and still get some sleep, as long as there were no delays. Still, there was the possibility of running into the chapter's nightly patrol, a band of highwaymen, or even a rogue Gant scout. The patrols kept the last two to a minimum, naturally, but there was always that chance something got through. And for what?

"Seems awful risky for having a playdate. Your new 'friend' is probably trying to set you up for a con. She asked for money?"

"It's not like that, man. Really!"

"Uh huh. Just keep an eye on your coins. Saint Baddis knows she's not in it for your looks."

Garman laughed as he dodged the half-hearted punch from his friend.

"I need to ask you to keep this quiet," Ronen said, putting a hand on Garman's shoulder. "I'm supposed to meet up with her again tonight."

Garman frowned. On the one hand, what Ronen was talking about went against the rules. On the other, though, this was his best friend. Aside from getting caught sneaking out after curfew, what harm would come from it? Besides, he was probably just feeling restless. All Adeptus got that way, especially when close to promotion to Journeyman. Ronen's Journey had been delayed slightly due to repairs at the compound and it had been eating at him. As soon as he received orders, and not trying to impress some girl, Garman was sure he'd drop the crazy talk.

"Okay, I'll keep quiet but," he said, raising a finger, "promise me you won't put me on the spot. I won't lie for you."

Ronen grinned as they walked into the barracks, the rising sun making the candles at the door unnecessary. He stopped to snuff them.

"Don't worry, little brother, they'll never know I was gone."

"What are you doing?"

Ronen stopped packing, turning to face the sleepy-eyed Novitiate. The younger boy hadn't made a sound as he approached. He'd go far in his training.

"I need to go out for a while, brother. I won't be gone long."

"How long is not long?"

"Don't worry yourself. Go back to bed. The Masters will have you up in a few hours." His smile was forced. This could cause problems, if it went on for much longer.

"Does Master Munn know about this?"

"Of course," Ronen said, his grin tightening, "he sent me on this mission."

"Oh, okay. Good journey, then." The Novitiate walked away toward the latrine.

No time to waste. Every moment in the chapterhouse increased the chances of discovery. Ronen shoved his stash of jerky into the pack and closed it, pausing at his door to check the hallway. All clear, for now.

He'd kept his head down in the week since he'd "confided" in Garman. He hated lying to his brother, but he knew Garman wouldn't—or couldn't—see things the same way. The "girl" he was sneaking out to see didn't exist, and was, in fact, a couple of men from a place called Ironhelm.

At the last meeting with his friends, they had mentioned that things were picking up, and they had to move on soon. If he didn't join them by the time they left, they'd be forced to leave him behind. The deadline was in a few hours, at dawn.

Garman wouldn't change his mind. Ronen had prodded the younger Adeptus carefully, feeling out his thoughts on abandoning the Order. Garman stubbornly stuck to his guns, countering each argument with Order dogma. Maybe in the future, after he saw how well Ronen was doing—the money, the responsibility, the *power* to make things better—Garman'd come around, but for now, at least, his friend was a lost cause.

One thing his new friends had implied was that he needed to make a good impression to their boss. Showing up empty-handed wouldn't do. The man had money, but craved information.

Ronen approached Master Superior Munn's office carefully. Earlier in the week, under the guise of polishing the heavy wooden door, he'd liberally oiled the latch and hinges. He entered the chamber soundlessly, and crossed the room to the Master's desk.

After a few minutes of searching, he crammed what he hoped was valuable information into his pack. The door closed as silently as it had opened.

Ronen made his way to the main hall with no interference and slipped out through the well-oiled metal door. On the previous occasions, he'd met his friends in the closest town, an easy run for any Windfist over ten. Tonight, however, they'd promised to meet him in a town farther south, roughly twice the distance. Not wanting to miss them, he'd decided to take a mount.

The stables were across the yard, however, and it would be a challenge on most nights to make it unseen. Fortune smiled on him tonight, though—overcast sky, no moon—he crouched low and picked his way across the open concrete and into the low-slung stables on the other side. The night breeze smelled of sage and distant smoke, urging him onward.

A few short minutes of work later, his chosen horse was saddled and ready to ride. He stifled the flash of guilt. It wasn't really stealing, since he'd leave the horse at the town farrier. Some BS excuse and his friend's coppers should convince them to return the horse to the chapterhouse and sell him a new mount. If not, well, it wasn't his fault if the farrier was crooked.

Ronen led his horse toward the main gate. The heavy outer doors usually remained open overnight but the guard on duty could throw a single lever and close them quickly if the need arose. The wrought iron inner doors, however, were closed, an ornate metal bar bracing them. It was enough to keep anyone too curious from trying to get in and bought time for the residents to get the main doors closed in case of attack. God help anyone caught between the two sets.

The night guard would be suspicious but some fast talking should get him through with no issue. He unlocked the door, swinging it open on whispering hinges.

"Going somewhere, Adeptus?" Master Munn said, approaching from the shadows. "It's either too late or too early for a joyride."

In his haste, he'd forgotten to check the roster. Master Munn had apparently pulled gate duty...or had Garman said something?

"I was just..."

"On your way to your chambers. Unsaddle that horse. Now." Master Munn reached out for Ronen's pack.

"No!" Ronen said and pulled back, twisting, the reins slipping from his hand. Master Munn was just far enough away that Ronen had time to grab the pommel. His horse, eyes rolling, stepped back as Ronen placed his foot in the stirrup, swinging his other leg over. Master Munn's sudden grip on his ankle pulled him off balance, causing the horse to jump. Ronen kicked without thinking, the realization of what he'd done hitting him just as hard as the impact of his boot on Master Munn's chest.

His horse reared at the unexpected movements just as Master Munn staggered, a steel shod hoof striking the master's forehead. He fell to the ground as Ronen recovered his balance. Eyes wide in horror, he knelt down next to Master Munn, pressing his fingers to the older man's throat.

Ronen breathed a sigh of relief—he felt a pulse. Something brightly colored at the Master's breast caught his eye. A corner of red plastic peeked out from under Munn's robe. He pulled on the chain it hung from, slipping it over the older man's neck.

Voices cried out from the hall, jolting him into action. Pocketing the chain, Ronen quickly swung up into the saddle and kicked his horse into a gallop.

Garman applied the salve carefully. The slightest touch brought a flash of pain but with it, pride. The design tattooed onto his cheek was less than a week old but represented years of dedicated study and training. He leaned in to look at his reflection in the polished steel of his favorite blade. The new wind streamer representing his recent promotion in rank was healing nicely.

He turned at the knock on his door, his hand flipping the blade to a standard grip, just in case.

"Yes?"

"Adep—excuse me, *Journeyman*," the younger boy said, entering the room with a sheepish look on his face. Like Garman, his cheek sported a tattoo. Unlike Garman's, however, his lacked the Journeyman and Adeptus streamers. Instead, he carried only the circle and shaft of a Novitiate. "The Master Superior is requesting your presence in his quarters. I am to escort you."

"Thank you, Novitiate."

The boy bowed slightly from the waist, arms crossed into the sleeves of his robes, before backing out into the hallway.

Garman finished his morning ritual, donning his formal cloak for an audience with the leader of his order. It wasn't often that Master Munn requested a one-on-one—looking his best couldn't hurt. He rolled his shoulders to settle the cloak into place, its weighted hem bumping against his ankle.

The walk to Master Munn's chambers was a quiet one, although several times the younger boy turned, mouth open, only to snap it shut and continue forward.

At the chamber door, the Novitiate stopped, knocking softly before stepping back.

"Enter."

"You asked for me, Master Superior?" Garman said, walking through the doorway.

Garman took in the room in a glance, habitually noting exits, concealment, and firing positions. As with most Windfist quarters, the Master Superior's was sparsely furnished—a simple bed shared one corner of the room with a sink and toilet with a large wardrobe squatting close by. Small and spartan as it was, the room represented a perk of rank—all other Windfist were required to share facilities with each other. The higher up you climbed, the less people you had to share with. No one but the Master Superior had privacy. As a Journeyman, Garman showered, shit, and shaved with six other young men.

"Welcome, Journeyman Garman," Master Superior Munn said, waving him to one of the two chairs in the room, a faded red leather piece in front of the small fireplace. Master Munn sat in its twin across from him. "I have a mission of grave importance for you."

"I'd be honored, sir," Garman said. He took a deep breath to rein in his emotions, hoping his outward appearance remained calm. *His Journey!*

Master Munn studied him, meeting his unflinching gaze with one of his own, no less intense coming from under the bandage wound around his head. The official story was there had been a riding accident. The rumor amongst the lower ranks suggested an altercation with one of the Journeymen. After a moment, he gave a slight nod.

"Information of a sensitive nature has reached my ears. Information that could prove vital to the fulfillment of our ultimate mission," the Master said softly.

Garman held his face impassive but he could fill his pulse accelerating. *Our ultimate mission? Surely he doesn't mean...*

The Master nodded slowly.

"Yes, my young Journeyman. It is early to tell, yet, but I have received word that we may have found what we need to end the Gant threat for once and all."

"What do you need me to do, Master?"

"You will report to Master Vilmund, near Old Kansas City, and deliver this," Munn said, removing a wax-sealed travel pouch from his robe. "It is for his eyes only, and you will follow his orders without question."

Garman nodded silently, mind racing. Master Munn continued.

"That is very important, Journeyman. If what has been found is what we think it is, it is too dangerous to be allowed to fall into the hands of anyone else. We, and the leadership in the Bunker, are the only ones who can be trusted to use it against the Gants and not against our fellow humans."

"Excuse me, sir, but isn't the Bunker a myth?" Garman asked, his eyes narrowing. *Is this another test?*

"No," Munn said, shaking his head with a small smile. "It's as real as you or I. However, it is not discussed where the conversation can be overheard. Communiques are limited to brief status reports when absolutely necessary. But I assure you, it is real... and it alone has the power to lead us back to our former glory."

"If this mission is that important, sir, shouldn't one of the older Journeymen, or even a Master, deliver it? I'm not sure I am the right person for the job."

The older warrior gave him a small smile.

Garman kicked out as the door crashed inward, toppling his chair backward, rolling as he made contact with the floor. Crouching next to the antique writing desk, he risked a quick glance toward the door just as the three Windfist Adepti entered, fanning out to block his escape. Garman reached up to grab the feet coming in through the window just over his head, yanking hard.

The boy's momentum carried forward and over, breath rushing out of his lungs at the sudden stop. Garman followed up with light taps to the kidney and back of the head before turning toward the others, whipping his cloak off his shoulder and around one arm.

He used the momentum, flicking his wrist and sending the weighted end toward the closest boy's face. The instinctive flinch let him close the distance and spin, bringing the cloak around hard into the next Windfist's stomach. He let go and snapped an elbow back into the boy behind him, moving forward at the whoosh of air.

Movement from the corner of his eye told him the last Adept was doing exactly what he'd expected—trying to flank him while he engaged. Garman dropped, using his legs to trip and bring the other crashing down beside him. He rolled, tapping the boy on the head as he stood up to square off against the last Adept.

Garman moved quickly, grabbing the young man's wrist and twisting it up, spinning into him as he did. A heave had the other on the floor next to his buddy, followed with a tap on the temple.

Garman looked at Master Munn for confirmation. At the other man's nod, he turned to help his brothers to their feet and retrieve his cloak. The four Windfist filed out, bowing to Garman as they passed. The door shut as Garman returned to Master Munn, in the process of righting the overturned chair.

"Trust me, Journeyman Garman, you are exactly who we want for this assignment. I'll go so far to say that I'm hesitant to take you on alone," Munn said, raising his hand to forestall Garman's comment. "I said hesitant—not unwilling. I know a few more dirty tricks than you do."

Garman couldn't stop himself from glancing at Master Munn's bandage, dropping his eyes and nodding in an attempt to hide it.

No luck. Master Munn caught it.

"I'll not beat around the bush, Journeyman. The Order has been compromised. This," Master Munn motioned to his bandaged forehead, "was the result of the actions of former Adeptus Ronen. I discovered him attempting to leave with sensitive information."

He held up a hand, while Garman's stomach dropped down to somewhere near his feet. Ronen had betrayed them? He'd been sure his oldest friend had merely received his Journey assignment. How could this be?

"I should have seen it coming. We've held ourselves above the rest of the world for too long, I fear, and our education has been lacking." Master Munn sighed, tension and weariness replacing his usual stoic expression. "We're still human and fallible, no matter how hard we pretend to not be. I let my guard down and therefore let us all down."

The Master Superior stood up straight, and held out the pouch. Garman snapped to attention.

"Your primary mission is as follows, Journeyman Garman: Report to Master Vilmund by the fastest route you can. Deliver this message. It will stay on your person at all times, to be read only by Master Vilmund. Await further orders from him. Delivery is your highest priority—let nothing stop you." A feral grin crossed his face. "Having said that, feel free to kill any Gants you come across."

Garman swallowed hard and forced his mouth into an approximation of a grin. This was it! He'd been waiting for this moment for years. He had to focus on his Journey now, he couldn't afford to be distracted by his friend's betrayal.

"I'm honored, Master Munn, I will not let you down."

"You'll leave at first light. Visit Brother Weiner to receive your load out and benediction," he said, placing a hand on Garman's shoulder. "We're counting on you, Journeyman Garman. It may sound overly dramatic but the future of the world rests in your hands. May the spirit of Saint Baddis guide you."

"Be polite, be professional..." Garman said.

"And have a plan to kill everyone you meet. Good luck, Journeyman. Dismissed."

"Saint Kalishnikov, we implore you, guide this warrior with your spirit—allow his weapon to seek his enemies and release them from evil with the application of high-velocity rounds," Brother Weiner intoned, laying his hand on the ancient rifle. "May this weapon never fail, even should it be immersed, or dirty, or used as a club. Hooyah."

"Hooyah," Garman whispered, breathing in the familiar, comforting scent of weapon oil.

Brother Weiner was one of the largest men Garman had ever seen. He stood well over six feet, his cloak and vestments only partially concealing his muscular build. A faint scar ran down the left side of his face from just below his ear nearly to his neck. His eyes were as hard as obsidian and, as Garman had learned painfully, never seemed to miss anything.

He removed a vest from the rack. Garman turned, allowing the older man to help him into it. As he shrugged the black leather garment into place over his buckskin shirt, Weiner began loading magazines into pouches.

"May your aim be true, Journeyman Garman, for the way may be difficult and ammunition scarce," Weiner said, taking a pistol from its place on the shelf beside him and raising it briefly above his head. "Take this sidearm with the blessing of JMB, peace be upon him. May those that wish to do you harm find themselves before the deity of their choosing, to be judged fairly after you have arranged the meeting. Hooyah."

"Hooyah."

Brother Weiner stepped back, the benedictions of the firearms complete. Brother Reinhardt took his place, intoning the prayer of the bladed weapons.

Brother Reinhardt was nearly as tall and large as Brother Weiner and even though much older, he carried himself with an ease that only partly concealed his still vibrant strength and agility. While his eyes were bright and he wore a near perpetual smile, no man who met him ever doubted this was a foe to be reckoned with.

"This is my knife; there are many like it but this one is mine. OORAH."

"Oorah."

"The path of the blade is a long one, for it begins where the path of the sidearm ends. Though it is last used, it is not of least importance. OORAH." His sidelong glance at Brother Weiner coincided, miraculously, with Brother Weiner's traditional rolling of the eyes. "The firearm may jam; the blade never does."

The two weapons masters had a long-standing history of friendly rivalry. Mostly friendly. Rumor had it Master Munn enforced a "voluntary" vow of silence on the two men during their Journeyman years.

"Of course," Brother Weiner said, "the path of the blade usually ends on the path to the infirmary."

"Oorah," Garman said, trying to cut off an old argument. He had places to be, after all. "Thank you, Brothers."

A sheepish look crossed both men's faces. Brother Reinhardt leaned in as though checking the sheaths strapped to Garman's vest.

"The slow blade penetrates the shield," he muttered with a wink. "Be careful out there, Journeyman."

Brother Poole, the order's administrator, stepped forward holding a jar. Garman closed his eyes as the face paint was applied.

"Saint Norris, aid this young man on his perilous journey. Bless these markings so that he may live as you did, conquering all trials and tribulations along his way. Lo, and the rattlesnake did bite him. And after three agonizing days, did it perish. Hooyah."

"HOOYAH!"

CHAPTER THREE

THE REST OF CHUCK'S WAY TO LARAMIE WAS UNEVENTFUL. THE terrain transitioned gradually from high desert to prairie. Inch by inch, scrubby sage and red dirt gave way to the gentle swell of rolling, grass covered hills.

Chuck had grown up shooting small game from the time he was old enough to hold his dad's smallest .22 rifle. He put this experience to good use over the next four days, scrounging up enough prairie dogs and small pheasant to eat quite well, all things considered.

Mindful of his experience with "Big-Eyed Jill," Chuck decided to avoid close contact with other travelers. Though he continued to act in the mannerly fashion that his mother would expect, he made a point of camping alone and never again sought anyone out for company or conversation. More importantly, he resolved to never again welcome anyone else to join him on the trail.

As he rode, Chuck considered this development. He was not, by nature, a solitary young man. Growing up, he'd frequently enjoyed easy friendships with other kids, when there were any to be had. Going it alone would certainly make for a long journey. The Bunker wasn't close, not by any stretch of the imagination.

Still, Chuck was a practical kid and he'd been taught to handle problems as they arose. First on his list: Get to Laramie.

His first indication was the way the broken-up path started to firm up under Millie's hooves. The asphalt started to reappear in longer and longer stretches. Some of them even maintained traces of yellow paint, like a shadow of an earlier time. His next clue was the hand-lettered signs proclaiming MARKET DAYS IN LARAMIE THIS WEEK!

Traffic increased along the road, too. Heavily laden wagons and coaches jostled through a crowd of more people than Chuck had ever seen gathered together in one place. More vehicles, too, horse- and oxen-drawn both. Some looked like proper wooden farm wagons, like what Pa had at home. Some, though, had clearly been adapted from prewar vehicles. In front of him, a team of draft horses pulled something that looked like a rusty, decapitated metal beetle. On his left, he recognized the bottom half of a minivan pulled by a pair of oxen. His ma had told him about minivans. She'd apparently ridden in one as a kid.

He held Millie to a walk but didn't dismount and followed I-80 past the barricades and into the center of town. It was an interesting place, Laramie. Before the war, it had been a small city, home to a university of some kind, according to Pa. Chuck could still see the twisted skeletons of what had once been high-rise buildings jutting up against the sky. No one lived or worked there now, of course. Old Laramie had been destroyed during the Bug War, like every other population center of note in the World That Was. The Gants that had overrun the place in the initial invasion were in turn wiped out by the firebombs dropped from airships. After the fires had died, survivors started over in a formerly suburban part of town, leaving the blackened skeletons of Old Laramie intact. Neither Pa nor Chuck could really figure why. A reminder, maybe, or maybe it was just too much effort to pull them down. Scavengers picked the buildings for useful materials—like the metal and cracking slabs of rein-forced concrete that ringed the new town's defensive perimeter, and that was about it.

Eventually, the roadway widened and disappeared beneath a layer of packed dirt. The sunbaked grass scent of the prairie vanished, beaten out by the smell of people, horses, and not-quite-adequate privy facilities. Someone, somewhere, was grilling meat and the scent of it made Chuck's stomach rumble. Overhead, the early afternoon sun glinted off a window somewhere. The minivan coach rumbled up ahead along his path and then came to an abrupt stop as the driver hauled back on the reins.

The driver hopped down from his makeshift seat. His shiny, bald head flushed red, his little eyes hard in his fleshy face. He stomped his bandy little legs as he walked purposefully around to the back of the coach. Then he lifted the canvas cover and opened up the luggage compartment and something Chuck never would have expected tumbled out.

It was a man. An old man, even older than Pa, with wrinkled dark skin and close-cropped steel-gray curls. Judging by the stench of alcohol that wafted all the way to where Chuck watched, the unorthodox passenger was also drunk as the proverbial skunk... and smelled about as nice. But as the fragrant stranger rolled in the dust-covered street, Chuck saw a distinctively oblong flat piece of metal on a ball chain fall out of the collar of the man's disreputable jacket.

The drunk was a veteran, just like Gunslinger. Just like Pa.

"Fouled my whole coach!" the driver shouted at the unfortunate feller. Then he reared back and kicked the man right in the stomach. He seemed to immediately regret this decision, as the drunk heaved and spat out what looked like pure bile on the driver's boots. Chuck didn't think the man's face could get any redder but it did. He balled up his fists and looked like he was about to commence murdering someone.

"Here, sir!" Chuck said, surprising himself as much as the driver. Whether or not the drunk was surprised was anyone's guess. He didn't seem overly responsive at the moment.

The driver glared at him, eyebrows raised in inquiry.

"I'll take him off your hands. Looks like you've had enough to deal with, an' all," Chuck said as he kneed Millie forward a few steps. The mare blew air out of her nostrils in a way that told her rider that she *did not* appreciate the stench. Chuck slid off of her back and crouched down to see if the drunk was still breathing. Above him, the red-faced driver continued to mutter about upholstery and cleaning and the cost of it all.

Suddenly the drunk lurched, then rolled to his back. He wore a battered leather jacket over clothes that looked like they'd been soaked in vomit. The old man let out a belch that watered Chuck's eyes and made his stomach flip-flop in protest. The driver backed away with a curse. Chuck watched the coach pull away and then shrugged and turned his attention to the derelict human at his feet.

"C'mon mister," Chuck said, reaching under the drunk man's shoulders and helping him to sit up. The drunk blinked owlishly for a moment or two, then looked over at Chuck and smiled. Not far away, Millie pawed at the ground with one hoof. She was impatient with the bad smells.

"Oooh, pretty horsey," the drunk said, his attention turning to the mare.

Chuck levered the man up with a heave—he was heavier than he looked—and got him standing. Or leaning, at least, which was probably as good as it was going to get. The drunk tried to take a step toward Millie and the mare snorted in derision and sidestepped away.

"Easy there," Chuck said. "Just leave Millie alone. She don't really like the way you smell right now."

"*Quoi?*" the drunk asked, in a drawn out, exaggerated tone. His voice sounded like yesterday's rust on an old tin can. "Do I offend?"

"You are rather fragrant, sir," Chuck said, smiling despite himself. The man seemed almost too clownlike. No one could be *that* drunk. "But if you come with me, I'll help you get cleaned up some. My name's Chuck."

"Jay Wyoming, at your serv—" He stopped to let out another miasmic belch, then paused and looked as if he were considering throwing up again. Then he smiled, his teeth white against the dark skin of his face and took Chuck's hand. "Service."

Chuck allowed his hand to be pumped up and down vigorously for a moment and then extracted it gently.

"Mr. Wyoming, I believe there's a bathhouse nearby. Then maybe we can get you something to eat?"

"And something to drink?" Jay asked brightly.

"Could be," Chuck said.

Chuck had been guessing about the bathhouse being close by but as guesses go, it turned out to be a pretty good one. A bit further down along the way, a squat building stood belching steam from a pair of pipes attached to the roof. A hand-painted sign depicted what Chuck took to be a bar of soap and several bubbles. He gently but firmly steered his new friend in that direction.

"Afternoon, gentlemen," the brunette inside greeted them. She looked to be about the age of Chuck's ma, with a leathery, seamed face and the high, curled hairstyle of a woman half her age. Her voice, too, sounded high and light, like that of a young girl, but with her ample curves and low-cut top, it was rather painfully obvious that the word "young" no longer applied.

"Ma'am," Chuck said, holding on to his drunk with his left hand and touching the brim of his hat with his right. "My friend here is interested in a bath."

"I am?" Jay asked.

"B'lieve so," Chuck said.

"Alright, then."

"What kinda coins you boys got?" the bath matron asked, her smile still friendly but her voice firm. "We don't take play money here. Nor barter. Cash only."

"Ogden copper, ma'am," Chuck said. "Will that do?"

"Sure thing, handsome. Two will get you a bath for half an hour, though you'll have to see to it your friend don't drown himself. Can't abide a man who won't hold his liquor," she said with a sniff in Jay's direction. By the look on her face, she immediately regretted that decision.

"I'll take care of him, ma'am," Chuck said. He reached into his coat and pulled out two of the small, rough-minted coins. "Thank you."

The matron took the coins and slipped them inside her ample cleavage.

"You're a nice boy," she said. "Taking care of your friend like that. Another two coppers and I'll wash his things while you're in there."

"I don't think it'll help, ma'am. I think we'll just burn 'em and buy new."

She laughed. It didn't make her look younger but it softened the edges of her face.

"I can help you with that, too," she said. "I keep a small selection in the bathing room. Half a silver will get you a basic kit. Shirt, jeans, underclothes, jacket."

Chuck handed this over without comment as well, hoping he wasn't making the same mistake he'd made with Big-Eyed Jill. But, he just couldn't seem to help himself. The old man was a soldier once, and down on his luck. It wasn't that much money and it just seemed like the decent, human thing to do.

"Well, that's fine then, young gentleman," the bath matron

said as she took the small silver coin and made it disappear after the coppers. "Go right through this door on my left. My name's Lula. You just call out if you need anything. Anything at all, handsome, alright?"

"Yes, ma'am," Chuck said. He quickly focused on steering Jay through the door to the left and thereby avoided thinking about Lula's implied offer. Jay, it seemed, had no such compunctions.

"Lula!" the older man called out, his voice rising and falling in an almost musical fashion as he strung out the syllables in an approximation of a cat in heat. "Lula, I looong for you. And I'm looong...for you!"

"Mr. Wyoming, please hush now," Chuck said in a low tone. "I don't want to get us thrown out of here after I've already paid the nice lady."

"Only for you, kid. Only for you. Or Lula. Oh Luulaa...."

Eventually, Chuck managed to get Jay through the door and into the steam-filled bathing room. Three large tubs filled the space, steam rising from the water inside. On the far wall, Chuck could see a number of shelves holding folded towels and items of clothing. A door with a window looked out toward the back but it was completely fogged over.

"Hot damn," Jay said as he caught sight of one of the tubs. With more coordination than Chuck thought possible, he shook off Chuck's hand and hustled over to the side of one of them. He dipped a finger in, whistled and then proceeded to strip himself out of his clothing and hop nimbly over the side of the tub. A fountain of water splashed out in response, causing Chuck to jump backward with a curse.

"Ahhh," Jay said, leaning back and closing his eyes. "This is more like it."

His voice was noticeably slur-less.

"Ah, Mr. Wyoming?" Chuck asked, his eyes narrowing slightly. "Forgive me, sir, but I'm beginning to suspect that you've been puttin' me on."

"Call me Jay, kid," Jay answered with a chuckle.

"Why?"

Jay raised his eyebrows and slowly opened his eyes.

"'S'my name, o'course."

"No, I meant why act drunker than you are?"

"Why not?"

"Well, you might not've gotten kicked by that driver, for one thing," Chuck said.

"Ah hell, kid, I've taken worse. That guy wouldn't know a real kick if it hit him right in the balls. Besides, if he hadn't done it, I never woulda met you. Now, if you don't mind, take those damn threads outside and burn 'em like you promised. They stink to high heaven. Leave the jacket. I'll just be in here, soaking my old bones. After my time's up, we'll eat and then talk more."

He closed his eyes and leaned his head back again.

Chuck pursed his lips and regarded the man who'd swindled him as cleanly as Big-Eyed Jill had done. Then he looked down at the pile of clothing and shrugged. He clearly wasn't going to get any more answers for a bit. Might as well make himself useful.

He kicked the clothes toward the back door. He wasn't touching them any more than he had to.

An hour's time saw them seated at the long, polished metal bar inside the building marked SALOON. Glass doors along the back bar, desperately in need of a good cleaning, housed bottles of warm beer, pickled eggs and jerky. At regular intervals above the doors, glass tubing spelled out names of people he wasn't familiar with, like "Bud Light" and "Sam Adams." Here and there, small faded signs stuck to the glass announced TWO FOR ONE PEPSI PRODUCTS or COME TO FLAVOR COUNTRY. Chuck had no idea where Flavor Country was, but it sounded too good to be true.

Mismatched tables and chairs took up the rest of the small building's floor area, crisscrossed with long shadows from the barred windows. A large, iron-barred door stood open, allowing the few midday customers to enter and exit through the smaller wooden swinging doors. Faded green, red and orange paint near the ceiling spelled out OH THANK HEAVEN.

He'd ordered food for them both. Jay had ordered drinks for them both. Chuck had wondered about the wisdom of Jay drinking more but when questioned, the old man just gave him a wink.

As they both sat at the bar with drinks in front of them and food on the way, Chuck contemplated his next move. Buy new supplies, certainly. Ditch this old bum, definitely.

"You're in my seat."

Chuck glanced to his right, looking for the speaker. He was

pretty sure that his new companion, now snoring face down on the bar, wasn't the source. Before he could turn, however, his shoulder was in someone's grasp.

"Mr. Marsh wants his seat, boy," the large man said, bald head in striking contrast to his full goatee. He jerked his hand and spun Chuck in place on his stool. "And Mr. Marsh wants it now."

"I'm sorry, sir, I'll—" In his haste to get up, Chuck's arm swept the bar top, taking his glass of beer with it. The contents spilled, soaking the other man, who Chuck assumed was Marsh. Chuck felt the flush rising to his forehead as he tried to stammer a reply. "Oh my gosh, sir! I'm so sorry."

The hand on his shoulder gripped harder, grinding tendons against bones. Chuck grimaced as he tried to squirm out from the large man's grasp.

"Do you know who this is, boy?" the bald man said with menacing glee. "This is Bill—"

"Murshle. Marsher," Jay said, raising his head as his eyes tried to focus. "Mill Warshle. 'Eard ya the fursh time. Now shaddup."

Apparently satisfied with his response, the drunk put his head back down.

The large bald man's eyes widened and he shoved Chuck away. The young man lurched forward and fell to the ground. He looked up just in time to see his erstwhile attacker looming over Jay's slumped form.

"Hey! Old-timer!"

Once again, Jay raised his head, the creases in his dark skin deepening as he squinted.

"That's Bill. Bad Bill Marsh. He's killed fifty men in five territories. You need to show him some respect."

"Can't he." The old man paused, a rumbling belch working its way up through his chest. He exhaled as he spoke. "Par'n me. Can'e speak for hisshelf?"

"Why I oughta..." The big man reared back, cocking his arm only to have it grabbed around the wrist by his apparently notorious friend.

"Easy, Bates. I'll take care of this," the man said in a low voice. Chuck stayed quiet, slowly scooting back as Marsh walked forward.

"Hi there, friend. I see you've had a hard night already. Why don't you get on out of here afore we take you outside?" Marsh said in a light, easy tone.

The old man seemed to consider it, a thoughtful expression on his face. He opened his mouth to reply...

...And puked. On Marsh's leg. Sour-smelling bile, mixed with rye and what looked like carrots, spewed forth, coating Marsh's pants and boot, but somehow not touching the floor or bar. Conversation in the saloon ceased, replaced by a horrified silence.

Marsh stood there in shock as the old black man staggered to the front door.

"Come back here!" Marsh said, starting after him, face red with anger. Jay disappeared from view. A moment later, Chuck heard the sound of a body hitting the ground. It was a distinctive sort of sound and it carried over the unnatural silence in the saloon. Marsh kicked the doors open and stalked outside.

Chuck scrambled, just beating the other patrons to the swinging doors, making it outside just as Marsh grabbed the old man by his collar, hauling him to his feet.

"I'm going to give you one chance, old man, before I put you out of your misery."

"Yap, yap yap. You givin' me a headache." Jay said, shaking himself free of Marsh's grip, then turning and walking away down the dusty street. Behind Chuck, gasps and murmurs rippled through the gathering crowd.

Before Jay got more than three steps, Marsh had drawn the pearl-handled revolver at his waist. The old man stopped at the sound of the cocking hammer.

"Go on then," Chuck heard Jay mutter. "If you're feelin' froggy, jump!"

Chuck cut his eyes to Marsh just in time to see the gunfighter's lips tighten. He fired, sending a deafening *crack!* through the flinching crowd. Dust exploded from a spot on the road a foot to the left of Jay's leg.

"Turn around," Marsh called out. "Turn around or so help me I'll shoot you in the back."

When Jay didn't immediately comply, Marsh squeezed off two more rounds, eliciting another collective gasp from the crowd as dust erupted from the right side of Jay's unsteady figure. He still didn't turn.

"You asked for it, you drunk piece of shit," Marsh growled, lining up his next shot.

The old man seemed to consider it, then took a stumbling

step forward, catching a toe and falling just as Marsh fired. The bullet passed through the space where the old man's head had been a mere moment before.

"Son of a bitch!" Marsh cried, his frustration openly replacing the arrogance in his voice. The old man rolled to his back and then slowly pushed himself to his feet, facing Marsh.

"Get 'im, Bad Bill!" someone yelled next to Chuck. It was Bates, the bald, goateed crony from earlier. The gunfighter took a deep breath, cocked his hammer again and took aim. Jay stood with a drunken leer and winked.

Marsh fired, just as Jay staggered to the right. The shot went wide.

"Goddamn it, stand still, old man!" Marsh bellowed, lining up his next shot. He fired, just as Jay pulled himself straight again.

The old man froze as the round struck him in the chest. He dropped, crumpling into a heap on the dusty street. Chuck felt bile rise in his throat as Marsh lowered his revolver with a smirk and started walking toward Jay. He should have done something, he should have...

Jay rolled to his back. Another gasp rose from the watching crowd. Marsh froze in his tracks. The old man reached into the pocket of his dilapidated old coat and pulled out a steel flask. He squinted, as he held it up to catch the light. Chuck could see that it had a bullet hole through the front and was dented outward in the back.

The old man shook the flask, touched a fingertip to the liquid leaking from the entry wound, frowned, and tossed it to the side. Then he reached into the opposite side of his jacket and pulled out another flask. He uncapped it, raised it in Marsh's direction and took a swig.

"Why, you..." Marsh roared and launched himself at the supine Jay. Jay reached up with both hands (having made the flask disappear faster than Chuck's eyes could follow) and grabbed the gunfighter by his ridiculously embroidered lapels. Then he rolled backwards, using Marsh's momentum to propel the two of them back and over his head, such that they landed with Marsh flat on his back and Jay kneeling on his chest.

"Only a coward shoots a man in the back, Billy," Jay said. "Your momma would be so ashamed."

Marsh struggled under Jay but the smaller, older man had

placed his weight carefully. He hooked the toes of his boots into the hollows of Marsh's hips and applied enough pressure to make the gunfighter howl.

Jay leaned back and then lurched forward as if he would empty his guts again, this time on Marsh's face. Marsh ceased struggling and lay very still and pale, his eyes wide. Jay heaved and the gunfighter flinched, screwing his eyes shut and twisting his head to the side.

A loud, long, majestic belch rumbled forth and exploded from Jay's lips. A surprised titter of laughter rippled through the crowd. Marsh's pale face flushed red.

Jay grinned over his shoulder at the audience. Then he bent and kissed Marsh, noisily, right on the tip of the nose.

"Nobody likes a bully, Mr. Marsh," Jay said. Then he listed to the side and somehow managed to clamber loosely back to his feet.

Marsh wasn't far behind. He rolled over and got to his feet but not before he pulled a wicked-looking knife from one boot.

"You're gonna pay, old-timer," he growled and reached out and grabbed a fistful of Jay's new shirt.

"Can't," Jay said cheerfully. "'M flat, broke and busted."

"You will be," Marsh said, before letting loose a laugh that sounded like he practiced it for maximum evil effect.

"Forgot something, didn't ya, Billy?" Jay said, still grinning.

"What's that?" Marsh sneered.

Jay reached into his jacket and pulled out a bedraggled quill. "A *pen*?"

"Mightier than the sword," Jay said and then stabbed the metal-reinforced tip into Marsh's cheek, just under his left eye.

Blood from this new wound ran down the side of his face and pooled in the dust of the street. Chuck thought it looked startlingly red against the dirty white of Marsh's skin.

"Old man, I can't let you murder that man in cold blood on my street," a stern voice said. Chuck looked up to see a stocky, short man with a star on his chest pushing his way through the crowd.

Jay got to his feet, swaying as he did so and touched his eyebrow in the sheriff's direction. Chuck nudged his way forward through the crowd in time to hear Jay speaking to the sheriff.

"Afternoon, Sheriff," Jay said, the words running indistinctly into one another. "We's jest having some fun."

"Your fun's over, old man. And you're lucky I saw him aiming at your back," the sheriff said as he bent and hauled Marsh to his feet. The lawman reached up and yanked the quill out of the gunfighter's cheek. Marsh howled again, clapping his hands to his face. The sheriff handed the pen to Chuck.

"You his friend?" The sheriff asked.

"Yes, sir," Chuck replied, after a moment's hesitation.

"Take him and get gone. You got business in my town, finish it before sunset. I'm inclined to feel obliged to you both for the entertainment, but as a rule I don't allow brawling in my streets. Sets a bad precedent."

"Yessir," Chuck said. He reached out for Jay's sleeve and pulled him away from the bleeding Marsh, the wide-eyed crowd and the hardened sheriff. Jay twisted against his hold, not to get away but so that he could turn around and wave goodbye.

"I'll miss you, Billy!" Jay called out, blowing another kiss as Chuck hauled him into a nearby mercantile store.

"Mr. Wyoming, sir."

"Jay, kid. Not 'Mr. Wyoming,' an' definitely not 'sir.'"

"Whatever you say, sir. Just come along now. Please."

They made the sheriff's deadline, but only just. The sun sank down behind them in a gorgeous orange-and-pink blaze as they rode out the gates and into the rising dusk. To Chuck's surprise, Jay had been carrying a fair amount of cash in his jacket. Enough to replenish Chuck's supplies, outfit them both for at least another week and buy a barely broke gelding from the livery stable. Jay didn't seem to have any trouble handling the spirited young horse and Millie didn't seem to mind the company, so Chuck figured everyone was happy with the arrangement.

They rode until the sunset's fire faded in the west. When the cool violet sky arched overhead from horizon to horizon, they found a creek and followed it away from the Eye Eighty till they found a likely campsite. They saw the horses watered and fed, built a fire and cooked some of the rations, then settled into a good meal in a companionable silence.

Chuck couldn't quite figure out how he'd ended up with a traveling partner. He was trying to think of a polite way to bring it up when Jay let out a belch, took another nip from one of his many flasks and saved him the trouble.

"So, kid, where we goin'?"

"Well, about that, sir—"

"Jay."

"Sir," Chuck said firmly, "I was just going to ask you...how long you figure you're going to be joining me?"

"Oh, awhile," Jay said.

"Well," Chuck said. "Meanin' no disrespect or nothin' but how do I know I can trust you?"

"Good question," Jay said, grinning, "'Cept at this point, you already have. I ain't hurt you yet, have I?"

"No, sir, but that doesn't mean you won't once I'm asleep with my guard down," Chuck said, thinking of Big-Eyed Jill.

"Verra true, kid. Verra true. Your Pa taught you well, it seems. He'd have to, to trust you with Fat Lady, there."

Chuck went very still. *How...?*

Jay gave him a grin and pulled the dog tags out of his jacket. They glittered in the flickering firelight as he tossed them over. Chuck reflexively reached out and caught it. He couldn't see well enough to read the name, but he could feel the raised texture of the letters on the second line: USA. United States Army. Just like his pa's. Just like the ones on Gunslinger's chain that hung around his own neck.

"You knew my pa."

"A long time ago, but yeah," Jay said. "Haven't seen Bullet in years. Recognized Fat Lady, though, when I saw you back in Rawlins. Thought I'd see what was so important that Bullet sent his favorite rifle out with a green kid."

Chuck thought for half a second longer and then shrugged and pulled at his own collar. At the end of the day, he could use someone to watch his back. It might as well be someone his pa knew. Even if he was an old drunk.

"This," Chuck said, pulling Gunslinger's tags free. The key, still threaded on the ball chain, twisted slightly and caught the firelight. Jay nodded thoughtfully.

"Your pa had that?"

"No, sir. A man named Gunslinger did. He came to visit my pa but ran afoul of some Gant cultists. He was more than half dead when I found him. All dead, now."

"Son of a bitch, that's why you came out to the middle of nowhere," Jay said softly, shaking his head. He closed his eyes, lifted his flask to his lips and took a long drink. "Do me a favor, son, put that away and don't take it out again. That ain't nothing but trouble, right there."

"This?" Chuck asked, startled. His pa had said it was important, but he hadn't said it was trouble.

"Trust me, kid, I know things," Jay said. He opened his eyes, lifted his flask and shook it slightly as if to call Chuck's attention to it, then put it to his lips for another drink.

"Yes, sir," Chuck said, tucking the key back inside the neck of his shirt. "So, Pa said it belongs to the Bunker. And I'm going to take it back to them."

Jay looked at Chuck for a long moment. Then his white grin split his dark face one more time. Chuck tossed the dog tags back and Jay plucked them out of the night air. He slipped the chain back over his head and then lifted his flask in Chuck's direction before taking another drink.

"All right, then, kid. Why not? Not like I'm missing bingo night at the VFW."

CHAPTER FOUR

GARMAN FOUND HIMSELF BADLY IN NEED OF A DRINK.

Since his departure from the chapterhouse, very little had gone right. The first two days, it rained. Cold food and wet clothes did nothing to raise his spirits.

Four days out, he'd been sidetracked by two local landowners. Apparently, there was some debate about who owed whom passage fees for a bridge that crossed the boundary stream that defined their respective properties.

Since the beginning of the order, in the last days of the Bug War, the Windfists had stood neutral between all factions. As an order, they claimed a higher purpose: namely, the eradication of the Bug threat. That focus on the benefit of humanity as a whole had led to the Order enjoying a unique status among the Territories. People saw them as unbiased arbitrators, and would look to them to settle disputes.

Garman had lost half a day investigating the background of the disputed bridge and handing out a judgment. Neither party had been particularly happy about his solution—that they jointly charge travelers the fee which they would split three ways—equal shares for each of them and a small tithe to the Order as thanks for clearing things up. But they'd agreed to abide by his decision, and signed a contract to that effect. He sent the paperwork to the nearest chapterhouse, making it their problem from now on.

Three days later, his horse came up lame. The nearest town

wasn't much more than a collection of tumbledown buildings and houses supporting the nearby mine. They didn't have a proper wall, just a makeshift stockade cobbled together from boulders and building materials scavenged from somewhere—abandoned dwellings, most likely. He didn't even think the place had a name, just another pile of dirt along the ruined highway. It did, however, have two things he needed—a stable, and a saloon.

He'd dropped off the horse, purchased another one with the Order's coins and gone in search of a drink while he figured out his next move.

The sign above the swinging doors proclaimed the establishment to be a saloon but he would have known that from the stench of smoke and spilled beer and the suspicious puddles in the dirt right outside the front door. Raucous sounds from inside proclaimed it to be full, despite the sun high in the sky. Garman rolled his shoulders and pushed through, his hands loose at his sides.

As he'd expected, the customers inside looked up at him as he entered. Most of the faces looked sweat-streaked and coated in rock dust: miners just off the night shift. A few eyes widened as they saw his tattoo, but no one stood up to challenge him, despite the buzz of tension just under the surface. That was a relief. He'd seen it before when on liberty—any time there was equal parts hard labor, hard liquor, and boredom, there'd be a brawl. Especially when some local tough drank his courage up. Garman wasn't in the mood to hurt anyone just now; he just wanted a beer.

There weren't many tables, and none empty, so Garman sat at the unoccupied end of the long wooden bar. The other patrons turned their attention back to a kilted old man at a table in the center of the room.

"Now, see, what we yoosta have was called 'airplanes.' They flew, like birds or dragons but you could ride in them," he said, sipping whiskey between puffs of his cigar. "No, really! I used to jump out of 'em, too. At least, until my knees gave out."

The crowd laughed, obviously used to the nutty tall tales. He did seem entertaining, no matter how crazy he was.

A few seats down, a pair of travelers, judging by the dust on their clothes, sat together. The older man's eyes lingered on Garman for a second. He was smiling though, friendlylike.

"Right on time," the older man said, white teeth gleaming against his weathered, dark skin.

"Pardon?" Garman asked, unsure if the man was talking to him, or to the young man sitting hunched beside him.

"Not you, Junior," the older man said, shaking his head. Judging by his slur, the beer in front of him wasn't his first drink of the day. "The kid! Now's the perfect time to talk to that pretty girl there. Look at her, she's all alone! Poor thing, prob'ly got stood up by one of these miners. She's jes' practically begging you to go say hello."

"I don't know, sir," the younger man said, shaking his head. "I thought you just *had* to have a drink. That's why we stopped in this nowhere town, isn't it? 'Best Beer in Deseret'? Don't you just want to finish your beer and go?" He did glance over at the girl, though, and his cheeks flushed pink.

Garman snorted in amusement. The bartender placed a mug in front of him, and the Journeyman took a sip. He narrowly avoided making a face. *Best beer in Deseret? Saints, I hope not!*

The Journeyman glanced over his shoulder in order to keep from making a face and saw the object of their conversation. She was, indeed, a pretty girl, sitting by herself at a table. The weak light from the window shone on the fancy trim of her evening dress... even though it was midafternoon at best. Her expression was one of haughty boredom as she idly fanned herself.

"Never know less y'try, kid! G'wan, just go talk to her. Ask her if she'd like a drink. I bet she'd love to talk to a young, handsome thing like you," the old man said, swaying forward in his seat. He caught himself on the other's shoulder, damn near shoving the boy out of his chair. The kid recovered well enough that Garman was impressed with his reflexes. He landed on his feet, then straightened up and looked over at the lady in question. He looked back at his companion, who made a kind of impatient shooing motion with one hand, while draining the kid's beer with the other. The kid shook his head, then shrugged and turned toward the lady's table.

"Ah, excuse me, ma'am," the kid said, his voice cracking slightly. Garman watched as the lady turned to look at him as if he were something that she'd found stuck to the bottom of her shoe.

She raised an eyebrow.

"Uh. He-hello. I, uh, was wondering... would... could I, uh, buy you a drink?"

She looked him up and down, her expression saying quite

clearly that no, he could not. Garman's heart went out to the kid as he shuffled his feet uncomfortably on the sawdust-covered floor.

Just then, a burly man with long black hair and mustache burst in through the swinging doors.

"What the hell is going on here?" he bellowed, as he stalked toward the hapless kid. Behind him, about half a dozen more men followed him inside.

The woman smiled and her expression reminded Garman of a particularly mean cat that had lived at the chapterhouse when he'd been a Novitiate. Before he realized that he was going to do it, the Windfist slid off of his stool. Not far away, the older man turned to look at him with dark eyes. Garman gave him a nod, then started to walk around the edge of the room toward the kid.

"Baby, he propositioned me," the woman said, her voice carrying a distinct whine to it. The kid stepped back, both hands up.

"You did *what?!*" the black-mustached man roared. The kid looked like he would try to explain but Mustaches wasn't about to hear it. He let fly with a haymaker that would probably crush the kid's skull.

If it landed.

Which it didn't.

Garman had just a moment to feel impressed before chaos broke out all around. The miners finally had their excuse to let loose, and did it with abandon. The kid had ducked Mustaches' first punch and launched himself forward to counterattack with a flurry of blows. One of Mustaches' bully boys stepped forward, picking up a nearby half-empty bottle.

Coward. Garman kicked a chair, sliding it into the man's legs before he could swing the improvised weapon. The man sat down hard, a look of surprise on his face quickly replaced by pain as Garman's foot made contact with his wrist.

The bushwhacker dropped the bottle, grabbing his wrist just as Garman pulled him over backwards, slamming him to the floor. What started as a howl of anger and pain was quickly cut off by the boot on his chest.

"Can't abide a man that'll hit another from behind," Garman said. "Why don't you sit this one out."

"You're doing great, son!" the old man at the bar said, nonchalantly dodging a flying beer mug. "Keep it up!"

Garman wasn't sure if he was talking to him, or the kid. As

he applied more pressure to the drunk's chest, he watched the younger man.

The kid was surrounded, more or less, by four men. He feinted toward the one at his twelve o'clock before throwing an elbow at the nine o'clock. Blood erupted from the man's nose as he staggered back in shock. The kid's foot snapped forward, catching the man in front square between the legs. An elbow to the back of the skull dropped him like a sack of meal.

Garman turned his attention to another man coming at him, rolling his eyes at the knife. He blocked the clumsy strike, the force of his defensive blow knocking the blade from the weak grip. Ridge hand to the throat sent the man to his knees, gagging.

Garman glanced back at the bar just as the old coot staggered, somehow narrowly avoiding a punch from the man next to him, before swiping the mug of beer off the table and stretching. His fist caught the man in the jaw, dropping him. The old guy looked mildly surprised as he took a swig, then raised the mug in salute at Garman with a wink. The Windfist gave him a small nod before turning back to the kid.

The kid avoided a strike from behind as he kicked right, taking that man in the knee. The thug at nine o'clock had recovered enough to try and connect with a kick of his own. The kid caught his ankle without looking, giving it a vicious twist. The pop of the knee dislocating was audible over the noise of the fight. Screams followed shortly after as the pain set in.

Six o'clock tried one more time, only to find his wrist locked in a two-handed grip. A split second later, he was flying over the young man's shoulder to land on his buddy, still green and groaning on the floor.

The kid straightened slowly, meeting the eyes of the other patrons. Not one held the gaze, suddenly finding something interesting—somewhere else—to look at.

"I'm really sorry, sirs, ma'am," he said, turning and bowing slightly toward the woman. "Please forgive me for defending myself. Have a nice day."

With this little speech, he touched his fingertips to his eyebrow at the lady, before extending a hand to Garman.

"Thank you, sir," he said. "My name is Chuck."

"Garman," he said, gripping the boy's hand. "Journeyman Windfist."

"Yes, sir. Appreciate the help. If things go like they usually do, we'd probably better leave now, before any more of his friends show up. You should come too."

"This happen a lot?" Garman asked, dropping the kid's hand and raising his eyebrows.

"Once or twice, so far," he said, giving him a grin and a shrug.

Garman found himself smiling back, though he didn't really know why.

"Keeps things fun," the old man said as he walked up, pulling on a thoroughly disreputable jacket. He let out an epic belch, then grinned at them both. "You headed east, Windfist? Imagine that. You c'n come with us out of town, then. Couple a poor wayfarers ought to be good company for your Journey, right?"

"If you say so." Garman rolled his eyes, stepped over the groaning bodies of their opponents and pushed his way out through the swinging doors.

"Where'd you pick him up?" Garman asked a few hours later. He and Chuck rode side by side following a singing Jay.

The old man had surprised Chuck, which wasn't totally unusual. But still, Jay had been positively charming as he wheedled the slightly prickly Windfist into riding along with them. In truth, it had been fun to watch, and Chuck already felt inclined to like Garman. Fighting beside a man had that effect.

Chuck looked over at the Windfist with an easy smile. The Journeyman sat with a look of stiff disapproval, but Chuck didn't mind. The trip had certainly gotten more interesting since Jay had tumbled into the dust at his feet. Now they had one of the legendary Windfists with them. Chuck had been somewhat distracted at the time, but he couldn't help but notice how well the other man fought. For the first time since getting scammed by Big-Eyed Jill, Chuck realized that he was actually having quite a lot of fun.

"Found 'im in Laramie," Chuck said. "He got poured out of a coach and I sorta got him cleaned up. He ain't bad, once you get to know him. Just try to stand upwind if you can."

"Hmmph," Garman said, "And is this useful along your Journey?"

"Oh, I don't know about useful, so much," Chuck said, "But, it's much more entertaining."

"A Journey shouldn't be 'entertaining.'"

"You say that in a peculiar way."

"What's that?"

"'Journey.' You say it like it's some kind of special thing. Mystical-like, or...a religious experience or something."

"It is," Garman said and gave Chuck a knowing and slightly smug smile. For a moment, the young man from the farm thought about pointing out that the Windfist wasn't too much older than he but his good manners held true.

"We must, each of us, take the sacred Journey for ourselves," Garman said. "Only by progressing through each test of fate can we grow into the warriors we are meant to be. We brothers of the Windfist order undertake our Journeys as the last step in our training. We seek out our enemy during its course."

"You think we're all s'posed to be warriors?" Chuck said, trying to keep the doubt out of his voice. Garman chuckled and gave him a nod.

"Of a sort, yes. It comes more easily to some than to others, certainly. But we, all of us, are bound by our common humanity to fight for our world and our right to exist. It's something that is, unfortunately, too easily forgotten these days," Garman said, turning to give Chuck a look.

"You, though," the Journeyman went on, "you seem a bit of a natural warrior. Someone gave you some solid training at some point."

"My pa," Chuck said, smiling as he thought of home. "He was a soldier in the war. Taught me an' my sis to defend ourselves. Uncertain times, as you said."

"Indeed," Garman agreed. His tone said that he approved of Pa Gordon's forethought. Chuck spared a moment to laugh—on the inside—at the thought of Pa wanting this monk's approval. Or opinion, for that matter.

"And did your father send you on this Journey of yours?" Garman asked.

"Yessir. Sorta. An old friend of his came to visit and died. Pa gave me his personal effects and asked me to see them to his friend's home, back east a ways." Chuck shrugged, hoping he sounded natural as he related this not-quite-lie. "I ran into Jay in Laramie and he knew my pa and his friend both, so..."

"Ah. An honorable mission, to be sure. Will you be traveling near Kansas City?"

"Could be," Chuck said, glancing forward. Jay didn't look like he was paying any attention to them but his horse slowed, then stopped altogether. Jay didn't seem to notice, as he was just hitting the chorus of some song about the bottoms of apples and furry boots. Chuck shook his head and turned his attention back to Garman. "Why d'ya ask?"

"That's where my own Journey takes me," the Windfist replied. "I cannot tell you what my task is, but it would be good to have companions as stalwart as you appear to be."

Stalwart?

"Uh, sure thing," Chuck said.

He would have said more but they'd caught up to Jay and the older man looked as if he were close to falling off his horse in the midst of his performance. Chuck pulled Millie up alongside, just in case. Jay listed to the side and rolled his head on his neck so that he could smile at the pair of them.

"Are we all friends now?" Jay asked, cutting off his serenade. "I don't think I could bear it if we weren't friends."

"We're friends, Jay," Chuck said, glancing at Garman. The Windfist shifted in his saddle, his face lined in disapproval, but he said nothing.

"Hot damn," Jay said, pulling himself back to something approximating vertical in his saddle. "A Windfist monk! Gonna be a helluva ride with you along, Junior!"

"My name is Journeyman Garman."

"You got it, Junior. So, where we goin'?"

Jay looked at Chuck and raised his eyebrows.

"Well, I have rather pressing business near Kansas City if you don't have anything better to do," Garman said, sounding rather deliberately casual.

Chuck suddenly had the suspicion that the Windfist wanted them along for his own reasons. Backup, perhaps. While that was flattering, Chuck would much rather the other man be upfront about his motives.

Not that he had many stones to throw at that particular glass house, as Pa would have said.

"Nothing we'd rather do than join you, Junior. I got an old friend near there," Jay said with a grin. "Couldn't have planned it better myself."

He reached into his jacket for one of his flasks and took a

swig before offering it to Garman. The Windfist shook his head, his face creasing with disapproval. Jay's grin grew wider and he held the flask out to Chuck.

Chuck looked at his two companions, shrugged and took the flask. Fire like a sunburn erupted in his mouth and down his throat. With a grimace, he fought through the burn, refusing to cough.

Garman gave a sniff and nudged his horse forward. Chuck capped the flask and handed it back to Jay.

"Atta boy," Jay said, his eyes glinting from within a nest of mahogany wrinkles. "Well done."

A few days later, Chuck's party arrived in Fewaf, a small settlement just outside of what used to be Cheyenne. Garman, though still somewhat prickly around Jay, seemed comfortable in Chuck's presence, and helped out with the hunting and foraging. His stoic, direct demeanor aside, Chuck found himself liking the slightly older Windfist. Trusting him, as well.

After an uneventful night, Jay had sent Garman off to secure tickets on the next train to Lincoln. Chuck, after securing the horses, had gone to the platform to watch the train come in. He hadn't wanted to show it in front of the others, but he was excited and fascinated by the massive, fire-belching metal snake crawling up the track. It hissed into the morning air as it slowed to a stop.

He turned at the sound of a frustrated grunt, and watched as a young woman struggled with a suitcase.

"Come on, Jennifer, no time to waste," an older woman said, looking down her nose with a sniff. She stepped onto the train from the platform, her face pinched like a sun-ripened prune. "This train was late to begin with; no need to make it more so."

Chuck walked over to where Jennifer strained to lift the heavy case. Pretty, about his age, with dark red hair, she was trying her best to keep her balance on the platform. The slight breeze threatened to tangle her legs in her somewhat faded, but very well-kept, homespun brown dress.

"Miss, may I be of some assistance?"

"Oh, no, I couldn't possibly ask you to," Jennifer said. "I can get it; it's just awkward. But thank you."

"It's no trouble at all, miss," Chuck said, ignoring her protests and taking the case's handle. While heavier than most of his bags, it wasn't much more than the sacks of grain he'd tossed every day, or the bales of hay, or the tons of manure... "I'll just get it up the steps for you. Should be easy after that."

"Thank you, so much," Jennifer said, rubbing the small of her back. "I never thought everything I owned would be that heavy. Sure didn't seem like that much when I packed it."

"I know the feeling, miss."

She climbed the steps, stopping at the top.

"Will you be taking this train, Mr. . . . ?"

"Just call me Chuck, miss, and yes, I reckon I will, since it's the only one 'round here for a while." He said, grinning. "Maybe we'll bump into each other again."

"I should hope so, Chuck."

He felt a flush crawl up his neck.

"Aww, shucks, I . . . well . . . ahem." He turned, looking over his shoulder at where Garman was paying the fare. "I should go help with the . . . um . . ."

Jennifer's smile made his frustration worse.

But then she said, "Well, I sure wouldn't mind having someone my age to talk to. Come find me when you get settled, okay?"

"Sure, miss. Be happy to."

"And call me Jenny!" She beamed at him again, before disappearing into the train car.

A black hand slapped down on his shoulder, snapping him out of his daze.

"Good lookin' young filly there, m'boy. Seemed interested in you. I wouldn't let that one get too far away, if you know what I mean."

"With all due respect, Jay, I rarely do."

The old man's wink did nothing to help his confusion. Fortunately, Garman came up, tickets in hand.

"We and the horses are booked to Lincoln. They'll be a two cars back. Twelve-hour trip assuming no issues." Despite his customary reserve, he seemed excited. Chuck figured it was his first train ride, too.

They quickly loaded the horses, gathered their gear and made their way past the watchful eyes of several rough-looking men. They wore matching uniforms—high-collared green jackets, heavy cotton trousers, and white helmets. Chuck assumed they were some kind of security, as they never strayed from the car near the end of the train.

Hauling the packs and saddlebags into the small passenger car required various contortions to avoid hitting the other passengers—as few as there were—with the awkward loads. Several minutes, and several apologies later, they found seats and stashed their gear. Chuck kept Fat Lady and his Marlin close, noticing that Garman made sure he had a few knives within reach. They traded a look coupled with a slight smile as they adjusted the pistols on their belts. Jay seemed oblivious.

"Well, it looks like we'll be seeing each other sooner than we thought, won't we?"

Chuck looked up to find Jenny smiling at him from the aisle.

"Um...hi, miss," he said. "Pleasure to make your acquaintance again."

"Howdy, li'l lady!" Jay stood, unsteadily stretching across Chuck and Garman's legs to extend a hand. "Pleasure is all mine. I'm Chuck's fun lovin' and rugg'ly han'some Uncle Jay."

Chuck caught the old man before he fell face-first into Jenny's cleavage.

"Whoops, p'arn me, miss. Must'a been a bump in the track."

They hadn't pulled out of the station yet.

"Chuck here was getting ready to go take care of the horses in the stable car. Why don't you tag along with him?"

"I was?" A hard nudge from Jay. "Ow. Oh, right, I was."

"I love horses! Do you mind, Chuck?"

"Yes. I mean...no? I mean..." He looked at his companions for help, finding none. "If you'd like to come along, I can't stop you."

"What the awkward young man is tryin' to say is, he'd be happy to have the company, miss." Jay slouched back down in his seat, seemingly pleased with himself.

Chuck stood, bumping into the luggage rack above him.

"Ow!" He rubbed his head as he felt himself blushing. At Jenny's barely smothered laughter, he grew even warmer. "If you'd just follow me, Miss Jenny."

It was the closest he could come to just using her given name.

As they made their way toward the stable cars, Chuck couldn't think of anything to say. How was it that Jay could pull off seemingly amazing feats of charm, while drunk and practically throwing himself at any female that moved, yet he could barely walk without tripping over something? Chuck knew he had a lot to learn about chatting up girls. He figured the best course of action would be to just talk horses to her for now. Keep it strictly business and educational.

The strong, yet not unpleasant, smell of horseflesh hit them as they entered the stock car. It had been cleaned quickly at the station, Chuck could tell, since the odor of manure wasn't as pungent as he'd expected. Clean straw, fresh oats and large hairy mammal all combined into the familiar.

"Oh, my," Jenny said, grimacing. "That's rank. I figured you'd be used to it?"

"I am." Chuck realized that Jenny had misread his expression. "Just got a bit homesick, is all. You don't have horses at home?"

She shook her head, holding her nose. Her voice became nasal.

"How do you handle the stench?"

"That's nothing. You should try herding goats after a downpour. Woof," he said with a grin. "This is 'clean' stable. Try taking a few big breaths."

"Okay." Reluctantly, she dropped her hand, inhaling deeply. "Oh, that does help. It's not so bad now. Which one's yours?"

Chuck walked over to Millie's stall. The big roan nuzzled his neck as soon as he came within reach.

"This is Millie. She's my mare." He patted her a few times before strapping on her feed bag. "That's a good girl, Millie. Millie, meet Jenny, she's a nice girl, too."

Millie whickered softly, nudging him before diving into the feed bag.

"Good girl, I put some carrots in there for you."

"You can tell a lot about a man by how he treats animals, you know."

He felt the flush rising again. "Oh? How so?"

"Well, a kind man is kind to everyone," the girl said, moving closer to him. Chuck would have stepped back to give her room but there was no place to move in the narrow stall. "Even animals. You treat her like she's a person, not just a beast of burden."

Jenny scratched Millie under her cheek. The mare sighed, angling her head and pressing into Jenny's hand. Didn't stop munching, though. Jenny looked at him over Millie's nose.

"You seem like a kind man, Chuck."

"I try to be but sometimes..." It wasn't very kind of him to blow people's heads off but it *was* necessary at the time. "What I mean to say is that I *think* I am, ma'am but there's times when you have to be mean. Like spurring a horse."

"I wouldn't know. Do you think I could ride Millie?"

"Um, sure." He started for the tack locker. "It might be a bit tight in here, since the stalls are only about twice as wide as the horses, but you could sit on her and turn her some, I guess." He trailed off at Jenny's giggle.

"No, silly, not now! After we get to Lincoln." She stopped, eyes growing slightly wider. "You were really going to saddle her for me?"

"Yes, ma'am. You said you wanted to ride and I thought you meant right now."

"Interesting," she said. Her smile grew somewhat less friendly, more conniving. "So, if I'd asked you to—"

She was cut off by the train's whistle, two long blasts. She glared.

"If I'd asked you to—OH!" The train lurched forward. Jenny staggered, falling into Chuck. She caught herself, using his chest. "My, aren't you strong."

"What were you going to say, Miss Jenny?" He felt himself grow hot again. Seemed like this girl was going to make his head blow steam like that train whistle.

"I was going to say—"

"Jennifer! There you are!" Jenny's older companion appeared in the doorway, holding a kerchief to her nose. "Come away this instant, before something foul gets into your dress."

The look she gave Chuck could have withered flowers.

"I tripped, honest!"

"I'm sure you did," she said with a sniff, then grimaced. "Come."

"Yes, Aunt Sil." Jenny curtsied. "Thank you for letting me meet your horse, sir."

She followed her aunt back into the passenger car.

Chuck watched them leave, not sure exactly what just happened. He fed the other two horses, made sure they all had fresh water, then made his way back to his seat.

He noticed Aunt Sil glaring at him from across the car, carefully positioning herself between him and Jenny. She also caught Jenny's small wave, stifling any further attempts with a sharp look. Jenny turned to look out the window, her shoulders slumping.

Chuck sighed, turning to focus on the land rolling by his

window. He found himself lulled by the gentle swaying of the car coupled with the clacking of the wheels.

He woke with a start at the sound of the whistle.

"Welcome to Cheyenne, boys!" Jay's grin was firmly in place as he swept a hand toward the scenery. "Largest city in what used to be Wyoming. Watch your step; besides the Gants and bandits an' all, it's dragon country."

Chuck leaned over to look up and out the window. He'd heard of the "dragons" that, along with the Gants, had destroyed the World That Was, but he'd yet to see one.

Of course, most people who saw them didn't last long. Dragons were hunters.

"Used to know a fine lady 'round these parts," the old man continued. "Really knew how to take care of a hungry traveler. Good cook too."

Chuck stared out the window. The "city," if you call it that, seemed to consist of the station, a few shacks, and the obligatory saloon. In the distance, piles of overgrown rubble dotted the landscape, rising in seemingly random, yet somehow regular groups. He couldn't decide if Jay was joking, or seeing things.

"Did this woman live under those hills, or in the saloon?" Garman asked. He was apparently thinking along the same lines.

"Oho! Watch it Chuck, Junior here seems to be growing a sense of humor!" Jay said, slapping Garman on the shoulder. "And here I thought the Windfist beat the funny out of all their recruits."

"The difference between wit and humor is that wit is dry," Garman said with a raised eyebrow. "And less odorforous."

"Easy there, Junior. Just funnin' ya a bit. To answer your question, she lived here a long time back. Not sure if she's still in these parts, or found a nice chap to settle down with. There used to be a fairly large town here, before the Gants came along. About sixty, maybe seventy thousand people."

Now Chuck knew the old man was full of it. *Sixty thousand* people, all in one spot? Goat patties, as Pa would say. Rawlins didn't have more than four hundred folks at one time, even during the fair. Laramie had seemed full to him, and he knew that had only been a few thousand, at most. He snorted.

The old man managed to correctly interpret the snort.

"Scoff all you want," Jay said. "There's a lot of country out there you ain't never been privy to, boy. Place called New York

City was the largest in the nation. Over seven million unhappy, crabby, downright unpleasant people jammed together in crowded bliss. One of the finest tributes to modern man's achievements. Buildings stretching to the sky, trains running underneath and the whole shebang humming along day and night. And right in the middle, Lady Liberty welcomed more of them with upheld torch, promising freedom. It was glorious."

Chuck looked out the window again as they started moving, envisioning buildings in place of the rubble, fifty, one hundred, even two hundred feet tall. Crowds moving in and around them, shoulder to shoulder, nose to nose. Like goats at feeding time.

"Ugh," Garman said with a scowl. He clearly was envisioning the same. "No, thank you."

"You Windfists are all about ending the Gants, right?" Jay asked. "Gettin' rid of all the 'lectrovores?"

"Correct," Garman replied.

"What do you think's going to happen when we get power back?" Jay said. "And why do it if it ain't to bring back the World That Was?"

"What you just described doesn't sound like a reason, to me."

"Ah, but let me ask you this—ever look up at the stars and wonder what else is up there?"

Garman nodded.

"We were on our way to finding out, son. Whole new wilderness to explore, worlds to find, adventures to have."

Garman frowned, then sat back looking out the window in thought.

As they continued, Chuck saw a few more shacks, scattered groups of people doing everyday chores: washing, weeding the small gardens, tending to livestock.

"I guess the dragons ain't as active this time of year," Jay said. "Kinda surprised these folks are out and about."

"Maybe the train scares the dragons," Chuck said. Jay shrugged.

The residents paid the train no mind, with the exception of the one older lady hurriedly pulling her clean sheets off the drying line. He couldn't help but snicker at how she shook her fist at the passing train, silently mouthing curses as soot settled on her freshly laundered linens. Ma would've probably started shooting. He stifled another wave of homesickness as he turned away from the scene to look across the aisle at Jenny.

Aunt Sil's steely gaze convinced him that was a bad idea.

With nowhere else to look, he decided to search his eyelids for holes, pulling his hat down and settling back into his chair. Visions of tall buildings and friendly women filled his head.

"Chuck. Chuck, wake up. Something's happening."

Chuck snapped awake as Jay's breath rolled over him, more effective than smelling salts.

"What's going on?" He shook fog from his brain, trying to focus through the disorientation. "We in Lincoln already?"

"No, son, I just got a feeling."

"I did mention issues," Garman said, drily.

He glanced around at the faces in the car—no one else seemed troubled. Garman shifted his gaze from the front door to the rear and back again, hand twitching toward his stowed weapons.

One of the men Chuck had flagged as security stood at the rear of the car. He was, to Chuck's eye, trying to look casual, but something in his demeanor didn't ring true.

After a few minutes, another man in uniform appeared, smiling as though he owned the world. Both newcomers were unshaven, sweaty and covered in soot.

The second man, slightly taller and leaner than his companion, spoke to the passengers.

"Welcome to the Barony of Ironhelm. As of right now, there's a small additional fee to utilize this here rail line. Now, if everyone cooperates, there won't be any trouble."

"This is an outrage!" An older woman, approximately his ma's age, stood up suddenly. "We've already paid for our tickets; you can't just rob us!"

"As I said, ma'am—this ain't a robbery, it's collecting a fee," he said, smiling a fierce, toothy grin. A gold incisor flashed in the sunlight through the train's dusty window. "Call it a 'security fee' if it makes you feel better. Now shut your pie hole and pay up. Unless you'd prefer to quit breathin'."

The woman sat down quietly, impotent defiance still written across her face. The older man next to her placed a hand on her arm, possibly to comfort her but more likely to keep her from speaking again. The Baron's man looked at his partner, then nodded.

A blur of motion and the old man rocked back, clutching his temple. Blood flowing between his fingers formed a ghastly river.

"Oh my God! Harold!" the old woman made to hug her companion, only to be stopped short.

"Now, leave old Harold be, ma'am, or my friend here will use his pistol as it was intended."

"Why?" the woman snapped.

"Because a lesson needed learnin' and it just ain't right to hit no old lady." His grin dropped as he looked over the rest of the passengers. "Now, anyone else got anything to say? No? Good."

The two men made their way down the car, collecting money from the passengers that had it, other items of value from those that didn't.

"Give 'til it hurts, folks, or you'll hurt 'til you give."

Jenny looked like she was trying to crawl inside her chair and hide. Unfortunately, her movements only drew the attention of the Baron's men.

"Oh, hello, pretty lady," the man said, his grin stretching into a leer. "You don't have to worry none—you don't have to pay us." A wink and a chuckle. "Not with money, that is. Just a kiss and you don't have to worry none a'tall."

The green-eyed girl's whisper was barely audible.

"No."

"I'm sorry, I couldn't hear you."

"No." The girl's voice became stronger, though not forceful. "I won't do it. I have money, take that."

"Oh no, sweetheart, you don't understand. I don't care what you have; I b'lieve I'll take what I want." The smile dropped, all semblance of cheer or goodwill gone. "And what I want is a kiss. At least for starters."

Chuck tensed. Jay placed a hand on his arm with a slight shake of his head.

Chuck forced himself to remain seated. Jay was right, he needed to keep a low profile. Garman would draw enough attention to the group as it was. But it just wasn't *right*. He shifted slightly, moving Fat Lady to where he could bring her around quickly, if necessary.

"C'mon now honey, no need to be shy." The security officer grabbed Jenny's arm, pulling her out of her seat and into his chest. "Just gimme a quick kiss and we'll see how you like—OW!"

He rocked back, three streaks of bright red appearing as if by magic on his cheek. As fast as the girl was, though, he was faster. The girl collapsed at his backhand, falling into her cushioned bench.

"Lousy bitch!"

Chuck was up before he knew what he was doing. In the time it took for the thug to turn toward him, Chuck brought Fat Lady around, driving the butt of the rifle into the other man's stomach. He followed with a sharp snap upward, enjoying the satisfying crack of the wooden stock against the man's face. Loverboy hit the floor with a thump.

He turned, ready to face the other security guard and found the man gagging, clawing at the hilt of a knife in his throat. He hit the ground with a gurgling wheeze. Garman gave him a nod, grabbing their gear.

"Are you all right, Miss Jenny?" Chuck said, kneeling, eye level with the young woman. "I don't think he'll be bothering you again."

"I am now," Jenny said. "Thank you."

"You'd better come with us. He ain't gonna be too happy when he wakes up."

"You will most definitely not be going anywhere, young lady!" Aunt Sil shrieked, clutching Jenny's arm in a viselike grip. "We are going to Lincoln and that's final!"

Garman pushed past him to retrieve his knife.

"Finish him and we'll get going, Chuck."

"No."

"What? You'll leave a living enemy behind you?"

"It ain't right. He's defenseless," Chuck said, drawing his bowie, handing it hilt first to Jenny. "If he tries anything, you'll need something better than fingernails."

Garman snorted, disgust plainly written on his face.

"Well, boys, we better get movin'," Jay called out. The old man had as much gear as he could carry on his small frame. "Figure our welcome is just about worn out. And let me say: Ain't my fault."

"This time," Garman replied.

"Yep. Not this time. Oh, brace yourselves." Jay grabbed a slim cord next to the window and yanked. Chuck and Garman barely had time to grab onto the seats next to them before the squeal of the brakes hit their ears. They lurched forward as the train braked, hard.

Jay led the way to the stock car, cheerfully ignoring the looks from the other passengers.

"Alright, Chuck, get the horses saddled. Garman, you see about getting that door open."

"What about you, sir?" Chuck headed for the tack lockers. Millie knew something was going on. She shifted in her stall, tossing her head and whickering.

"I'm going to make sure there ain't no trouble from the other guards." The small man dropped his load and headed for the door.

"Won't you need some help?" Chuck asked.

Jay started giggling and was still giggling when he left the compartment. From out the door they could hear his guffaws.

"But he ain't even armed," Chuck pointed out, plaintively.

Garman ignored him, examining the drop-down door.

"Locked from the outside. I'll head out and get it open."

Chuck nodded, concentrating on his task. His nerves on edge, he was still able to get the horses saddled and gear loaded fairly quickly.

The sound of bolts being thrown back came just before the flood of blazing sunlight as the door dropped to the ground. Garman hurried up the ramp, taking his mount's reins from Chuck's hand.

"We need to move. I heard more men toward the front car. Couldn't tell how many but that sound will draw them toward us."

Chuck nodded, leading Millie and Jay's horse out onto the scrub grass. As if in response to Garman's comment, a shout came from the backside of the train. Sounds of a brief scuffle followed. Jay appeared from around the corner.

"All set? Great. Let's go."

"We heard something. Was there... did you?" Chuck said, handing Jay the reins.

"Nah, nothing big. Just convinced two more of the security team they should rest a spell," the old man said, winking as he pulled himself up into the saddle. "Also made sure it would take awhile for this thing to get movin' again."

"Chuck!"

He whirled at the scream from the stock car. Jenny stood in the entrance, terror on her pretty face. The thug from earlier stood behind her, bracing her against his chest, Chuck's knife to her throat. The gun in his other hand pointed in Chuck's general direction.

"Now just hold on a minute there, boy," the man said through the blood running from his pulped nose. He bent close to take a long, dramatic sniff of Jenny's hair. "I think you forgot something valuable. She's a fine young thing, isn't she? Hate to mess up her dress Now drop that rifle."

"Just let her go, mister. She ain't done nothing to you," Chuck said, bending slowly to put Fat Lady on the ground in front of his feet, keeping eye contact all the while. "This is between you and me."

"She means something to you and I owe you one," the man said, grinning his blood-smeared, gold-glinted grin once more. With his eyes still locked to Chuck's he bent and gave Jenny a noisy, smacking kiss. She whimpered and squirmed but the thug held her tightly.

"Besides," he went on, light wisps of her hair moving with his breath. "She said 'no.'"

A quick movement and Jenny's mouth opened in a soundless gasp as the tip of the knife pierced her throat. She went limp, the weight of her body pulling her captor's arm just enough that his bullet went wide.

He would never get a second shot.

Chuck drew his pistol, long hours of practice making the move smooth and deadly. His shot painted gray matter inside the walls of the stock car before Jenny's body hit the floor.

Chuck started forward, only to stop at Garman's hand heavy on his shoulder. He brushed it off angrily and turned to face the Windfist as time and sound came back all in a rush.

"Lemme go! She needs help!"

"She'll be fine," the older boy said. "She's still breathing, and we need to put as much distance between us and this train before they get to the next stop."

"He's right, son," Jay said. "We got bigger fish to fry, remember? Sucks but we gotta let her be and get a move on."

Even Millie seemed to agree, nickering and stomping her feet.

"Those gunshots will have alerted anyone nearby," Garman said. He stepped back and mounted up, then spun his horse to survey the horizon. "We need to move."

As if in response, a shout drifted back to them from the front of the train.

Chuck took one last look at Jenny's limp body, silently offering a prayer for her, as well as asking forgiveness for his part in her situation. He swung into the saddle, then lightly kicked Millie's flanks to follow the other men.

They rode hard for almost thirty minutes, switching between full gallop and a fast lope, to get as much distance between any pursuit and themselves. They finally slowed, horses lathered and breathing hard, to walk along a small stream flowing between mesas. Jay called a halt.

"All right, I've been watching and haven't seen signs of any-one coming after us yet." He shaded his eyes against the setting sun. "Getting to be too dark to ride fast here soon. I say we set up camp and keep an eye out, get started moving fast in the morning."

Garman nodded.

"Chuck," Jay said, "you okay with the plan?"

"Yeah," Chuck said with a shrug. "Guess so."

"All right, then let's get up to that cut over there; looks like a good spot."

A short time later, with the horses fed, watered and brushed, Chuck stretched out on his bedroll next to the small cooking fire. Garman was in position a few yards away, having volunteered for first watch. Jay sat nearby, watching silently, taking the occasional pull from his ever-present flask.

"You're still bothered by what happened." It wasn't a question.

"She got hurt, Jay. And it was my fault."

"Yep, she did. Not so sure about it being your fault, though."

"If I hadn't done anything, she might still be okay."

"Now, you don't know that, son. Remember, she had a mind to say no before you did anything. Can't say for sure whether she made the right choice but it don't matter what we think. She made that decision on her own and stuck by it. Can't blame yourself for other folk's choices."

"Garman was right. Should've killed him."

The old man nodded, offering his flask. At Chuck's headshake, he took a pull.

"Well, I woulda, in your shoes. But I ain't you, and neither is Junior over there. Main question is, would you be able to live with yourself had you done it?"

Chuck grew silent, turning it over in his head.

"Thought not. You tried, you did what you thought was honorable, you stuck to your code. She got hurt because there are bad people in the world. That's it. At the end of the day, there are less bad people, because of you and what you stood up for. But, maybe, just maybe, there were people on that train that saw you and it made them want to be a better person. That girl was free, Chuck. She made her decision the first time she said 'no.' You showed her, and more importantly, other people, that good men are still around."

Jay put a hand on his shoulder.

"You're a good man, Chuck. Now, let's get some sleep."

Chuck nodded, rolling himself in his blankets. Sleep came slowly but eventually it came.

CHAPTER FIVE

JASMINE SHADED HER EYES WITH ONE HAND AS SHE SQUINTED into the burning blue of the sky. A breeze whispered past, cooling the sweat that beaded along her dark hairline. The air tasted of heat and the iron red dust of the desert. She stood on a bluff overlooking a jagged slash of canyon. Up ahead, a cry like that of a hawk echoed off the rocks. Behind her, she heard a horse whinny nervously in response.

"Lady Moore?" one of the men to her rear asked. He sounded as nervous as the horses. She held up a hand, demanding silence, as another of those piercing screams bounced off the rocks around them.

The horses began to neigh and whinny even more and Jasmine could hear the men cursing as they struggled to control the beasts. She didn't bother to look back. Horses were not her problem and she'd warned the men to stay back. Not her fault that they felt the need to hover.

A *whump, whump* sound came from in front of them and a sudden smile split her otherwise proudly arrogant expression. Great leathery wings rose out of the canyon before them, glistening copper and green in the relentless desert sun. Jasmine felt a surge of joy and love pulse through her in time with the dragon's wing beats as it rose up above them. Downdrafts tugged at her hair, whipping it back from her face. She lifted her hand and pointed.

The dragon banked slowly, dipping one ten-foot wing and

entering a lazy turn to the left. The sunlight briefly illuminated the shimmering gray-blue of the dragon's belly. Then he flared his wings and landed on the rim of the canyon, not ten feet away from Jasmine. Powerful hind legs touched down first, followed by winged forelimbs. He dipped his head at her approach, slightly mangled feral pig held delicately in an iridescent beak capable of breaking a man in half. As she stepped forward, he laid the pig on the ground and looked to her, eyes wide as he sought her approval.

She bent and examined the pig. He'd taken it from above and snapped its spine with the first bite, from the looks of things. All in all, a neat, clean kill. Jasmine approved.

As was her custom, Jasmine closed her eyes for a moment and whispered her thanks to the pig for his sacrifice. Then she pulled a short knife out of her arm-sheath and sawed off the pig's ear before standing and smiling at the dragon.

"Good work, Quetzalith," she murmured. "The rest is yours."

The dragon let out a rumble and bent to begin tearing at the pig carcass. Jasmine watched for a moment, then stepped even closer and reached out to stroke the long, backward-sloping skull crest. Quetzalith let out a deep, gravelly moan of pleasure and continued feasting. The pig's blood was very red against the glossy sheen of Quetzalith's black beak.

"Why d'ye take the ear?"

Jasmine turned to see Byron, one of the Baron's lieutenants, standing back a few yards from her. He wore the standard uniform of the Baron's sworn men, though the Baron would be disgusted to see it now. Several days of hard riding had creased the nap, sweat stained under the arms, and several of the shiny brass buttons were missing. The retainer's long hair, protruding from under his pith helmet, was lank and oily—so covered in road dust that Jasmine couldn't have said its color. He had a tight grip on the reins of his white-eyed horse and Jasmine felt a surge of revulsion. Though he'd asked his question politely, Jasmine didn't have a lot of patience for those who would disregard the natural terror of terrestrial animals in the presence of a dragon.

But still. He was the Baron's vassal. And nominally, so was she.

"Tribute," she said, her rich voice carefully devoid of judgment, even as the horse plunged and tried to pull away. Byron cursed and kicked his mount, opening up bloody wounds in the horse's flanks with his spurs. Anger pulsed through her and Quetzalith paused in his eating and began to glare balefully at the man.

Jasmine took a deep breath and forced herself to calm. She didn't know how or why but Quetzalith was remarkably sensitive to her emotions. As tempting as it would be, the last thing she needed right now was for Quetzalith to alienate the Baron by slaughtering one of his lieutenants. So, she ran her mind through the calming exercises her father had taught her as a child and waited while the loathsome man brought his pitiable mount under control.

"How do you mean, 'tribute'?" he asked, wiping the sweat from his eyes.

"He is a predator," she said. "An apex predator, which means that he has no predators of his own. I've had to teach him to respect me. Part of how I do that is by insisting on taking a part of every kill he makes."

"How d'ye teach 'im that?"

Jasmine turned toward the man, letting her face empty of all emotion.

"I convinced him young that I am the deadlier predator," she said. "And I never let him forget it."

There was more to it, of course. She had raised Quetzalith from a flapling. There was true affection between them now, but it never hurt to remind these rough men that she was not afraid to be ruthless. As if to underscore her point, Quetzalith looked up from his feast and snapped his beak in Byron's direction. That set the lieutenant's horse to plunging in panic again and Jasmine allowed herself a wintry smile. She gave Quetzalith's crest one more caress before stepping away. He'd splashed pig's blood on her, but she didn't mind. It only served to underscore the point she was trying to make.

It helped that the Baron held her in such high esteem, she admitted to herself as she walked back to where the other three men waited with her horse. To a man, they looked miserable in their uniforms, though they'd at least managed to avoid Byron's slovenliness. Not for the first time, she found herself thanking her lucky stars that the Baron liked her tight-fitting leather vest over a thin cotton blouse and trousers. Otherwise, she'd have been forced to wear some ungodly fanciful creation as well. Possibly a gown.

Jasmine didn't have anything against gowns under the right circumstances but when one was out on a hunt, they weren't at all practical.

"Let us return to Ironhelm," she said. "Quetzalith has fed and—"

She broke off just as Quetzalith lifted his head and looked down the road to the north. A rising dust cloud indicated riders approaching at speed. Quetzalith abandoned the rest of the pig carcass and took two running steps forward before vaulting into the air using his fore and aft limbs. His great wings snapped out and he beat hard to climb above them. Not for the first time, Jasmine spared a wistful hope that she could fly with him. It wasn't possible, of course. He'd never fly with her added weight... but a girl could dream.

"It appears we have company coming," she said and walked toward her own mare. She accepted the reins from the youngest of the Baron's men and swung into the saddle with ease. Something prickled along her spine. High above, Quetzalith circled on the afternoon heat and waited.

They didn't have to wait long. The dust cloud soon resolved itself into a trio of riders, riding hell-for-leather down the long, dusty road from Ironhelm. Jasmine glanced up but Quetzalith's lazy circles continued, which meant that he didn't see a threat coming for her. So she had that going for her, which was nice.

The trio thundered up, horses and men alike caked in road dust and sweat.

"Water!" Jasmine ordered, snapping her fingers. She could hear them fumbling behind her and one of her escort thrust a full canteen into her waiting hand. When the riders slowed to a stop in front of them, Jasmine nudged her mare forward and held out the canteen to the lead.

His hand shook with exhaustion, slopping the water out of the neck of the canteen as he lifted it to drink. Long streams cut through the red-caked dust on his chin and neck. Below him, his horse panted. Jasmine waved two of the Baron's men forward to assist the other two riders and waited for the lead to drink his fill.

"Much obliged, Lady Moore," he said. Gasped, really, as he handed back the nearly empty canteen.

"Did you come directly from Ironhelm?" she asked, keeping her voice calm. Impatience would help no one in this situation.

The lead rider nodded, swiping his face with his dust-caked sleeve. It left a bloodred smear across his forehead. Jasmine suppressed the urge to reach forward and clean his face like a mother.

"The Baron's compliments, my lady. He requires your presence at all haste," the lead rider said, through the deep gulps of air.

"Of course," Jasmine said softly. She ruthlessly shoved down the irritation that always accompanied a summons from the Baron. "Has something happened?"

"He wishes to brief you in private, my lady. He begs that you will not delay in returning to him posthaste."

"Well," she said. "That's clear enough. Gentlemen, there is a stream for your horses nearby. Continue about twenty yards further down the road, then turn toward the canyon. There's a small footpath that follows along where the rim crumbles away. Dismount and lead your horses about another fifty feet and you'll find a spring."

"With respect, Lady Moore, the Baron instructed us to escort you home."

Another stab of irritation. Like certain of his men, the Baron had no respect for the sanctity of animal life. It was but one of the things she hated about the man.

"Fine," she said, her pleasant smile firmly in place. "Then we will wait while you water your horses."

"But he said posthaste!"

"Then you'd better hurry, hadn't you?"

Despite the urgency of the summons, Jasmine set a deliberately moderate pace for the trip back. Consequently, they arrived at Ironhelm's outskirts shortly after dusk. They rode their exhausted horses through the darkened town while Ironhelm glowed with gaslight ahead. Here and there, Jasmine caught sight of a villager's face as they pulled back behind a curtained window or ducked into a darkened doorway. She smiled determinedly and waved but fear of the Baron's men seemed to outweigh whatever goodwill she'd acquired since she'd come to live in this place.

She sighed inwardly against the sadness, but it wasn't, truly, a surprise. The Baron ruled through fear and intimidation, no matter how pretty he tried to make it look. Gilt paint on the signs and streetlamps did nothing to hide the hollow, hungry look in the eyes of the townspeople. There wasn't much she could do about that. So she turned her face to the ostentatious edifice ahead and continued on.

Ironhelm's large, castellated fortress had been constructed with two purposes in mind. First, it was a defensive fortification against the giant insects that still occasionally roamed these wild lands. Most had been exterminated in the Bug War, of course, but everyone knew that you couldn't kill them all off. Just when you thought that you had, another outpost nest would pop up. As far as she knew, there were few queens in this part of the country but even a minor nest of workers and scouts could overrun the village. Stone walls and a defensible position made sense.

Second, it was imposing. Castles meant strength, the Baron's primary concern. And it matched his ridiculous aesthetic sense. Despite the hundreds of empty buildings that could easily have been modified to be just as secure, nothing would do for the Baron but a castle out of his mind's own twisted fairy tale. It was his symbol of power.

One of them, Jasmine thought as Quetzalith's shadow briefly covered her. *Quetzalith and I are another.*

Domesticated dragons—one could never call a dragon truly "tame"—were extremely rare. The fact that he had one at his beck and call gave the Baron a significant amount of cachet. Plus, what good was a castle without a dragon to guard it?

They continued toward the stone gates, past the point where the dirt track became cobblestone patches in ruined asphalt. The gates towered above them, with armed men watching them from the windows and crenelated roof. The iron-bound wooden doors swung outward with a hydraulic hiss and Jasmine and her escort limped in on their blown horses.

"Lady Moore!" A voice called out from the wooden catwalk that ran over the door behind the gatehouse. Jasmine slewed around in her seat to see another of the Baron's lieutenants. He clattered down the stairs as she sat back in her saddle, causing her mare to stop.

"The Baron wishes to see you immediately," the lieutenant said. Overhead, Quetzalith circled again, waiting for Jasmine's signal to land.

"I will attend him as soon as Quetzalith is settled," Jasmine said calmly, as she swung her leg over the mare's haunches and dismounted.

"I beg your pardon, my lady, but the Baron said *immediately*. He specifically added that the dragon could wait."

"I see," Jasmine said, ruthlessly suppressing the fuming rage that boiled up from within. "In that case, have these horses seen to and call the vet. At least one of them is favoring a foreleg."

"At once, my lady," the lieutenant said, relief in his tone. Behind her, Byron started to chuckle nastily.

"Looks like himself missed ya, Lady Moore," Byron said, sneering.

Jasmine turned to look at him and smiled her wintry smile again. Then she raised her hand and dropped it down, curling the fingers into a fist as she did so. Quetzalith let out a scream. Jasmine knew it was just acknowledgement and curiosity that she was calling him to land here, instead of up in their normal tower. It sounded terrifying to untrained ears, however, and even the exhausted horses shuffled and plunged.

"Gentlemen, I suggest you remove these horses before Quetzalith lands. I will return as soon as I am able," she said with a smooth, icy tone. Then she turned toward the stairs leading up to the Baron's main hall.

Behind her, people and animals dove for cover as the dragon made his approach. Jasmine usually tried to keep him discreetly out of the way as much as possible, given the instinctive, visceral terror that most life forms—including humans—felt in the presence of a dragon. But, to put it bluntly, she was pissed off and hearing the screams of fear brightened her day just a little bit.

Quetzalith snapped his beak at the guardsmen on the gatehouse as Jasmine reached the doors to the main hall. She looked over her shoulder at him in mild reproof, though she couldn't be too angry. Not at him, anyway. The guardsmen, were, predictably, backed up against the stone wall and starting to raise their weapons.

"Offer no threat and he won't hurt you," Jasmine called out before she opened the main hall door. "Shoot at him and I don't imagine you'll survive much longer. And if you do, you shan't survive my return. Quetzalith, behave yourself."

And with that, she opened the door and walked into the main hall.

"Terrifying my men again, Lady Moore?"

The Baron's voice echoed through the vaulted space, coming

from the raised dais on the far end of the hall. Jasmine paused, allowing the door to swing closed behind her, before walking unhurriedly up the center aisle of the room. On either side of her, rows of empty trestle tables waited for the evening's dinner, when the Baron's retainers and staff would crowd together for a meal and often rowdy celebration. As usual, she buried the lingering flicker of annoyance at the tables. The Baron's insistence on his idea of an "appropriate aesthetic" had caused no end of headaches, and even a few fatalities. Despite the perfectly good modern furniture available for the looting, the Baron had insisted his men cobble together trestle tables for his great hall, so that he could play the mighty lord sitting over all of his men.

Several fireplaces lined the walls. Though it was summer, the temperature dropped quickly in the desert at night and teams of servants moved efficiently from one to another, lighting small blazes that crackled pleasantly. The gaslight sconces high on the stone walls brightened perceptibly as someone opened the line further. A side door opened and the scent of roasting meat and vegetables wafted out. Jasmine's stomach growled but she pushed hunger and fatigue away and smiled at the man waiting for her at the far end of the room.

William Schilling, self-styled Baron of Ironhelm, stood as she approached, his lean, six-foot frame draped in the finest clothes available: leather pants, a bright blue button-down shirt open at the throat, and, of course, a ridiculous black velvet half-cape that he must have found in the ruins of the old Amarillo Community Theatre. Jasmine was pretty sure that's where he'd found the prototype for his court's livery, anyway.

His standing to greet her was less a sign of respect than a move to enhance his already elevated position. Thinning blonde hair, surprisingly gray-free for his age, framed an almost gaunt face. Sharply angled cheekbones enhanced the deep hollows under his pale-blue eyes. This expression remained flat, what she recognized as barely restrained anger at her deliberately measured pace. She'd have to play it carefully. While he wouldn't take his annoyance out on her directly—probably—the Baron had a tendency to do things that would cause her emotional distress. He loved his power and had no hesitation in using it as cruelly as possible.

"My Lord Baron," she said with a smile that she'd practiced

enough so that it looked genuine. She came to the edge of the dais, watching as his smile became part scowl.

"My Lady Moore," he said, his voice tart. "I asked you a question."

In response, she inclined her head and performed a curtsey, though it probably lost some of its effectiveness without skirts to spread.

"Forgive me, my lord," she said as she straightened, looking him right in the eye. "I find it necessary from time to time to remind certain of your men that I am not to be trifled with."

"Give me their names," the Baron replied, "and I will handle them."

"With respect, my lord, that would be counterproductive. I can best be of service to you if the men follow my orders because I give them, not because they fear what you will do to them if they do not. I greatly appreciate your offer of assistance; however, it is not required at this time."

The Baron harrumphed as he resumed his seat, then tilted his head and smiled at her. She returned the smile, though it turned her insides cold.

"I am pleased to see you, Lady Moore," he said. His voice held a silky edge that made her skin crawl.

"And I, you, my lord." The lie came easy after years of practice.

"Perhaps after dinner, we may discuss just how pleased," he said, leaning forward to take her hand. She allowed him to draw her up onto the dais and pull her onto his lap. His free hand stroked her shoulder and neck up under her hair. She shivered involuntarily, praying he would take it as arousal, not revulsion. Despite his polished exterior, the Baron's hands were rough.

"As always, I am at my lord's disposal," she said softly, hating that it was true.

"And I am so pleased that you are. Unfortunately, I have some ill news that I must discuss with you first." He pressed a kiss to her temple and then set her back on her feet and indicated that she should sit in the chair next to his own.

Grateful for the reprieve, she complied.

"I received a disturbing report that I should like you to investigate," he said, his demeanor changing from that of a lover to that of a leader. She had to give him credit for that, at least. He did know how to get things done.

"Of course, my lord."

"Five days ago, a security team left here, bound for Fewaf. They were to relieve the other team at the depot, and guard the rather large payroll. They should have arrived at Kimball yesterday. They have not. Nor has the cargo."

"Do you think that they stole the money and made a run for it?"

"It's crossed my mind," the Baron said. "It's also possible that there was some difficulty and my men were killed. Either scenario is unacceptable, of course, but my response depends on what, exactly, happened. The situation cannot be left as it is and it is not an opportune time for me to leave. I must send someone I trust, who can make decisions in my stead. That means you, my love."

Jasmine blinked. In the seven years since she'd come to live here, this was the first time that the Baron had shown her so much trust. Preference, yes. Trust and authority to act for him? No.

Interesting.

"Well, my lady?"

"Apologies, my lord," she said smoothly, "I was just thinking through a plan. When shall I leave?"

"Tomorrow morning and take a sizeable force. Say...a large squad, fifteen men. Captain Conason will lead your escort and ensure you return safely to me."

Ah. There was the other shoe. So, she was trusted but only so far. Good to know. At least James Conason was a tolerable man, unlike Lieutenant Byron. Perhaps...perhaps there was still an opportunity to be had, if she paid close enough attention.

"I'll send word ahead to have my private engine readied for your trip. Is there anything out of the ordinary you require? For my pet, perhaps?"

"That won't be necessary, my lord." She ignored the insult. "I prefer riding and Quetzalith isn't fond of trains."

"Nonsense, my dear. I have a private car for reasons such as this. Time is of the essence," he said, taking a sip from his glass. "Not to mention, the sooner you arrive, the sooner you can come back to me."

Yes, wouldn't want me too far out of your grip for too long.

"Since haste is of importance, I must insist. Besides, it would be a waste to not use it, especially for something as silly as the dragon's feelings." His voice dropped, becoming sinister. "You know how I hate waste."

He paused, letting her mind fill in the potential consequences of refusal.

"As my lord commands," she said in the way she knew he liked. His face brightened again at her agreement.

"Excellent! Your leathery friend will be comfortable, I'm sure, in the stock car."

The Baron smiled as he stroked her cheekbone with his knuckles. Jasmine tilted her head into the caress, suppressing a shudder when he leaned in to kiss her lightly upon the lips. She closed her eyes so that he wouldn't see the loathing therein.

Jasmine finished preparing herself. Dinner was always a formal affair.

Despite the surroundings of the main hall (which had always looked entirely medieval), the Baron had a borderline obsessive love for what he called the "Steam Aesthetic." Thanks to the history lessons her mother had drilled into her when young, Jasmine knew that he was attempting to recreate the formality and elegance of the Victorian Age. However, apparently the Baron had never had those same lessons and was working off of some bizarrely mishmashed template he'd cobbled together from things he'd read and seen as a young child. Thus, he thought it entirely proper to insist on completely impractical, ornate velvet uniforms for his guardsmen, even though good leather would have done the job in a much better way.

At dinner, the Steam Aesthetic required that his "court" all be seated together in the main hall. He and his chosen few, including Jasmine, would be seated at a table on the dais, which contained a salt cellar. All the other diners would be seated at the trestle tables below the salt. Again, Jasmine knew that this was a convention which far predated the Victorians but to try to correct the Baron's understanding of the Steam Aesthetic was to court destruction. He was very proud of it.

Food would be served by an army of footmen, again dressed in uncomfortable and impractical livery. Luckily for all, the Baron required the services of a skilled chef and so the court ate tolerably well. He often had singers and a string quartet playing during the meal, which would have been pleasant, except that he insisted on old songs from before the War rewritten for strings. Some of the arrangements worked, some manifestly didn't. Sadly, the Baron seemed to be a huge Rush fan and the rhythmic screeching that replaced Geddy Lee's lyrics always gave Jasmine a headache. She hadn't minded the original "Tom Sawyer" when her father had played it on his hand-crank phonograph...but she thought she just might scream if she heard the Baron's musicians' cover one more time.

Jasmine let out a sigh and smoothed her hand down the deep amethyst silk of her bustled gown. She rather liked this one, with its sweetheart neckline corset and ruched skirt that ended a few inches above her knees, showcasing her stockinged legs. In the back, the bustle fell to the tops of her calf-high boots. It was an ensemble that was ornate enough to please the Baron but still allowed her freedom of movement if needed. Plus, it was pretty, and she liked to wear it.

The clock on the mantle of her fireplace made a whirring sound and emitted a soft *ding* to signal the hour. Time to head downstairs. The Baron appreciated promptness in his court. He was often late but that, like so much else he did, was simply to signal his dominance.

Jasmine took one last look in the polished glass of the antique mirror, then turned to where Quetzalith lay curled on his nest of quilts next to the fire. The dragon stared at her with one eye.

"I will be downstairs," she said. As ever, she wondered whether or not he truly understood her. Her father had said that dragons had approximately the same level of intelligence as the smartest working dogs. They would respond to command words and the tone of their trainers' voices. Jasmine, however, thought that estimate was low. Quetzalith always seemed to get the gist of what she was trying to convey.

She walked to the great shuttered window that dominated one quarter of the west wall of her tower room. With a flick of her wrist, she unlatched the barn-door style shutters and pulled them far enough open that she might look out. The sun had finally dipped below the distant hills and the sky spread out before her in streaks of yellow, orange and pink. Somewhere near the horizon, someone's campfire blazed into view. A tiny speck of burning light that filled her heart with longing.

Jasmine stepped back and resolutely closed the shutters. She did not lock them. This was, of course, expressly forbidden by

the Baron, but she didn't care. The Baron's dinners were often a
hell of politicking and backstabbing. If something went horribly
wrong for her, at least Quetzalith would have a way out. Fortunately, no one ever came up to the tower room without Jasmine.
They rightly feared Quetzalith's wrath too much to try.

She walked back to the dragon and stroked his crest for just
a moment in reassurance and then sighed as the clock whirred
again. She squared her shoulders, assumed the arrogant half-smile
that was her trademark poker face, and headed for the door.

Jasmine's heart sank the moment she walked into the main
hall. Bodies crowded close on all sides and the string quartet
sawed away at some old song with a frenetic, volatile energy.
That usually meant that the Baron was in an even crueler and
more capricious mood than normal. Fantastic.

She took a deep breath before moving through the crowd
at a steady pace. People ducked out of her way, aware that the
Baron was likely to punish anyone he thought wasn't paying the
proper respects to his favorite.

As usual, he wasn't in evidence when she arrived at her seat
upon the dais. She stood a few feet away from her chair, waiting
for him with equal parts dread and impatience. The sooner he
arrived, the sooner they could eat and be finished with dinner.
However, his presence was always a difficult thing to bear.

"My Jasmine." His voice came from behind her, close enough
that she could feel his breath. It slid around her neck, encircling
her throat as his hand touched the small of her back. She turned
to greet him with a smile that she hoped looked as genuine and
tender as it had appeared in her mirror. His answering smile
shot an icy spike of fear through her guts. He was in a mood.

"My lord," she replied, dipping into a curtsey designed to
show off the lean muscles of her legs. He usually liked her legs.

Anger bubbled inside; a tar pit in her heart.

"Sit with me, my lady," he said, his voice a velvet caress.
She straightened and put her hand in his outstretched one, then
allowed him to lead her to the table. The dull roar of the mill-
ing crowd stilled as the pair of them stepped forward into the
light. The Baron paused for dramatic effect, his eyes scanning the
assembled guests and what he called his "nobles." Once again, his
lack of formal education shone through, but she knew better than

to inform him that a mere "Baron" was the least of the landed nobility. He didn't appreciate such corrections at all.

"Good evening, my friends," the Baron said with a smile. "I am so pleased to see you all gathered together. Come, let us dine upon the bounty of my table."

Jasmine kept her smile from slipping at either the awkward phrasing of these words, or at the way his hand tightened painfully around hers. A footman jumped forward to pull out Jasmine's chair. She seated herself and the Baron followed suit. Only then did he release her hand. Jasmine was careful not to shake it out or otherwise indicate that he'd hurt her. Instead, she reached casually for her wine glass, taking a sip while she scanned the room.

The Baron must have made it known that he required the presence of his entire court for tonight's dinner. Jasmine saw several faces that she'd thought were posted far away at the various trading posts that made up much of the Baron's financial empire. Besides the local mines that produced natural gas and copper, the Baron had stakes in several other business ventures that ranged from the respectable to the dastardly. He'd used his men to create a stranglehold on the ancient railroad network that existed in these parts. People who tried to scratch out a living in lands controlled by the Baron had to pay increasingly high protection fees... and if they couldn't pay, then their lands would be confiscated and their children sold into slavery. Indeed, the Baron's slave distribution network was one of the largest sources of his personal wealth.

It was also one more reason why Jasmine loathed the man.

The food had been good. For a little while, Jasmine had hoped that that alone would mitigate the strange and dangerous mood she detected from the Baron. Conversation flowed along the head table, the Baron engaging in the various debates with relish. Jasmine, as usual, didn't say much.

"You know, my lord, you really should look into expanding your trade network further east. There are quite a few enclaves along the Mississippi River that would pay top dollar for your copper." The speaker was one of the Baron's toadies. Privately, Jasmine couldn't stand the man. He was one of those self-important types who insisted on speaking as if he were an expert on every subject... even when he wasn't. Plus, he'd gotten overly familiar with her once about two years ago.

They'd been out watching Quetzalith hunt one day. The Baron hadn't been looking and James had managed to run his hand down her back to cup her buttock. A roar from Quetzalith had brought the Baron's attention back to Jasmine and James had dropped his hand quickly. Afterward, she'd quietly reminded him that the Baron didn't appreciate anyone touching her in an inappropriate fashion. He'd taken her hint and been exquisitely polite to her since.

She still couldn't stand him.

"Is that so, James?" the Baron asked, his voice stretching out in a drawl. Fear ran like ice under Jasmine's skin. That tone didn't bode well.

"Indubitably, milord. Why, with a proper trade route established via my proposed Kansas City spur, you could double your current income. Then, if you can acquire enough additional labor to expand and build a full rail yard there, you could see exponential growth in the next few years!" James said, smirking. He had an avaricious glint in his eyes.

"Oh, James, that's very interesting. Very interesting indeed." The Baron toyed with the stem of his wine glass. "And how do you propose that we begin with plans to build a spur to this area?"

James puffed himself up even more at the Baron's apparent enthusiasm. Jasmine fought to keep her face neutral as her mental alarms started screaming. Something was about to go very wrong.

"Well, milord. As you may know, I do have some small contacts with the enclave at old Kansas City," James said.

"Small contacts? Would you mean, by chance, the mayor of the enclave? The one whose hostile takeover you financed with the money that I gave to you to fortify my rail yards in Kansas? The one who pays you a monthly percentage of the 'commerce taxes' that he extorts from those who try to do business in his pathetic, ugly little ruin of a town? The one who would charge me an extortionate rate to do business there?"

"Milord!" James sputtered, his face turning red "I—I do not think he would..."

"You know, James. I find it amusing that you believe I value your opinion on these matters. As though we're equals. It's cute. You have a wife, correct? How long have you been married?"

"Uh, um." James spluttered at the abrupt change of subject. "Ten years, milord."

"Ah, yes, I remember now. And two children, is it?"

"Yes, milord. A son and daughter."

"Right—your son is the elder; he's about ten, if I recall. Bit of string bean. Could use some muscle. I'll send him to the mines. What is that old saying? What doesn't kill you, makes you stronger?"

"Milord? I . . . I don't understand."

"Oh? Allow me to make this perfectly clear: You're mine. Your family is mine. You were allowed a certain amount of freedom due to your usefulness overriding the, frankly, highly irritating aspects of your personality. That has ceased to be the case. As of this moment, you no longer have money, rights, or say in your fate."

"My apologies, milord! I had no idea that I have offended you!" The blood drained from James's face as tears welled in his eyes. Jasmine watched him realize that everything—family, wealth, status—had just been erased at the whim of the man before him. "How may I make this up to you?"

"You can't. All you can do is become something to amuse me. Your expression right now is a good start. I anticipate the look of helplessness in your eyes as your wife is drawn and quartered in front of you will be even more so. Especially the accusation in her eyes because she knows it was your fault. I look forward to that; it should give me at least a few hours of enjoyment." He leaned forward, spearing a small slice of roast with his fork, contemplating it thoughtfully before continuing. "You will never see your son again. You will, however, see your daughter, daily, as I raise her as my own, showering her with gifts and giving her everything you can't. She will grow to understand that her father is worthless, learning to despise you as the years go by, until I decide that you are no longer amusing. Then, I'll let her decide if the filth in front of her is worth saving."

He took a bite, chewing slowly as James begged for forgiveness, savoring the meat and the moment, before motioning for the guards.

"Take him away. Break his ankles and bring his family to me."

Jasmine forced herself to watch the velvet-coated guards walk up to the table and hoist the blubbering man to his feet. Then they frog-marched him down the center of the room and out the front door as the entire court watched in perfect silence.

The Baron leaned over and took her hand with a slight smile as the large doors closed behind the guards. James's muffled howls of despair trailed into the distance. Jasmine blinked, then returned the Baron's smile and squeezed his fingers lightly.

"I love you, my lady," he said softly, with a bit of an emphasis on the "my."

"And I you, my lord," she replied, evenly.

"You will enjoy having a daughter, I think. I believe her name is Keelie."

"A lovely name. I am certain that I shall."

He laughed and stroked her hair.

"You look very pretty tonight, my Jasmine. I do enjoy that color on you. Please do not worry, love. No one could supplant you in my affections. The girl will be our daughter, nothing more. She is too young to tempt me, anyway."

I was only fourteen, Jasmine thought. But she said nothing. Only smiled and gave a tiny, submissive nod.

Upstairs, Quetzalith screamed his rage into the cold, dark night.

Jasmine planned to leave at dawn. Before she met her escort in the darkened courtyard, however, her instincts told her that she had to make one other stop.

She was fortunate that she wasn't required to attend the execution. Baron Schilling had accepted her plea of fatigue, especially with the promise of "resting up for him." She had excused herself from his bed shortly after fulfilling that promise, citing an early departure.

"Keelie?" she called quietly as she pushed past the wooden door into the room not far from her own tower chamber. She heard the sound of muffled weeping, then a sudden stillness.

Smart girl.

"Keelie, it's Jasmine. Lady Moore. I'm not going to hurt you. I wanted to see you before I left."

A rustling. The sound of someone pulling covers up to hide themselves.

Jasmine sighed and made her way with the help of the burning night light to the heavy, four-poster bed that dominated the furniture in the room. She moved the curtains aside with slow, deliberate, telegraphed motions and sat on the side of the bed.

"I'm not going to hurt you. I only want to help you, sweetheart."

"You're not my mother." The words came from under the heavy quilt. Even muffled, they dripped with acid rage.

"No," Jasmine agreed. "I will never be your mother. Your mother is dead. Tragically taken from you. I am sorry about that, but I can't change it."

A sob. Just one. No further answer. Jasmine sighed.

"Listen, Keelie," she said to the grieving, angry girl. "I can't stay long but I have to tell you something very important. It's your choice if you want to remember it or not. It's your choice whether to tell the Baron I said it or not. He won't be happy about it. He might even kill me for saying it . . . but you need to hear it."

"I'm never telling him *anything*!" Keelie spat.

"I can't blame you for what you're feeling, sweetheart. But believe me when I tell you that that kind of thinking will get you killed."

"I don't care. I want to be with my mommy."

Jasmine's eyes burned with unshed tears. She reached out a hand and stroked the lump of blanket as it shuddered with more sobs.

"I know what you're feeling," Jasmine said.

"How could you?" Keelie snapped from under the quilt. "You're his lady!"

"I'm his lady because he killed *my* parents."

The shudders quieted. Jasmine drew in a deep breath.

"I was fourteen. He and his men came to my home. Killed my parents. Killed all of the dragons except for Quetzalith, who was still an egg, and brought me back here to be his dragon tamer . . . and his lady," she added, letting some of the grinding bitterness into her voice.

"Like you, I hated him. But I had to pretend otherwise, or else I knew he'd kill me next and then Quetzalith would die. I had to stay alive for Quetzalith's sake. Just like you have to stay alive for your father's sake and your brother's. If you keep the Baron happy, he'll do just about anything for you . . . as long as he's in the right mood. It would be better for you if I didn't have to leave right now but I do. So you have to learn quick. I hear you're a smart girl. Is that true?"

Keelie sat up for the first time and let the quilt and blankets fall away down into her lap. Her brown hair would have been pretty, had it not been a tangled, tear-matted mess. She pushed it away from her red-rimmed green eyes and nodded.

Jasmine smiled.

"Good," she said. "Then you will understand what I'm saying. Don't give in too quickly. He will be suspicious. Be wary of him but excruciatingly polite for the first several weeks. Let him see that you're afraid of him. He will shower you with gifts and luxuries, things to make you smile. Make him work for it but eventually, let him see you looking happy and content.

"Things are going to be very bad for your father, I'm afraid," Jasmine went on. "The Baron is going to humiliate him and debase him in every way, so that he will appear worthless in your eyes. Again, do not allow this to happen right away. Let it be slow and steady."

"What about my brother?" Keelie asked in a small voice.

"He is a trickier problem," Jasmine admitted. "He's to be sent to the mines and I don't see a way to stop that right away. Perhaps in a year or two, you can ask the Baron for him as a personal servant or guard or something... but leave that for now. It's too soon. He will have to survive as best he can."

"He's strong," Keelie said staunchly. "He'll survive."

"I'm sure he will," Jasmine said. She was sure of no such thing. He was just a child.

"How long will you be gone?" Keelie asked her.

"I don't know," Jasmine said, guilt pulling at her. She knew very well how long: forever, if she could swing it. But she couldn't leave this girl without hope. "Maybe a few days, maybe a few weeks. But listen, this is very important. You must watch everyone, observe everything and trust *no one*. Especially if I don't return. Remember what I said. It will keep you alive."

"I trust you," Keelie said softly, reaching out her little hand. Jasmine felt her heart shattering in two places.

"You shouldn't," she cautioned, but she took Keelie's hand anyway.

"But I do. Thank you, Lady Moore."

Jasmine nodded and squeezed her fingers lightly before letting go.

"Now lie down and get some sleep. He will likely let you sleep in today, but I would expect him sometime this afternoon. Remember what I said. Listen to your instincts and trust no one."

"No one but you," Keelie agreed as she laid back down. Jasmine covered her up with the blankets and then, before her stupid motherly instincts could get her in any more trouble, turned and slipped back out the door.

CHAPTER SIX

THE TRIP FROM IRONHELM TO KIMBALL GAVE JASMINE TIME TO consider her next move. Ten plus hours sitting in the private car would be preferable to days on the trail to most people. She didn't consider herself "most people," however. Out in the heat and the air, she felt like she could breathe. Granted, the Baron's men that usually accompanied her served as a reminder that she wasn't fully free, but it was close as she could get. She was thankful for any time she had outside of the keep, even if it was still within the Baron's growing territory. The steady motion of the car served as a background rhythm to her meditations as her brain worked on several of the knotty problems she faced.

The first and most immediate was the question of finding her quarry. The Baron had given her what little description he'd been able to glean from the scant eyewitness accounts that had filtered back to Ironhelm. That in and of itself had infuriated the Baron. It seemed that though there were other passengers, no one had gotten a good look at the perpetrators who had assaulted his men.

Or, if they had, no one was talking. Jasmine wasn't surprised. The Baron was often fond of quoting the old adage that it was better to be feared than loved. Much like his other historical anachronisms, he held this ideal close to his heart. Therefore, Jasmine hadn't risked telling him that Niccolò Machiavelli had added the caveat that the fear instilled should never be excessive, for that could be dangerous to the prince. That above all, a prince should not interfere with the property of their subjects, their women, or the life of somebody without proper justification.

Jasmine had actually read *The Prince*. It had been one of the hundreds of books in her parents' collection. Had the Baron kept any of them, read them, he would have had a much better chance at being who he thought he was. But he hadn't. He'd burned them, along with everything else from her childhood.

The train's whistle pulled Jasmine out of her musings. She blinked and refocused her eyes on the rolling hills and dusty terrain. They were approaching a dust-choked cluster of buildings marked by a brand-new water tower. Ahead, the train's whistle sounded again as it approached the town. Three blasts. End of the line. The beginning of their mission.

The train depot had the dubious distinction of being the largest and most well-maintained building in town. It squatted long and low under the new water tower, next to the iron web of tracks that led into the depot and the attached rail yard.

As the train eased to a halt, Captain Conason approached. Tall, at least a foot taller than she, the captain exuded strength. Jasmine could swear she heard the uniform seams straining as he saluted.

"Lady Moore, we've arrived in Kimball," he said. "How would you like to proceed?"

"Unload the horses, get the men prepared for the next stage. I'll see to Quetzalith. It's best if everyone involved is well clear before I let him out."

"Yes, milady." He paused, briefly, before continuing. "I don't think that will be an issue. I'll have a perimeter established to keep the locals at distance."

She nodded. The man was thorough and observant, showing foresight.

He saluted, leaving her to gather her belongings and disembark.

As she stepped onto the platform, several groups of men came to attention, moving to positions at a considerable distance. Foot traffic stopped, leaving a clear area between herself and the stock car. Impressed, she walked to Quetzalith's stall.

"Hello, my friend," she said, approaching the dragon. "Thank you for being patient. It's time to fly again."

Once more, she couldn't help but think that the dragon understood her words. Excited by the sight of the open door, Quetzalith bobbed his head and snapped his beak as she released the bolt on his stall. The dragon walked forward slowly, shaking his wings free as he stepped onto the ramp. A quick look at her asked the question: Fly?

She simply gestured for takeoff.

Massive wings spread as he took several jerky steps, beating the air with powerful strokes. In seconds, he was airborne, circling into the late-afternoon sky.

Jasmine watched him for a few seconds, jealousy and joy fighting for her emotions. She turned to Captain Conason.

"Remain here," she said, "I wish to speak with the conductor and your presence makes people nervous. I will call if I need you," she said.

Captain Conason gave her a nod, then glanced overhead, as if to look for Quetzalith. But the dragon circled high above, content to soar through the enticing thermals that rose from such a vast amount of grassland. Jasmine knew that he could be at her side and flaming within moments, so she was inclined to just let him play. He so rarely had the pleasure.

Jasmine turned her back to the captain and his men and walked up the dusty steps to the wide double doors of the train depot. She pushed her way inside and noted that the dim waiting room was nearly empty. A small family sat in one corner, sleeping children leaning against drowsy-looking adults. She gave them a nod, trying to ignore the way the mother's eyes went round at the sight of her. So. They knew who she was then.

A hand-lettered sign pointed her to the left, and down a short hall she found the conductors' office. She knocked politely on the door. A few moments later, a dark-skinned man of indeterminate age wearing a conductor's uniform pulled the door open.

"Yeah?" he asked, his tone supercilious and impatient. Jasmine tamped down on a surge of irritation.

"I am Lady Jasmine Moore," she said. Using the title the Baron had granted to her often seemed absurd—it was rare that she did. But there were times it proved useful. The conductor straightened up, his expression smoothing into far more respectful lines.

"My lady! What c'n I do fer ya?" His voice held a note of sycophancy that rubbed her the wrong way.

"I have been sent by the Baron to investigate a recent incident aboard the train three days ago. It appears there was an issue with the security team. Are you familiar with the situation?"

The man's dark face paled, just slightly.

"Y-yes, my lady," he said. His eyes darted, finding somewhere, anywhere, else to look. "Though only afterwards. I didn't...I weren't there..."

"I am not here to hold you responsible," she said coldly. "I merely require that you give me a factual account of what happened."

"Well, miss—"

"My lady," she corrected him sharply. People who behaved as he did seemed to expect a certain amount of arrogance. She was happy to give it to him, especially if it helped loosen his tongue.

"M'lady. I apologize, m'lady. We don't often get people of quality out this far."

"The incident?"

"Yeah, well. The incident." The conductor pulled himself up straight and tugged at the bottom of his jacket.

"A few miles out of the mountains, your boys started to circulate, doin' their rounds. There was some trouble in the main passenger car. Some floozy bein' a cocktease, or somethin'. These three fellas took exception to your man giving her the business and they fought. Your men, well, they didn't make it."

"I see. And where are these men now?"

"Your men? Over t'the undertaker's."

"No. The three who killed my men."

"Oh." He gave Jasmine a lopsided grin that she was certain was meant to be disarming. It only irritated her further. "They hightailed it out the back of the train and disconnected the baggage car and the caboose. Those're still a few miles west of here," he said, pointing.

"And you sent no one to look?"

"We did! Just as soon as the train came in. Seems they did something to the couplings, blew it all to Hell. They're dangerous men, m'lady! Murderers!"

Jasmine closed her eyes for a moment and willed her temper to calm. It wouldn't do to have Quetzalith come blasting his way in here simply because this man was a waste of air.

"I see," she replied as she opened her eyes. "Thank you for the information. I will be certain to mention your...actions... in my report to the Baron."

"Yes, m'lady. Thank you, m'lady," the conductor replied as she turned her back on him and strode back out into the punishing sunlight.

"What news?" Captain Conason asked as she reappeared.

She didn't slow but went right to her mare and swung herself into the saddle.

"The conductor is a fool," she said. "The Baron's men seemed to be equally so. The three suspects escaped, uncoupled the baggage car and damaged it. The Baron indicated that he was interested in the contents of that car. We ride west along the tracks and see what we can find."

The captain gave her a nod. She kicked her mare into motion, he and his men following closely behind.

"Some few miles west" turned out to be four hours' ride down along the railroad tracks. The moon, bright in the clear mountain air, gave plenty of light as the group of them approached the abandoned car and caboose.

Jasmine signaled Quetzalith to land beside the railroad berm and dismounted. Captain Conason and his men fanned out to surround the car, weapons at the ready. The captain's vigilance made Jasmine have to hide a smile. If there had been anyone nearby, Quetzalith would have seen or smelled them. The car was empty.

Still, it didn't hurt to be cautious. She drew her "Mare's Leg"—a short-barreled, lever-action rifle—from her saddle holster and approached the front of the unhitched car. Quetzalith continued to sit quietly as she climbed the metal stairs, then tried the sliding door.

It was locked. Interesting. Who abandons a railroad car and then locks the door behind themselves?

The lock was no real problem, even though it consisted of a steel bar bolted to the floor. She could have picked it, of course, but that would have alerted her escort (and eventually the Baron) to the existence of her lockpicks and her ability to use them. She had a better idea.

With a quick tap from the stock of her Mare's Leg, Jasmine broke the glass out of the window set in the top half of the door. She took a moment to make sure all the glass was safely out of the frame and then squeezed her body through the opening. It was a tight fit but she was slim-hipped enough to make it. Once inside, she simply pushed the bar out of the way and slid the door to the side.

Moonlight poured in through the windows, making long shapes that twisted over blanket- and tarp-covered piles of cargo. Jasmine took a few steps into the car, looking for something...

Ah! There! An additional cage built into the back wall of the car. It, too, was locked, the mechanism intact. Again, fascinating. The Baron's precious cargo was certainly locked in this compartment. There was no way that the perpetrators wouldn't have figured that. But then why did it appear to be completely unmolested? In fact, except for the window she'd broken the entire car looked pristine.

What was going on here?

"Captain," Jasmine called out, without looking over her shoulder. "One of your men has some bolt cutters, I presume. Please have them brought in to me."

"Yes, my lady," he called back and a few moments later, Captain Conason himself walked in through the door, his boots crunching on the broken glass she'd left in her wake. She gestured to the lock. He gave her a nod and hefted the bolt cutters before walking forward.

Man of few words; I can appreciate that.

He settled the cutter jaws on the chain and twisted his head, stretching in preparation. Jasmine watched as his chest expanded with a deeply indrawn breath. He paused for half of a heartbeat and then applied brute force, squeezing the wide-spread handles of the bolt cutters. His breath hissed from between his clenched teeth as his muscles strained under his uniform. With a final "HAA!" of effort, the captain drove the teeth of the cutters through the metal of the lock, rewarding them both with a loud snapping sound.

Jasmine raised her eyebrows. That had been impressive.

Conason let the lock fall to the floor of the car with a dull *thunk*, then stepped back and gestured for Jasmine to open the door.

She gave him her wintry smile and did so, then stepped inside the small space. Sure enough, there was a strongbox sitting in the center of the floor. She put in the combination that the Baron usually used and lifted the lid.

An errant beam of moonlight glinted back at her from the gold bars within. Jasmine exhaled slowly and closed the box, then turned to look over her shoulder.

The captain stood there, watching her.

"The Baron's cargo is here," she said softly. No need for the other men to hear. Conason would tell them what he needed them to know. "But it seems that those who killed our men have fled. I am reluctant to leave this here, unattended. And yet we cannot let those murderers go free."

He nodded.

"I think," she said slowly, "I think you and your men must stay. Send a rider back to the town and get an engine here to tow these cars. There is too much here for us to carry it ourselves, even if we were to divvy it up. And..." she trailed off, not wanting to say it out loud.

Captain Conason nodded again. He'd seen the gold. He understood. The temptation might be too great for his men if they divvied it up into individual portions. Even if there wasn't so much there.

"Quetzalith and I will follow them. They likely fled on horseback. That should leave enough of a trail for him to track them. I will send word back as soon as I can."

"Take John Reborn," he said.

"No." She shook her head. "He will only slow me down. Quetzalith will keep me safe enough."

"They killed four armed men and used an explosive to damage the coupling. There's a good chance they won't be easy targets," he said, implacable. "Take him and two others."

She looked at him for a long moment, her heart sinking. Her gut told her that he would not be dissuaded. Finally, she nodded and turned away.

"Fine," she said, moving toward the door. "We leave now."

As she'd predicted, her quarry's trail was easy to follow. She and her escort were able to make up the lost time quickly, using Quetzalith as an advance scout. The dragon was well trained, alerting them to changes in direction, allowing her party to cut around hazards. Based on the small campsites along the trail, she figured they were no more than twenty-four hours behind after their first full day.

A few hours after noon on day two, he spotted them. At least, she assumed it was them, as she couldn't imagine another reason anyone would be heading into the plains at speed.

On her order, the dragon flung himself into the air, climbing in a spiral above their position. He'd circled once, twice and then given a screaming cry that meant he'd seen something.

Her mare and the other horses were well rested—some hard riding wouldn't harm them. She kicked the mare into a lope and followed the dragon. In a short time, they found a gully adorned with broken sage brush, angling off to the north. They rode single file, Reborn in front, Jasmine next, then Kyler Anderson and Skye Jonas following as they negotiated the twists and turns of the dried-up creek bed. Jasmine glanced at the sky every few minutes, keeping Quetzalith in sight. As best she could tell, the gully ran due north, despite its torturous route. Before too long, a few hours at most, the sun would start to sink behind the hills off to their left and they'd be riding blindly into what could very well be an ambush.

If not for Quetzalith, that was.

The dragon's eyes, better than any eagle's, would see trouble long before it threatened his person. And if something did threaten her, Jasmine knew that he would bring flame like the wrath of an angry god to keep her safe. Once and only once had this failed to be true, when the Baron had captured her, and that hadn't been his fault. Hard to wreak vengeance when one was still encased in an egg.

With a bit of effort, Jasmine turned her mind away from those well-worn but useless lines of thought and focused on the task at hand. Quetzalith's instinct to destroy anything that threatened her was part of the problem in this case.

She wanted to find the group that had killed the Baron's men...but she didn't want them dead.

"What's that?" Chuck squinted up at the sky. A shadow raced across his face for the second time. "Too big for a bird."

"Dragon," Jay said. "Well, air quotes, 'dragon.' More of a pterosaur."

"A what?" Chuck asked.

"Kids," Jay sighed. "Waaay back, there were big lizards. Dinosaurs. Some could fly. Pterosaurs. That 'dragon' is a pretty big version of that. Came across the Rift with the Gants."

"Dinosaurs were technically avians, not lizards," Garman pointed out didactically. "And their precise evolutionary relationship to Abominations is unclear. Strange to see one here. They feed primarily on Gants and thus tend to stay close to nests. It may indicate a nearby Gant nest."

"Yup," Jay said. "Weird that it's alone, though. They're usually in packs. Looks like it's circling. Most of the ones I've run into tried to make me a snack."

"What do you think, sir?" Chuck tried to keep the fear from his voice. Gants were bad enough, but Fat Lady could handle them. Dragons? He could probably hit it on the wing but if he missed...

"Gotta hunch," Jay said. "Let's see how it plays out."

"We should find cover," Garman said, looking around.

"We finally agree on somethin'," Jay said.

"What's that pet of yours doing?"

Reborn's tone—scratch that, his presence—set Jasmine's teeth on edge. Bad enough he was here in the first place, but the bastard's attitude was making it worse.

"He's hunting." Jasmine said. "Looking for our quarry."

"Taking long enough."

Quetzalith was a speck against the pale blue sky. Suddenly, he dove sharply, free falling about a hundred feet before pulling up.

"What's that mean?" Reborn said.

"Not sure. Could be he found something." He had definitely found something. She had trained him to circle in order to "point" without alerting the prey or attacking it.

"Hmph. Probably a rabbit."

No, idiot, she thought, *he found who we're looking for.*

A plan began taking shape in her mind.

Jay raised the spyglass, focusing on the small dust cloud in the distance.

"Looks like four riders. Three male, one female. If I had to guess, I'd say the lady is the scout and that dragon is hers. Seems to be staying close to her, at least."

Garman studied the area.

"There's a small gap between the mesas ahead. Some decent scrub, a rock fall and we can take the high ground."

"Not as good as heading 'em off at the pass," Jay said, smiling. He shook his head at Chuck and Garman's looks of confusion. "Kids. Okay, what do we have in the way of weapons?"

"I have Fat Lady, my Marlin, and two Colts," Chuck said.

"Kukri, two .45's."

"And that AK in your bedroll," Jay said. Garman's face clouded. "Right, 'Adept's weapon.' Okay, Junior, I want you over there, where they'll come in from. Use pistols from behind after they pass you. You're the gate, closing the trap. Get control of that girl quickly, so she can't use her dragon against us."

"Why do you think the girl is controlling the dragon?" Garman asked.

"'Cause they'd never have a girl along less she was important," Jay said. "And what is your doctrine about the word 'why' when the shit's about to hit the fan?"

"'During critical action conditions the word 'why' is irrelevant to conditional remediation,'" Garman recited.

"Which translates as 'shut the hell up and do what I fucking tell you,'" Jay said. "Chuck, you stay high with the Marlin until they get into the thick of it. I'll hang back some and make sure no one slips past Junior here."

"As if that's a possibility," Garman muttered.

"How will you do that, sir?" Chuck asked, more to move past the Windfist's offended pride than anything.

"I'm small and hard to see," Jay said, smiling. "Are you able to take out at least two of the men quickly?"

"Yes, sir, I can take out the first and probably the second once you give the word. At the very least a solid body shot to put him down."

"Good. Positions. They'll be here shortly. Now," he continued, letting out a sigh. "Questions, comments concerns?" When there didn't appear to be any, he gave them a grin. "Let's be banditos, boys!"

"That damn dragon ain't doin' nothin'," Reborn said. "Ain't he 'sposed to be looking out for these scumbags?"

"He's riding thermals." Jasmine didn't try to hide her irritation. "Getting into position to scout ahead. If he sees something, he'll let me know." As if in response, Quetzalith let loose a short blast of flame.

"What was that?"

"Indigestion."

"Oh." Reborn nodded toward the mesas in their path. "I don't like that."

"No way around it. And, the trail takes us right through here," Jasmine said. "On the bright side, it isn't a box canyon."

Reborn gave her a dirty look.

The dragon let loose another burst of flame, banking to circle back above her.

They're ahead, she thought, *most likely where it narrows. I'm going to need to make a move soon.*

Jasmine stopped, raising her hand above her head in a circle, then dropped it sharply to point at Reborn.

"What the hell?"

The dragon hit Reborn hard, claws first, taking the man's torso with him as he regained altitude. He made it about fifty feet before he dropped it, a long trail of intestines and gore following him.

"WHAT THE—" Skye's shout cut off as the back of his head exploded.

Anderson had just enough time to snap off a quick shot at Quetzalith before doubling over in his saddle.

Jasmine's horse lurched, just as the feel of cold steel caressing her throat sent a shiver down her spine.

"Keep still. You don't want to give us trouble." The man's voice growled in her ear. "Let's just keep that abomination of yours airborne and out of range. Understand?"

"I do," Jasmine said as she slowly raised both hands over her head. She was pleased at how steady her voice sounded. Quetzalith circled uneasily overhead but as Jasmine didn't make a fist, he knew she wanted him to stay aloft.

"There's a Mare's Leg next to my knee, a knife in each boot, and one in my sleeve. Other than that, I'm unarmed," Jasmine said. "I...uh...want to talk to you."

"Is that so?" her captor asked.

Jasmine paused for a moment, then swallowed carefully. The blade never wavered. He held the flat of it against her skin, so it didn't cut her—but a twist of his wrist and she'd be damn near decapitated.

"Do you think you could put your knife away?" she asked, a bit tartly, all things considered. It was hard for her not to retreat into attitude and arrogance when threatened.

"With that thing of yours overhead. No thanks. You just behave and keep it aloft—"

"Him."

"What?"

"*Him*," she said, anger growing. "*He* is not an 'it.' *He* is a dragon and his name is Quetzalith. You needn't be such an ass about this."

"*It* is an abomination," the blade holder said, a bit of his own anger causing him to sneer. Jasmine felt him draw in a breath against her back, as if he would say more, but just then two other riders came down into the trail and he clammed up.

"Afternoon, kids," the shorter, darker of the two called out cheerfully. "Let's go find us a place to camp and then we'll have us a nice long parley."

"Follow him." The man behind her put pressure on the knife. Jasmine rolled her eyes and did as he said.

Not quite how she had planned, but close enough.

Chuck looked across the fire at the woman they'd...captured? Rescued? He didn't rightly know. Things had moved pretty quickly from the time the dragon—Ket-something—he couldn't wrap his tongue around the Spanish-sounding name—had dropped out of the sky and kicked off their ambush. He'd done as Jay had said, taking out the two men, and the next thing he knew, they had a girl and a dragon along for the trip.

Jay let out a long, almost musical burp and sat back, patting his slightly rounded stomach. On Chuck's other side, Garman huffed his disapproval while lifting another chunk of roast pork to his mouth. The Windfist had spent most of the meal alternating between glaring at Jay and glaring at the dragon girl. Chuck was starting to wonder if Garman was ever happy.

"All right, missy," Jay said, completely oblivious to Garman's looks. "How's about you tell us your story now?"

"If you like," the girl said. Chuck thought she had an odd lilt to her voice, as if she were used to speaking and eating in much fancier circumstances than these. She'd helped to cook the feral pig the dragon had caught, though, and seemed comfortable enough on the ground eating with her hands. Maybe she wasn't as fancy as all that.

"My name is Jasmine Moore. I'm a dragon trainer, lately working for Baron Schilling. My dragon is Quetzalith," she said, glancing at Garman. Chuck did the same, noticing the Windfist narrow his eyes just a touch at the name.

"Quesa-whosit?" Jay asked. Jasmine smiled, a dimple flashing into existence.

"Quetzalith. Say it like Ket-za-lith."

"Oh! Quetzalith," the old man said. "Play on Quetzalcoatl and Pern! Got it. Nice to meet you, fella," he said, leaning back and looking up at the dragon. Jay had chosen a campsite in one of the twisty canyons near the ambush. Once he'd delivered their dinner, the beast had found a convenient rock outcropping not far from Jasmine and perched. Chuck had the feeling that the dragon was keeping an eye on all of them, to be sure they wouldn't harm his mistress. Oddly enough, he didn't feel threatened. Actually, it was a bit of a relief to see that the lady had her own protection and therefore didn't need his.

Quetzalith stopped his own meal of a second pig (minus the ear Jasmine had taken) and craned his impossibly long neck down to look at the small black man staring up at him. Chuck could hear Garman's breath hiss out between his teeth and a glance showed that the Windfist had his wicked kukri in his hand.

"No, don't," Chuck whispered. "Jay's all right, just watch."

They all sat very still as Quetzalith stared at Jay. Despite the threat of immediate immolation, the old man seemed perfectly relaxed, smiling at the beast.

"Quetzalith, these are friends," Jasmine said, her voice clear and firm enough to echo faintly from the rock walls of the canyon around them.

The dragon looked at her, then back at Jay. Then he turned his attention to Garman for a long moment. A deep rumble, accompanied by a hiss of steam issued forth from the beast's beak.

"Quetzalith," Jasmine said again. Her tone held a note of warning. "Friends."

The dragon rumbled once more, as if to say that he wasn't rightly sure, before looking at Chuck himself.

The thing had huge eyes. The pair of them bored into Chuck and he felt, for just a moment, as if his entire mind were exposed to the elements. The beast's yellow irises, nearly glowing in the flickering firelight, closed like a pair of fists and brought the pupil to a pinpoint.

"We're friends," Chuck said. He hadn't really planned to speak but he couldn't seem to stop himself. "We're not going to hurt your lady. I give you my word."

Quetzalith stared at him for a moment longer, then bobbed its massive, elongated head once before swinging it to look at his mistress. Jasmine looked at Chuck with an unreadable expression and made a quick hand gesture to the dragon.

"Eat," she said softly. "I'll groom you after."

The dragon returned to his feast and Chuck felt himself take a breath as the sudden tension eased.

"Well," Jay said, sounding delighted. "That was entertaining!"

"Did he understand me?" Chuck asked, looking across the fire at Jasmine again. She shook her head slightly and shrugged.

"I honestly don't know," she said. "He understands some of my words. Commands and the like. He understands the word 'friend' to mean 'do not attack unless I say.' But the rest of it? Your guess is as good as mine."

"I thought you were some kind of dragon trainer," Garman said.

"I am," Jasmine said, irritation creeping into her tone. "But I'm not a mind reader, so forgive me if I can't speak to Quetzalith's deeper understanding or inner motivations, Windfist."

"What can you speak to, then?" he shot back. "You're the so-called expert and yet so far I've heard nothing but 'I don't know' out of you. Where'd you get your training, if you're so knowledgeable?"

"Garman..." Chuck said softly.

"No, it's all right," Jasmine said, her voice icy. "You want my story? Fine, here it is. I was fourteen years old when the Baron attacked my family's training Weyr, burned it to the ground, slaughtered my parents and killed all of our dragons but Quetzalith. He was mine, you see. Just an egg at the time. The Baron's plan was to abduct me and my egg, rape me into submission and force me to raise Quetzalith and use him to further his ambitions of empire. Of course, when he killed my father in front of me, he destroyed the only training manual I've ever had. So what I know, I've figured out myself. With Quetzalith. We've raised each other in a more hostile and treacherous environment than you can possibly imagine from behind the walls of your comfortable monastery. So don't you ever question my education, Windfist. I promise it was more thorough than yours."

"Miss Jasmine—" Chuck said.

She threw up a hand and whipped her head away from Garman

to stare at Chuck. For the second time that night, Chuck felt pinned by a pair of intense eyes.

"Stop," she said. "Stop right there. I neither need nor want your pity. It won't change what happened to my family, or to me. So save it for someone that you *can* help. Because all I want from you three is a way out."

"Sure thing, doll," Jay said. "We're headed east. You want to come along? You and Quetzalith? Make it worth our while and you're in."

Chuck started to protest, but he thought he saw Jay give him a small shake of the head. It wasn't much and Chuck wasn't even certain he'd seen it but it made him pause.

"I can pay you," Jasmine said. "I need to get to Pittsburgh. I can pay you two hundred Ogden silver. Half now, half when you get me to my uncle's house."

"You have an uncle?" Jay asked. "Where was he when you were fourteen?"

"At sea," she said, her voice sad. "Not his fault. He left with my father's blessing. I don't think he knows I'm alive. But he's a dragon breeder, too, or was. So even if he doesn't acknowledge me as his niece, he'll welcome me because of Quetzalith. A trained, fully grown male dragon is incredibly valuable in stud fees."

"This is a terrible idea," Garman said. "Her Baron will be after us, not only for killing his men—again—but also because he's going to want the abomination back."

Fire blossomed against the night sky, singeing the air above their heads.

"Shaddup, Junior," Jay said softly. "Y'ain't helping here."

"He is not *my* Baron, Windfist," Jasmine said.

Garman got stiffly to his feet. He inclined his upper body to the angry girl in a short bow.

"I apologize," he said. "But taking you along is too great a risk to our mission. Chuck, you have to see that. How are we going to hide a freaking *dragon*?"

"You won't have to," Jasmine answered. "Quetzalith can take care of himself. He is perfectly comfortable flying for a full day at heights so high even I cannot see him any longer. And he is as much of an asset as a liability in this."

"How, pray tell?" Garman asked.

"You said it yourself. The Baron is coming after you anyway, because you've killed four—now seven—of his men. That's why I was sent after you in the first place. Quetzalith can watch our rear like no other, alerting us to pursuit hours before we'd otherwise be aware. And then, of course, there's the fact that he can breathe fire. It's a useful feature, as I suppose even your limited imagination can grasp." She said this last politely, as if she were delivering a compliment rather than an insult. Chuck found himself snorting in amusement.

"Your call, kid," Jay said, turning his head to look at Chuck. "I'm for, Garman's against. Yours is the deciding vote. What do you think? Do we take this job?"

Chuck turned to look at Garman. The Windfist still stood, his face pinched with disapproval. Across the fire, the girl sat apparently at ease, though her back was straight. He could see her hands trembling. Next to him, Jay lounged with a flask in one hand.

And up above, Quetzalith watched him with those piercing eyes.

"We do," Chuck said, his voice firm. "We'll take you to Pittsburgh but you pay us when we get there, uncle or no uncle."

He was inclined not to charge her, but Jay apparently thought it was important to do so. If that was the case, then Chuck refused to get hustled again. So.

"Agreed," Jasmine said, relief in her tone. Her smile, complete with dimples, flashed back into existence. Chuck thought he heard Garman suck in a breath beside him.

"Be aware, abomination trainer," Garman said, just as politely, "that your 'champion' seems to attract trouble. I can only imagine that your abomination shall increase the odds of that happening."

"Aw, hell, junior," Jay said as he leaned forward to offer Jasmine a nip from his flask. "Lighten up. We always have a good time, don't we? Don't we?"

"Fine," the Windfist said, dropping back to his seat. "But don't say I didn't warn you."

"Hell, at the very least, it'll take some of the attention off of Chuck," Jay said, settling in for the night.

Chuck snorted a laugh and leaned back to look at the dragon again. The fascinating creature dipped his head one more time, tucked it under one massive wing and appeared to go to sleep.

CHAPTER SEVEN

THEY SHARED A CHILLY BREAKFAST, IN TERMS OF BOTH TEM-
perature and tone. Jasmine and Garman seemed content for the
moment to ignore each other as much as possible and only speak
to each other when absolutely necessary. Those conversations, at
least, were excruciatingly polite and formal but the whole thing
made Chuck's skin itch.

Then there was the dragon. True to Jasmine's word, Quetzalith
had taken off shortly after dawn and climbed so high as to be the
tiniest speck in the sky. Chuck could find him but only when Jasmine pointed him out. Even so, Chuck couldn't shake the feeling
that the great beast was watching him with those powerful eyes,
tracking his every move. It unnerved a man, to say the least.

Once they got on the road, Garman had dropped back a
few lengths, muttering darkly about guarding their rear better
than any abomination could . . . and the need to guard against
the abomination itself. Jasmine seemed inclined to scout ahead,
keeping one eye up at Quetzalith and following some cue that
Chuck couldn't read in his flight pattern. So Chuck found himself
riding next to Jay for most of the morning.

The old vagabond didn't seem to be showing quite as many
signs of complete inebriation this morning, though he did take
a nip from his flask every so often. They rode in silence for the
first little bit, as the sun climbed into the sky behind them in a
blaze that promised some heat later on.

"Why'd you charge her?" Chuck asked, turning his head to spit a line of tobacco juice off to the side. He'd been going over the events of yesterday in his head and this part didn't seem to make sense. It just didn't seem like Jay.

"Hmm?" Jay asked before leaning to the side and spitting out a precisely aimed stream of tobacco at a nearby tiny ant hill. The hill immediately exploded into activity. Those in the immediate path of the liquid missile curled up and died, while their fellows swarmed over their lifeless bodies in chaotic panic.

"The girl. Jasmine. Why'd you tell her we'd only take her to her uncle's for a price?"

"Oh, that. We need to have a talk about women, kid," Jay said with a grin.

"Jay, no, please. I ain't...I won't try...with her...and I grew up on a farm so...no."

"Not what I meant, kid," Jay said, shaking his head. "Pretty girl but the vibe's not right. She's a survivor, that one. She'd probably gut you as soon as look at you if you tried. And that's why I charged her."

"Pardon?"

"See, kid," Jay said, shifting in his seat. The old man's voice lost some of its characteristic easy humor and he sounded almost serious. "That girl? She's been through more shit in her young life than you and Garman combined and it didn't break her. But it did change her. It made her hard, but brittle hard. She can't take charity, especially not from a group of men. But if she pays us, it's a job and she's still relying on herself."

"Oh," Chuck said. He chewed on this idea for a few minutes. He knew the need to be self-sufficient. Pa had drummed into him that while everyone needed help sometimes, that accepting charity was a dead last resort and should only be utilized if circumstances were life-or-death dire. But he'd also been taught that it was a man's honor and place to care for a woman, especially if that woman were in distress. It didn't sit right with him to take Jasmine's money to see her to safety but, once again, he felt like Jay knew what he was about. So he'd keep quiet for now and let things develop.

Nothing said he couldn't give the money back to her later. Or slip it into her bags one night, or something. That thought cheered him and he straightened up in his saddle and gave Jay a nod.

Jay gave him a wink in return and held out one of his flasks.

"Sun's barely up, Jay," Chuck said, smiling in spite of himself.

"Suit yourself," Jay said. "Sun's over the yardarm somewhere."

"Seems to me water might be a bit more fortifyin' than what you got in there."

"You fortify your way, kid, I'll fortify mine."

"Yes, sir."

Baron Schilling sat, silently contemplating the man in front of him. A member of the security team, he had been present the day of the unpleasantness Jasmine was investigating. Freshly groomed, in a new uniform, the man shifted uncomfortably in front of the heavy oak desk.

"Now, explain to me, Mr...Wilt was it? Exactly what happened again."

"Yessir, milord." Wilt cleared his throat a few times. "Well, you see, it was like this, sir. We boarded the train in Fewaf, and started makin' the rounds. So there we was..."

"Were."

"Excuse me, milord?" Wilt looked confused.

"The word is 'were.'"

"Oh. Okay. So were we was, was on the train..."

Schilling pinched the bridge of his nose, trying to keep his frustration in check. He made a mental note to require literacy tests for future hires.

"Are you feeling okay, milord?"

"Yes, Mr. Wilt. Just a moment of exasperation. Please continue."

"I get that too sometimes, milord. Usually clears up after a shot of vinegar though."

"You were saying, Mr. Wilt?"

"Yessir. I were up front, keepin' an eye on the engineer, making sure he was safe and all. Everything seemed to be goin' well, on schedule, you know. Next thing I know, the train stops. A few minutes later, I hear a gunshot. I looked back down the train and saw three fellers riding off. Jumped down quicklike to see what for and found Brewer in the stable car with his head blown off. Went to find t'others, and they was dead, too."

"I see." Schilling took a sip from his water glass. "Tell me, Mr. Wilt, why did you do nothing?"

"Well, um, you see..." Wilt looked down as he shuffled his

feet, clenched fists crushing his hat. "I ain't proud of this but they'd killed Brewer, Gilinski, Ashford, and Taylor. Those men weren't soft, sir, and I didn't want to tussle with no one that could do that."

"Your honesty is appreciated, Mr. Wilt, even if your cowardice is not."

"Thank you, milord."

"Can you describe the men?"

"Well, Brewer was kind of tall, lanky..." He paused at Schilling's grimace. "Vinegar, milord. Works every time."

"Describe the *attackers*, Mr. Wilt."

"Oh. Them. Well, I didn't get a great look at 'em; they were moving pretty fast. But I did see one of them was one of those Windfist fellers when he boarded."

The Baron looked up sharply.

"You're sure about that?"

"Yes, milord. Dressed like one of them. Had one of them tattoos on his face, too."

Schilling leaned back, steepling his fingers in front of his chin.

"Do you think you would recognize it, should you see it again?"

"Oh, yessir."

"Excellent, Mr. Wilt." He picked up a small silver bell, giving a short ring before setting it back on the desk. Lieutenant Sampsei entered, his large frame at attention. He snapped a crisp salute, palm out, tip of his middle finger almost touching his graying red hair. Schilling nodded.

"Please show Mr. Wilt to the waiting room and escort the young man waiting there to me."

Lieutenant Sampsei saluted again, motioning for Wilt toward the door and following him out.

Windfist weren't known for running from perceived injustice. It was odd that one would be involved in an attack and leave, rather than reporting to the local authorities. Something was happening and he'd be damned if he wouldn't take advantage of it.

Were the monks mobilizing? Had they heard about his connections to the Gant cultists and the advances in controlling the insects? One Windfist in the middle of nowhere didn't necessarily mean anything but...coincidence was a funny thing. Sometimes it was just that—coincidence. However, he hadn't made it this far by ignoring correlation. This whole situation begged for further investigation and since he hadn't gotten a report from Jasmine, he would have to proceed without her. A knock came from the heavy oak door.

"Come in."

Lieutenant Sampsei entered, saluted, then motioned for the next visitor to enter.

The young man walked into the office, lack of any sense of decorum or humility apparent on his tattooed face. The whelp didn't even possess sense enough to act as though he was in the presence of his better. If his clothing hadn't identified him as Windfist, his bearing and attitude were a dead giveaway. Some education appeared to be in order.

"I am Baron Schilling," he said, leaning forward. "My men tell me you claim to have information?"

"Yeah."

"I'm all ears, young man."

"What's in it for me, Your Grace?" The Windfist's sneer robbed the title of any respect.

Oh, how easy it would be to make this little snot regret his impertinence. That could wait, though. For now, more flies with honey.

"We will discuss compensation when I determine how useful you are, my boy."

"I figure I must be pretty useful, since your men came to me."

"Boy," Schilling put as much contempt into the word as he could muster, "while true that my men look for *things* that may be helpful to my plans, it is never guaranteed that what they find is what I need. Much like collecting flotsam in the sewer: What may look interesting in the water, may only be shit when examined closely."

The Windfist looked as though he'd been slapped.

"Now, I ask again, boy, what do you have for me?" Schilling dropped his hands to his lap, hidden behind the desk.

"Do you know who I am?" The boy took a step forward, fists clenched. "I am—"

"A Windfist." He squinted for effect. "Excuse me. *Former* Windfist. Adeptus, by the tattoo. Wyoming chapter, by your clothing. Impulsive moron, by your actions. Did I miss anything?"

All but the last had been reported to him by his men. But no need to tell the idiot that information.

Let him think I see all.

"Yeah, you missed the part where I kick your ass," the young man said, taking another step forward.

And stopped at the distinctive click of a cocking hammer.

"Ah, I did miss something," Schilling said. "Eunuch. Should you take one more step, I'll make it happen. I know you are highly trained, capable and fast. What I don't know, and I'm certain you don't either, is if you're faster than a bullet."

He didn't take his eyes off the Adeptus. But he did allow a slow smile.

"Lieutenant, call the rest of your detail, please. I want this boy taken to a cell and starved. After a few days, have him whipped. We'll revisit this topic when he is more suited to acting civil."

Boots thudded in the hall at Sampsei's shout. Watching the range of emotions—from anger, to understanding, to fear—play across the kid's features was almost worth the irritation.

"Wait!" The boy raised his hands, looking over his shoulder at the door. "Wait, just wait. I'll tell you what I know."

Schilling nodded, making a "proceed" motion with his free hand.

"My Master Superior had documents, reports, from other chapters. There was talk about the Gantists being able to control the bugs. Attacks on settlements, wagon trains, stuff like that."

"Yes, and? Rumors of coordinated attacks have become more commonplace."

"Yeah, but these were witnessed, by Windfist." A note of pride entered his voice. "So you know it's true."

"So?" Schilling sniffed. "This news is nothing to me."

In actuality, this was interesting. It seems the knowledge he'd sold to the cultists years ago was finally coming to fruition. In the process of taking what had once been Amarillo, he'd looted the local universities for anything of use. Without electricity, most of the equipment was useless; however, the libraries had provided thousands of volumes on a wide swath of subjects. It was how he'd built his empire—in a society forced to regress technologically to the steam age, knowledge of Industrial Revolution–age tech was priceless. Witness his growing railroad empire, for example.

The cultists had been highly interested in entomology, of course, with engineering and chemistry coming close behind. What he saw as an amusing pastime, they saw as coming closer to their gods.

It seemed an opportune time to strengthen that alliance.

"I've not heard anything that makes you more than a waste of my time. Lieutenant, I've changed my mind. Have this boy dragged behind a horse. Perhaps his screams will provide a momentary amusement."

The soldiers moved closer, carefully. Schilling had a suspicion that, had he not still held the pistol on monk, his men would find themselves seriously injured. Windfists were nothing to trifle with.

"I can be of service, Milord Baron." Ah, there was the tone he was waiting for: humility. Schilling raised a hand again, stopping the soldiers' advance.

"Oh? How?"

"Your men, the ones I met, we talked. Talked about how to change things. Make 'em better."

"Did you now."

"Yeah. Talked about how the Windfist ain't done nothing much in a while. How things ought to be," the boy said, clasping his hands in front of his chest. "Milord, I know I can talk to my brothers. Make them see things my way. I can get into the chapterhouses without a fight. Talk to the guys my age. Bring them to you."

The former Windfist's eyes flashed with passion. "I can bring you an army, milord."

The Baron had considered this before, however briefly. If there was even a small percentage of disillusioned young men in the ranks... well, the promise of wealth and power was a strong aphrodisiac.

"For now, consider yourself lucky. You've earned a brief reprieve while I consider your proposal," Schilling said, uncocking the pistol. "Lieutenant, please escort... What was your name?"

"Ronen, milord."

"...Mr. Ronen to a room in the east wing. Mr. Ronen, I suggest you utilize the bath. Your odor would gag a vulture. I will send for you when I have an answer," he said, the cold smile returning to his lips. "To be honest, Mr. Ronen, I wouldn't get too accustomed to the luxury. I'll most likely kill you in the morning. Dismissed."

The former Windfist finally seemed to grasp the situation, bowing deeply and leaving the chamber without another word. Schilling addressed the remaining guards.

"Please bring Mr. Wilt back in."

Moments later, Wilt was again in front of him, hat in hands.

"Mr. Wilt, I trust you noticed the young man I summoned?"

"Yessir, milord," Wilt said. "Had the same tattoo as the one up North."

"You are certain?"

"I sure am. Same kind of clothes, too."

"Thank you, Mr. Wilt. Please enjoy a few days rest and relaxation. You may go."

"Yessir, milord, much obliged, milord."

The coward near prostrated himself before taking his leave. Schilling leaned back in his chair as the door closed behind Wilt, thoughts churning.

The reports from the Windfist, the death of his men, his informant's disappearance—all happening very close to one another. It couldn't be coincidence. He'd heard other rumors, that the Gantists were searching for someone—someone that found something important to their cause. Had this Windfist on the train been trying to protect this item? If so, it fell to reason that he'd head for his people.

It seemed Mr. Ronen might be useful after all, if for nothing else, a tool to gather information.

And if he proved useless, at least his death would be entertaining.

Schilling poured whiskey into his tumbler, noting the level of liquid in the decanter. He made a mental note to have another bottle brought from his private reserve soon. Yet another perk of leadership—he had an iron grip on the best alcohol in the area.

He made sure, decades ago when rebuilding Amarillo into Ironhelm, that his forces controlled any trade goods. It allowed him to create a "company store" type situation, controlling the availability of certain items and therefore maintaining supply. Left to their own devices, the lower classes would fail to use the items to the best advantage, trading willy-nilly or wasting resources. For the good of his subjects, he had to maintain strict order.

A light knock on the door interrupted his thoughts.

"Enter."

Ronen entered, followed closely by Lieutenant Sampsei.

"Ah, Ronen," Schilling said, allowing a slight smile to play on his lips. "I see you took my advice and utilized the plumbing facilities. I no longer confuse your odor with that of week-dead skunk."

To his credit, the boy kept his anger harnessed; only minuscule tightening around his eyes betrayed his emotions. Schilling would prefer to see that fire erased completely, but could work with what he had, for now.

Ronen bowed stiffly.

"Yes, milord, thank you. Your hospitality is appreciated."

Schilling sipped slowly, drawing the silence out.

"I have decided that your offer is agreeable. It would be a waste to ignore your talents and training and, as you said, you have an advantage when it comes to the Windfist. Also, it seems one of your chapter had a hand in damaging my property. I would like to bring him to justice."

"Milord Baron, I will not disappoint you." Was that relief in the young man's eyes? If so, good. A few hours contemplating his mortality had worked wonders on his attitude. "I know I can deliver."

"We shall see," Schilling said. "Do I need to emphasize the cost of failure?"

"No, milord," Ronen said, shaking his head emphatically. "My life is in your hands."

"Yes. It is. You will travel to Old Kansas City, visiting any Windfist chapters nearby, to recruit your former fellows. Along with your primary mission, it is important that you gather any and all intelligence on other Windfist activities. In this time, information is worth its weight in silver. Changes are afoot."

"Yes, milord, I understand. One of the reasons I came here was to get involved with your vision. The men I came with spoke at length about it."

"Indeed." Schilling drained his glass, motioning for Ronen to have a seat. "Let me tell you about my vision.

"I was your age when the ants came. It was a different time, as I'm sure you're aware. Everything was simpler but complicated. Information, communication, it was all at your fingertips, at all times. We, as a species, had become conceited. We were the masters of our destiny, shaping the world to our myopic visions. Did you know that we went to space?"

At Ronen's head shake, he continued.

"Hard to believe but we did. The shooting stars you see on occasion are our legacy. Fantastic machines to transport men into the inky black above us. Fantastic, yet fragile. You see, I remember watching them leave the Earth, only to see them crash back again. Happened once practically over my head. Tragic, but a necessary reminder of what happens when we overstep our bounds."

He poured another drink, taking a long draught before continuing.

"I believe the Gants were our saviors, really. You see, we'd strayed. Equality for all and some such nonsense—a conceit of those that spent too much time as the dominant species. The Gants came and put paid to the notion that *we* were the top of the pecking order. I wish to put humanity back on the correct path."

"Which path is that, sir?"

"Have you ever read Verne? Doyle?" A headshake from Ronen. "No? Pity. I see the time period they wrote about as the ideal, myself. A place for everyone, as is the natural order, none of this . . . forced equality that became so prevalent. As you can see, the people that live under my benevolence are well taken care of. But they know their place. Every cog does its job, the machine runs smoothly. A lesson from my father that has proven true time and again."

"I see."

"Another lesson from my father: Find the right people, put them where they do the most good. Eliminate the wrong people from the equation, or place them where they will do the least damage.

"You have a unique opportunity. Make the most of it. I will have a detail and travel accommodations arranged for you tomorrow, so you can start at the earliest possible moment. Sampsei will brief you on the details, and collect everything you took from the chapterhouse. Good night."

Ronen stood, snapping to attention, arms at his side, head held high.

"You will not regret this, Milord Baron. You have my word."

Schilling nodded to Sampsei, who escorted Ronen from the chamber. Things were coming together.

CHAPTER EIGHT

THE SUN STARED DOWN FROM A CLOUDLESS SKY. CHUCK'S PARTY worked their way east, following game trails and dry streambeds out of the canyonlands. Every now and again, they came upon a straight stretch of ground that may have once been an old road. There wasn't much left but several unnaturally straight scars cutting across seemingly endless rolling hills. They used these when they could, as it was easier going all around.

After their noon break on Jasmine's fourth day, Garman abruptly took the lead, Jasmine dropping back to ride beside Chuck and Jay. Chuck wasn't sure what to say at first, but Jay opened up with a question about the dragon and she seemed happy to discuss Quetzalith all day.

"Wait a minute." She stopped mid-story, as something caught her attention. She reined in her horse and looked around. "Why are we going south?"

"What?" Chuck felt his face heat. She was a good storyteller and he'd been engrossed in the tale of her initial attempts to train Quetzalith. "We're just following the old road..."

"No," Jasmine said, angrily. She raised her arm over her head and a tiny speck in the sky grew at an alarming rate. "What's going on here? We've turned south and passed at least two intersections where we could have turned back east. Where are we going? Do I need to be concerned? Are you double-crossing me, old man?"

"Me?" Jay asked, his eyebrows raising up his forehead. "Not me. Kid's in charge."

Jasmine turned to look at Chuck.

"We ain't double-crossing you," he said, trying to sound placating. "I didn't even think about it, but Garman's got something to do near Old Kansas City. Order business. We were on our way there before we found you."

"Before *I* found *you*, you mean," she said, suspiciously. "And you didn't think to mention this 'Order business' before now?"

"Uh. No," Chuck said, sounding shamefaced even to himself.

She stared at him for a moment longer, then pressed her lips together. Overhead, Quetzalith's shadow grew ever larger, until the dragon loomed over their heads, wings spread wide, buffeting the air around them. The horses snorted and danced in protest, Millie whinnying her deep disapproval. Chuck looked down long enough to try and calm her, then looked slowly back up at Jasmine.

Who threw her head back and burst into laughter.

Chuck blinked. That was not the reaction he'd been expecting.

"Seven hells, look at you!" she said. "You look like a five-year-old about to be spanked and sent to his room! Gods above, you really aren't trying to double-cross me, are you?"

"No, ma'am," Chuck said softly, feeling his face burn even more. Next to Jasmine, Jay started chuckling as well. Chuck tried to throw him a glare but he had the feeling that the effect was spectacularly unimpressive.

"No. I don't believe you are. In any case, my gut says to trust you and I trust my gut. All right, farm boy. Let's go see to your friend's 'Order business.' Because blush or no blush, I believe you're aware of what Quetzalith will do if it turns out that my gut was wrong. Aren't you?"

"Believe so, ma'am," Chuck said.

"Good boy," she smiled and kneed her horse forward into a trot after Garman. Chuck pursed his lips and urged Millie forward to follow her. Overhead, Quetzalith let out a ringing cry and began climbing back up into the sky.

"Wish she wouldn't call me 'boy,'" Chuck muttered as the still-chuckling Jay pulled up alongside him.

"Count your blessings, kid. You got off light for that one. Shoulda told her before."

"S'pose so. Why'd you say that, though? I ain't in charge of nothing."

"Ain't you?" Jay said, looking sidelong at him. "Coulda fooled me."

"What do you mean?"

"Well...Garman said it, I suppose. This is your Journey. We're just all along for our own reasons. The way I see it, that puts you in charge. Might as well embrace it."

"But that makes me responsible for everyone."

Jay's face split into a wide grin and his eyes sparkled with a wicked, edged sort of humor.

"Guess it does, at that."

Chuck sat quietly for a few moments, then whispered, "Fuck."

"You said it, kid!" Jay laughed. "You said it all right there."

"Wait..." Chuck said after another few minutes' thoughtful silence. "If I'm in charge how come you're the one who's always deciding what we do?"

"Cause age and experience wins over youth and enthusiasm, boy. Remember that, too."

Several days later, they found a Windfist outpost on the edge of a prairie ghost town. Crumbling buildings squatted next to a wide, flat field that, while long, was a significantly different color than the rest of the grass in the area. As they approached, Chuck could see the decaying hulks of prewar vehicles: some he recognized, some he didn't. Some of them even had what looked like wings jutting out from the sides.

"What was this place?" Chuck asked as they rode toward the closest entrance: a gaping hole in the rusted jaws of an ancient twisted metal fence.

"Brenner Field," Jay said. He pointed to a barely-legible sign hanging from a portion of the fence remains. "There used to be a bunch of these airfields all over the country. If you were rich enough or passionate enough to have your own airplane, you kept it at a place like this."

"Now it's an outpost belonging to the Windfist Order," Garman said, impatiently. He'd waited for them to catch up and now he nudged his horse forward through the fence.

"No appreciation for flying the friendly skies, that one," Jay said. "Can't say I blame him, though. Most guys in his line of work would've had to jump out of them, into extremely *unfriendly* skies. Puts a damper on enjoying the ride."

Jasmine followed behind him, skepticism tinged with naked longing on her face as she gazed at the sad corpses of the so-called flying machines. Chuck followed her and Jay brought up the rear. A hot wind whipped over them, rustling the grass as they rode toward the tall single tower that jutted into the sky up ahead.

"Did people really fly in those things?" Chuck asked as they drew closer to the derelict machines. "They look so . . . heavy compared to Quetzalith."

"People did," Jay said with a bit of a smile. "And if you think those are clunky and heavy looking, you oughta see a C-130. Or a Jolly Green Giant."

"A what?"

"Never mind," Jay said, shaking his head. "Kids."

Up ahead, Garman had ridden straight to the base of the tower, dismounting near the door. He tried it—locked. So far, no one had answered his authoritative pounding.

"No one home, Junior?" Jay asked as the three of them caught up with the Windfist.

"There should be," Garman said, his face creased in a frown. He pounded twice more. "I don't understand. Someone should always be awake and on watch. They should have seen us as we came through the fence."

"Maybe they did, and they don't want to talk to you," Jasmine said sweetly. Garman glared at her over his shoulder before pounding on the door again.

"They are my brothers," Garman said. "They would have recognized my cloak. They have no reason not to speak to me."

"I can think of some," Jasmine murmured again. Jay snorted a laugh. Chuck sent her a look that he hoped was quelling.

"Not helping, ma'am," he said softly.

"You're right," Jasmine said. She didn't sound particularly contrite, but she dismounted from her horse. "My apologies, Windfist. If you move to the side, I can probably open that door for you."

"It's locked," Garman said.

"Really? Wow. What a shocking development," she said in that light, pleasant tone. Her eyebrows arched prettily. "And here I thought you were just making that terrible racket for the sheer joy of noise. Fortunately for us all, I've brought my picks."

She reached inside her boot, drawing a pair of slim metal tools that looked as if they'd been fashioned from ladies' hairpins. Garman scowled at her for a moment and then stepped aside, his boots sounding harsh on the dusty area in front of the door. Chuck, feeling useless, hitched the horses to a nearby rail.

It wasn't a quick process but eventually, the dark-haired dragon trainer twisted her hands over as the lock made a satisfying *thunk* sound. She removed her picks from the keyhole, stashed them back inside her boot and then stood up and stepped back.

"It's all yours, Windfist," she said, her dimple dancing. Garman gave her a rather stiff nod, wrapping his big hand around the metal doorknob. The other hand held his kukri.

"Stay alert," he said in a low whisper. "My brothers may be hurt, or under duress, or something worse inside."

Chuck wondered why Garman felt it necessary to whisper after making such a godawful racket earlier, but the Windfist was already opening the door, so he went with it. He drew a pistol, noting that both Jasmine and Jay held guns of their own.

The door opened silently on well-oiled hinges: evidence that someone, at least, had been maintaining the tower until very recently. They filed into a small room at the base of a square spiral of stairs. A window at head-height let in the intense afternoon sunlight. Dust motes danced in the square beam as it slanted down to the floor.

Garman cautioned them once again by laying his finger on his lips and then began to walk up the stairs. Chuck had to give it to the big man: He moved with incredible lightness, even on a metal staircase. Jasmine, Chuck and finally Jay followed, stepping as quietly as they could, though none of them seemed to have Garman's almost preternatural gift for stealth.

The stairs went up for a fair ways. Chuck counted four complete cycles around, each illuminated only by a single window, until finally they came to another metal door. Garman tried the knob on this one and it turned slowly in his hand. Chuck felt his breathing quicken in anticipation of action as the Windfist held up three fingers and slowly counted them down. Three. Two...

One.

Garman burst in the door, knocking it aside with his shoulder. He stepped past the door to the right. Chuck followed, his revolver up at the ready, breaking left before turning to sweep around.

Behind him, he could feel Jasmine and Jay brushing past, bringing up their own weapons, ready to meet the imminent threat of...

Nothing.

It was a large room surrounded on all sides by windows. At some point, two of the large windowpanes had been broken out and replaced by cut boards. Even so, the room offered an impressive near 360 degrees of visibility. Four pallets lay around the edge of the room, each of them stripped of any blankets or other bedclothes. Shelves lined the walls under the windows but they were largely empty. Chuck spotted what looked like a jar of canned beets that had been left behind.

"Well," Jasmine said into the silence. "This is anticlimactic."

"They should be here," Garman said, his voice hard with anger, or fear, or maybe both. "A Windfist never abandons his post. I don't understand."

"Maybe they got called away," Chuck offered but Garman shook his head and holstered his gun.

"No, if that was the case, the chapterhouse would have sent a replacement. Something must have happened. Something else. We're likely not safe here. We should move on. I will inform the chapterhouse in Old Kansas City. The Master Superior there will know what to do. And he will need to know about this abandonment."

"Are you sure they didn't just decide that watching grass grow wasn't worth their time, Junior?" Jay asked. "I mean, it ain't like there's a lot out here for them to keep track of."

"Every post is vital, old man. They wouldn't just abandon it without good reason."

"If you say so, Junior."

"I say so, old man. And it's Journeyman."

"Yeah, you told me."

"How far away is it?" Jasmine asked Chuck.

"Old Kansas City?" He dug out his map, studied it for a minute, then continued. "Looks like a few days. We'll need to stop and resupply before we get there."

"The leader there has no love for the Baron," Jasmine said, thoughtfully. "So, we're not likely to face much from his bully boys in town. I like this plan."

"We didn't ask for your approval," Garman snapped at Jasmine as he kicked at one of the bedrolls. She just laughed at him and turned to lead the way down the stairs. Jay rolled his eyes and followed after her.

"It's not her fault, man," Chuck said, reaching out to the Windfist. "You don't have to take it out on her."

"I know," Garman said. "It's just...they should *be* here. I've got this feeling that something's terribly wrong and I can't put my finger on what. And then she makes some kind of stupid comment or laughs that stupid laugh of hers and I can't concentrate on anything but how *wrong* it is that we've allied ourselves with an abomination like that."

"Jasmine? She ain't hardly an abomination, Garman. And I'll thank you not to talk about a lady that way in my presence."

"Not Jasmine, the dragon. That thing came through with the Gants. It's unnatural and it doesn't belong in our world. But here we are, letting it hunt for us, scout for us, treating it like some kind of damn pet when it could burn us all to ash where we stand."

"But it ain't going to burn us, because of Jasmine. Look, man, I know you don't like Quetzalith and that's okay but you gotta be polite to the lady, alright? We're doing a job for her, it's just common decency."

Garman took a deep breath and clapped Chuck on the shoulder.

"You stick by your principles, Chuck. You're a man of honor. I respect that about you. For you, I will try to be more civil to the dragon tamer and her...thing. I just hope that my doing so is not putting us more in danger."

"How so?"

"By sullying the purity of my warrior spirit. I pray that the Saints Kalashnikov and Baddis will not abandon me for keeping low company and that Saint Norris will continue to watch over our Journey together," Garman said, folding his left hand over his right fist and bowing his head.

"Amen?" Chuck said, because all of a sudden it sounded a lot like religion and he tried to be respectful of such things. Garman looked up with a small smile that didn't quite reach his eyes and clapped Chuck on the shoulder again.

"Oorah. Onward to Old Kansas City?" Garman said, gesturing to the doorway that led to the stairs.

"Sure thing, buddy," Chuck replied. "Wouldn't miss it."

CHAPTER NINE

ARIEL SLAMMED BACK INTO HER OWN BODY, WHIMPERING AT the memory of the joy that had so thoroughly ravaged her entire being. She blinked and realized that time had passed.

She was in her own bed, in the alcove she shared with her parents. The sun shone its harsh light through the dirt-caked window.

She'd lost the entire night.

Moving as if she might shatter, Ariel carefully sat up. Every movement made her head pound and she felt like she might throw up. There was a little water in the pitcher by the door. It tasted flat and old but she drank it anyway. It helped, a little.

Her parents were gone, no doubt up with the sun and working hard at maintaining the mechanisms that kept the Nest alive and producing electricity for the holy ones. For the first time, Ariel understood their fanatic devotion to duty. If a Blessing was to be their reward, she could finally see why they'd all but completely neglected her, leaving her to mostly raise and educate herself among the other acolytes. For even now, she felt a deep yearning to do whatever she could to get back to the chamber, to feel that overwhelming rush of pleasure ricochet through her again.

Something splashed onto her hand. Ariel looked down and realized it was a tear. She touched her face to find a thin tracery of wetness.

I do not want it.

It was unthinkable but she thought it anyway. That joy, that ultimate reward—it frightened her, worse than any Holy Warrior's mandibles. To lose her sense of self to the point where nothing else mattered but the Blessing? To lose larger and larger chunks of time, as she had done this morning? To yearn, even as she now yearned for more of the same?

I do not want it!

Without even realizing it, she was on her feet. She took the bag of wild onions and berries she'd gathered, added an empty bottle, her scavenged fire starter, a spare tunic, and a knife. The bottle she could fill from the river.

The irony did not escape her. The very thing that drove her parents' every action, including leaving their daughter to fend for herself as a child, gave Ariel the exact mindset and skills to reject it.

The rest of the acolytes would be expecting her to take her place somewhere in the machinery or on the Dam. They'd expect her to work diligently, and present herself to the acolyte leaders for additional tasks, so that she could earn another taste of the unholy Blessing that the Child offered.

They'd never expect her to walk out the door of the compound and just keep walking.

But that was exactly what she did.

Three days later, Ariel huddled against the cold metal of the ancient boxcar, trying to turn her brain off. The incessant rumble and vibration of the car numbed her backside and spine. Her mind wasn't so easily conquered. Nor was her stomach, stabbing hungrily at her from inside—a constant reminder that she'd eaten the last of her food two days ago, when she'd decided to hop the train.

She choked back a laughing sob as she thought of that "decision." Starving to death, crouched in a half-frozen ball on the filthy floor of a not-quite-empty boxcar, Ariel couldn't decide if she'd done the right thing or not.

She had turned back twice during those first twelve hours. Neither time had been intentional. She'd merely been wandering, her only goal to get away from the sickening lure of the Blessing. Twice, though, her steps had brought her back to a bluff that looked down over the lake and the Dam. Twice, she'd nearly started down the path back. Redemption? Destruction? She still wasn't sure.

"If I go, I need to go *far*," she'd said out loud the second time. The highland wind had ripped the words from her mouth so that she'd barely heard them. She'd felt them, though. Their truth had resonated through her being. She had to go *far* away. Otherwise the Blessing would pull her back and drive her mad and she would lose all that she was in its pursuit.

So she'd done the only thing she could think of. She'd headed south, to a spot not far from the depot where the acolytes received new converts and traded for the few items that the Nest couldn't provide for itself. She'd waited until nightfall and then hopped on an empty car that had just left the station. She hadn't moved much since. Not even when the train itself stopped to take on water, fuel, or presumably, other passengers. At least, a few other passengers had hopped on during the last stop, though Ariel didn't think they'd paid for their fare. Like her, they'd stolen onto the boxcar and hidden in the shadows of the open door until the train started moving.

At first, Ariel hadn't paid them much mind. There were three of them: thin, hungry looking men. She couldn't tell their ages because their faces were so smudged with dirt, though one of them had a fringe of greasy hair around his chin. They'd taken up residence on the opposite end of the car and Ariel didn't think they'd even noticed that she was there until the sun had come up a few hours ago. One of them had immediately put his head back and commenced snoring. She wondered if he was drunk. She'd heard stories of drunks, though she'd never seen one in person. The lure of the Blessing was too great for those at home. No one would risk being unable to work and so losing out.

Now, though, the late-morning sun slanted in through the open door to Ariel's left. No matter how she ducked down, she couldn't hide the feminine shape of her face from that thin light. It wasn't strong enough to heat the interior of the car, or give comfort to her chilled fingers and toes but it was more than enough to highlight that she was a girl.

"Pretty."

Ariel stiffened and opened her eyes. One of the three men had moved closer and now crouched down directly in front of her. He reached out with dirt-stained fingers and touched her face. She swallowed hard and tried not to move.

"Soft."

"Nillon, come away from the girl," one of the other men called out from the other side of the car. Nillon wrinkled his nose and rolled his eyes.

"I weren't hurting her none," he said, looking over his shoulder. His voice had a definite whine to it. "She's so pretty. I ain't seen a woman in *ages.*"

"You ain't gonna see her, neither. Now get back over here."

"You ain't my daddy, Big Joe," Nillon whined.

"I thank every God every day for that. Now get your scrawny ass back over here before I make you. She's young. She ain't for you." Big Joe's voice dipped into a sort of growling threat and Nillon let out a huffing sort of sigh. But he dropped his hand from Ariel's face and stood up. She tried not to look up at him, as she didn't want to give him any encouragement but her impression was that he was tall and cadaverously thin. He smiled down at her and his crookedly brown, broken-toothed smile was enough to make her shiver in fear before he lurched back to the other side of the car. She dropped her eyes to see Big Joe looking at her, a troubled look on his bearded face. He saw her looking and gave her a small nod, as if to say that he'd keep her safe from his friend Nillon.

Ariel didn't nod back, she just tried to hunch lower, bringing her shoulders up and tucking her chin down. She suddenly became aware of her thudding heartbeat and all trace of fatigue seemed to have flown in the face of her sudden fear. She didn't know what Nillon might do. She simply knew that he scared her.

And yet, it didn't take long until the rhythmic thumping and ever-present whirr of the train's passage pulled at the edges of her awareness. Her body's exhaustion further dragged at her, until her head nodded back against the cold metal of the boxcar and her eyelids slid shut.

Ariel never knew whether it was the slowing of the car, or the hand tugging at her clothing that woke her up. She opened her eyes to see Nillon's rotten smile inches from her face. She drew breath to scream but all that came out was a sort of terrified croaking noise.

"So pretty," Nillon said as he pulled at the collar of her tunic one more time. He seemed to be trying to pull it down or tear it.

Truesilk didn't tear easily, however, and his dirty face creased in frustration. Ariel struck out, batting at his arms with her hands but hunger caused a lassitude and weakness in her body. She felt like she was moving underwater.

The blast of the train whistle split the air around them, making Nillon jump and let go of her tunic. Ariel scooted back and to the right along the wall of the boxcar. She couldn't go far, however, and found herself trapped in the corner. Nillon gave her another grin and lurched toward her as another whistle blast reverberated through the metal of the car.

"Godsdammit, Nillon!" Big Joe roared. Apparently, he'd been asleep, giving Nillon the confidence to try his luck with Ariel once more. The train whistle had woken him just in time. He got to his feet and charged, impacting the smaller man with a *thud*. Ariel squeaked as they hit the floor of the boxcar next to her, making the dirt jump up into the air. On the other side of the car, the third man snorted, smacked his lips and opened his eyes.

"Wha—?" he asked, his voice querulous, like that of an old person to whom no one listens. "Why're ye fighting *now*?"

His eyes, so bloodshot that they looked rimmed with red even from across the car, found Ariel as she tried, once again, to make herself as small as she could. Next to her, the combatants rolled, fists flying as they fought to pummel each other.

"Oh," the drunk said. "Lemme guess. Nillon tried to cop a feel and Big Joe took exception?"

Ariel surprised herself by nodding. The drunk nodded back, then looked around.

"Welp," he said, squinting out of the open door. "Good news for you. Looks like we're slowing. You'd better jump now, sweetheart. Nillon never sleeps and a train whistle's the only thing that'll wake Big Joe."

He was right, Ariel realized. She peeked out the door closest to her and saw that they were, indeed, slowing as they came into one of the innumerable towns that had sprung up along the railroad. She had no idea where she was, but hadn't that been part of her plan? If she didn't know where she was, she couldn't find her way back. And if she couldn't find her way back, then going forward was her only option.

Plus, she was starving. And she'd finished the last of the water in her bottle last night, before the men had gotten on.

Dehydration and hunger had weakened her to the point that she was easy prey for anyone like Nillon and she couldn't exactly forage while on the train. Better to get off and take her chances in this small town. Or perhaps outside of it.

While the battle raged on next to her, Ariel pushed herself slowly to her feet and stepped over to the doorway. The drunk gave her a friendly nod as she positioned herself. She nodded back, in thanks for his advice, and took hold of the bag she still carried looped across her chest.

The train lurched, then slowed at an increasing rate. Ariel took a deep breath and made her jump to the berm beside the tracks. In midair, she realized that she probably hadn't planned that very well. She tried to bring her feet together, but she was too late. She landed heavily on one foot, then the other. Then her knees. Then her face.

She lay still for a moment, then rolled to her back. The sky burned a brilliant, aching sort of blue. Her mouth was full of dirt. She was so hungry, she almost swallowed it.

With a groan, she pushed herself to her feet. Everything hurt but she was fairly certain that nothing was broken. Ahead of her, the train lumbered on, slowing but not stopping in the little town ahead. Ariel watched it go, then gave it a shrug and started walking along the tracks. Her ankle twinged at her but she ignored it and limped on.

Eventually, she came to a sign that proclaimed the town's name to be New Falls City. It seemed to be a very young place. The wooden boards that made up the buildings were still the bright yellow-tan of new wood. The road itself still had grass tamped down in the middle of it. The ring of hammers on nails underlaid the sounds of horses' hooves and people's conversations as they did their business.

After a moment's hesitation, Ariel stepped forward and joined in the flow of the crowd. Young it might be, but New Falls City was clearly booming, for the wooden sidewalks were packed with people of all ages and situations. Judging by the number of men coming and going in mining gear, the local mines were running shifts at all hours. One must have just changed out, for about half the faces she saw were coated in sweat and dust from being underground.

The crowd carried her forward, past a saloon and a mercantile, to some kind of central square. In the center of the square, a low circular wall and a line of buckets made Ariel's mouth go absolutely dry. And she thanked the Queen Almighty when she saw the sign that marked it a public well.

She pushed forward, using her elbows to fight her way through the current of moving people. Eventually, she stumbled off the wooden sidewalk into the square and half-ran, half-limped toward the well. She grabbed a bucket from the line, tied it to the rope that lay anchored and coiled next to the edge of the well and dropped it in. A gratifying splash echoed up at her a moment later.

Her arms were almost too weak to haul the bucket back up. Tremors rippled through her back and shoulders and her hands burned from the slick, heavy hemp of the rope. She dropped it once and couldn't help but let out a sob as the bucket splashed down to the bottom again.

"Here, ma'am," a voice said. "May I give you a hand?"

Ariel looked up to see a tall, brown-haired young man, roughly her age, smiling at her. His hazel-blue eyes had warmth in them—her first instinct was to smile back. Unlike Nillon, this man's teeth were white and even and his face made her think of open blue skies. But logic told her that he could just as easily be a threat as Nillon and so she backed hastily away.

"See this here?" He pointed to a contraption of gears that Ariel had not noticed. She had been so focused on getting to the water that she had not paid attention.

"You thread the rope in like this, then you can turn the crank and it'll haul the water up for you. It's much easier."

"I know how to use a pulley mechanism," Ariel said. To her surprise, her voice, though sounding rusty and disused, carried a note of disdain. Of course she knew how to use a pulley. She'd just been overly focused on the water itself. Yet more proof that she had allowed herself to become unacceptably dehydrated.

"Well, then, there you go," the man went on, seemingly undeterred. "Have yourself a good day, ma'am."

He lifted his hat and turned to walk toward a group of others standing not far away. His companions, two men and a woman, wore expressions that varied from dismay and worry to amusement.

"Why'd you do that?" Ariel heard one of them, the younger of the two men, demand as the helpful man approached their group. The four of them dove back into the movement of the crowd and Ariel couldn't hear anything else.

Water. She was losing her focus.

She squinted her eyes against the bright sun and forced herself to focus on the pulley mechanism. It really was primitively simple, especially for someone raised from birth to be a mechanic for the Nest. She turned the crank, the bucket of water rising smoothly toward the arm.

Once again, Ariel's hands shook as she unlatched the bucket but this time it was with eagerness. She raised it to her lips to take a long, deep drink of the sweet, cool, delicious water. She had never tasted anything so delicious in her life, even though she knew very well that it was only her dehydration talking. Cool runnels spilled down over her chin and neck as she drank her fill.

She stopped, stomach churning. The last thing she wanted was to throw up all of that water but if she did, she wanted to be able to replace it quickly, so she waited by the well for a good few minutes. Now that her thirst had been satisfied, hunger took over at the top of her priority list. She still didn't have any money but the town wasn't terribly big yet. Perhaps she could find work with the construction crews. She certainly knew enough about machinery and engineering to be able to assist in the building of these crude structures. The nonbelievers simply did not have the same technology as the acolyte communities. Sad, perhaps, but a testament to the goodness of the Almighty Queen.

Ariel clamped down hard on the emotional ache such thoughts engendered. She had made her choice and must now suffer the consequences. With that thought uppermost in her mind, she turned to practicalities and reached into her bag for her bottle.

She was contemplating the possibility of acquiring another water receptacle when a shout rang out across the square. Ariel looked up to see the crowd on the sidewalk parting as a trio of men pushed their way through.

"Sister!" the lead man called in a deep, commanding voice. Ariel's mind went blank with fear. He was dressed, like her, in a tunic of truesilk. He was an acolyte. They had found her. They were going to take her back.

She capped off her water bottle, trying her best not to slosh the contents out, before stowing it in her bag. Then she got to her feet and bolted across the square.

"Sister, wait!" the acolyte's voice followed her. She ducked into the crowd and through it, earning an elbow to the head for her trouble. Another passerby let out an angry shout of protest as she staggered past. Ariel mumbled an apology and drove on, trying to put distance, people and obstacles between her and the pursuing acolytes.

Up ahead, a narrow alleyway between two newly erected buildings beckoned. Ariel plunged into the shadowed gap. The scent of wood varnish wrapped around her, clawing down into her nose and throat. Her head started to pound in time with her steps. She stumbled again, pain lancing up her ankle. She threw out a hand, catching herself heavily against one of the buildings, the wood rough and tacky under her touch. The world tilted and spun. For the second time that day, Ariel's face slammed into the dirt.

Still, though, fear pushed at her. They would find her. They would realize she had deserted the Nest. Maybe they would take her back, to enslave her will to that of the Nest in the hopes of a Blessing. Maybe... maybe they'd just kill her.

None of those options seemed especially palatable. Ariel pushed herself woozily to her feet and kept going. The lack of a commotion behind her indicated that she had eluded immediate pursuit but getting out of town seemed the logical next step. Too bad she hadn't been able to acquire some food. She'd just have to forage along the way.

Ariel exited the narrow space between the buildings out into fresher air and immediately felt better. Her headache remained but she no longer felt dizzy and unstable. She slowed to a brisk walk and reached into her bag for her water bottle.

"Queen's wrath!" she swore, realizing her left hand was covered in sticky varnish and caked-on dirt. She tried wiping it on her tunic but that only succeeded in making the truesilk sticky.

With a shake of her head and a dissatisfied sigh, Ariel let her hand fall and continued trudging past the piles of new lumber and marked-out lot lines. Onto the rolling prairie.

Not far out of town she found a small stream cutting through the tall grass at the bottom of a gully. For the lack of anything better to do, she turned to follow it. At least that way, she'd have water and a relatively good chance of finding edible plants. Not to mention small animals, like frogs and the like, if she were really lucky.

It was a better alternative than dying, at any rate. Ariel settled her bag on her shoulder and carried on.

✧   ✧   ✧

She had stopped at dusk. Her body spent from adrenaline and weak from lack of food, she made camp at a likely spot near a bend in the creek. She had even managed to light a fire without burning herself, thanks to the antique fire striker she'd placed in her bag. She even made a little soup in her water bottle, using the wild onions and cattail stems gathered during the day's trek. Not the most appetizing thing she'd ever eaten but not the least, either. At least it was nutrients. That was the important part.

She ate, and then laid down next to the tiny fire ringed with streambed rocks. The wind had picked up once the sun set and the chill made her skin prickle up in tiny bumps.

The moon started to rise and Ariel's eyes drifted closed, only to snap open at the sound of a footstep crushing the tall grass behind her. Then she heard something else: a clicking sound, like that of a set of mandibles tapping together. Her breathing accelerated and Ariel had to force herself not to jump up and run. She would never outrun a Holy Scout or Warrior. The best she could hope for was to distract her. Which would be even harder if she had an acolyte escort. But maybe...

She wrapped her left hand around the long stick she used to stir the fire. She took a deep breath and twisted her hand, trying to rub some of the varnish off on the stick. Even after her day's exertions, the sticky substance still lingered, tacky and annoying with its venomous fumes. Those fumes, however, gave her an idea.

Ariel worked the stick while she listened to the sounds of movement getting closer behind her. She very slowly flipped the stick around and nudged it into the glowing coals of her fire.

"Sister." It was the deep voice from the man in the town.

Ariel rolled, whipping the stick out of the fire in a blaze of sparks and coming face-to-face with the faceted eye of a Holy Scout. She shrieked, striking at the segmented lenses reflecting hundreds of glowing torches back at her. The scout let out a shriek of her own and reared back, giving Ariel room to get her feet under her.

As she did so, a tiny ember drifted down to the front of Ariel's tunic, landing squarely in the smear of varnish. The tunic went up with a *whoosh*. Heat assaulted her senses.

She screamed, flinging the torch away. Slapping at her chest made her left hand go up in flames as well. With nothing else to do, she turned and leapt over the coals of her fire to land on the crumbling bank of the tiny stream. She dove forward, hoping that there would be enough water to put out the searing pain in her chest, face and arm.

Blessed coolness followed the heat; oblivion followed close behind. Just before she slid into merciful unconsciousness, Ariel thought she heard gunshots and the sound of voices yelling.

Chuck waited on his belly as the wind whispered through the tall grass all around them. Next to him, Jay kicked his leg lightly to get his attention. Chuck lifted his head to look at the older man. He was holding out his binoculars.

Chuck took them with a nod of thanks. The moon was just rising and there wasn't much light other than the glow from the girl's campfire down near the creek bed below. Chuck put the lenses to his eyes, carefully looking away from that night-vision-destroying light.

There. Movement behind her. From the depressions in the grass, it looked like two or three men ... and something big.

As the moon broke over the horizon, the ambient light increased a tiny bit. Not really enough to notice but enough that Chuck was able to make out the curving carapace and outsized mandibles of a warrior Gant.

Chuck lowered the binoculars and looked at Jay. In the building moonlight, he could see Jay point up. High above them, unseen in the blue-black sky, Chuck knew that Jasmine's dragon circled, watching their drama unfold.

Jay had turned to pass the binoculars to Garman on his other side when the girl down below screamed. At first, Chuck thought it might have been Jasmine, but the timbre of the voice was wrong and it came from the wrong direction. Jasmine remained at their camp, a few miles away, guarding their horses and stores.

Chuck looked back just in time to see the light from her fire flare as she hit the Gant in one of its eyes with a flaming stick. Then chaos erupted. The Gant reared back in pain, nearly taking out one of the men as it swung its mandibles in panic. The girl seemed to ignite, flames springing into life on her hands and body. The men who had been sneaking up on her camp swore as more fire erupted from her burning hands and spun away into the grass nearby.

Garman swore. Jay chuckled. Chuck raised his rifle to his shoulder.

"All right, boys," Jay said. "Let's be heroes."

Chuck sighted on the man closest to the burning girl and stroked the trigger.

The man fell, shot cleanly through the ears. One of his companions followed clutching at his chest.

"Yes!" Garman cried in triumph. He tossed his rifle to Jay and started to skid down the rise toward the Gant, clearly intending to attack the insect.

"Sonofabitch!" Jay swore, juggling Garman's rifle with his own while getting to his feet. "C'mon, kid. Time to save two idiots."

Chuck figured he'd better follow suit. The three of them headed down the hill just as the fire caught the grass and smoke started to drift upwards.

A sleek shape arrowed down from out of the darkness above. A brilliant stream of white flame lit up the night, engulfing the hulking shape of the Gant and the remaining man standing nearby.

"NO!" Garman screamed. He broke into a run toward the burning insect.

"Damn it, Windfist!" Jay shouted after him. "You're going to get yourself killed! Or that damn dragon's going to set us all on fire!"

"Jay," Chuck asked, looking around. "Where's the girl?"

"That was mine!" Garman shouted at the dragon, shaking his fist at the sky. The beast was once more a shadow among the stars. "That kill was mine!"

"Ah, shut it down, kid!" Jay said, sourly. "You weren't going to kill that Gant with your bare hands, anyway. It saw you coming a mile away! It was just waiting for you to get within reach, so it could eat you. Now quitcher bitchin' and help me put out this damn grass fire before the whole prairie goes up!"

Luckily for all of them, the aflame Gant writhed out of the grass and into the sandy, rocky area where the girl had made her camp. Quetzalith apparently had surgically precise aim: None of his flame breath had spread, so the only fire they really had to worry about was the one that the girl had started with her flaming stick.

Jay pulled his filthy neck bandanna up over his nose and walked up to the smoldering grass. He waggled his eyebrows once at Chuck before doing the last thing Chuck could have possibly imagined.

He unbuckled his belt, dropped his pants and began to piss on the fire.

Garman turned and threw an arm over his nose, glaring at Jay. "Seven Hells, that stinks!"

"Well, yeah, it stinks," Jay said, "I'm pissing on a fire. C'mon, get your tool out and join in! We gotta get this put out before it spreads much further. And it's just you an' me since Chuck's gotta go find that girl and see if she's okay. Don'tcha Chuck?"

Chuck still hadn't located her.

"Try that way, son," Jay said, pointing with one hand toward the creek as he put away his firefighting equipment. "That's where I'd go if I was on fire. C'mon, Windfist! Don't be shy! Gotta get this grass nice and wet!"

Chuck turned and ran in the direction of the creek. She lay like a broken thing, face down in the water. The scent of burnt meat made his stomach roil in protest and fear. He slid down the tiny bank to her side and reached out with trembling hands to move her hair away from her face.

Her breath fluttered warm and soft against his hand.

Relief poured through Chuck like a river through a gorge. He rolled her over, letting the newly risen moon wash over her features and injuries. Her tunic was ruined, her eyebrows gone. In the uncertain light, it looked like her face was otherwise unmarked. Her hand, though, looked raw and blistered.

He slid one arm under her shoulders, another under her knees and carefully stood up. The wet stones rolled under his heels and he nearly dropped them both but he managed to keep his feet, barely.

"Got her, kid?" Jay asked. Chuck looked up to see the older man standing not far away.

"Yes, sir," Chuck said. "Fire out?"

"Yep. She okay?"

"No, sir," Chuck replied. "Burned up and half-drowned. You know any medicine, sir?"

"Not much. Maybe Jasmine does. Wait. Did she get any bug blood on her?"

"Maybe a little. She stabbed it in the eye pretty good."

"Heard a rumor bug blood has some healing mojo."

"Let's hope there's truth to the rumor, then," Chuck said as he looked down at the girl's face. Pretty, even without eyebrows.

He'd thought so when he'd seen her at the well and he thought so again now. "She's gonna need it."

They brought the girl back to their camp. It took much longer to get back there than it had to come out. Most of that was because Chuck insisted on carrying the injured girl. She wasn't overly heavy, underfed as she was, but he didn't want to jostle her. So he walked slowly, barely keeping one eye on Garman's back in front of him in favor of staring down at her face.

"She ain't going nowhere, kid," Jay said, his voice soft in the darkness. "Not unless she kicks it. And then her face ain't going nowhere till you put her down."

"I know," Chuck said. "I just want to make sure she keeps breathing."

"Let's just get her to the camp and we'll see what's what."

Fortunately for Chuck's peace of mind, the girl's breathing continued, uninterrupted, throughout the long journey. He wondered if she'd hit her head on the rocks in the stream. She looked as if she were simply sleeping.

When they finally arrived at their camp, Jasmine hustled forward to meet them.

"What happened?" she demanded. "Quetzalith brought me a fragment of charred carapace! Did you encounter Gants?"

"Gant," Garman said, his voice sour. "One warrior. Alone. And your abomination blasted it before I could do *anything!*"

He stomped into the cleared area around the fire and dropped into his habitual cross-legged sitting posture. With a huff that sounded exactly like that of an angry toddler, the Windfist pulled his rifle into his lap and began going through the motions of cleaning it.

Chuck would have ordinarily laughed at his companion's temper tantrum but right now it just made him tired and irritable. There was a wounded girl to consider.

"Jasmine," he said, "do you know any medicine? She got burned in the fight."

"Quetzalith?" Jasmine asked, her eyes widening with horror. "He wouldn't—"

"No, she did it herself, trying to fight off the warrior with a burning stick when we attacked. And the warrior wasn't alone, neither. There were cultists with it."

"They don't count," Garman muttered.

Next to Chuck, Jay laughed. That, apparently, didn't help. Garman's scowl only deepened as he hunched further into his task.

"I don't know much," Jasmine said. "But bring her here by the fire and let me take a look."

Jasmine stirred up the fire to provide as much light as possible while Chuck laid the girl on his bedroll.

"I'll get you guys some water and then make some chow," Jay said softly. "Garman's gotta get the sulk out of his system. Let me know if you need anything else."

"Thank you, Jay," Jasmine said. She knelt next to the girl and started looking at her injuries.

"She was burned on her chest and hand," Chuck said. "And her face a little bit, too, though not as bad. I found her lying in the creek. I was afraid she'd breathed in some water but I think she's okay. Jay said something about Gant blood being good for healing, so we smeared some on her. Got some in one of his flasks, too. Just in case."

"Yeah, her lungs sound good," Jasmine said, as she bent down to listen to the girl breathing. "I think it's just the burns...as well as exhaustion and malnutrition. We need to get some food in her as soon as she wakes. Something easy, like soup. In the meantime, I have a salve I use for sunburns; let's try that on her hand, face and chest, then wrap them with clean bandages."

"I have a clean shirt in my pack," Chuck said.

"Cotton?"

"B'lieve so."

"That will do. Cut it into long strips, a couple of inches wide. Let me get the salve from my things and we'll get to work," Jasmine said. She pushed herself up to her feet and walked with her usual purposeful stride over to the other side of the fire. Chuck didn't want to leave the girl alone, so he waited until the dragon trainer returned before getting his shirt.

While he prepped the bandages, Jasmine took the water that Jay had provided and tried to clean the girl's burns. It didn't help matters that she was filthy overall. Chuck found himself wondering how long she'd been on the run...and what she was running from. She was dressed as a cultist but she certainly lacked their usual vacant-eyed intensity. Not to mention, she'd run from the other cultists in town, and had fought them when they approached her camp. Had they abducted her? Or was she simply a runaway? He hadn't had much experience with them, until recently. He'd never heard stories about people leaving the cult, though.

"Hold her hand steady, I'm going to try and clean her burns," Jasmine said, bringing Chuck's attention back to the here and now. He did as the dragon trainer instructed, even after the girl woke up and started to whimper.

"Hush, I know it hurts," Jasmine said. Chuck could tell that she intended her voice to be low and soothing, even if the girl didn't seem to be too soothed by it. "You managed to get dirt and I don't know what else in these burns on your hand. There. That should do it. Chuck, hand me the salve and be ready with the bandage."

Chuck did as he was told but he found his eyes tracking back to the girl's pale, pain-pinched face. She was looking at Jasmine with something like terror in her eyes.

"Hey," Chuck said, to try and distract her. The girl cut her gaze over to him, but the fear didn't lessen. "Remember me? From the well?"

The girl shook her head wildly, then paused. Her eyes narrowed as she caught the edge of her bottom lip between her teeth.

"The pulley," she whispered. Her voice sounded dry and cracked as desert mud. Chuck grinned and nodded. Next to him, Jasmine snapped her fingers without looking up and held out her hand. Chuck started, then handed her the rolled-up plaid bandage. For a moment, he'd forgotten that they were midway through a round of doctoring.

"Do you want some water?" Chuck asked as Jasmine wound the bandage around the girl's hand. The girl nodded again and Chuck reached under her head to help her lift up enough to drink from his canteen. Water splashed down the sides of her face and dampened the collar of her filthy clothes but more of it got into her mouth and she drank greedily.

"Not too much," Jasmine murmured. "We don't want her to puke."

The girl apparently heard that, because she backed off of the canteen herself. Chuck eased her to the ground, then capped the canteen and sat back, content to watch her face and wait for further orders from Jasmine.

"There, keep that as dry and clean as you can and we'll see how it looks tomorrow." The dragon trainer gently placed the girl's now-bandaged hand on her stomach. "Now for your chest..."

"I'll go," Chuck said, sitting back on his heels and preparing to rise.

"No!" Jasmine said sharply. "I need your help."

"But..." Chuck protested.

"Don't bother arguing with me—I need you, so you stay put. Grab her shoulders and hold her in place. Unless you'd rather have Jay or Garman looking at her naked chest?" Jasmine tilted her head slightly. "Jay would probably be a gentleman, though he'd definitely say something off color. That would make her even more uncomfortable. Garman, though. You know what he thinks of me; how is he going to view a cultist girl?"

"He's not that bad..." Chuck said.

Even to his own ears, the protest sounded weak. Jasmine simply looked at him with raised eyebrows until he sighed and nodded. He settled back down and placed his hands on the girl's shoulders.

With quick, neat movements, the dragon trainer cut away the uncharred remains of the girl's tunic. Chuck clamped his eyes shut but not before he got the impression of creamy white skin that sloped and curved in interesting ways. The middle of it, though, was a mess.

Her clothing had burned quickly, as far as he could tell, leaving nothing behind except the occasional fragment. Most of her chest looked badly sunburnt, the dark-red area clashing with the pale skin around it. Along her ribs, close to her left arm, things got worse.

A fist-sized area, white and rimmed with red welts, oozed clear liquid. Several blisters dotted her skin, faintly pulsing with her heartbeat. Jasmine cursed softly.

"Okay, Chuck," she said, "this is going to be bad, but it needs to be done. You've got to hold her down no matter what. Are you ready?"

Fighting nausea, he nodded.

He felt the girl tense as Jasmine poured water slowly on the wound, her jaws clamping shut hard at the first touch. Her whimper damn near broke his heart. It took everything he had to maintain his hold on her shoulders, though, when Jasmine began gently scrubbing the dirt and debris from the burn. The girl's screams pierced the night, agony and anguish wrenching at him. He held on.

"I know it hurts, ma'am," he said, voice cracking, "but it has to be done. It'll all be over soon, I promise."

He didn't know if she heard him or not. Or if she did hear him, if it helped.

Jasmine repeated the process, carefully working around the raised blisters. Each time she touched cloth to skin, the girl screamed—each scream weaker than the last. But she didn't pass out.

When it was all over, Chuck felt his whole body trembling. Jasmine seemed to be doing a little better, though her face was pale in the firelight. The girl lay gasping before them, eyes closed.

"Let's wrap her up in a blanket so she doesn't get cold," Jasmine said. "She'll have to sleep with you tonight so that you can keep an eye on her."

"Why me? I don't know nothing about...well, anything. Shouldn't you be keeping an eye on her instead?"

Jasmine swiped an errant lock of hair out of her eyes with the back of her wrist. She looked exhausted and half-sick from the last hour's labors.

"Chuck, you're a smart kid but sometimes you don't notice shit. She's terrified of me."

"What? No. She knows you won't hurt her—well, not if you didn't have to—for medicine reasons," he foundered to a stop as Jasmine shook her head.

"Me torturing her by cleaning her burns would be bad enough but it's more than that. Didn't you see how she looked at me?" Jasmine pulled her collar aside to bare her upper chest. A magnificent tattoo of Quetzalith in flight stretched from collarbone to collarbone. "Cultists hate dragons. Her parents probably scared her as a child with threats of dragons swooping in to grab the bad little cultist children. I wish it weren't the case, but it is. She has to get some rest, poor thing. She has to feel safe and only you can give her that."

Chuck looked down at the girl. She continued to lie still, breathing shallowly, apparently not noticing (or caring) that they were discussing her as if she weren't there. He considered her for a moment and then bent close enough to speak softly to her.

"Ma'am," he said, "Miss Jasmine thinks I need to sleep beside you tonight, to make sure you're okay." Briefly, his thoughts flashed back to Big-Eyed Jill, way back when. He pushed that thought aside and focused on the girl before him. "I'd sure like to know that that's not a problem for you. I promise to be a gentleman and keep my hands to myself."

Slowly, her eyes opened.

"Better you than her," the girl whispered, confirming what Jasmine had said.

"She's really very nice..." Chuck started.

"Please," the girl whispered again, her eyes widening with fear and pain. "I can smell the dragon on her. I can't...it's...please."

"All right," Chuck said. "It's okay. I'll keep you safe. What's your name?"

"Ariel."

"Ariel. I'm Chuck. I'll keep you safe. I promise."

Perhaps it was a bit of a grandiose promise to make. After all, there were a thousand things that could come out of the night to harm them. More cultists, Gants, not to mention the various natural predators and creepie crawlies that lived in the area. Most of those things would be dissuaded by their numbers and guns, to say nothing of the fire-breathing lizard in their midst, but not all.

Still, it seemed to reassure her. Ariel nodded once and closed her eyes, allowing her body to go limp. Chuck looked up at Jasmine, who sat watching him with a grave expression on her face.

"The girl is sick, starving and hurt. I don't need to tell you to behave yourself, do I?" she asked quietly.

"No! I don't...what?"

"I have eyes, boy. Never make the mistake of thinking that I'm stupid. I didn't survive the Baron's court by failing to pay attention," she said. "It doesn't matter. It's not my business, as long as you hold up your end of the bargain and get us to my uncle's. I'm just warning you, in case your little head starts thinking louder than your big one. We don't know anything about her."

"We know she's hurt, like you said. And starving and scared and alone. I'm not going to take advantage of her or anything like that," Chuck said. Jasmine seemed to switch gears faster than he could blink and it left him feeling like he'd been run over by a train. "You were the one who insisted that I sleep with her!"

"Good. I like you, Chuck. I'd hate to have to kill you." Jasmine gave him a smile that, while tired, reached all the way to her eyes. She slowly pushed herself to her feet and walked over to the other side of the fire.

Chuck looked down at Ariel and then started to tuck her into his bedroll. He was half tempted to try and sleep outside of it, giving her privacy and leaving absolutely no doubt as to the purity of his intentions. The night wind had picked up a bit of a chill, however, so he wrapped her up in all of his blankets but one. When the time came, he'd stretch out beside her and wrap the outermost around himself. At least that way they'd stay warm and hopefully she wouldn't be too uncomfortable.

She watched him with passive eyes as he tried his best to gently move her into the blankets. He didn't want to jostle her more than he had to. By the time he got her settled, Jay approached them both with a cup in each hand.

"Jasmine said you'd want something to eat, little girl," the old man said with a smile. He squatted down on his heels beside her and held out the steaming cup. Ariel stirred herself and lifted her hands, but her left was wrapped in bandages.

"Here, I'll help," Chuck said and nearly knocked the girl over in his haste to get to Jay. The old man chuckled and pulled the cups out of reach.

"Sit down, son, before you hurt somebody. Here's yours. You eat that and I'll help our miss, here." Jay sounded like somebody's kindly grandfather, rather than the drunk old reprobate that Chuck knew him to be. "And what was your name, angel?"

"Ariel," she said. "And I'm not an angel."

"None of us is, sweetheart," he said, settling himself on the ground. "I'm Jay. Chuck, help the girl sit up a bit and then I'll help her drink some of this broth. It's not much but you probably want to go easy until your stomach is used to having food in it again."

Chuck put his cup on a nearby rock and managed to situate himself behind the girl. He didn't want to lift her up too high, but he managed to support her head enough for her to take several sips.

"Were those men chasing you?" Jay asked, still using that gentle tone.

"I think maybe they were."

"Can you tell us why they might?"

"I'm not sure," Ariel said. "Unless it's because of the turbines."

"Turbines?"

"The Nest's power turbines. I know how to repair them. So do some of the others, but they're ... not always reliable. The Bliss ... anyway. I didn't think anyone would notice that I was gone, but maybe they have. I wonder if one of the turbines went down." She took a deep breath and focused her eyes on Jay's weathered face. "You won't take me back, will you? I can't ... I don't want to go back. Not ever."

"Miss, we're not going to take you anywhere you don't want to go," Jay said, and Chuck made a fervent noise of agreement. After that, her eyelids fluttered closed, her breathing shallow and even. Chuck laid her back down before turning to his own meal.

"Where's Garman?" He realized that the Windfist was gone.

"Up on the ridge, playing lookout. He'll cool off up there and come wake me for second watch. Jasmine's got third. You just take care of Ariel ... huh," Jay said with his funny little grin. His eyes nearly disappeared into a nest of dark wrinkles. "Ariel and Jasmine. Looks like we've got a pair of princesses on our hands."

"What?"

"Kids." He shook his head, getting to his feet. "Never mind. Get some sleep, son. Your girl's going to need you before morning. I'm betting Jasmine's going to want to change those bandages when she takes her watch."

Somewhere, a coyote yipped in the distance, the wind whistling harmony as it flowed through grass nearby.

Chuck nodded and then carefully laid himself beside the sleeping girl before pulling the outer blanket over himself. The smoky-sweet scent of Ariel's hair teased at him, cutting through the uglier scents of charred meat and medicinal salve. He closed his eyes and willed sleep to come.

CHAPTER TEN

ARIEL WAS STRONGER THE NEXT MORNING BUT STILL TOO WEAK for a day of traveling. She did confirm that Gant blood helped, and her burns looked considerably better. Jasmine suggested that they spend the day in camp, giving her a day to rest and the rest of them time to figure out what to do with her.

"She comes with us," Chuck said. The iron in his voice surprised himself.

He, Jasmine, Garman and Jay had gathered after noon, near Quetzalith's perch in order to talk privately. Chuck could look over and see the girl as she slowly sipped a cup of broth. Her smudged face, pale against the darkness of her lank hair, made her look fragile. A dirty china doll a breath away from breaking.

"Look, I know you like her," Garman said, "but she's a cultist. You and I both know that they're not reasonable people. They're like mindless drones with only one goal . . . to do the will of the Hive."

"I don't think she is," Chuck said, shaking his head. "She ran from them, remember? She lit herself on fire to get away from them. Maybe she was one, once, but she's definitely not now."

"She could be a plant, put here by the cultists for some reason of their own." Jasmine looked up from grooming Quetzalith. "Any reason they might be after you?"

His heart skipped slightly. Could she know about the key? He decided to ignore the question.

"No, she's not a plant."

"You don't know that."

"I do!"

"You don't." Jay spoke up for the first time. He gave Chuck a slightly apologetic grin. "Junior here's right for once, kid. You don't know it. I don't think it's likely but it's possible. You can't forget that, ever."

"So what?" Chuck fought to keep his voice down. The last thing he wanted was for Ariel to hear this exchange. "We just abandon her out here?"

"Hell no," Jay said. "Nobody's suggesting that. But you gotta figure out something to do with her, something that isn't going to jeopardize your mission."

"Assuming you mean the mission to get me to my uncle's and not some other mysterious errand, I quite agree," Jasmine put in. She patted Quetzalith's neck and ducked under to continue applying some kind of oil to his hide. "And I have a suggestion. But it might require more than she's willing to give."

"What do you mean?" Chuck asked. "I won't let you hurt her."

Jasmine leaned around the dragon's head to give him a disgusted look.

"As if I would," the dragon trainer said, disdain dripping from her words. "I'm not talking about hurting her. I'm talking about hiring her. As my assistant. She can help me groom this guy and do other chores. And once we find my uncle, if we're going to stud Quetzalith . . . well. There will be plenty of work for her. And then you three can leave her with me and go on about your business."

"It has merit, kid," Jay said, raising his eyebrows.

"But she's terrified of Quetzalith," Chuck protested. At the sound of his name, the dragon swung his head to look at the group of them. Behind them, Ariel let out a muffled gasp, as if proving his point.

"She's terrified of everything," Garman said, throwing his hands up in the air. "Are you going to protect her from all of it?"

"If I have to," Chuck said. He could feel his face growing hot with anger. "It seems no one else is willing, so I don't see as I have much choice."

"Kid, relax. Junior don't mean nothing," Jay said. "But he's right. You can't protect her from life. It's like the girl on the train. Ariel made her choices, now she has to live with them, even if it means facing her fears. Jasmine's suggestion is a good one. Why don't you at least let her present the option to the girl?"

"What if she says no? What then? I'm not abandoning her," Chuck said.

"For Baddis's sake, Chuck, no one's suggesting that!" Garman said. "But we gotta do something with her!"

"We can cross that bridge when we get there, kid," Jay said. "Why don't you go ask her if she'd be willing to get to know Jasmine and Quetzalith a little better?"

"Fine," Chuck said, "but in a while."

He didn't really have much of a reason to delay, except that he felt like his friends were backing him into a corner and he didn't like it. He kicked at the dirt and turned his back on them, muttering something about making sure Ariel ate.

Garman watched Chuck walk away and felt his own frustration ratchet up a notch. To be completely fair, it wasn't all the kid's fault. Fact was, he was seriously worried about what they'd found back at the outpost. It hadn't looked like there'd been a struggle or anything but his brothers wouldn't just abandon their post. From the time that they were tiny recruits, they'd had responsibility and loyalty conditioned into them. He would sooner hack off his own arm than abandon his assigned mission ... even one as bizarre as this was turning out to be.

"Stupid kid's not thinking with his head," Garman muttered, forcing his thoughts back to the present. At his words, the dragon rustled his wings and Jasmine let out a little chuckle. Jay threw them both a look and then started to whistle and walk away.

"What?" Garman asked her, suspicious.

"Nothing," she replied, laughter threading through her tone. He suspected the joke was at his expense. Exasperation kicked his frustration up another notch.

"No, something's funny," he insisted. He couldn't do anything about his missing brothers, or about Chuck's bullheaded blindness but he could damn well stop this girl and her abomination from laughing at him behind his back. "Share the joke."

"Fine," Jasmine said, turning to face him. She folded her arms over her chest and looked at him with an amused, lofty expression. "I just find it amusing that you say 'not thinking with his head' like it's a bad thing. Like paying attention to emotion and instinct isn't what keeps us alive more often than not."

"It *is* a bad thing," Garman said. He ignored the whisper

of thought that said that she might have a point. "Emotions get people killed."

"False," Jasmine said, holding up a finger. "People get people killed. Or accidents do. But rarely are emotions to blame. Unless you're talking a heart attack in the throes of passion—but I suppose a Windfist monk wouldn't know anything about that, would you?"

"I know enough," Garman shot back stiffly. "I'm not a eunuch."

"Oh! Gay, then? Because I know you don't allow women into your little club."

"No! I mean—the Windfist Order is not a 'little club'!"

"Relax, there's nothing wrong with being gay. The heart wants what it wants, after all."

"No! I mean, you're right, there isn't anything wrong with it but I'm not gay. I like women."

"I see. I suppose the order has groupies, then? Women who find your pretty tattoos and bulging muscles to be sexy?"

"What? I don't know... I mean, maybe... yes. There are women like that, but I don't, I've never..."

"Never? So, I was right, then. You don't know what passion feels like."

"What?" Garman's head was spinning. How had this happened? "I am passionate about my mission, about the order!"

"Mmhm," she said. Her smile both infuriated and confused him. "How well does that mission keep you warm at night?"

"That doesn't make any sense."

"Exactly," she said, stabbing a finger at him. Her smile turned triumphant. "It doesn't make any sense at all. Fact is, you think that you can operate without any human connection. And that's a lie. Everybody needs somebody. So, don't go judging Chuck for having a heart and wanting to do right by Ariel."

"I wasn't! It's honorable that he wants to help her, even if she is a cultist. But I cannot let him compromise our mission because of a pretty face," Garman said, his voice rising.

Quetzalith turned to stare at him. Garman stared right back. He'd be damned if he'd let an abomination intimidate him.

"Easy, sweetheart," Jasmine crooned to the dragon, stroking the side of his neck. "The monk isn't going to hurt me. Give the kid some credit, Windfist. He's not going to compromise your mysterious mission. But you berating him about having feelings for the girl is only going to piss him off. I'm just saying, let it be. Let nature take its course."

"And what? Let him lose his heart to some cultist that could just as well be a spy as not? *You* said that, remember?" Garman asked, stabbing his own finger back in her direction.

"Of course I remember. And I still think it's a possibility. That doesn't make it any less Chuck's choice in how he responds."

"I..." Garman fell silent. It *was* Chuck's choice. So why did it bother him? He surprised himself with his next words. "I just don't want him to get hurt."

Jasmine looked at him for a long moment, then her smile softened, losing its sardonic edge.

"You care about him, Garman. That's good. But he's a grown man, even if he's young. He's entitled to experience life," she said, her tone almost gentle.

Garman bit the inside of his cheek and felt his face settling into a scowl. If he was fair—and he generally tried to be—she was right. Not that it made him feel any better.

"I *have* been with a woman," he said then, blurting it out defensively and hating himself for it. To make things worse, her smile only deepened and sympathy touched her eyes.

"Yes," she said, still in that gentle tone. "But have you ever loved?"

He didn't have an answer for that. Or not one that he wanted to share, anyway. He turned and started walking back toward the fire.

"Me neither," he heard, or thought he heard her say as he walked away.

Ariel moved away from the relative security of the camp. After resting for most of the day, she felt strong enough to take a walk. She wanted some time alone, so she had waited until after dusk, then snuck away while everyone else was occupied with other tasks. These people seemed harmless but they made her nervous. She needed to think.

As she did back at the Hive, she looked to the night sky, letting the sheer size of the star-speckled black void overwhelm her. As always, it was comforting, though she couldn't explain why. The feeling that she was just a small, insignificant being hidden away from the world gave her solace. She could hide, simply a speck of dust in the dark.

A voice came from behind her, muttering angrily. She shivered as she recognized the Windfist's voice. Garman, that was his name.

"I don't need them. I have a mission and I could certainly complete it on my own. And faster too."

"Then why do you not leave?" she said, walking toward him, even though he interrupted her solitude. "It is not required that you stay with them, is it?"

He tensed as she came into view, weight shifting to the balls of his feet as his fists clenched. He relaxed slightly, flushing as the realization he wasn't alone set in.

"No, I could leave anytime. What are you doing away from the camp? Chuck was looking for you."

"I wanted to see the stars," she said, matter-of-factly. "The fire light makes it difficult."

He snorted.

"And Ketzell...Ketswal...the dragon makes you uncomfortable."

"Yes. Jasmine too."

"Hmph. Jasmine. Yeah." He fell silent, his annoyance clouding his face.

They walked together silently for a few minutes until he exhaled loudly.

"That woman is frustration in people form," he said all at once, the words tumbling out in a rush. "Where does she get off telling me what's right and wrong?"

Ariel stayed quiet, letting him vent his feelings. He scared her—not as much as the dragon trainer—but certainly enough to make her hesitate to comment. Her limited experience with people outside the Hive didn't give her much to say on the matter.

Garman didn't seem to want answers, anyway, content to rant about Jasmine uninterrupted.

"Her dragon takes my kill and she gets mad at me?" he said, throwing his hands in the air in frustration. "Everything I say gets twisted into knots. She constantly picks apart every action I take. It's as though her favorite pastime—no, her only pastime—is to make me look the fool in front of everyone!"

Off to her left, brush crackled.

"Garman..." It occurred to her that they had walked some distance from the campsite. They should probably turn around and head back. Comforting or not, the sky wouldn't protect them from any predator that decided to wander by.

He ignored her, too focused on his rant.

"She's so high and mighty, looking down on me because I didn't grow up in some lofty damn castle, surrounded by servants and bootlickers."

More rustling. If it was an animal, it was bigger than a rabbit.

"All she cares about is that damn dragon and whatever she's trying to find out east. Doesn't give one thought to anyone else's priorities. Can't see the damn forest for the trees."

The rope loop came out of nowhere, landing at Garman's feet mid-stride. He only had a moment of surprise before it pulled taut, tripping him. He hit the ground, hard. Ariel opened her mouth, only to have it covered with a dirty hand. Sour breath assaulted her ear.

"Don't you try nothin', pretty. You jest keep quiet."

Three men came out of the brush as Garman got his hands underneath him. The man holding the lasso gave it a hard yank, pulling the Windfist backwards. With no leverage, all he could do was try and turn to face his attackers. Two of the men grabbed Garman's arms and sat on his chest, pinning him to the ground. The weight kept him from screaming but these men were taking no chances. One untied the bandanna from his neck and shoved it into Garman's mouth.

"Git them wrists in front of him, boys," the older man said, keeping the rope taut as his scarred face in a twisted semblance of a grin. "We'll truss him up good."

Moving with quick, decisive motions of long practice, the men secured the warrior monk's bonds and gag before standing up.

"Good work, boys. Now get that pole we cut so's we can get on out of here," the leader said. He took a long look at Ariel and scratched his jaw. Scabs broke open, leaking a thick fluid mixed with blood. "Guess we'll take the gal too. Git 'er tied but make it so's she can walk. Don't figger she'll be givin' us any trouble."

The younger men bound Ariel's hands behind her, cinching the rope tightly. She gasped as pain shot up her burned arm, thankful that her hands quickly started to go numb. They left her feet free but it didn't seem prudent to try and run. Yet. Maybe, if they were focusing on Garman, she could try but she'd have to wait until the closest to her was distracted.

In moments, the group was off, making their way almost silently through the tall grass. Garman, tied to a sapling slung between two of the younger men, struggled to no avail. The man behind her kept a tight hold of her, hot breath on her neck. The leader of the group tailed them all.

"Jay, Ariel's gone," Chuck said as he walked toward the older man, trying not to sound concerned. With the argument earlier, he didn't want to seem overly worried. "I thought she might be, um, indisposed, so I waited for her by my bedroll, but she hasn't been back yet. It's been a while."

"I'm sure she's fine, son. Might have gone to take a bath in the creek."

"I checked there too," Chuck said, bracing himself for the ribbing that was sure to follow. Even though his thoughts had been chaste and honorable, he just knew that Jay would give him grief about trying to catch Ariel nekkid. Wouldn't put it past Jasmine, either. "I swear, I wasn't trying to sneak a peek or nothin'. I called out first, so's she'd have time to get covered up."

"Okay, now that's odd. Didn't figure she'd wander off too far."

"She's probably fine, guys," Jasmine said, looking up from her spot near the fire. "Just needed some time away from all of us. We make her nervous, you know."

"You might," Chuck said, "and Quetzalith there definitely does, but Jay and I don't."

"She's probably off thinking by herself, like Garman," Jasmine said. "He walked off after you left to go sulk. Or train. Or whatever other crap those monks do."

"Well, that's another thing, ain't it?" Chuck said with a frown. "He's been gone a while, too, right?"

"Kid, you're getting worked up over nothing," Jasmine said, rolling her eyes. She smiled at him though, so he didn't take it too hard.

"I dunno, girly, Chuck may be onto something," Jay said slowly, rubbing his jaw. "Wouldn't see Junior stayin' away for too long. He's itchin' to get on the trail."

"Is there any way, you could, I dunno, have the dragon go look for them?" Chuck asked. He met the trainer's eyes, waiting for the inevitable laughter. "I mean, that's how you found us originally and that way if they are just wandering around we won't miss them or nothin'. Please, Miss Jasmine."

It sounded lame in his ears as he said, it but he couldn't think of a better argument. To his surprise, Jasmine's smile grew.

"It won't hurt Quetzalith to take a lap before he goes down for the night, I suppose," she said, looking at Jay. Her eyes twinkled in the firelight. "He's cute when he's all sincere and worried, ain't he?"

Chuck felt his face go red. But if the teasing went along with the searching part, it was worth it.

"Thank you, Miss Jasmine. I really do appreciate it," he said. "It'll help me feel better."

She stood, approached Quetzalith and started making hand symbols.

"Search. Find. Return."

The dragon nodded his leathery head once before launching himself into the air. The powerful downstrokes of his wings flattened the fire, sending a dancing party of sparks onto the grass nearby. Chuck hurried over to stomp them out before anything caught.

"All right boys, I think we's about far enough for right now," the leader said. He made his way to a small clearing in the grass. "Cinch that rope up, Jeffy. Them Windfist are sneaky tough bastards."

"Yessir." The ropes bit into Garman's wrists as they pulled them tighter. "I think we should'a grabbed them other young'uns, too, Paw."

"And that's why I do the thinkin', moron. What were we gonna do, walk right up and ask them to come along? We got lucky with these two." He leered at Garman, as he spoke, his milky eye practically glowing in the starlight. "Windfist is usually too hard to sneak up on, ain't ya? 'Cept you."

A trickle of drool escaped from the corner of his mouth.

"This girl's a sweet one, Paw. You shore we can't eat them?"

"No, stupid, they're worth too much."

"All of them?" Jeffy whined. The sound of it grated on Garman's nerves. "What about just one foot?"

"I said no! I swear, if I have to tell you agin, boy..." the older man said, shaking his fist. "You 'member what happened with the last one, donchoo? Couldn't help yerself, got carried away, dincha?"

"Yer right, Paw," Jeffy said on a heavy sigh. "I jest thought that maybe, you know, this time..."

"Of course I'm right. Now git that idea outta your mushy skull. Him we can sell, or maybe ransom. We need her for breedin', or we git more puddin' heads like you."

Jeffy slunk off, deterred. For now, at least. In the sudden silence, Garman thought he heard something. Something flying? Would Jasmine send the dragon out to look for him? It didn't seem likely. However, if Chuck or Jay had insisted . . . Maybe?

It seemed like a long shot but the only one he had. They had, he corrected. It was his fault Ariel was in this predicament. Had he not been focused on his irritation with Jasmine, had he been paying attention to his surroundings, they wouldn't be here. On the plus side, this did undermine her point about emotions. He'd make sure to bring it up when he saw her again.

If.

He put the thought out of his mind, concentrating on what he could do to get free. The ropes binding him were tight but maybe . . .

He slowly started working his hands, trying to get enough slack to free them. His captors began setting up camp, unpacking bedrolls, cooking utensils and a wicked set of knives. Flint struck, kindling blazed.

Well, at least if they do eat me, they won't eat me raw.

A flash of flame pierced the starlit sky. Brief, no more than a blink before it faded. His captors, concentrating on their tasks, missed it completely.

For the first time since meeting him, Garman sincerely hoped it was Quetzalith.

"There!" Jasmine said, pointing into the darkness. "He's found them."

"Are you sure?" Chuck asked. He didn't doubt the dragon had found *something* but . . . "There's a lot of critters out here, how do we know it's them?"

"He wouldn't have signaled if it was food, Chuck," Jasmine said. She threw him an irritated glance. "He isn't easily distracted. My orders were to find Garman and Ariel."

"Yes, ma'am. Sorry, ma'am."

Quetzalith landed on his perch, kicking up a cloud of dust. Chuck shielded his eyes as Jasmine made more hand signals. The dragon made some sort of reply, shaking his head and clicking his beak. She frowned, repeated the sequence. Same results.

"What did he say?" Chuck felt a bit silly asking. "Are they in trouble?"

"I . . . I don't know," Jasmine said. "He's indicating 'herd' or 'pack' but that could mean a few different things. People, deer, wolves, I'm not sure."

"That settles it," Chuck said. "We need to go check it out. They could be in trouble."

"I'll stay here," Jay said. "Someone's got to watch the horses, tend the fire and whatnot. Y'all have fun."

Chuck checked his pistol, slung his Marlin and turned to Jasmine.

"I'm going but I need you to help me," he said. He tried to sound tough but knew she could see the worry in his face. "Will you come, Miss Jasmine?"

She nodded, checking her own weapons.

"Lead the way miss."

Ariel felt helpless. It seemed to be becoming a trend and it bothered her. The last day of water, food and rest had done wonders for her constitution but she was a far cry from taking on four men alone. Especially with both hands tied behind her back. She had to buy time for Garman to work himself loose.

"It is not a good idea to eat people," she said, trying to keep the quaver out of her voice. "You don't know if they are sick, or diseased."

"Oh, we ain't worried much about that, pretty," Paw said as he walked over, stroking her cheek with a filthy hand. "Meat's meat. 'Sides, if we do, we'll cook 'em up pretty good. Kill anything bad off."

"Not necessarily. I have heard of people getting very ill."

Mostly true—there had been an incident in the Hive a few winters ago. A group of acolytes had been caught in a severe snowstorm while foraging. A week had passed before the lone survivor had made it back to the Nest. No amount of help or treatment could restore him to his former health. It took time but he eventually admitted to eating the remains of the other acolytes to survive. Aside from guilt and remorse, he'd eventually developed physical ailments.

"Ain't been problem yet, pretty," Paw said, eye twitching. He seemed not to notice. "I reckon we'll be fine."

"Have you ever eaten someone like him before?"

"Hunh?" Paw seemed to consider it. "No, can't say I have."

"Then it seems to me you have a unique opportunity."

Garman's shocked expression spoke volumes. Good thing he was still gagged.

"Hm. You got a point there," Paw said, scratching his chin, smearing pus and blood.

"I am certain that you could find another young man to sell, if you really needed to."

"Well..."

"How would you cook him? If you decided to eat him?"

"Oh, we'd just roast him, I guess," Paw said, turning toward Garman. "Jus' set up a spit and keep it turnin'."

"If I were you," Ariel continued, "I would boil him. Keeps what fat he has contained in the pot and helps tenderize the meat. You will need a bigger fire, though. Nice and hot."

"Now look here, missy, I don't need you tellin' me how to cook. Been doin' this for nigh on..." He counted on his fingers. "Plenty of time now."

"I understand," she said, shrugging. "Not everyone has the patience for slow cooking."

She ignored the choked snarling from the bound monk.

"Dang it, girl, now you got me hungry," Paw said. His good eye lost focus as he thought about the situation for a moment. Then he snapped his fingers with a jagged grin. "Guess we'll just cook a part of him now and save the rest for later."

"You could do that, I suppose," Ariel said. She made a show of frowning, as if thinking hard. With a head shake, she said, "No, I do not think that will work."

"Why the hell not?"

"First, there will not be enough for everyone. I suspect you risk Jeffy disobeying your orders," she said, nodding. "Second, you will have to worry about him bleeding out. If he dies in transit, the meat will not be as fresh. You would not want to lose any flavor. Lastly, what if the wound spoils? Think about how much you will lose. If I were you, I would want to savor every last bite."

She glanced at Garman. The Windfist's hatred poured out of him in waves. She swallowed hard and steeled her nerves, hoping he'd understand what she was trying to do.

"Shoot!" Paw said, kicking a small rock into the brush.

"Dangit, girl, yo're right. I knew you was a keeper when I saw you in town."

"Hm. I was thinking, 'If it were me, what would I do to enhance the flavor?'" Ariel said. She could see she had the old man's full attention. He made a motion for her to go on. "I bet if he ate some wild berries on the trip, it would give just a hint of sweetness. You could make a sauce, tonight, and give it to him to drink. I saw a patch nearby."

"Yah, that might could work," Paw said, eyes narrowing. "I suppose you want me to go get them?"

"Oh, no," she said, shaking her head. She let her voice drop to a whisper. "I mean you could but that would leave me here with Jeffy. He scares me."

"Hm. Yo're right agin. That boy ain't trustworthy," Paw said, clearly torn and unsure what to do. "An' if I go with you, he'd prolly try and eat that Windfist afore we got back."

"I could go get them myself, but I would need my hands."

"That's true," Paw said slowly. His wary expression grew more intense. "You ain't tryin' to trick me into lettin' you free, are ya?"

"Oh, no! I would never! It is too bad you do not have a longer rope; you could tie it around my waist. It would make me feel safer as well, so I could just follow it back. I do not want to get lost."

"Oh! Why din' you say so?" Paw said. His face brightened. "We got us a long one right over there. You jest sit tight, pretty."

She waited until his back was turned to steal another look at Garman. The Windfist continued to glare at her, disgust written on his face. She shook her head slightly, hoping he understood.

Paw came back with the longer rope, cinched it around her waist and untied her hands. A sudden flare of pain came from her burns—freedom brought renewed sensation.

"There," Paw grunted, handing her the coil. The other hand pulled the slack tight. "That'll keep you from wandering off. Now, if anything scares you, you sing out and I'll come a runnin'."

"Thank you," she said, swallowing her revulsion to gently take his hand. "I feel safer already."

Ariel started toward the darkness at the edge of the clearing, letting the rope out as she walked.

The dragon's flame came from this direction, she thought, looking at the night sky. *The stars confirm the camp is this way.*

Jasmine and her dragon still sent shivers down her spine but, she had to admit, they were much less terrifying than her captors. What she needed was time. She reached the large bush she'd seen earlier, moved behind it and sat down.

She could likely find her way back to Chuck on her own, but it was risky. Still weak, in the dark, with who knew what else was out here...she would have a much better chance if Garman accompanied her. Besides, he had done nothing to harm her. Leaving him felt *wrong*.

No, she needed to help him.

"Pretty?" Paw called out, his voice floating through the grass. "How you doin'?"

"I am fine," she said, shaking the bush. "Just found some berries. I will be a few minutes."

Ariel tugged the knot at her waist. With the limited use of her left hand, untying it was nearly impossible. It would take more time and strength than she currently had. She looked at the remaining length of rope in her good hand and an idea began to form.

She carefully wrapped some of the slack around the sturdiest branch available. A quick tug confirmed it wouldn't come loose on its own. She was far enough away from the fire that darkness engulfed her as she slowly crawled away, angling around the small camp. If her luck held, she could reach Garman without being spotted. At regular intervals, she gave a gentle tug on the rope.

While she made her way through the tall grass, Ariel kept an out for anything useful. Several times, nettles scraped her exposed skin, sending sharp, stinging pain through her. Teeth clenched, she remained silent, focusing on her goal. Garman should be close...

The last two coils in her hand caused panic. If she didn't reach him soon, her plan fell apart. There! Firelight wove through the grass, bright beams painting stripes across her arms. Garman lay in front of her, watching the men intently. She reached forward with her bandaged hand, slowly parting the grass next to his head...

Searing pain exploded through her hand, thorns piercing the bandage. Her cry came unbidden. Garman whipped his head around, straining at his bonds.

"What the hell?" Jeffy jerked his head toward her, his features blurring with the sudden onset of tears. "Paw! She's over here!"

Paw yanked hard, snapping the rope taut. The branch she'd

used broke with a loud *crack!*, grass whispering as it sailed into the prairie. Paw hauled the rope quickly hand over hand, reeling it in as fast as he could. Ariel felt the loop around her waist tug, then yank, pulling her toward the old man. She pitched forward, instinctively throwing her hands out to break her fall. Her scream pierced the night as she hit the ground.

Chuck tensed at the sound, every nerve on edge at the high-pitched scream. He started to charge ahead, only to find Jasmine holding him by the bicep.

"Hold on," she said, her voice pitched low. "We don't know what's waiting for us. Getting killed doesn't help her or Garman."

Chuck forced himself to take a deep breath, then nodded.

"We need a distraction. Quetzalith can dive in, startle them, giving you time to close. I'll have him do it twice. On the second, you get in there and get to work."

He nodded. It was as good a plan as any, given the urgency.

"Get ready," Jasmine said. She snapped her fingers at the circling dragon, calling his attention to her signals. "I'll hang back and cover you with the rifle."

She raised a hand, dropping it sharply. "Go!"

Chuck sprinted, following the sound of Ariel's screams.

Ariel clawed ineffectively at the dirt with her good hand, desperately trying to find something—a stick, a sharp rock, anything—useful. Paw stood over her, one foot firmly on her back, pinning her to the ground.

"Now, if there's one thing I can't stand," he said, "is a woman that don't know her place. You need some learnin'."

He pressed down, forcing her burned chest into the dirt. Pain erupted through her body, her cries muffled as her face hit the ground. She struggled, panting, to push with her good hand in an attempt to relieve the pressure on her wounds. Paw's answer was to apply more.

Ariel clenched her teeth, desperately trying to bear the agony, to no avail. Her scream tore through the air.

To be answered from above.

Strong gusts of air flattened the grass. The foot on her back disappeared as Paw hit the ground next to her, cursing. Ariel took the opportunity to roll, gasping at the sudden relief.

"What the hell is a dragon doing in these parts?" Paw bellowed. He recovered quickly, bounding to his feet and running for his pack. "Boys! Shoot that damn thing!"

Ariel watched as the dark shape gained altitude, powerful wings beating the air into submission as it banked. Several shots rang out. The dragon screamed once more, the sound growing louder as it dove again.

Another volley of shots. To her surprise, one of the men fell, rifle clattering to the ground. Movement at the edge of the clearing caught her eye.

Chuck strode into view, face grim, jaw set, pistol leveled at his next target. He pulled the trigger, dropping Jeffy's other companion. Paw whirled, rifle spitting fire as he shot from the hip, only to fall as two bullets ripped into this chest.

Ariel felt hands at her shoulders as she was hauled to her feet. Jeffy's hot breath tickled her neck, the sour smell of rotting teeth assaulting her nose. Cold steel pressed against her throat. Chuck turned, leveling his pistol.

"Come any closer. I'll giv'er a new smile," Jeffy said. For emphasis, he applied more pressure, creasing Ariel's neck. "You can't drop me a'fore I cut her."

Chuck lowered the pistol.

"Good thing I don't have to."

Warm blood and bone fragments showered the back of Ariel's head a split second before the sound of a rifle shot reached her. The knife fell from Jeffy's lifeless fingers, his body following shortly after.

Ariel stood still for a second, releasing the pent-up air from her lungs. Chuck ran forward, catching her just before her legs gave out.

"I'm here, Miss Ariel," he said, tenderly shifting his hold to avoid her chest. "I got you, ma'am. I'm here."

"*We're* here," Jasmine said as she strode into the clearing, slinging her rifle over her shoulder.

"Yes, ma'am, we're here," Chuck amended. He didn't take his eyes off of Ariel. "Can you cut Garman free, Jasmine?"

"If you insist," Jasmine said, walking toward the bound Windfist with a knife in her hand and a calculating expression. "Do we have to remove the gag?"

Chuck ignored her, easing Ariel to the ground. She tensed as Quetzalith landed somewhere behind them.

"They were going to eat Garman," Ariel said, quietly. "I-I tried to help him escape."

"Shh, it's okay, they won't hurt anyone now. I'm going to check on Garman, just stay right here. We'll leave in just a minute."

He stood up and walked over to Jasmine. She'd cut the rope at the Windfist's ankles and now attacked the one around his wrists. The gag was still in place.

"There," she said, as his bonds fell free. "Okay, tough guy, now you owe me one."

Garman, looking embarrassed, pulled the gag from his mouth. He rubbed his wrists, wincing as the circulation returned.

"I owe you both my life," he said.

"And?" Jasmine prodded, a small grin playing across her lips. "Who else?"

"And..." Garman said, face contorting as he ground his teeth. He sighed, raising his eyes to look pointedly at Quetzalith. "And the dragon."

"You know, he'd appreciate it if you used his name and spoke to him directly," Jasmine said. Ariel could not tell if she actually believed that, or if she was just toying with the monk.

Garman shot her a glare but to his credit, stood and walked shakily toward the dragon.

"Quetzalith, I owe you my gratitude, as well as my life," he said stiffly. He stood at attention, raising his hand palm down to touch his eyebrow in salute. "Thank you."

Ariel did not know if the beast understood him, but the dragon dipped his head and spread his wings slowly.

"Well, I'll be damned," Jasmine breathed. "I didn't teach him that."

"We should get moving. Grab anything that looks useful," Chuck said, looking around the camp. "Miss Ariel, are you up to walking?"

"Yes," she said, pushing herself carefully to her feet. "I can walk."

In a few short minutes, the others had scoured the camp, collecting weapons, ammo and items of worth that could be easily carried. They ignored anything that looked like meat.

Paw's body let out a faint groan as they passed him. To Ariel's surprise, the older man clung to life. They stopped.

"My boys.... You killed my boys..." Paw forced his words

through clenched teeth. "I'll find you. I'll hunt you down and make you pay..."

"No, you won't," Garman said. The firelight glinted off a knife that was suddenly in his hand.

His dark eyes held no compassion, only determination. As he crouched next to the injured man, Ariel turned her head, shivering.

She buried her face in Chuck's chest at the soft crunch behind her.

CHAPTER ELEVEN

JAY, APPARENTLY NAPPING NEXT TO THE FIRE, OPENED AN EYE as they approached.

"I see you found 'em," he said. "What happened?"

"I failed to maintain situational awareness," Garman said. "Stupid. Novitiate-level stupid."

He stared, frowning into the darkness. Jay raised an eyebrow at Jasmine.

"Scavengers," she said, spitting the word. "Tried to grab a quick payday, or a meal."

"Hmph. Those fellers been out in the badlands too much. That and collecting poisons for trade. Heavy metals and radiation ain't good for unprotected people."

"Like most vermin, useful in certain ways but not someone you'd want to be around," Jasmine said, nodding in agreement. "Do anything for money and not above taking ethical shortcuts."

"Do you think there will be more close by, waiting for that group?" Chuck asked, glancing at Ariel. "Is it safe to stay here?"

"No way to be certain," Jasmine replied. "But my understanding is that they spend a long time hunting and trading. We'll probably be fine; anyone associated with them wouldn't be surprised if they were missing for a while."

"Good, I don't think Ariel is up to moving out again tonight," Chuck said, scrubbing his free hand over his face. The adrenaline had worn off. He was ready to lie down and let weariness carry him into oblivion.

"I'll take first and second watch," Garman said, moving to the edge of camp. "Chuck, Jasmine, I owe you both a decent night's sleep."

Chuck didn't argue. He made his way to the bedroll, lay down and shut his eyes. He felt, but didn't stir at, Ariel climbing in next to him.

The sun hit them like a battering ram as it climbed higher in the cloudless sky. Quetzalith and Jasmine went out to hunt and reconnoiter. They returned with a pair of antelope and news that the surrounding area was empty of cultists, Gants and scavengers. Or, at least, if any of those were out there, they were holed up somewhere not visible from the air.

Chuck made several trips down to the creek, filling canteens and their cooking pot. Jay whipped up a stew from some of the antelope meat and Jasmine found some wild onions and mushrooms to actually make it flavorful.

Slowly, Ariel began to interact with the rest of the group.

Chuck brought her some of Jay's stew, insisting she eat every bite. Garman sat not far away, breaking down and performing the cleaning ritual for each of his weapons.

"Why do you do that?" Ariel asked softly at one point. Chuck looked up, but the girl was watching Garman as he swabbed the barrel of his spotless rifle with a bore brush.

"To clean them," Garman said, curtly.

"They do not look dirty," Ariel said.

"They aren't," he said without taking his eyes off his work. "Because I clean them."

"Be nice, Garman," Chuck growled softly. Garman glanced at him with a raised eyebrow before turning to Ariel with a snort. It was the first time he'd looked at her since the conversation had started.

"It's a ritual of my Order," Garman said. "We fieldstrip and clean our weapons to calm us, to care for the machinery and to invoke the warrior spirit that they carry."

"Warrior spirit?" Ariel asked. If she'd had eyebrows, they would have climbed up her forehead. "A gun is a machine. It has no spirit."

"You wouldn't understand," Garman said, loftily. "It's a Windfist ritual."

"Is that what your order is called? Windfist?"

"The Windfist Order, yes. We are the keepers of the human legacy, warriors against the abominations that would infest our world and wrest it from us. I don't suppose you'd know anything about that, though, cultist girl."

Chuck sighed, shaking his head at Garman. He didn't know what happened before he'd arrived at the scavenger camp, but it hadn't helped Garman's opinion of Ariel. Ariel, though, didn't seem discouraged by his comments.

"I have seen those markings before," she said, "the ones on your cheek. Are those from your order?"

"Yes," Garman said, warily.

"Some members of my hive had them. Some that were obsessed with the Blessing," she said. "They could not work, eventually wasting away."

"What do you mean by Blessing?" Garman asked. A shiver went down Chuck's spine at the way they said the word, like it was important, or mystical. Whatever it was, Chuck didn't like the way it sounded.

"It is a gift from the young Gants, the larva," Ariel said with a frown. She was obviously having trouble describing it. "It is as though every moment of joy you have ever felt happens to you again, all at the same time. Your skin tingles, your heart races, you have fantastic visions. It is the most terrifying sensation that can be experienced."

Chuck watched a tear roll down her cheek, unnoticed.

"I don't believe you," Garman said, scowling. "No Windfist would succumb to a Gant. And certainly wouldn't become a cultist. Our discipline protects us."

"Don't be so quick there, Junior," Jay said from his seat not far away.

"No. A Windfist is above such things."

"Windfists are still human, son," Jay said, almost gently. A small hint of a smile tugged at the corner of the old man's mouth. "Vegas wasn't built because people could control their urges."

Chuck watched the emotions play across Garman's face. The monk stared down at the pieces of rifle in his lap, swore, and reassembled it faster than Chuck would have thought possible. In seconds, he slung the rifle and surged to his feet. Without another word to any of them, he stalked away up the ridge.

"I do not mean to cause problems," Ariel said softly. "I am not good at talking to people."

"He's had a rough day," Jasmine said from across the fire, where she sat sorting through the herbs she'd foraged. "I think our Windfist friend has had several of his worldviews challenged recently."

"Why are you being so nice to me?" Ariel asked her. Chuck opened his mouth but shut it again at Jay's peremptory gesture.

"What?" the dragon trainer said with a smile. "Did you think that I was going to cut you open to let Quetzalith feast on your insides?"

"Are you?" Ariel asked. Chuck had no idea how she could sound so calm about it. Only when he looked closely did he realize that her delicate hands were trembling. He clenched his own hands into fists and ground his teeth.

"Not unless I find out that you're a cultist spy," Jasmine said silkily.

"Jasmine!" Chuck exclaimed, warning and censure in his tone. Woman or not, he didn't like the idea of anyone making Ariel afraid.

"I am not," Ariel said.

"Make me believe you," Jasmine invited.

"I cannot do that. I cannot make you believe anything. You have to evaluate the available evidence on your own," Ariel said.

"Jasmine, she's not a spy..." Chuck started to say through gritted teeth. Jasmine forestalled him by holding up a hand.

"You're right, little sister," Jasmine said. "And right now the evidence is inconclusive. So that leaves me with my gut. My gut tells me that you're not lying. But I want you to understand that if you are, I'll find out. And Quetzalith will roast you alive."

"I am not your sister," Ariel said. "Nor am I little."

"Perhaps not, but I find it's better to build bonds with one's traveling companions. You're adrift and lost in this world. You don't know what's what or whom you can trust. That's part of the reason I think you're telling the truth. Either that or you're just a phenomenal actress."

"I am not acting."

"No," Jasmine said with another smile. "I imagine you're not. Not as literal as you are. Unless, again, that's just your cover. Either way, for the time being, I'm going to treat you as genuine. Which means that my heart goes out to you. I want to help you, if I can. So I call you 'little sister' to reassure you of my reluctance to harm you."

"Conditional reluctance, you mean," Ariel clarified. "As long as I am not a spy, you are reluctant."

Jasmine tipped her head to concede the point.

"And you?" Ariel asked, turning to Chuck. "Do you think I am a spy?"

"No!" he answered. Jasmine chuckled.

"No, he doesn't," she said. "In fact, he gets angry when any of us mentions the possibility."

Chuck shot her a glare which only made the dragon tamer laugh harder, causing Jay to join in. The young man rolled his eyes at the pair of them and then turned to take Ariel's hand.

"I don't think you're a spy," he said. "I promised that I'd protect you and I mean to stand by my word."

"Why?" she asked, though her fingers curled around his. He could feel the slender fineness of the bones in her hand.

"Because... because you need help and I was taught to help a lady in need."

"I am not a lady."

"You are to me."

"Damn kid," Jay said and whistled. "That's a good line. Did you hear that, Jazz? Good line, right?"

"Indeed," Jasmine said, her eyes bright with laughter. "Kid's got a bit of game, it seems."

"Learned that from me," Jay said, nodding sagely. "Sure'n hell didn't learn it from Bullet. That boy never had no game." Then he threw Jasmine a wink that had her laughing all over again.

"What are they talking about?" Ariel asked quietly. Chuck just shook his head.

"They're just being silly, don't worry about it."

"All right. May I sleep with you again tonight?"

Chuck forgot how to breathe. After a few seconds of opening and closing his mouth soundlessly, he nodded.

Garman had apparently returned in time to take the last shift before dawn. Chuck woke as the monk shook him. The eastern horizon had started to lighten to a pearly gray and the young man could just see the shadowy forms of their companions as they moved slowly from their bedrolls.

"Since the lady seems better today, I thought we'd press toward Old Kansas City," Garman said softly. That was all he said out loud, but Chuck could read the apology in his eyes and in the gentle way he woke them both.

"Good plan," Chuck said, his voice like gravel. He tried a smile that felt more like a grimace, but Garman smiled back. "Let's get some food and get moving."

They did just that, eating the reheated remains of last night's stew beside the banked fire before breaking camp and heading out. When the sun broke fully over the eastern horizon, they were already on the trail toward the closest small town where they could purchase a horse for Ariel. Once again, Pa's map proved accurate, as they found the town just before midday. They bought a horse and some supplies from a huge prewar building that had been refitted as a combination general store and livery stable. According to Jay, this was fitting, because the building had once been the type of store that had "everything."

"You had to have a membership card to get in, though," Jay said. "I kept mine for a long time. I really missed those bulk packs of toilet paper you used to get."

"Jay, that's not proper talk around the ladies," Chuck said.

"Why not? Everybody poops, kid."

"Yeah, but you're not supposed to talk about it!"

After two days ride across the wide windswept prairie, Chuck saw a flat silver ribbon winding along the horizon off to their left. He felt his interest perk up. It had been a long two days in the saddle, where the only entertainment to be had involved teaching Ariel to ride and listening to Jasmine tease Garman. According to Jay, there hadn't been much out here even before the war, so it wasn't strange to see so few signs of human habitation even now. But two days surrounded by nothing but grass, sky and wind was a lot, and the river offered a welcome change to the scenery.

"That's the Missouri River," Jay said. "The Mighty Mo. Southern Federation claims everything on the east side. And Old Kansas City, too, though you might not tell that to the folks as make their home on the west enclave. City sits where the Kansas river joins to the south."

"If they all live in the same city, why do they disagree?" Ariel's confusion showed on her face. Her riding had improved during the last few days as she worked with the sweet-tempered older gelding they'd purchased for her. She still looked like a bag of potatoes slumped in the saddle, but she could at least trot, canter and lope. And she never complained, though Chuck knew her muscles had to be screaming by the time they camped every day. She certainly moved stiffly at night.

"Some old, bad blood," Jay said. "Goes way back, almost two hundred years. Folks like me were slaves on the east side, free men on the west."

"You mean soldiers?"

"No, people with brown skin."

"Seems illogical."

"You nailed it, girly," he said, smiling. "But that's people for you. Prolly don't even know why they're fightin', just that they should be. Remind me to tell you about the Hatfields and McCoys sometime."

"And the chapterhouse is just on the other side." Garman shifted forward in his saddle, causing his horse to high-step.

Within a few hours, the city came into view on the horizon.

"Ah, good ol' Kansas City," Jay said. "Yoosta be a major hub for just about everything. Planes, barges, roads, you name it, it came here. Got hit pretty hard during the war but you can't keep a good city down. Bounced back pretty good in the last twenty years. Whatever your game, there's a hustle for you in KC."

"Crossing the border might be a bit tough," Jasmine said, pointing. Chuck looked in that direction, squinting. The setting sun behind them wrapped the east in shadows. It took a minute but eventually Chuck could make out the tiny silhouette of an oblong-shaped object on the east side of the river.

"What's that?" Chuck asked, trying to sound clinical and unconcerned. He failed.

"Looks like an airship," Jay said, squinting. He stood up in his stirrups, leaning so far forward his horse sidled under him in protest.

"Ain't seen one of those since the war," he said. "Musta refit it. Didn't think we had any flyable anymore."

"How is it flying?" Garman asked. "It doesn't have wings like a bird. It just floats there."

"That bag on top?" Jay said, pointing. "It's got gas in it that's lighter than air. Not sure what, been hard to find helium lately."

"Maybe they figured it out," Chuck said. "But why would that make it hard for us to cross, Jasmine?"

"Because of the flames," Jasmine said, pointing again. This

time, when Chuck turned to look, he could see a stream of fire pouring down from the side of the bottom of the airship. Unlike Quetzalith's pinpoint jet of flame, this looked like a spill of some kind of liquid that burned as it fell.

"Shit," Chuck said, then he felt his face heat up. "Beg your pardon, Ariel."

"For what?" Ariel asked softly.

"For...hell. Never mind."

The girl shrugged and turned back toward the others.

"We can't go around it?" Jasmine asked.

"Only one way across the river," Jay said. "Unless you want to go hundreds of miles either direction."

"Not particularly, no."

"Then, girlie, we gotta go through Old KC."

"More importantly, I must get to the chapterhouse," Garman said, the tension in his voice making him sound self-important. "They must know about the outpost and...other things."

At that, the Windfist kicked his horse into a gallop. With a shrug toward the others, Chuck followed, more slowly. Ariel moved to stay close to Chuck—and far from Jasmine, he noted. The dragon tamer and old man fell in behind.

By the time Garman had to slow enough that they caught up with him, Chuck could start to see the details of what Jasmine had called the "enclave." Mostly it was dirty shacks, leaning in the prevailing wind and constructed of a mishmash of materials. Towers of smoke rose from the parts nearer the water. The narrow, twisty streets were full of people, mostly looking with angry or fearful eyes in the direction of the smoke.

"We're sure this is a good idea?" Jasmine asked softly. The streets and the growing crowds of people had forced them to ride close together. "This looks like the makings of a riot. The people on the other side might not let us across. Especially if they're busy burning this enclave to the ground."

It seemed that's exactly what was happening. As they got closer, it became apparent that the dirigible overhead was floating back and forth, roughly following the line of the river, continuously pouring flame on this bank. It moved slowly, lumbering through the air like an ungainly sky-beast. Judging by the ugly and terrified mood of the crowd around them, though, it was good enough at raining destruction.

"I am a Journeyman Windfist. We have recognized neutrality in any petty disputes," Garman said, steel in his voice. "They *will* let us through."

"Do they know that?" Jasmine asked. "Because I don't think they're going to realize that this is just a 'petty' dispute."

Garman's face flushed with anger. Before he could answer, a scream echoed up ahead and the press of bodies around them ratcheted up. Millie stamped and sidled, tossing her head. Chuck could hear the others trying to soothe their mounts as he bent to mutter calming words in her ear.

"This way," Ariel, of all people, said. She awkwardly pulled her horse into an alleyway where the press wasn't so bad. Chuck and the others followed, as the dull roar of the crowd built steadily behind them.

"We have to get down to the river!" Garman shouted. He looked near-frantic. "I must get to the chapterhouse."

"Fine," Chuck said, "but we're not getting there through a crowd that's about to panic. Let's cut south to the edge of the enclave and see if we can't work our way back around to the crossing point."

Another scream echoed behind them, followed by the crash of glass shattering. All the horses spooked but Ariel's, which, already unsettled by having an inexperienced rider, reared. The terrified girl clung to her saddle and barely managed to stay on. Just as it seemed she'd get it back under control, the horse bolted down the alleyway.

Chuck cursed, kicking Millie into a run after them. The thunder of hoofbeats behind him told him Garman, Jasmine and Jay were in hot pursuit as well. All around them, more screams, more crashes and bangs echoed through the darkening air. A roaring sound seemed to rise like the night all around them, though that may have just been the blood in Chuck's ears.

He leaned forward, his heels urging Millie to run faster. The mare's ears lay flat against her head, but she trusted her rider and did as he silently asked. Slowly, they began to draw alongside Ariel's horse. The girl clung, white-knuckled, to her saddle horn. Chuck reached out, stretching his arm to its limit and barely caught the flapping rein. Carefully, gradually, he and Millie nudged closer to the panicked gelding while he gave the rein a firm, steady pull. The gelding, comforted by the presence of another horse, as well as Chuck's confident commands, slowed. Eventually, he came to a halt in an open space on the edge of the enclave. His sides heaved but he looked otherwise unharmed.

Ariel looked half-dead from terror.

"Are you all right?" Chuck asked, fumbling with her reins.

"I am unhurt," Ariel said, gasping. "What are you doing?"

"I'm fixin' your reins as a leading rein. Then I'll tie it to my saddle, here. That way your horse will have to stay with Millie," he said, suiting actions to words. The growing clatter of hoofbeats meant that the others weren't far behind.

"But won't that make it difficult to get through the crowds and the buildings?"

"Maybe. But I won't risk him taking off with you again."

"Why not?" she asked, her voice trembling.

"Because I promised I'd keep you safe."

"But why?"

Chuck studied her, certain that she was toying with him. But Ariel didn't look like she found it amusing, or like she was trying to get him to admit to anything. She looked terrified and genuinely confused. Slowly, as if she were the one in danger of bolting, he reached up to touch the back of her clenched hand.

"Because..."

He never had to finish that terrifying sentence. Garman, Jasmine and Jay careened into the open area at just that moment.

"Fires have spread," Garman said, his voice curt and businesslike. "The mob is panicking. This whole place is a tinderbox. We need to move."

The minute the words left his mouth, a distant explosion sounded. The horses sidled again but Ariel's mount was still tired from his earlier panic and the others held their mounts steady.

"Right," Chuck said. "You're sure your Windfist colors will get us through?"

"I'd lay my life on it," Garman said.

"Yes, but you're laying ours on it as well," Jasmine murmured.

"Do you see another option?" Garman asked, his head whipping toward her in anger. She simply shrugged.

"This is our option," Chuck said quietly. "So put your cloak on, brother, and everybody stay close. We head for the crossing."

"I'll take point," Garman volunteered. He looked around to orient himself. Jasmine lifted a hand and pointed.

"That way," she said. He gave her the barest of nods and then turned to face that direction.

"Give me her leading rein, kid," Jay said as he pulled alongside Chuck. "And you guard our rear. Jazz and me'll keep the girl safe for you."

Chuck could almost feel Ariel stiffen at the prospect of being close to Jasmine, though she said nothing. He nodded, untied the leading rein and handed it to the old man. Drunkard he may be, he'd yet to fail Chuck when the chips were down. Another explosion, this one closer, boomed across the sky. Millie danced and tossed her head.

"Let's move out," Garman said. "Stay together and move fast. Don't stop for anything if you can help it."

It wasn't long until they encountered the panicked mob. From afar, it hadn't looked like the enclave had housed that many people, but the few streets that were not blocked with rubble were absolutely packed as the mob tried to move away from the fire. Waves of stampeding, terror-stricken people rushed at them, forcing them to ride bunched together. The air smelled scorched, and hot winds carried the scent of fire and ash.

One of the men came at them, screaming wildly. His face, smudged black with soot, twisted with grief or anger or fear. He reached up to grab Jasmine's rein, causing her horse to rear. Garman struck out faster than thought, catching the man under the chin with the butt of his rifle. He stumbled backward, falling under the press of bodies. Ariel let out a little scream and Chuck felt a sick fear settle in the pit of his stomach.

Above them, Quetzalith let out his own scream, almost lost in the roar of the crowd and the distant fire. Jasmine's head whipped up and she waved her hand over her head.

"No!" she cried. "You'll make them worse! I'm fine! Garman, we have to move, Quetzalith thinks I'm threatened. He wants to flame this entire crowd!" she cried.

"I'm doing my best!" Garman shot back. He was, too, using his larger horse's bulk to break a path through the surging crowd. It was harder because they were moving against the tide, toward the destruction that rained down on the enclave from the airship above.

"Jasmine, can Quetzalith take that thing out?" Chuck asked.

"Maybe," she said, hesitantly. "But if they're armed at all, they'll shoot at him and I won't risk him if I can help it."

"Might not be able to help it."

"Cross that bridge when we come to it," she said, voice hard.

Chuck let it be for the moment, simply fighting to stay together with the others. The press of bodies increased, past the point of "uncomfortable" and on into "dangerous" territory. With no other options, they had no choice but to push on.

Abruptly, they were through. Garman's horse stumbled just a bit as she exited the mob of panicked pedestrians, her hooves squelching in the slick mud underfoot. With no rain recently, Chuck couldn't figure where the mud played in, until he looked around and realized that the buildings around them were unmistakably burnt. The airship was behind and to the north. They'd passed into the fire zone.

"Someone musta tried to fight the fire here, at least for a little while," Chuck said. "Garman, see if you can follow the mud to the river. I'm betting that's where they got their water and it might be the safest path. Don't wanna ride through embers if we don't have to."

"Roger," Garman said, turning back to his task.

"Jazz," Chuck said, using Jay's nickname for the dragon trainer. "Is your boy okay?"

"Better now," Jasmine replied with a quick smile of thanks. "The crowd made him nervous. He doesn't like it when I'm in danger."

"Are you not always in danger?" Ariel asked, her voice carrying just a hint of a tremble. Jasmine turned her grin on the girl.

"Pretty much. Maybe that's why he's so cranky all the time," she said. It was clear that Jasmine was trying to make a joke, but Ariel's eyes only got wide and her face went pale. Paler. She cut her eyes down and hunched her shoulders inward. Chuck saw Jasmine's smile falter.

"What say we get movin' before that airship turns back around?" Jay asked. He had a flask in hand and shrugged as he took a sip before continuing. "Not that I'm in favor of bein' in such a rush all the time. But, you know. Being fried crispy doesn't sound too good either."

"The old man's right," Garman snapped. "We're wasting time. Let's go."

After the madness of the crowd, it seemed as if they rode through an empty wasteland of soot and mud. Chuck felt his hackles rising as they moved further and further into the destruction.

Try as he might, he couldn't catch a glimpse of anyone but he knew what he was feeling. They were being watched.

The others seemed to sense it, too. Garman kept his head on an aggressive swivel. Ariel shivered and leaned toward Jay, who loosened his guns in their holsters. Jasmine simply looked worried, glancing up repeatedly at the sky, as if wondering if she dared call Quetzalith down to them.

As they got closer to the river, the burned-out devastation got worse. Soon, they were picking their way through unrecognizable piles of cinders and ash. Warped, blackened metal lay in twisted heaps here and there on the ground, forcing the horses to carefully high-step in places to avoid being cut. A breeze eddied through, bringing with it puffs of ash and the stench of scorched air. Up north, the airship stilled, then began a ponderous turn.

"They're coming back around," Jasmine said, her voice tight.

"I see the water…and the bridge! Let's ride!" Garman shouted, kicking his horse into motion. The other horses responded to their lead mare, kicking up ash and soot as they sprinted for the battered, patched architecture of the bridge.

Off to their left, the airship belched more flame out over the enclave as it accelerated south. Chuck bent low over Millie's neck, urging her on and praying that Ariel's gelding would keep it together, and she would stay on her mount.

Finally, the expanse of the bridge stretched before them, arcing over the dark ribbon of the river. A line of barricades stretched across the foot of the bridge, bristling with spikes and rifle barrels.

Garman let his reins go and stood up in the saddle, spreading his arms dramatically. His distinctively mottled cloak rippled out and caught the light of the mirrored lanterns trained on the street leading up to the bridge.

"I am Journeyman Windfist Garman! I am on a mission of grave importance for my Order! I invoke Windfist neutrality and call upon you to allow me and my party to pass!"

A bit overdone, perhaps. Chuck had to admit, though, that the monk's voice echoed magnificently over the water, cutting through the background roar of the fire.

At first, nothing happened as they continued to approach the roadblock. Then a handful of the barrels disappeared and one of the wooden barricades swiveled haltingly to the side, as if being dragged by many hands. Those things didn't look light, or easy to move.

Chuck, beads of sweat along his hairline, heard the roar of flames getting louder. He kept his eyes on Ariel's back, trying his best to ignore the rising heat as they thundered onto the bridge and toward the barricade.

"Come on!" A voice came from ahead, behind the fence. "You can make it! It won't flame you once you're with us!"

"If it's yours, then order it to stop!" Chuck shouted out.

"It ain't ours anymore! Just keep riding! You can do it!"

A fine layer of soot had settled over the surface of the bridge, making the footing treacherous. Millie slipped more than once and Chuck worried that she'd come up lame on the other side. Better lame than burnt to death, though. He urged her forward.

Sides heaving, the horses clattered through the tight opening in the barricade. They jostled one another as the riders tried to keep from getting inadvertently speared by the spikes that jutted out in all directions. As soon as Chuck was in, nearly twenty men went back to work on the barricade, pushing it back into place.

"What is that?" Jasmine demanded, pulling her horse to a halt.

"Airship, ma'am. We used to call it a 'dirig,'" one of the men behind the barricade said, over his shoulder.

"I know what it *is*, thank you," Jasmine snapped at him. "I meant, what is it *doing*? The whole enclave is going to go up in flames. People are going to die!"

"Pardon me, ma'am," the man said stiffly. He walked forward. He wore a high-collared, lightweight blue jacket over light brown homespun shirt and jeans. Unlike the others, however, his had six small brass buttons sewn onto the collar, suggesting that he held a higher rank. "People have already died."

He pointed behind him, to a building built into the side of the bridge. More people in the same uniform hustled in and out, several of them wearing what looked like a white armband with a red cross on it.

"Infirmary?" Jay asked. The soldier nodded. "I thought the airship wasn't firing on you guys?"

"It wasn't but it fired on plenty of civilians. Some of them ran this way. Exceeded my orders to do so but I let 'em in. Prob'ly gonna be hell to pay but I couldn't leave kids out there to get incinerated. Especially when it's their own damn people who stole the thing!"

"Kids?" Jasmine gasped and slid down from her horse. She

took off at a jog for the building. Several of the men moved as if to stop her but Garman, of all people, spoke up.

"Let her, she's got medical training," he said.

Chuck cut his eyes to Jay. They had all heard Jasmine protest that she didn't know much more than first aid, but neither of them said anything. If nothing else, she'd be an extra pair of hands to help. And if there were kids...

"The airship was stolen?" Garman asked.

"Yeah, this afternoon. Bold as you please, a group of them enclavers comes outta nowhere and swarms her where she was docked off the end of this here bridge. Lost a couple of good men when they threw 'em overboard. She ain't been used in years, y'see. I been here about twenty and never seen her fly." He ran a hand across his forehead, smearing sweat-soaked soot. "We had only a skeleton crew there, while the rest of us manned this crossing point. Keeping all them enclavers from sneaking across without the proper paperwork. But then, next thing ya know, the damn dirig is *rising*. I sent a runner to see what in the hell was going on but then we heard shots fired, so I called all hands to the barricades. Think they got my runner; he never reported back in."

"Are you certain it was a group of enclavers that swarmed the airship?" Garman asked.

"Can't think who else it would be. Weren't none of my men and they weren't wearing any other kind of uniform."

Garman raised his eyebrows and looked over at Jay again. Not wearing a uniform didn't mean that they were necessarily people of the enclave. Especially not when they seemed so determined to burn it down.

"How come they didn't come fire on your position here?" Jay asked. "Seems that if they were enclavers, that'd be their first move, if their goal was to bust the border."

The soldier straightened up, chin jutting forward.

"Not that we think you're wrong," Chuck said hurriedly, holding his hands out in a placating manner. "But, how did you know your men would be safe, as well as us and the enclaver kids you let in? Once they started pouring fire, that is."

"Oh, well." The soldier's posture relaxed slightly, though he did glare suspiciously at Jay for a moment before he went on. "See, that's the thing. They can't."

"What? Why not?" Garman asked.

"It's an old dirig. And the steering mechanism don't work as good as it used to. Leastways, it never has. That's why we always kept it tethered. And when they swarmed it, it was still tethered to the cable that runs along the riverbank. It can't come this far out over the water."

"So it can't go any further inland, either?" Garman asked. Before he got an answer, Ariel spoke up.

"Jasmine is coming back," she said softly. "She looks upset."

"Upset" doesn't quite cut it, Chuck thought as the dragon tamer walked toward them.

She came to a halt about midway between the infirmary and the barricades, in an area that was slightly less crowded. Most of the men turned to watch her as she raised both hands over her head, clasped them and then pointed with both hands toward the shadowy hulk that hung, motionless, at the base of the bridge.

For a second, nothing happened. Then a brilliant white bolt of flame blasted through the sky toward the airship's bag. The bolt struck and Chuck just barely had time to launch himself toward Ariel and drag them both to the ground before the sky erupted in an explosion that seemed to stretch from horizon to horizon.

Chuck was fairly sure men were shouting—he could hear the muffled sound of metal clattering on stone and wood—but most everything else was lost to the ringing in his ears. He took a second to look Ariel over.

"You all right?" he asked her, his voice echoing weirdly through his head.

She nodded, eyes wide, hands clapped over her own ears. He nodded back, did his best to give her a reassuring smile and took her hand. Then he pulled them both to their feet.

Jay was picking himself up, dusting off his sleeves. Garman, already on his feet, argued furiously with the soldier, whose face seemed to be alternating red and white. He gestured at Jasmine, at the burning skeleton of the airship as it drifted to the ground and at the men all around them. Jasmine stood unconcerned, watching a small dark shape circling in to land.

Chuck decided he'd better grab their horses. In truth, he was grateful that they were too tired to have bolted already—and he was equally grateful that Quetzalith was angling in downwind. Of course, he couldn't do the same for the men around him, who looked at the landing dragon with equal parts horror and disgust.

Quetzalith flared his wings and touched down next to Jasmine, then dipped his head for her caresses and murmured praise. The soldier pushed roughly past Garman and charged up to them, which made Quetzalith raise his head and let out a warning squawk. Jasmine, too, looked up at the uniformed man, her face calm.

"We haven't been introduced," she said, pleasantly. "Lady Jasmine Moore and this is Quetzalith. And you are?"

"Sergeant Chris McVey and, begging your pardon ma'am, but *what in the hell were you thinking*?"

"Excuse me?" Jasmine's eyebrow shot up, a subtle note of warning entering her tone. Garman tossed a worried look at Chuck and the group of them hurried over to try and help.

"What did you... Do you know what you've just done? You've just destroyed the last functional airship on the continent! We had orders to protect it at all costs!"

"Then you shouldn't have let it be taken, I suppose," Jasmine said coolly.

"*It was tethered! It wasn't going anywhere!*" Sergeant McVey, face nearly purple with rage, clenched his fists. Quetzalith eyed him warily. "*All we had to do was wait until they ran out of fuel for the boiler! They would have come down! But you had to go and destroy it!*"

"Sergeant..." Garman said. "Surely it isn't that serious. You said it yourself, the dirig was an antiquated piece of equipment."

"*We had orders!*" McVey screamed, spittle flying. "My unit has protected that ship for decades! It was too important to be destroyed! Those orders came from National Command Authority itself! Protect the ship *at all costs*!"

"Do you know what you have inside your infirmary?" Jasmine's tone stayed pleasant, conversational. Chuck felt the sudden urge to shiver.

"Wha—?" the sergeant asked, taken aback by the sudden shift in conversation. "We have... refugees. Kids."

"That's right. Kids and families. Who were attacked by that thing. One little girl has burns over the entire right side of her body. She probably won't survive the night. Because you let that thing be taken."

"What? No, my men..."

"Were doing their jobs, yes. But they were overwhelmed when someone charged the ship. I heard about it all inside."

"Enclavers. It was enclavers that took it, to try and bust the border, no doubt."

"False. Those families in there are from the enclave and they were just as surprised as you. More so, in fact, because they never expected to have liquid fire dumped on them from above," her lips stretched into a tight smile, eyes glinting like icicles as she spoke.

"Well, coulda been a small group ... dissidents ..."

"Possibly," Jasmine said. "But then why would they kill their own people? In any case, whoever took that airship needed to die. So they are dead."

Chuck shuffled a bit at this. Not that he disagreed with her. The men who would do something this horrible got what they deserved, but the idea of such arbitrary justice made him uneasy. He liked Jasmine but who was she to decide who lived and who died?

Now, however, was probably not the time to raise the question.

"But ... But ..." the sergeant sputtered.

"Look, Sergeant McVey," Chuck said. "We've got a, uh, Windfist mission to do. Seems you don't need us here any longer."

The man blinked, then focused on Garman's facial tattoos. He cut his eyes to Quetzalith, then to Jasmine, then back to the Windfist. He seemed unable to speak.

"Right," Garman said. "We'll be on our way, then. Thank you, Sergeant. I'll report your assistance up through my chain of command."

With that, he turned and mounted his horse. Jasmine did the same, giving the sergeant another icy smile. Chuck, Jay and Ariel followed suit.

Sergeant McVey opened his mouth, as if he would order his men to stop them but Quetzalith chose that moment to open his wings and launch. Chuck could hear the muffled screams and curses from the men gathered at his back. He glanced nervously around, hoping that none of them took it into their heads to shoot at either them or the dragon. Their vulnerability itched at the back of his skull and he didn't like it.

Nothing happened.

They continued onward over the curve of the bridge and then down the other side into a quiet, broad street that looked to be well tended. There were even trees growing on either side, with street lanterns at regular intervals. Houses and darkened storefronts lined the thoroughfare and all of the buildings were built of brick. Scorched and obviously reclaimed brick but brick nonetheless. The whole place looked prosperous, a far cry from the shantytown across the river.

"Bit diff'rent on this side," Jay said softly. When Chuck looked his way, the old man gave him a mirthless smile.

"Why?" Chuck asked.

"Why is it different? Why else? Money. KC's always been a crossroads. Lots of commerce flowing through here. Folks make good on being the middleman." He shrugged. "Then they clean up a spot, make it safe for families. Other folks want to move in there. So on. The money builds. That's why the bridge is guarded. To keep this area safe."

"But you just said they wanted to bring people here, to build the money," Ariel said. "Why did they keep those people in the enclave out, if that is what they are doing?"

"Pay attention, young lady," Jay said, not unkindly. "Money. The enclavers don't have it, so they don't get to cross to the sunny side of the street."

"What street?" Ariel asked. Her brows pinched together in a frown as she fought to follow Jay's rambling explanation.

"It's an expression, girlie. It means that they're stuck living in squalor until they can pull themselves out."

"No wonder the men at the bridge thought they'd been attacked by enclavers," Jasmine put in. "I'd attack, if it meant feeding my family. What a horrible system!"

"Do you think so?" Jay asked mildly. He might have said something else but Garman interrupted them all with a joyous shout that felt entirely wrong for the quiet, darkened street they rode on.

"There it is!" the Windfist called out. "The chapterhouse!"

At first, Chuck couldn't see what had him so excited. Up ahead, the houses and buildings thinned out and a wide field stretched open. A twisted, cobbled-together fence stretched around the wide, empty space. It wasn't until Garman led them along that fence to a gate that Chuck realized what he was seeing. It was like the outpost they'd visited ... What had Jay called it? An airport. Only this was on a much grander scale.

In through the gate and the horses' hoofbeats softened as the surface of the street changed from gravel and dirt to that black, crumbling asphalt. A road turned and followed the fence line around the perimeter of the wide-open space toward a low cluster of buildings in the distance. Here and there, metal poles stabbed up out of the ground, occasionally in a line leading toward a wide swath of asphalt. Jay had called it a runway at the other place but these runways (Chuck counted two) were unbelievably large by comparison. They stretched off into the darkness and even under the light of the moon, Chuck couldn't see the far end.

"Something's wrong," Garman said, dread soaking through his voice. "Where is everyone?"

"Now, Junior, don't get your panties all in a wad," Jay said. But Chuck noticed that the old man loosened the rifle in its saddle holster. "It's late, they're probably sleeping."

"Without a watch?" Garman snorted. "Unthinkable. Every night, without fail. 'The price of freedom is eternal vigilance.'"

"Thomas Jefferson had a point, but I don't think he was talking about guard duty," Jay said.

"Who?" Garman asked irritably, reining his horse to a stop. "Never mind, old man. I know what I'm talking about. Something is wrong; it's too quiet,"

"Jasmine," he said, "how well can Quetzalith see in the dark?"

"He found you and Ariel." The dragon trainer came to a halt. The rest of them followed suit. "Do you want him to check out what's ahead?"

"Yes. Have him fly over those buildings there. That should be the main chapterhouse. I want to know if there are men, horses, that sort of thing."

"In this moonlight, he can't get too close without being seen," she said. "And you Windfists are likely to shoot at a dragon, am I right? So he'll stay high but he can see movement and tell the difference between animal and man."

"Good enough," Garman said. "Let's wait here until we know more...if that's all right with you, Chuck." The Windfist looked a bit sheepish. Chuck shrugged and gave Garman a grin that was meant to be reassuring.

"This is your mission, Garman," he said. "You're in charge."

"Thanks," Garman said quickly, returning the grin. "So, yeah, we'll wait here, let the ab...dragon check things out and report back."

Chuck watched Jasmine's eyebrows climb at Garman's slip and quick correction, but she didn't say anything. Instead she lifted her hands and made a series of gestures that ended with her pointing in the direction of the buildings. The dark shape of Quetzalith dipped a wing in acknowledgement and then arrowed through the moonlight toward their objective.

The buildings lay quiet and ominous up ahead and Quetzalith stayed high as he circled several times.

"What does he see?" Garman asked Jasmine, his voice tense. Jasmine turned in her saddle and gave the Windfist a long look.

"I don't know," Jasmine said. "It's not like I can read his mind. He sees something interesting, either men or beasts. That's all I can say."

Garman looked slightly embarrassed by her rebuke and Chuck could hear Jay's soft chuckle. The Windfist just nodded, turning to watch as the dragon circled again before flying back toward their position. He landed as close to Jasmine as her mount would allow. Millie trembled.

A strange sort of conversation ensued. Jasmine would make a sign with her hands and Quetzalith would respond by moving his head. Once, he leaned back and spread his wings slightly.

"He saw riders, a group of many, which usually means more than three," Jasmine said. "Behind the buildings, a little ways away. Not moving."

Before she could say more, a flaming comet arced from the roof of one of the buildings toward them, searing its way through the moonlit night.

"Move!" Chuck kicked Millie into a gallop, grabbing for Ariel's reins as he did. Quetzalith let out a scream of rage and launched into the air, his wings stroking for height as Jasmine kicked her horse into motion.

"Scatter out!" Chuck yelled, though he kept Ariel's leading rein. "Makes us harder to hit!"

Another flaming projectile flew toward them. The first impacted the ground ten meters behind them, where it crackled in the dead, dry autumn grass. Chuck looked back to see a tendril of smoke whisper up into the night.

"This whole place could go up," he shouted. "Head for the buildings!"

If this place was like the other Windfist outpost they'd seen, there would be more concrete near the buildings. Of course, that was where someone was firing great flaming missiles at them, so that complicated matters. Still, it seemed that in this situation, doing anything was better than doing nothing.

The horses ran flat out, spooked by the scent of fire so close once again. Whoever was shooting stopped for a moment. He'd have taken it for a good sign, except gunfire started peppering the ground around them.

"Get in close, it's our only chance!" He kicked Millie to even greater speeds. The mare stretched her neck out, sprinting toward the dubious safety of the buildings, hooves skidding on asphalt and gravel. They finally encountered the concrete apron.

"Over here!" Garman shouted. "I found the door!"

He dismounted before his horse came to a complete stop and ran for the door. He turned the handle as he slammed his shoulder into it.

It only opened a few inches.

Chuck slid off of Millie and set to, leaning his shoulder next to Garman's as they muscled the door. The gap widened slightly as something heavy scraped against the floor inside, making Chuck's teeth itch with the sound. Someone must have secured the horses nearby, because Jay and the girls joined them after a few moments.

"We'll go in one by one," Chuck said. "Garman, you first. Be ready, we weren't exactly quiet coming in and we still don't know who was shooting at us and why."

Garman nodded, drew his kukri, then looked at Jasmine and ducked in through the door.

A heartbeat later, he called softly and Jasmine slipped through, followed by Jay, then Ariel. Chuck brought up the rear.

The inside was a dimly lit, concrete hallway of sorts. Chuck looked around but saw no one. The only sign of habitation had been the pile of broken furniture against the door.

"There have to be only a handful of them, at most," Garman was saying when Chuck joined the group. "Any more than that and there would have been guards."

"Right," Jay said, "makes sense. That's why they barricaded the door."

"We should keep a sharp eye out," Garman said, ignoring the older man. "If it were me, I'd trap the stairs, or do something to funnel intruders into a planned kill zone. So be ready for ambush."

"And who will be going first?" Ariel asked, her voice shaking with a fine tremor.

"I'll take point," Garman said.

The cultist girl shook her head. "From a purely logical stand-point, it should be me," she said.

Chuck opened his mouth to speak but Garman cut him off.

"You're right but Chuck won't let you, or will insist on going first instead. I'll take point. If there is a trap, I'm likely to recognize it first and if any of my brothers are left alive..."

"Challenge accepted, Junior!" Jay called down from the first landing. "That part's clear! Y'all come on up!"

Garman looked up, his temper showing hot on his face, especially when Jasmine chuckled quietly behind him.

"We agreed that I should go first!"

"The hell we did! No one agreed to diddly squat, so I figgered I'd go ahead and do something," he said, striking a dramatic pose: hand on hip, one foot resting on the next step, complete with his infectious grin. Chuck found himself smiling in response.

"Ol' Jay leads the way...all the way!" the old drunk called out as he started to climb again. "As usual!"

Garman grumbled something unintelligible and stomped up the stairs after the old man. Jay winked down at Ariel and then scampered up, staying ahead of the growling Windfist. Jasmine let out a low laugh and followed, with Ariel and Chuck bringing up the rear.

They rounded one landing and started up another when Jay suddenly stopped, holding his arm out to still the others. Garman came up to his shoulder and peered up the stairwell.

"What is it, old man?" Garman asked, craning his neck to try and see further up the concrete squared spiral of risers.

"Not up there," Jay said, his earlier gaiety gone. "Look there."

He pointed straight ahead, at eye level, where the next landing started. Garman squinted, leaned further over Jay's shoulder, then abruptly straightened, eyes going wide.

"Where does it go?" Jay asked, pointing to the wall.

"What is it?" Jasmine asked.

"Tripwire. Badly concealed," Garman said, sounding gruff. "Sloppy work."

"Clean enough that you didn't see it right away," Jasmine pointed out softly. Garman either ignored her or didn't hear. Chuck gave her a look, which *she* ignored.

"Not sloppy," Jay said. "Rushed. Like they were short on time or something. Something surprised them? Anyway, it runs up that wall to that grated vent there. I'm betting there's something nasty in there waiting to spray out. So everyone step carefully over the wire and don't touch the wall going around the corner."

"Got it," Chuck said and took the opportunity to gently take hold of Ariel's elbow. She looked down at her arm, then at him, her expression puzzled.

"So's you don't lose your balance," he said.

"Why would I?" Ariel asked, pulling her arm away. She didn't look offended, or uncomfortable, just confused. Chuck felt mortification heating up his face.

He moved forward, stepping with exaggerated care over the tripwire before beckoning the rest of them onward.

When Chuck approached the wire himself, he could see why Garman missed it. Even if it was sloppy or rushed, it was damn near invisible to *him*. Funny that Jay of all people found it. That old drunk had sharper eyes than he let on. He stepped carefully over the wire and followed along behind, trying to keep his eyes open for the next trap.

Two flights up, Jay found another tripwire.

"That's two for the old man, Junior," Jay cackled, clearly enjoying showing Garman up. "Wanna bet I find more than you? Loser buys."

"Windfist don't bet," Garman said. His face stayed blank, though the words came out through clenched teeth.

"Horseshit. I've known a *lot* of Windfist. They don't bet when they think they'll lose. You scared you'll lose?"

"I fear no such thing." Garman paused, frowning. "Fine, I accept."

"That's more like it," Jay said, slapping him on the back. "I'll even let you go first, give you a fightin' chance."

Garman grumbled, taking the lead. He stopped at the next landing, examining every square inch before motioning the rest to join him.

Jay winked at Chuck as he passed. Chuck couldn't help wondering if the old man had shamed Garman for fun, or as a lesson.

Probably both.

Either way, it worked. Garman found two more traps on the way up. Jay found three.

They reached the top landing. Garman and Jay both examined the steel door and, finding it clear, opened it.

The room, for lack of a better term, stretched in front of

them dark and mostly empty. Vague shapes hunkered at regular intervals, offering cover for any would-be attackers.

"Move from cover to cover, singly," Garman said. "Don't bunch up. Mind your step but move quickly. We will be exposed to potential attacks anytime we are in the open. I'll go first."

He looked at each of them.

"Don't forget to cover me. Ready?"

Everyone nodded. The Windfist moved out, feet silent on the hard floor. He made it to the first object, a large column roughly eight feet tall and just as wide. Chuck didn't realize he had been holding his breath, until Garman motioned for the next person. Jay motioned for Jasmine to follow, then Ariel. He turned to Chuck.

"I'll go next. You make sure no one blows my black ass to Hell," he said, grinning, and Chuck couldn't help but grin right back. Jay moved out.

They leapfrogged their way through the massive area, from one column to the next. Chuck kept a close eye on each smaller room off to the side. Most looked like saloon bars, metal counters dividing the rear of each room from the main area. A few were completely open; some had a few tables and chairs inside.

About halfway through, Chuck's nerves were on edge. Nothing moving besides the five of them, no noises, no lights. It was eerie. With every leap forward, he felt more keyed up, expecting *something* to happen.

Jay eased around the next column as Chuck ran up. Over his head, a large sign labeled DIRECTORY made him chuckle. On it, a large, faded dot read "You are Here."

Where the hell else would I be? he thought.

"Hang on," Jay called out softly. They waited, wondering what was in store for them this time. The older man reached behind him and grabbed a handful of Garman's cloak, pulling the Windfist forward.

"Look there," Jay said, pointing at a glass wall. It was easy enough to see through, past an open area that looked down on the main floor below and into another glassed-in area.

This one appeared to be twin to their own, except that it did hold lanterns. And people. And lots and lots of guns, judging by the number of rifle barrels leaning against the glass wall. Chuck only counted three silhouetted figures moving...but with all those weapons, his party's numbers didn't mean "winning."

"That your boys?" Jay asked Garman. The Windfist leaned forward, peering through the glass, then shrugged.

"Could be," Garman said. "That room would command a view of the grounds very well. It might be where they holed up. But where's the threat? I just don't get it!"

"Let's go ask 'em," Jay said. "We'll work our way around to the right and call out. You do the talking, give them the secret password or something to let them know it's you and see if you can't get them to not shoot at us. Sound good?"

"That's your plan? Asking pretty please don't shoot at us?" Jasmine asked.

"You got it, girlie. Brilliant in its simplicity, isn't it?" Jay said with a grin. "I always like the simple plans. Unless you have a better idea?"

"I suppose just, you know, *leaving* isn't an option?" she asked. Garman looked at her and even Chuck could see the anguish in his eyes.

"No, I have my orders," he said firmly. "And I have to find out what's happened here. Something is very, very wrong."

"Then I guess not," Jasmine said, giving him a little smile.

With another nod at everyone, the Windfist took his place at the head of the marching order, leading them down the long, curving hallway toward the observation deck they'd seen.

As they got closer, the hallway and windows started bristling with spikes that looked like they'd been fashioned of furniture and scrap metal. Garman's comment about kill zones bounced inside his head. He tried to put it out of mind as the Windfist led them to the base of the throat and called a halt.

Jay looked around, then raised his eyebrows at Chuck.

"You mind a slight change of plan?" he asked Garman. "I think I can make a good impression. I'll use my grace and tact." He pulled a flask from his jacket, took a swig and held it up. "This is Grace..."

Jasmine snorted but no one else said anything. Garman just nodded. Jay took a few steps forward, then stopped. After a moment of confusion, Chuck realized there was another tripwire he could barely see.

"Hey boys, I see you've got this hall wired to blow," Jay called out in a voice that echoed through the eerie stillness. "We ain't here to hurt ya. In fact, one of your brothers is with us and he's concerned. What ya say about havin' a little parley? We got a Journeyman, a farm boy, two gals and the town drunk. About as nonthreatening as you can get."

A voice came back to them after a moment.

"Stay right where you are! Put the weapons away or we blow the place."

"Bit drastic, don't you think?" Jay said. "Just settle down now, we'll holster the iron but you gotta calm down a bit, friend."

"Don't tell me what to do, old man, just put the weapon away."

Jay moved with exaggerated slowness, motioning for the others to do as they were told. Chuck slung the Marlin carefully, keeping it from getting tangled with Fat Lady. Garman slid his kukri back into its sheath with a grimace. Jay nodded, turning back to the speaker.

"That better, boys? Can we come in and talk like civilized men now? My friend here's been powerfully anxious to get to you."

At the end of the hallway, where the spikes had narrowed the space to a single body's width, a door opened slowly.

"Not too fast," the still-unseen voice warned.

"Go on then," Jay said, clapping Garman on the shoulder. "Be easylike, though. These brothers of yours are a bit skittish."

Garman hesitated, his face carefully composed and blank, hands seemingly relaxed. Still near to his kukri and pistol, Chuck noted.

"Send the women first. We know you won't shoot near them," the voice said.

"Whoa, now, pard," Jay said. "That's a mighty big request."

"We can take out all of you now, or you can get the women out of harm's way."

"How is that getting us out of harm's way, exactly?" Jasmine muttered.

"Okay, boys," Jay said. "We get your point. Ladies, after you."

Jasmine started to protest, but stilled when Chuck threw her a look. Truth was, she was more than capable of caring for herself, but he wasn't so sure about Ariel.

He cut his eyes to the former cultist girl, who still watched him with a look of puzzlement and then back to Jasmine. The dragon trainer seemed to understand his unspoken plea, because she gave him a slight nod.

"Fine," she said. "Ariel, stay close."

She reached out, took the other girl's hand and stepped over the tripwire. Ariel cast a nervous look back at Chuck but didn't shrink away. Chuck nodded and waved to her to go on ahead. Jasmine would keep her safe.

Ariel nodded in return and followed Jasmine over the tripwire. The spiked hallway narrowed so far that the two of them crowded close as they walked single file toward the open door. But their hands stayed linked.

Jay followed next, then Chuck. Garman brought up the rear. As soon as he passed through the doorway, Chuck became uncomfortably aware of at least four rifle barrels pointed at him and his companions.

"You're with him!"

"Whoa, whoa!" Jay said, spreading his hands. "Him who? Chuck?"

"No, not *him.*" Chuck figured the Windfist speaking had assumed the role of leader. At the very least, he acted senior to the others. He stabbed a finger at Garman, wrapped in the same cloak that the man himself wore. "The traitor. He's from Sheridan!"

"I'm no traitor," Garman said, his voice cold. Chuck recognized the look on his face as well. The Windfist was sizing things up, looking at all the angles. "You will not accuse me again."

Chuck realized that the other group had the same expressions. While he had no doubts that he, Garman and Jasmine could take them—especially if Jay did his usual trick of getting in the way at just the right time—he wasn't sure if they could do it without putting Ariel in danger. The room was too small, the Windfists had the advantage.

"AT EASE!" All eyes focused on Jay. For one split second, Chuck could swear the old man seemed taller, sober and *in command.* But only for a second. His sloppy smile came back. "Now, traditionally, we'd all grab a beer and chew this over, civilized-like. We're fresh out. Got any?"

The leader shook his head.

"All righty then," Jay said reaching into his vest. He pulled out his ever-present flask. "We move on to the paint thinner."

He took a long pull before handing it over to the leader. He looked at Jay for a long moment, then at Garman, then shrugged and took a sip. His face twisted in a grimace.

"Yeah," Jay said, "it'll put hair on your chest, burn it off and grow it back again. Now what's all this about?"

The Windfist leader took a deep breath, then seemed to wilt.

"I'm Adeptus Stephens," he said. "By the way."

"I'm Jay. That's Chuck, Jasmine and Ariel. Your brother is Garman."

Stephens nodded at each of them in turn, his eyes lingering on Garman as he bit his lip.

"This is a hell of a situation, sir," Stephens said, looking between Garman and Jay as he spoke. "I don't even know where to start. Begging your pardon but I don't even know how much I should trust you and that breaks my heart. Honestly, I just don't know what to do."

The Adeptus looked both very young and very tired in that moment. Chuck abruptly realized that he couldn't be much older than fifteen.

"Tell me why," Garman said. The hairs on the back of Chuck's neck rose. His friend's voice was low, flat and devoid of emotion.

"Three days ago, a group of brethren rode in, one from your chapterhouse," Stephens said, gesturing to the small patch on Garman's right breast. "Three Journeymen. They had another guy with them, wearing some kind of old-fashioned-looking uniform."

"Old-fashioned? Like the regiment in town?" Jasmine asked, her eyes narrowing intently. Stephens looked at her, startled to hear her speak up.

"No. I mean, yes. Prewar but not immediately prewar. *Old*, old-fashioned, Before Saint Baddis's time," the Adeptus replied. "Big guy, though. Didn't say much. Anyway, the lead Journeyman says that they're trying to meet up with a brother on a Journey—you, in fact."

"Me?" Garman asked, narrowing his eyes. Stephens nodded.

"Described you to a T. Gave your name and everything. Said they were trying to reach you, so they didn't know how long it would be until you checked in, so the Master Superior let them stay. Not a big deal, right?" He took a deep breath that sounded suspiciously like a sob and then plunged onward.

"Except that yesterday they attacked us. Well, that's not exactly right. I guess we attacked first but that was because Master Vilmund..." He broke off, choked up and gestured to the corner. Chuck turned to look and realized that a man lay on a pallet of blankets, clearly badly wounded.

"Your brother, Journeyman Ronen, he got all of us together,"

Stephens went on, his voice thick. "Adepti and below. He started preaching sedition to us, talking about the plight of the enclavers and how wrong it was that the citizens of Old KC have so much while they have so little. He started talking about the unrest in other areas. At first I didn't see much wrong with what he was saying but then he started talking about violating our neutrality and that's when I knew something was off. I spoke up, but he shouted me down. Several of us left the meeting and went to fetch Master Vilmund. Your brother struck him, as you see there, and the next thing we knew, we were under attack."

"Who attacked you?" Garman growled.

"More soldiers dressed like the silent one. Old-fashioned uniforms but modern weaponry. Ronen called upon us to join him in overthrowing the Masters. He fired on those of us who refused. We four only got out because we were closest to Master Vilmund. He fought so savagely, we didn't know how badly he'd been hurt until we managed to hole up here and he collapsed." The young Windfist's face started to crumple with grief. He looked quickly away and composed himself.

"How did you manage to break the attack, son?" Jay asked, gently.

"We didn't." Stephens sniffed as he fought to retain control of his emotions. "We had the hallway rigged to blow, like you saw. We were just hoping to take as many of them with us as we could, when suddenly an explosion happened out to the west. I think they'd attacked the Southern Federation position at the river, too, because someone was pouring Greek fire down from the sky. But then there was the explosion and everything seemed to stop. We could hear them shouting in confusion and then someone must have ordered a retreat. We haven't heard nothing from them since."

"An explosion?" Garman asked.

"Yeah, over there," Stephens answered. "Big fireball, looked like it was hovering over the river."

Chuck's head snapped up, looking first at Garman and then at Jay. The old drunk's eyes narrowed.

"Jay, you think—?"

"It's a trap," Jay said, his words falling like steel onto stone. "The airship was likely a diversion and when Quetzalith destroyed it, they realized we were here."

"And I walked right into it," Garman said. Chuck hadn't ever heard him sound that angry before.

A cough sounded from the corner and the figure on the pallet started struggling to sit up.

"Master!" Stephens said and rushed to the injured man's side. The other three Windfists, silent until now, looked at one another and slowly lowered their weapons.

"Help me . . . sit," the Master Superior Vilmund said. Stephens pressed his lips together in a line of disapproval, but he did as his Master said.

"Master, you need to save your strength," Stephens said.

"For what? I'm dead already, boy. I need to talk." He looked up and his eyes met Jay's.

"You?" the Master said, disbelief creasing the pain on his face.

"Hiya, Vil," Jay said. His voice was gentle, like when he talked to Ariel and seemed almost sad. "You look like shit."

"Should see it . . . from here . . ." the old Master said, coughing up a laugh. And a spray of blood that made Chuck's heart sink. He didn't know much about medicine, but he could tell that the old man was right. He didn't have long.

"Take it easy, Vil," Jay said. He walked over to the wounded man and took a knee beside him.

"Don't take orders . . . from you . . . anymore. Who's . . . the kid?" Vilmund asked, looking at Chuck.

"Bullet Gordon's son. I'm taking him in."

"Bullet? Why?"

"Gunslinger tried to get to them." Jay paused, placing a hand on the Master's shoulder. "He found it, Vil."

The Master Superior Windfist laughed again, a harsh, hacking sound that made more bloodstained spittle fly. Stephens pressed his lips together in a white line of misery and began easing his Master back down to the pallet.

"You have to rest now, Master," Stephens pleaded, his eyes suspiciously shiny. "Please."

"Not yet," he said. "Journeyman—come forward."

Something hard hit the outside window, causing a resounding *thud*. Chuck jumped, as did most of the rest of the others. Jasmine and a couple of the young Windfists went over to look. Chuck stayed where he was, eyes riveted to Jay's face.

"Journeyman Garman reporting as ordered, Master," Garman

said. He stepped forward and, like Jay, took a knee next to the injured man's pallet. "I have an eyes-only message from Master Munn for you."

"Save it son, won't do me much good to see it now."

"But Master," Garman said, reaching into his cloak, "my orders are to deliver this and await further instructions."

"Consider it delivered." A fit of coughing interrupted him. He fought it back and continued. "Your new orders are to go with Jay to the Bunker. Find the National Command Authority. Tell them what you saw here."

"The what? Master, I don't understand. We don't bear allegiance to any of the Territories!"

"We do, my son. The one the others came from...the United States of America."

Garman's eyes went wide and he looked at Jay, who met his gaze steadily.

"It still exists?" Garman breathed, as if he couldn't believe it to be true.

"It does, as long as there are men like us to defend it. We swore to support and defend. That's our purpose. The order's purpose."

Master Vilmund reached feebly down his leg, fingers straining toward his cargo pocket. Stephens gently opened it and guided the Master's hand inside. Vilmund sighed and nodded at Stephens, who helped him lie back down once more. In his hand, the Master Windfist held a small book bound in green cloth.

"Take this," he said. "It has the...details you need."

"I will, Master, I promise," Garman said. He took the little book reverently, tucking it inside his own cargo pocket on his thigh.

"Oh, bloody flaming hell!" Jasmine suddenly swore as another loud *thump* rattled the windows. "We're under attack!"

That got everyone's attention. Stephens leapt to his feet and started shouting orders at the other three Windfists. Each of them ran to what were clearly pre-briefed stations, their faces grim. Stephens himself opened a door in the back wall that Chuck hadn't noticed and jumped inside.

"Who's attacking?" Garman asked, as he hustled to join Jasmine at the window. "Is it the rebels again?"

"Looks like," Jasmine said. She pointed down to a mounted

man wearing a cloak that resembled Garman's. Chuck got to his feet and started walking toward the window. He was halfway there when Jay called him.

He looked over to see the old drunk leaning down, listening to the dying Windfist's whispered instructions. Jay lifted his eyes, beckoning for him with one hand.

Chuck shrugged, doing as he was bid. Jay was obviously keeping secrets, but he'd kept them alive so far with his habit of lucky blundering. Chuck was starting to suspect that was due to neither luck or blundering at all. But now was clearly not the time to discuss it.

"Get the others and find Stephens," Jay said in a low voice. Chuck nodded and turned for that back door. He realized that the reason he hadn't seen it when they first walked in was because it had been built to disappear into the wall around it. Only a faint seam betrayed its presence. He pushed on the door and it swung open to reveal a ladder going up. A creaking noise echoed down the ladder from a light-filled rectangle about eight feet up.

Chuck entered the tube and climbed the cool metal rungs as quickly as he could. The lit rectangle turned out to be a doorway that opened into a space a little smaller than the observation deck below. However, instead of having two walls of windows, this area resembled the tower back at the outpost, with a 360-degree view of the surrounding area.

Despite the wide views, the space felt pretty cramped. It also reeked of the heavy, cloying scent of burnt pitch. Chuck figured that the claustrophobia was mostly because of the massive machine squatting in the middle of the floor, on top of what looked like some kind of turntable. The machine itself resembled a crossbow but bigger than any bolt thrower Chuck had ever seen... as was the spear resting securely in the firing position. Behind the machine, Stephens frantically cranked away at a winch that seemed to be twisting the rope mechanism that, Chuck assumed, would fling the spear when released. The whole thing was damned impressive, truth be told.

"Here," Chuck said. "Let me take over. Your Master wants you downstairs."

"You know what to do?" Stephens asked, breathless.

"I'm a quick learner," Chuck replied.

"It doesn't appear complicated," Ariel said, from where she

stood by the door. Stephens jumped and nearly let go of the crank at her sudden appearance. Chuck wasn't sure why, but he felt like that would probably be a bad idea. The Windfist recovered quickly.

"Fine," he said. "Crank here until you can't, then secure the handle with this lever, here. Don't forget that or this thing will cut you in half, got it? Then turn the table to point out whichever window you want. Make sure the window's open and then hit the release lever here. Oh, and there's pitch and matches over there to light the spear heads if you want."

"This what you shot at us when we rode in?"

"Yeah. Called a 'ballista.' Pretty cool, ain't it?" the young Windfist said with the shadow of a grin.

"Yeah. You'd better go," Chuck said, moving to take the boy's place at the winch. Stephens scurried out the door and down the ladder while Chuck started cranking. Ariel walked toward the dais, her face a study in fascination as her eyes devoured the intricate mechanism of wood and metal.

As the rope twisted tighter, it got harder and harder to crank the winch. When Chuck found himself using all of his strength and all of his body weight to keep the winch handle from unwinding, he reckoned he had it good and tight. He flipped the safety lever and went to take a look outside.

A force of about a hundred men had assembled in the open area below. Chuck could see the glint of moonlight on the shiny uniform buttons they wore. About half of them were mounted and there were two wagons with covered cargoes.

"Either ammo or supplies," Chuck muttered. He shrugged and found himself wearing a small grin. This ought to be fun.

Ariel looked up and blinked, her eyes focusing back on him from the faraway stare she'd had.

"Do you want to try and hit one?" she asked.

"Seems like a good idea, don't you think?"

"I suppose it would delay them a bit. That's what we want, right?"

"You got it."

The girl stood and went to the window, her eyes narrowing in concentration. Then she looked back at the ballista.

"We need to elevate this," she said, her hair whipping as she looked from the window to the ballista and back. "Give me a second."

"Sure," Chuck said. He opened the section of window by sliding it back over its neighbor. A breeze drifted in, carrying the
sounds of horses and men. He spared a moment to hope that
Millie and their own mounts were okay before turning to the
pot of pitch sitting over a low, shielded stove.

Chuck glanced around and located a paintbrush about the
width of his hand. He took it and the pot and painted the point
of the ballista bolt. It was messy business, pitch glopping everywhere, and he felt a fair amount of urgency to move quickly.
When finished, it wasn't pretty but he got the bolt point covered.
He set the pitch pot back on the stove, grabbed the matches and
lit the point up.

A tiny blue flame raced over the spiky planes of the bolt
head, followed by a wash of heat and orange. Chuck shook the
match out, then hustled back over to the rear of the mechanism.

Ariel had been busy. Somehow, without disturbing the arming
crank or the safety latch, she'd managed to tilt the entire swiveling dais. He glanced underneath and saw that she'd tinkered
with the metal ring mechanism that sat atop the center post.

"What did you do?" Chuck asked, blinking. Would it be safe
to swivel?

"Well, I disconnected this brace here..." she started, pointing
to an attachment point under the turntable. She never finished the
sentence, though, because a rattling sound down below heralded
the presence of an automatic weapon. Chuck cursed and pulled
her down to the floor with him.

"Never mind," he said. "Let's give them something else to
think about."

Ariel nodded, rising to her hands and knees to turn the ballista
toward the window. Apparently it was not only safe to move on
its tilted angle but the turntable was also kept well oiled, turning
without sound. Chuck did his best to aim down the length of the
bolt without rising from his knees and released the launch lever.

The bolt leapt forward, arcing through the night toward the
massed forces. Cries of alarm echoed up from the enemy below,
punctuated by the scream of the horses. Chuck was just starting
to think about going to the window to see where he'd hit when
an extraordinarily loud *boom!* knocked him off his feet. He hit
the floor midway through a shower of tinkling glass, as all of the
huge observation windows shattered. Chuck covered his head with

his arms and waited for the ringing in his ears to stop, feeling the sting of a thousand tiny cuts on his exposed skin.

"What did you hit?" Stephens asked. Even muffled by the ringing, his voice cracked with excitement. Chuck looked up to see the Windfist Adeptus hurrying forward from the hatchway. Garman, Jasmine and Jay followed into the little room, making it seem even more cramped than below.

"Ariel?" Chuck called out, his voice sounding tinny and far away in his own ears. The stench of gunpowder filtered in through the window, mixing with the heavy pitch smell.

"Here, I'm all right," she said faintly.

"One of the supply wagons, I hope," Chuck said, craning his neck upward to look first at Ariel—she seemed to be all right—and then at Stephens. "What are you all doing up here?"

"Vil said there's a back way to the ground level through this room. Stephens is supposed to show us out," Jay said, his boots crunching on the glass underfoot. "So quit layin' about and let's get a move on."

Chuck gingerly put his hands down on the floor and levered himself back up to his feet, only to find Stephens looking gleefully at the destruction below. A crater now sat where the supply wagon had been but moments before. The explosion had ripped a sizable hole in the enemy force and velvet-clad bodies lay strewn in a roughly circular pattern from the central crater. As they looked, however, some of those bodies started to move and at least one of them got a shot off in the general direction of the tower. The bullet *whizz-cracked* as it passed near enough to them, breaking Stephens out of his happy trance.

"Come on, we don't have much time," the boy said, as if he hadn't just been staring out of the blown-out window. Chuck fought the urge to roll his eyes and merely reached out to help Ariel to her feet.

The way turned out to be a hidden hatch underneath one of the windows. At some point, there had clearly been equipment there, because there were still wires sticking out of the wall. The door opened onto a tiny crawlspace with a ladder. It looked barely large enough for Stephens. Chuck and Garman would have a tight fit.

"According to Master Vilmund, this used to be an access hatch to the terminal's main circuit system, whatever that means," Stephens told them as he shimmied down the ladder. "Goes all the way down to the basement. I guess there was some equipment and stuff down there before the war. The bugs destroyed this place pretty quickly in the first wave and after we took it back, the Order built the chapterhouse here."

He continued to chatter as they descended. Chuck gestured for the ladies and Jay to precede him down the narrow chute, then grinned conspiratorially at Garman.

"Your brother's a bit of a chatterbox," Chuck said. Garman looked up at him, his face somber and troubled.

"He's nervous. Downstairs his dying Master gave him a near-impossible task. He's to see us safely out of here. He's too young, though."

"Ain't we all?" Chuck asked, reaching out and clapping Garman on the shoulder. The Windfist lifted the corner of his mouth in a tiny smile, then climbed after the others down into the passageway.

Chuck took a minute trying to brush the majority of the pulverized glass from his hair and clothing. He didn't want that raining down on the others below. More shots followed the first and he could hear distant shouts as the enemy got themselves organized into a frontal assault on the main entrance to the terminal.

"Company's coming," he called softly as he lowered himself, legs first, into the chute. The toes of his boots found the metal rungs of the ladder and he began to climb downward, hoping he wouldn't kick Garman in the head.

"If they went in the front door, they're toast," Stephens called back, his voice high and crackling with forced excitement.

Garman was right, Chuck realized. The Adeptus was scared. Maybe not for himself but for his brothers and his lost Master. An ache stabbed into Chuck's chest at the thought. Poor kid. Best to keep him distracted.

"Why's that?" Chuck asked, calling down into the darkness below.

"We've got the entire main floor of the terminal covered from our observation deck. There's only the one way in—the way you came. And the whole thing is booby trapped. They may get in but we'll make 'em pay. And I'll get you out first. That's the important thing. That's the mission. Here we go, the basement entrance is just here. Stay tactical, people. We're in closer proximity to the enemy now."

A dim light filtered up from below. He could hear the whisper of boots against concrete and feel a change in the air. It felt cooler, with a touch of moisture and the faint scent of mildew hanging everywhere.

Garman tapped him on his calf. A look down told Chuck that the Windfist was clear of the ladder. He picked up his feet, sliding the rest of the way. An open doorway led into a dimly lit, vast concrete space. Here and there, he could see crates and boxes stacked in neat piles between rectangular pillars, stretching into the darkness ahead. The Order had obviously used this space for storage.

"This way," Stephens whispered, forgetting his own imposed silence, gesturing them on down a clear pathway between the pillars. He stopped at one of the boxes and flipped it open.

"These are old," he said, "but sometimes they still work." He reached inside, pulling out a handful of foil-wrapped cylinders. Jay let out a low whistle.

"Didn't think there were many of these left," the old man said, his voice barely carrying. Pa had spoken like that when they went hunting.

"Just this pallet," Stephens replied proudly. "The Masters would never let us use 'em. Said we needed to develop our dark vision...but..." For a second, grief and fear ravaged his mask of cheerful excitement.

Chuck understood. No reason to hoard supplies if this place was about to be overrun or, more likely, demolished when Master Vilmund and Stephens's remaining brothers blew the place sky high. He felt for the brave kid.

"Anything else we should take?" Garman asked.

"Whatever you want," Stephens said with a smile that didn't come close to reaching his eyes.

"Medical supplies?" Jasmine asked. "Since someone appointed me team medic, I could use a few things."

"Over there," Stephens said, pointing to a nearby group of crates marked with a red cross on a white background.

"I'll come," Jay said. "Might be medicinal liquor." He threw a broad wink at Garman, who merely snorted and followed along. Chuck and Ariel stayed with Stephens.

"What are these?" Ariel asked softly, holding out the packet that Chuck had handed her.

"Look," Stephens said. He took it from her hand and tore the foil wrapping away, revealing a slender cylinder about six inches long. He took this and bent it hard enough that Chuck heard a faint *crack*. A soft red glow began to filter through Stephens's fingers, intensifying as he shook the cylinder.

"Master Vilmund said they used these for light when the bugs attacked. They're all chemical, so they don't attract Gants." He handed it back to Ariel, who peered into it, as if she could see the light-creating mechanism inside. The red light played over her cheekbones and she looked absolutely delighted.

"Fascinating," she breathed, her lips curving in a tiny smile. Stephens smiled back. Instantly, all of Chuck's empathy for the kid disappeared.

"Come on," Chuck said. "We don't have all night. Get us to our horses so we can get out of here."

"Oh, right," Stephens said, tearing his eyes away from Ariel. He gave Chuck a guilty look. "You left 'em by the back entrance, right? It's just this way."

The kid took off down the middle of the basement again. Ariel, still fascinated by the chemlight, followed along. Chuck tried not to feel like he'd done something wrong and gestured to Garman to hurry the rest of them up.

They stopped one more time to ransack a stash of ammo cans near the exit and then Stephens led them up a short half-dozen concrete stairs to a metal door.

"Hold up, kid," Jay said as the young Windfist reached for the door handle. "There's likely to be some fellers outside. Might want to come up with a plan."

"Oh, right," Stephens said, sounding embarrassed. "Ahh... right. A plan."

"What's on the other side of this door?" Garman asked briskly.

"Um, a covered set of about six stairs, then an open walkway toward the outbuildings."

"The stairs are in a well? Concrete, like these walls?"

"Yeah."

"Okay," Garman nodded. "This is what we'll do. I'll slip out and neutralize anyone near the doors, then you guys can follow."

"Better yet," Jasmine interrupted, "I'll go. Those men? They belong to the Baron. I recognized the uniforms. They know me. Their first instinct will be to obey what I tell them to do."

"That's a terrible idea," Garman said, grimacing. "What if they shoot you?"

"They won't, because then the Baron loses Quetzalith. At most they'd try to overpower me and take me back to him."

"Oh, like that's any comfort!"

"Well," she said archly, with a mischievous grin, "I expect you'll be a gentleman and persuade them to do otherwise."

The dragon tamer gave the Journeyman a broad wink and before he or anyone else could stop her, pushed through the metal doors.

Jasmine pulled her shoulders back and lifted her chin—her customary "command" pose. She climbed the concrete steps in what she hoped was a brisk but unhurried fashion. A soft sound behind her indicated that someone (probably Garman) had followed her out in stealth.

"Gentlemen!" she shouted, in part to cover any other sounds from her companions, in part because it was her plan. "What is the situation here?"

"Who—? *Lady Moore*?" a young voice called out. Jasmine's eyes adjusted quickly to the darkness and she could make out a pair of velvet-clad soldiers turning to face her.

"Yes, of course it's me," she said, allowing carefully calculated impatience into her tone. "I need a report! What is the status of the situation on this side of the compound?"

She walked out of the concrete stairwell toward the confused pair, hoping to give her friends time to maneuver in the darkness behind her. She gestured behind the two guards, hoping to get them to turn, and was partially successful.

"We, ah, we were looking for you?" the talkative one said. He turned to look around nervously, probably trying to locate Quetzalith. "Were you...are you all right? Were you captured?"

Jasmine didn't have to answer.

Garman flowed from behind her and, clamping his hand over the man's mouth, twisted his head back. Quicker than thought, Garman drove his knife repeatedly into the base of the neck. With a spray of blood, the talkative guard was dead.

On her other side, the guard's partner stood, openmouthed, as Garman turned toward him. He recovered quickly, firing three shots before Garman's kukri took his head. It landed with a soft *thump* near her feet, mouth open in permanent surprise.

"Shit." It sounded like either Chuck or the young Windfist, Stephens.

Jasmine watched the body fold, crumpling to the ground in slow motion, blood fountaining from the stump on its shoulders.

"That could have gone better," Jay said. He grabbed Stephens by the elbow and urged him forward. "C'mon, we gotta move. Those shots will bring company."

Jasmine shook herself and stumbled forward into a lope. Garman came up alongside her, rifle in his hand.

"You okay?" He might as well have been standing still; his breathing wasn't troubled at all, either by the run or anything else that had just happened.

She had blood in her mouth. That fact suddenly intruded on the fog and hum left by the gunshots. She swiped at her lips, swallowed past a throat gone dry and focused on putting one foot in front of another.

"Yeah," she said. "I'm good."

A shadow passed over them as they ran next to the dubious cover of the terminal building. Jasmine didn't need to, but she glanced up to see Quetzalith's wings silhouetted against the blue-black sky. He circled over them, at an altitude that she hoped would keep him safe.

They rounded the corner of the building and Jasmine could see their horses clustered together. Chuck let out a low whistle—his mare lifted her head in a whinny and started toward them. The other horses left off eating the grass that had grown up around the foundation to meander in their direction as well. They'd just about gotten mounted when the platoon of twelve velvet-clad soldiers showed up.

Jasmine didn't see where they'd come from. She was midway through swinging her leg over her horse's saddle when Quetzalith attacked with a scream of rage. She looked up, horrified, to see him diving. Wings tucked close, he arrowed for a point somewhere between them and the way they'd entered the Windfist compound. She felt her stomach open up into a pit of dread as she turned to watch his strafing run.

Fire blossomed against the cool of the night as Quetzalith spat his liquid flame in a wide arc. Clearly, his goal was to engulf the entire platoon of men standing between them and the exit. A surge of triumph warred with the sick fear in her belly. She hadn't told him to attack! He must have thought that she was in danger...but he'd just exposed himself to enemy fire with that low dive.

The dragon snapped his wings open, angling them to pull out of his dive, into a climb. His wings flashed darkly in the moonlight as he reached his apex, then whipped his body around one wingtip and reentered the dive for another pass.

Screams and the scent of cooking meat drifted toward them on the night breeze. Jasmine bit her lip hard enough that she tasted blood once more.

"Not so low," she whispered. "Please, sweetling, not so low this time."

He didn't hear her. Instead, the dragon seemed almost gleeful as he exhibited his raw power once more. If anything, Quetzalith pulled out *lower* this time, whipping his head from side to side as he spat fire blasts at anyone wearing velvet and not yet aflame.

The crack of a rifle split the air. Quetzalith's glide faltered.

Jasmine was in motion without realizing that she had ever started. She kicked her horse's flanks, mercilessly urging the beast to run faster toward the fiery carnage ahead. Quetzalith let out a bellow of pain and banked toward them, losing altitude rapidly.

A bullet flew past her. She hardly noticed. Behind her, someone was shouting her name but she hardly noticed that, either. Only Quetzalith mattered. She had to get to him. She had to see what was wrong.

The dragon touched down with his hind legs, skidding and leaving deep furrows in the grass. Jasmine cried out and kicked her horse again, only to feel herself wrenched to the side, nearly toppling out of the saddle. Someone had grabbed hold of her horse's bridle, turning them away.

"NO!" she screamed. "What are you doing?"

Just then, the ground heaved beneath them, causing their horses to shy. The sky split open on a roar of sound and a blinding flash, a hot wind flattening the grass all around them. The top half of the terminal building disappeared in smoke and flames.

The Windfists had sprung their trap.

Behind her, Quetzalith let out another bellow and took off again. She swiveled around to try to watch him. His wingbeats weren't steady. Something was wrong.

"Jasmine!" Garman said, still holding her bridle. "We have to go! There will be more troops coming!"

"But he's hurt!" she cried. Her eyes burned with anger, hot tears streaking down her cheeks, turning icy in the night wind.

"He's flying! He'll be okay. Come on, we've got to get out of here!"

She twisted and turned in the saddle, trying to follow Quetzalith's shape against the sky. A wisp of cloud covered the moon for a moment and he was gone. She let out a sob and slumped in her seat. A sense of helplessness flooded through her, feeding the tears that streamed down her face.

Garman looked back at Jasmine, worried. She hadn't moved since he'd gotten her horse pointed toward the exit and the rest of the group. He knew she was concerned about Quetzalith, but the dragon had taken off again, so his injury couldn't be that bad, right?

Plus, they had other things going on at the moment. The six of them were riding hell-for-leather toward the perimeter gate they'd used earlier. Even Chuck's mare Millie was running flat out, carrying two riders. Ariel sat behind Chuck, Stephens riding her gelding. Every now and then, the wind brought them the sound of shouts. Someone was after them, either the surviving members of the platoon that Quetzalith had attacked, or another group.

Their only hope, as he saw it, was to get lost in the old city beyond. Garman just hoped that the dragon had given them enough of a head start.

When they reached the gate, Stephens reined in and slid down with a grimace. He kept one hand pressed to his belly. With the other, he swung the gate open, then led the horse back over toward Millie.

"Here you go, ma'am," he said, offering Ariel the reins. "You'll be needing your mount again."

"Brother!" Garman said. "What are you doing? We don't have time for this!"

Stephens looked up at Garman. He slowly removed his hand from his abdomen, revealing the blood-soaked evidence of a gut wound. The sickly-sweet stench of a perforated intestine rose in the air between them. Despair hit the Journeyman Windfist like a blunt object to the head. That was not survivable.

"You're right," Stephens said, voice calm, hands steady as he reached up to help Ariel slide down. "You don't have time. You guys get through the gate and I'll hold them here as long as I can to buy you time. The ruins of the old city are a warren just a block or two east of here. That's your best bet."

Garman swallowed hard, then nodded. Ariel looked at Chuck, who gestured to her to mount up.

"Right," he said. "Jay, you take point."

The old drunk nodded, lifting his right hand to his eyebrow as he nudged his horse forward. Stephens looked startled but copied the gesture. Garman felt tears threatening to close his throat and he swallowed hard.

"You're a good kid," Jay said as he lowered his hand. Then he did something truly extraordinary. He leaned over in his saddle until he could touch Stephens's blood-covered hand. Then, using the Adept's own blood, he added the Journeyman's half-barb to Stephens's tattoo.

"Godspeed, Journeyman Stephens," Jay said. Then with a "Ya!" the old man kicked his horse into motion through the open gate.

Garman stared after Jay, then looked to Stephens, who regarded him with a faint smile.

"Guess your Master never told you about him, huh?" Stephens asked. Before Garman could answer, the...Journeyman?...slapped his horse's rump and he was following the others out into the ruined streets of Old Kansas City.

After a moment, he heard more shouts, followed by more gunshots behind them. Then there was nothing at all.

CHAPTER TWELVE

HOOVES POUNDED ON THE TURF. ARIEL HOPED FERVENTLY THAT the horses would not come up lame on the treacherous, asphalt-strewn ground.

"This way," Jay called. "Stick close to the river. I got an idea." Somehow, even after everything, the old drunk still sounded cheerful.

Chuck steered Millie to follow Jay's horse, helping Ariel with her mount. They ended up picking their way through the deserted ruins that used to be the east end of town.

"How's ol' Q doin'?" Jay asked at one point.

"He's hurt, that's all I know," Jasmine said, her voice tight and clipped with worry.

"How long will he stay aloft?"

"Until he can't, if I don't call him down first. If he wasn't injured"—she took a deep breath— "he could soar for days."

"It's gonna be okay, girl," Jay said gently. "I got a plan."

"Plan? What plan?" Garman spat as he edged past her to the front of the group and pulled his horse to a halt. "All we're doing is running scared! We should—"

"What? Turn and fight? You got a mission, Windfist, remember? Don't make your brothers' sacrifice worthless."

For a split second, Ariel thought he saw a glint of steely anger in Jay's eyes. Then he blinked and the cheerful drunk was back.

"Trust me, Junior," Jay said. He reached out and patted

219

Garman's cheek—right on the Windfist tattoo. Then he winked and reached into his jacket for his flask.

"Why should I?" Garman shot back, jerking away. He nearly caused his horse to shy. "And what was that with Stephens's tattoo?"

"Have I misled you yet?" Jay lifted his flask in Garman's direction, clearly choosing to ignore the rest of the question. Garman answered with a muttered growl but he otherwise let off. The whole group started moving along again.

By the time they got free of the city, the sun had crept over the horizon. A thick fog squatted over the river, making it so Ariel could barely see past the hind end of the horse in front of her. Behind her, she heard Chuck ask Jasmine if Quetzalith would be able to find them.

"He'll find me," Jasmine said. Though her face still creased with worry, her tone was all rock-solid confidence. "He always does. If he can fly, he'll find me."

Before anyone could say anything, a deep, bellowing note sounded through the fog. It made Ariel jump, which made her horse shift nervously under her.

"Perfect," Jay said. "Couldn't have planned it better if I'd tried. Our ride is here!"

Another deep note billowed out, the fog in front of them swirling. It parted as a gray behemoth resolved out of the mist. Another long, low blast sounded as it glided toward the bank.

Jay dismounted, Ariel and Jasmine following suit. The old drunk had a grin the size of his entire face and he was nearly dancing with excitement.

"I knew I remembered right! Give it a minute, kids, they'll lower the gangplank and send out the welcome wagon. Chuck, we're gonna need some money."

Maybe it was the fog, but Ariel felt like she had stepped into a surreal dreamworld as the boat did exactly that. It drifted to a stop next to a jut of the bank where someone had once built a kind of dock. A hatch appeared in the side; a long metal tongue clanked and creaked as it slowly extended out to the rotting wood.

Another moment of eerie stillness, then a booming voice greeted them.

"Well, hell! Goes to show what I know. I didn't imagine we'd have paying customers at all with this damn fog! And here you lot are!" A pause. "You are paying customers, aren't you?"

A figure emerged from within the boat and began to walk toward them. Ariel could not help but gape. The man was *huge*. Tall, broad, shaved completely bald, with a beard that, while long and full, was obviously neatly trimmed and cared for. He walked down the plank like a man stepping out of his own castle, his teeth flashing white in a grin as he looked at them.

A grin which turned slightly suspicious as he saw the small black man leading them.

"Mother*trucker*. Jay, you son of a whore. You intend to pay for your passage this time?"

"Sure thing, Bun," Jay said with his usual cheeky grin. He waved Chuck forward. Chuck sighed, grabbed his money stash and approached.

"Chuck, this is my good friend, Jack. Or Bun-bun. Bun, this is my good friend Chuck. He likes to pay for things."

"How much?" Chuck asked.

"Where you goin?" Jack/Bun-bun countered.

"Pittsburgh," Jay said. "You guys still make that run?"

Jack pursed his lips and considered.

"Could be," the big man said. "You and these horses?"

"And another passenger to join us later . . . probably."

Both of Jack's eyebrows climbed halfway up the shiny dome of his head at that.

"A latecomer? Huh. Okay. Be about ten days. You ready to leave?"

"The sooner the better!" Jay said.

"How much?" Chuck asked again. He sounded slightly testy. Probably due to his question being diverted.

"What kinda money you got?"

"Ogden."

"Huh. Nice. Ten silvers each, for the whole trip. Berths and food included. Liquor you gotta buy at my bar. Or drink your own, I don't care. When's your other friend joining us?"

"Unclear. He's out and about just now," Jay said evasively.

"Fine. Long as he can get a boat out to us or swim or whatever."

"Fair enough, we'll take it!" Jay's voice dropped slightly. "You ain't gonna wreck this one, are ya?"

Jack grunted.

Jay clapped him on his massive shoulder and gestured expansively at Chuck as if to say "Pay the man!"

Chuck scowled at the old drunk, muttering something about booking passage on a damn cruise liner. Jay gestured again. Chuck shrugged then counted out the silver pieces. All of them fit easily in Jack's massive hands.

"All right then," the big man said jovially. "Now that we're all friends, welcome aboard the *Long Tall Sally*."

"Not me," Jasmine said in that same, empty voice. "I'll wait here for Quetzalith."

Heads swiveled in her direction.

"Jasmine, you can't," Garman said, finding his voice first. "Ronen and the others are looking for us. They'll find you and you won't stand a chance alone."

"I can't leave without him," she said.

"But you said he would find you through anything," Chuck said. "We can't just leave you, ma'am. We made a deal."

"I absolve you of the deal. I'm not leaving without Quetzalith. He's hurt, and I don't know if he'll be able to track me on the river. You guys go on. I'll hide or something if the Baron's men get close."

"That doesn't make any sense!" Garman shouted, causing Jay, Ariel, and Chuck to all make shushing noises. "How will the beast find you if you're hiding? I know you'll be so concerned with him that you'll find the highest point and make a damn *target* of yourself! It's like you *want* to be captured. Is that it? Do you want to go back to your old lover, the Baron?"

Ariel sucked in a breath of air, her eyes flicking from Garman's white-faced fury to Jasmine's dead-eyed stare. She hadn't forgotten how casually and matter-of-factly the older woman had related the horrors she'd suffered in the Baron's custody. Ariel would have expected Jasmine to explode with anger and lash her barbed tongue up one side of Garman and down the other for saying that, but she just blinked and looked away.

"Think that if you want," the dragon trainer said. "I'm not leaving without my dragon."

"But you said he'd find you!" Garman cried, heedless once more of the noise.

"He always has," Jasmine said. "And he will again. But he's hurt, and I can't take the chance that he won't be able to keep up with the riverboat."

"Jasmine—" Garman said again. He surged toward her, his

face twisted in anguish. He wrapped his hands around her biceps and froze, staring into her uncaring eyes. Ariel opened her mouth, though she had no idea what she would have said, when suddenly it struck her.

Garman cared for Jasmine.

It was the only thing that made sense. Why else would he argue so hard against her leaving the group, when earlier he'd addressed her with suspicion and distrust. Confusion bubbled up in Ariel's brain. She wasn't used to dealing with human emotions like this. What was she supposed to do? Jasmine didn't seem to be able to function without Quetzalith, but at the same time, could she urge Garman to abandon the woman he so clearly cared about?

And all the while, the skin between her shoulder blades itched, as if someone or something were waiting in the fog to pounce and destroy them all.

"Jay," she whispered to the wizened black man beside her. "I think we should get going."

"Damn straight," he muttered, taking a pull on his flask. Then he turned, gave her a wink, and put the flask back inside his battered jacket.

"What's it going to be, Jay?" the big riverman asked.

"All of us," Jay said, walking toward Garman and Jasmine where they stood locked in their contest of wills. "Come on, children. It's time to go."

"I'm not—" Jasmine started to say.

"Yes, dear girl, you are. Junior's right about the Baron's men. They won't treat you kindly. And Quetzalith can fly for days. He'll find you. Chuck?"

"Yes, sir?" Chuck asked, stepping forward. Ariel could see an echo of her own confusion and misery on his face.

"Get her legs. Garman, hang on tight. Jasmine, it's time to go."

"No!" she screamed, and started to kick as Garman hauled her in close to his body. She thrashed and writhed, trying anything she could to fight her way free. She arced backward away from Garman and then rammed her head into his chest, causing him to cough. He held doggedly on as she kicked out, catching Chuck in the jaw and sending him reeling backward onto his butt.

She let out a scream and whipped her head forward again, closing her teeth about the ridge of Garman's collarbone. The

Windfist howled, but he tightened his arms around her body and just hung on until Chuck could get back to his feet.

"No!" Jasmine screamed again, her voice wild and raw. "I won't! I won't! You can't make me love you!"

Jay's face went pale, and he met Garman's startled look.

"Bloody hell," the old man said. "Just...shit. Just hang on—"

Another scream rent the night around them. The fog suddenly swirled in a weird eddy as a huge shape loomed overhead. A blast of flame cut through the wetness of the fog and startled Garman to the point that Jasmine was able to break free of his grasp. She took off running as Quetzalith back-winged to land heavily beside the riverbank.

"Thank all the saints," Garman whispered. "But—"

"Yeah," Jay said.

"Is that a dragon?" Jack asked, causing the men and Ariel to swivel their attention back to him. "Don't tell me that's your 'additional guest.'"

"Uh, yessir, actually," Chuck said. "He's Jasmine's, and she didn't want to leave him."

"Huh. Well, I've hauled weirder cargo. He can have the top deck, out of the way of my crew. He'll have to hunt for himself, though. I don't keep livestock on board."

"We'll take care of it," Jay said. "Let's just get them on board before she changes her mind."

"I don't normally hold with abducting young women onto my riverboat, Jay," Jack said, his tone darkening.

"I know," Jay said. "But trust me, she'd rather be with us than here when the Baron's men arrive. She ran from him once."

"Did she now? Tough chick. Fair enough. But she sleeps with the other girl, and if she wants off at the next stop, she gets off."

"Deal."

"Then welcome aboard once more."

Chuck wasn't wrong about the boat. As they made their way aboard, Jack described the *Long Tall Sally* in expansive terms as a "luxury river cruiser." And it certainly *looked* plush. Even the stable stalls below decks were sparkling clean. The smell of new, freshly mown hay filled the space. It was enough to help calm the horses, who weren't super enthusiastic about getting on a boat in the first place.

"The *Sally* is a throwback, y'all understand," Jack said, gesturing to a bronze plaque on one of the bulkheads. "She was active on the Mississippi as a floating hotel and casino right up until the Bug War. We had to make a few adjustments once we lost electrical, but thanks to our ingenious boiler-room mechanic, we've got hot and cold running water for your suites and our full kitchen. My chef would have my skin if it were otherwise.

"I've a groom to come see to the horses daily," Jack went on. "But you're welcome down here at any time, of course. Horses seem to do better when their people visit often. We'll keep your lot stabled close to one another. I gather you've been traveling together a bit?"

"A bit," Chuck said, reluctant to say too much too fast. He still wasn't sure how much he could trust this giant of a man, but he had to admit that the stabling situation scored points in his book.

"Cool. Once you get your mounts settled, head back up the ladder and I'll meet you on the deck above," Jack said. He left with a friendly wink at Ariel and a clap on Jay's shoulder.

"Boy's a bit skittish just now," Chuck heard Jay say.

"No problem. Not my business," Jack replied. He didn't seem to have any heartburn with it. Chuck reluctantly added to the mental pile of points in the big man's favor.

"C'mon, Millie," he murmured to his tired mare. "Let's get you brushed and fed."

The group of them cared for their horses, mostly in silence. Chuck could feel exhaustion pulling at the edges of his mind, making his hands and feet slow. He tried to concentrate on one thing at a time—focusing on the brush patterns in Millie's coat as he combed her, listening to the tinkle of grain as he poured it into her feed bucket—It just seemed easier to do that than to think about the larger questions that loomed ahead, or the pain they'd left behind.

Eventually, he ran out of chores, noticing that he alone remained belowdecks. He looked up and gave Millie's nose one more pat.

"Enjoy your grain," he told the mare. "You've earned it. Now I suppose I'd better go try to see to the rest of the crew. I wish they were as easy to please as you, though."

Millie eyed him as she munched away, her expression enough to make Chuck snort a laugh. Clearly, she thought he was an idiot for wishing such a thing. Millie was a horse; his other friends were people. People were always harder to please than horses. That was just the way of the world.

Feeling marginally better, Chuck eased out of Millie's stall and down the narrow passageway to the ladder. He found Jack waiting for him at the top.

"You take good care of your horse, kid," Jack said. "You raise her?"

"Kinda, yeah," Chuck said.

"I can respect that," he said, stroking his beard. "See, some men see horses like another tool, like a gun or a knife. They only give as much care as needed to keep the tool functional. Some see them more like a dog, a loyal companion. Which a good horse can be, for sure. But some men hide in taking care of their horses. They lavish more affection on them than they would a woman. They worry and fret over it. Hell, the only animal I know that's more self-sufficient than a horse is a cat, but not for these men. They'll neglect all of their human relationships in favor of their damn horse. Me? I never saw the sense in that, considering it's an animal apt to bite or kick me at the first opportunity."

"Millie wouldn't bite or kick me, sir," Chuck said, not sure whether he was being insulted or not. "She's a good horse who just carried me through a warzone without flinching."

"So she's a battle buddy. I can respect that, too." A small smile curved his beard. "Just remember, she's not the only one you have."

He stood to the side, gesturing for Chuck to precede him. Not that there was much room to get past the giant in the narrow ship's passageway.

"Now, your cabin is there on the left. You're sharing with Jay and the other guy. The ladies are up one deck. They get a better room because, well, they're ladies."

Chuck nodded. That made perfect sense.

"Dinner's one more deck above them, once you're ready. Don't come into my fine dining establishment stinking of gunpowder and sweat. Understand?" He winked. "We've got fine clientele on this ship and we mean to keep it that way."

"Yes, sir." Despite everything, Chuck felt a tiny bubble of amusement well up within him. Though huge and intimidating, this giant clearly had a sense of humor. Maybe it was just reaction but he found himself chuckling.

"Right," Jack said. "I'll see you later. Try to keep Jay under control, too. And remind him that I toss card cheats overboard. Have a pleasant trip!"

With that, he turned and made his way nimbly up the ladder. Chuck wouldn't have expected such a big guy to be able to move with such ease but Jack was obviously all about defying expectations.

Chuck walked down the hall and entered his room.

He'd barely gotten his clothes off before falling into bed. Not even the reek of smoke, sweat and whatever he'd rolled in had kept him awake. Only the sound of the ship's horn—hours later, judging by the sun—had gotten through his exhaustion.

Remembering Jack's comment about appearance, he filled the small clawfoot tub, climbing in with a sigh. Almost immediately, the water turned gray with caked-on grime and trail dust. He felt a bit guilty about draining the tub and refilling it, until he remembered the price.

"For ten silver, I'm taking as many baths as I please, dammit."

He stayed in until the water grew cold, dried off and put on clean clothes. His stomach reminded him about dinner.

Though the stables had been nice and his room more than adequate, Chuck found out what "luxury river cruiser" really meant when he joined the others in the dining room.

The highly polished wood floor gleamed in the light from shiny brass wall sconces. At least a score of round tables draped in spotless white tablecloths stood in a rough semi-circle off to the left. They faced what looked like a raised stage covered by a curtain of blue velvet. To the right, Jack himself stood behind a long wooden bar, polished to that same glowing gleam as the floor. Pretty women scurried back and forth from the bar to the tables and occasionally emerged from a swinging door opposite that Chuck guessed led to the kitchen. Each of them wore a uniform: short skirt, stockings with the line up the back of the leg, a jacket that looked like a cut down, feminized version of a man's formal coat and a tiny round hat perched upon their piled-up hair.

Chuck couldn't help but take a good long look. He didn't know if any of these ladies was named Sally but he didn't imagine it was much of a stretch. They certainly *seemed* long and tall.

"Chuck!" Jay called, waving his hands from the bar. "Come on over here and have a drink! Ol' Bun here was just telling us about this new singing act he's got on board. Really classes up the joint, does it, Bun?"

"I'll let you judge," Jack said, a hint of a smile curving his lips.

"Where are the others?" Chuck asked as he approached.

"Ladies ain't here yet. Jack's got 'em in a berth with a heated shower. I'm betting they're getting clean."

"And dressed," Jack added. "I took the liberty of having some gowns hung in their closet as a loan. I thought it might help them feel comfortable in fine company."

"You thought of that?" Jay asked, raising his eyebrows.

"What? Hard to believe? You know I'm a detail man, Jay. Details are what matter in this business. Besides. Tay never wears a gown twice to perform. We've got gowns coming out of our ears. Good thing she brought her own seamstress."

"Gentlemen," Garman said as he walked up. Chuck looked over at his companion and did a double take. Instead of the usual dark-colored pants and vest, both with multiple pockets, the Windfist had donned some kind of more formal uniform.

The neatly pressed pants were a similar shade of dark blue as his standard pair, different in that they had a bright red stripe running up the legs. Also neatly pressed, Garman's light-brown shirt collar rode high at his neck, accented with a dark green necktie.

Over this, he wore a dark green suit jacket that reminded Chuck of the soldier at the bridge. Garman's hadn't been worn as often, that much was obvious. The OKC sergeant's jacket had been dirty, worn and patched; Garman's looked brand new. Shiny brass buttons held it tight over his chest, leading down to a wide leather belt. The patch on his left shoulder was the same as the one on his standard vest—his chapterhouse design, only larger. A small copper pin shaped like a pitchfork sat high on the wide lapels.

His boots appeared to be the same pair he normally wore, only now polished to a bright shine. Chuck figured he could see his face in them if he got close enough. Even his wide-brimmed hat was clean and brushed.

Bet anything he's got knives and guns under that jacket.

"Where you been, Junior?" Jay asked as he lifted his drink to his lips one more time. "And what's with the fancy clothes?"

Jay, of course, looked as disreputable as always, leather jacket and all. Since he'd left home without his Sunday best, Chuck had put on what he had, a mostly clean shirt and jeans. As a result, he looked about the same as usual.

He felt very underdressed.

"Your friend here said this was a luxury dinner. I figured a little formality couldn't hurt," Garman said with a smile.

"You look good, Windfist," Jack said with a rumble of approval in his voice. "But you're printing on your right hip. You want to adjust that? Some of my clientele get nervous when they think violent men are in their midst."

"They don't know you too well, do they, Bun?" Jay asked with a hiccup.

"Perhaps not, but that never stopped me from taking a man's money. His delusions aren't my problem. Drink, Windfist?"

"Beer. Thanks," Garman said.

Before Jack could deliver the beverage, the Windfist held up a hand as his gaze locked on something near the door.

Chuck, too, looked up and felt his mouth gape open. Ariel and Jasmine had entered the room. He'd never seen either of them looking the way they looked right then. Beside him, Jay let out a low whistle.

Jasmine caught sight of them, glancing back to say something to Ariel before leading the way to the bar. The dragon tamer wore some kind of slinky, dark-blue sparkly fabric that covered her shoulders, leaving her arms bare. It also had a deeply plunging neckline that revealed a pendant nestled between her breasts, just below her tattoo. The dress hugged her tightly from collarbone to hips, then swirled and flared out to just brush against the toes of her silver shoes. She gave them a small nod as she approached, but her red-rimmed eyes still seemed empty.

But Chuck couldn't focus on that right away; he was already busy staring at Ariel.

Unlike Jasmine's dress (which, he learned, plunged to her waist in the back, leaving the long slope of her spine bare), Ariel's had a high neckline and long sleeves. It was silver in color and like Jasmine's, it sparkled in the light of the room. Unlike Jasmine's, Ariel's dress ended several inches above her knees, revealing a set of long, sleekly muscular legs, encased in some kind of black, closely woven tights. On her feet, she wore a pair of black boots that stretched to her knee, featuring a heel that only accentuated the lean curves of her calves.

"Try champagne," Jack said, his voice filtering through the sudden roaring in Chuck's ears and recalling him to himself. Well, that and the way that Jay reached out and pushed his mouth closed hard enough to make his teeth clack together.

"Champagne?" Garman asked, sounding as poleaxed as Chuck himself felt.

"Champagne. Offer some to the ladies. They'll like it. You're welcome," Jack said, pushing forward five delicate-looking fluted glasses. Garman blinked furiously, then took two. Chuck followed suit. Jay grinned at them both and took the last one before downing the contents.

"Champagne?" Ariel asked as she and Jasmine joined the three men. Some kind of fragrance—sweet, a little spicy and warm—wound through the air teasing at Chuck's senses. "What is that?"

Chuck blinked hard and thrust one of his flutes toward Ariel, nearly sloshing the bubbling liquid out of the glass.

"For you," he said roughly.

"Is it good?" Ariel asked quietly.

"It's beautiful," Chuck said. "Uh...I mean. Yes. It is. I mean, I think so. I've never tried it."

Ariel brought the glass to her nose to give it a sniff. She scrunched her face up as the bubbles tickled.

"It's very bubbly," she said, her voice doubtful.

"Jack said that you'd like it," Chuck admitted. If she didn't like it, he didn't want her to think it had been his idea.

That got a smile out of her. She cut her eyes to the bar, where Jack stood polishing a glass and watching their group's various interactions. The big man gave her a wink and she lifted the glass toward him, smiling, as if to say thanks.

Her smile lit up her entire face and Chuck felt envy and gratitude tangling inside him. Gratitude toward Jack for getting her to smile. Envy because he hadn't been able to do the same.

"He's a very nice man," Ariel said. "He left me this dress to borrow. I'm glad he did; I did not have any other clothes."

"I'm glad he did, too," Chuck said, before he could stop himself. *That* got her attention back on him. She looked puzzled, though, as if she couldn't figure out why he cared about such a thing.

"Wanna try it together?" he asked, trying to forestall any of her super-awkward questions.

"All right," she said. Chuck gave her a smile that he hoped was debonair and tapped his glass lightly against hers.

At least, that was what meant to do.

In reality, he hit her glass just a little too hard. Instead of a light, airy *clink*, he produced a crashing sound that made him think that perhaps he'd shattered the glass entirely. Which would, he was certain, not only be his luck but would also cause the excruciatingly large and intimidating Jack to look unfavorably upon his behavior.

Not a good option.

"What did you do that for?" Ariel asked, her eyebrows drawing together in further puzzlement.

"I...ah...I think it's tradition," he said.

She shrugged.

"All right," she said again, lifting the glass to her lips. Chuck took his own drink, unable to tear his eyes from her full-lipped mouth. Would she like it? Would she smile again? Would...

The gas lamps in the dining room dimmed, brightened, then dimmed again. Chuck glanced around to see uniformed staff stationed beside the wall sconces, performing a choreographed dance of covering each lamp with a shade, then uncovering it, then fixing it back into place. Somewhere, a set of chimes sounded out five notes and the dull roar of conversation stilled.

"Ladies and gentlemen," Jack's voice filled the room. "Please make your way to your tables for the dinner and entertainment portion of the evening!"

Before he could overthink it and mess it up, Chuck quickly offered his arm to Ariel. She stared at it for a moment before glancing over at Jasmine. The dragon tamer had wound her own arm through Garman's and this seemed to give Ariel the clue she needed. She tentatively laid her fingertips on Chuck's sleeve and he felt a surge of warmth flow through him.

"Did you like it? The champagne?" he asked quietly, steering them through the crowd after Jay. Apparently, the old man knew which table they'd been assigned, for he wove his way up to one right next to the stage. Chuck led Ariel to her seat before taking his own.

And immediately began mentally kicking himself for not pulling her chair out, as Garman did for Jasmine. He stared down at his plate, wondering if he should say something, when Jay called out a hello to the leggy serving girl handing out baskets of rolls.

"It was strange," Ariel said. "It felt a little...well. I'm not sure."

Chuck didn't really have time to react to this odd statement even if he'd wanted to, because their dinner was suddenly served. The fare seemed simple enough but after weeks of trail rations and Jay's cooking, it smelled delicious. He tucked into his food and didn't register anything else for a while.

"Mind if I join you for the show?" Jack asked several minutes later. He had approached the table as the servers began clearing the used plates and utensils. Someone put a steaming carafe down in front of Chuck, the warm scent of coffee reaching out to him. Without waiting for permission, Jack sat down next to Jay and reached for the carafe.

"Show?" Garman asked. "Did you hear that, Jasmine? There's a show."

Jasmine looked up from her plate, her eyes dull. She hadn't eaten anything.

"Would you like your meal wrapped up for you?" one of the serving women asked Jasmine.

"Yes," Garman said, just as Jasmine shook her head in the negative. The dragon tamer frowned up at him.

"You have to eat something," the Windfist said, dropping his voice. Judging by the expression on the faces around the table, they all heard him anyway.

Jasmine pursed her lips as if she would argue, then she shrugged, letting the matter drop. The server nodded, whisking the plate away without another word. Chuck looked over at Jay. That wasn't like Jasmine at all. He thought about asking what was wrong but he was pretty sure he knew. They hadn't talked since Quetzalith had returned to them so suddenly on the riverbank. The dragon had been badly enough injured that Jasmine had spent all of her time and energy since boarding in nursing him. At no point had they talked about her fighting them, or her outburst during the struggle.

The lights pulsed again, then dimmed even further, casting the dining area into darkness. Next to them, the curtain on the stage rose, revealing a man sitting at a drum set, illuminated by a spotlight. He began to play a hard, driving rhythm, stilling all conversation and bringing everyone's attention to the stage. The tinkling notes of a piano joined in as another light came up to reveal a man sitting at a small piano. Next came the violinist, a woman wearing all black, followed by a man with an upright bass. She wove a quick, spiky little melody through the bass line and the drum beats. The whole thing built into a quickening, almost frenzied climax...

Then stilled. The lamps went out.

A single breathy note rang through the darkness, cutting through the hanging silence. Slowly, the stage lights came up and the band began to play once more. This time, a singer joined them on stage. She was tall and thin, gowned in a red sheath that seemed to glow in the footlights. Her lips matched her dress exactly and her blue eyes and platinum blonde hair shone as she belted out her song.

> Well it's a dark, cold world
> People hard as chitin
> Between the steam and the fear
> The truth becomes clear
> No one is coming
> We're on our own here.
>
> So pass me a mag
> And pour another round
> We'll make it out alive
> Or we'll burn it to the ground
>
> I know the curve of your face
> The hot slide of your skin
> I know the taste of your laugh
> At this crazy mess that we're in
> Because no one is coming
> We're on our own here
>
> So pass me a mag
> And pour another round
> We'll make it out alive
> Or we'll burn it to the ground

The violinist stepped in, playing more of the dizzying melody. Chuck drew in a breath, feeling his pulse accelerate in time with the music. He glanced around and found the faces of his friends rapt. They, too, seemed lost in the music.

> *And maybe I'll lose your love*
> *Like I've lost all the rest*
> *And maybe you'll run from me*
> *And say it's for the best*
> *But no one is coming*
> *You'll be on your own here*
>
> *So pass me a mag*
> *And pour another round*
> *You'll make it out alive*
> *Then I'll burn it to the ground*
>
> *Yeah, baby pass me a mag*
> *And pour another round*
> *I'll get you out alive*
> *Then I'll burn it to the ground*
> *Yeah, I'll burn it to the ground!*

Once more, the violin climbed, supported by the throbbing bass line and the haunting piano melody. The drums drove onward, pushing everything to its inevitable conclusion. Chuck felt tears in his eyes and a tightness in his chest as the instruments faded into silence and the lights dimmed once more.

Then just when he thought it was over as the darkness became complete, the singer let out another breathy murmur:

> *Cause no one is coming*
> *I'm on my own here.*

A pause, like a collective indrawn breath, and then the entirety of the dining room erupted into applause and cheers. The lights flashed back up, the singer smiling before them all.

"Thank you," she said. "And welcome aboard the *Long Tall Sally*! My name is Taylor and we are the River Runners Band."

With that, the band launched into another song Chuck didn't recognize. This one wasn't nearly as gut-wrenching, though. It had more of a fun, playful feel.

Across the table, Jack sat back in his chair, laughing. Chuck thought he saw the gleam of wetness in the big man's eye but he wasn't going to say anything.

"Girl's good, isn't she?" Jack asked.

"Damn straight," Jay said, his voice carrying a note of awe. "Who is she?"

"Taylor? She's my steam mechanic's daughter. Hell of a singer. Great girl, too. She'll come down to the bar after her set. I'll introduce you, if you like."

"I most certainly would like," Jay said eagerly. Jack's face stilled, then he drew his eyebrows together in a frown.

"Jay," he said softly. "She's a lady."

"Of course she is..." Jay started, then paused, looking more closely at his friend.

"Oh," he said, all trace of drunkenness gone from his tone. "It's like that?"

Jack paled, looked away, then pushed to his feet and walked back to the bar without another word.

"Well, I'll be a Gant queen. I never expected *that*," Jay said.

"What?" Garman asked. "What just happened?"

"Didn't you see him?" Jasmine said, speaking up for the first time since they'd sat down. She sounded soft, subdued and very sad. "He's in love with her."

"With the *singer*? She has to be half his age!"

"That's probably why he doesn't want to talk about it," she said, tiredly. She pushed her chair back and got to her feet. "I find I'm not much for company tonight either. Good night, everyone."

"I'll walk you to your room," Garman said, getting to his feet. Once again, when Chuck would have expected her to deliver one of her tart set-downs, she merely shrugged and turned to go. Apparently, it didn't matter much one way or the other to her. Garman offered his arm once again but either she didn't see it, or she didn't care, because she just walked back toward the ladder leading below decks.

"She is not feeling well," Ariel said softly. Chuck looked up to find the former cultist watching him watch the dragon tamer leave. "She is...very upset about the way you and Garman fought with her. She knows it was necessary, but it brought back bad memories. And she worries for Quetzalith."

"I know," Chuck said.

"Is it because she raised him from an egg?" Ariel asked, tilting her head to the side in curiosity.

"I think that's part of it," Chuck said. "But more than that, Jasmine's been through some bad stuff. She loves him."

"Love," Ariel said. Slowly, as if tasting the word. "Love is what you feel when you wish to mate, yes? The reproductive urge?"

Chuck swallowed hard. And immediately began coughing as he choked on air. On his other side, Jay let out a cackle and pounded him between the shoulder blades.

"Not quite, girlie," Jay said. "That's part of it, sometimes, but really that's just lust. And lust is a mighty fine thing...but love is better."

Looking slightly relieved, she leaned forward to look past Chuck at Jay.

"So she doesn't feel that lust for the dragon? That is good to know. That seems...wrong somehow."

Jay cackled again and Chuck wished he could be anywhere else. In fact, he started looking around for possible avenues of escape, only to catch sight of the big bartender, Jack.

He stood, arms crossed over his chest, looking like a man deep in the throes of religion. His wet eyes stared at the singer with a look of heartfelt longing edged with sorrow.

"So what is it, then?"

Chuck turned his attention back to Ariel. Her big blue eyes looked intently at him, as if it were extremely important that he give her an answer.

"I...I don't..."

"The kid here ain't never loved anyone but his family," Jay said, coming to Chuck's rescue. "See, that's the thing. Love happens in a buncha different ways. Jack loves Taylor because she's beautiful and talented and I'm betting because she has a personality that fits with his own. At least, I hope so. Jasmine loves Quetzalith because she raised him like a mother and because, like Chuck said, the two of them have been through a lot together."

"Do mothers love their children?" Ariel asked. Her brow creased as if she turned this thought over in her head.

"They ought to," Chuck said. Something clenched inside his chest as he realized that she wasn't being sarcastic. She really didn't know a mother's love. "A real mother fights to the death to protect her children from harm."

"Or teaches them how to handle the harm that's unavoidable," Jay added with a little shrug. "Or does her best to do those two things. Not everyone's as tough as your ma, boy."

Before Chuck could respond to that, the music ended with a flourish. Taylor's clear, high voice cut through the applause that followed.

"Thank you, everyone. We're going to take a short break before our next set. In the meantime, enjoy dessert!"

The lights on the stage dimmed and the lights of the rest of the dining room brightened. The serving girls began to circulate once again, carrying trays of delicate concoctions that almost looked too pretty to eat.

"C'mon, you two," Jay said. "Let's go to the bar. I want to meet this girl."

The old man pushed out of his chair and then stumbled as he nearly ran into one of the servers.

"Excuse me, please!" the young woman said, deftly sidestepping. She managed to keep her laden dessert tray level and unspilled but Chuck noticed that Jay's hand whipped out and snagged one of the small bowls from atop its surface.

"Oh, no, m'dear. Excuse me!" the old man said, touching the brim of his imaginary hat. "Unpardn'ble of me, getting in your way like that. My momma's rollin' in her grave!"

The server gave a startled little laugh and then moved on along her route. Jay smirked after her for a moment, waggled his eyebrows at his two young companions, then grabbed a spoon from the table and took a bite of whatever it was he'd grabbed. Chuck shook his head and got to his feet before pulling Ariel's chair out for her. This time, at least, he'd remembered.

"How can his mother be rolling if she's dead?" Ariel wanted to know. She placed her hand into Chuck's outstretched one and allowed him to help her to her feet. "That doesn't make any sense."

"It's just an expression," he said. "It means she'd be scandalized or somesuch. He was just teasin' the waitress. Probably so he could get away with stealing the dessert."

"Did he steal it? I thought food was included in our passage."

"It is," Chuck said. "But he wasn't supposed to just take it like that."

"Why not?"

"Well . . . it just isn't done that way," Chuck said, foundering.

"Unless you're cute about it," Jay added. "Which I was and am. Don't fuss yourself, princess. It's just a thing."

Ariel's face showed her dissatisfaction with Jay's explanation, but she didn't press any further. She gave a little shrug and tucked her arm into Chuck's. The three of them set off through the tables and the circulating servers toward the bar.

Taylor was there, elbows on the bar as she talked animatedly to Jack. Her face lit up in a grin larger than the professional smile she'd worn on stage. She'd been lovely then but that genuine smile made her even more beautiful.

"And it worked!" the singer said, excitement filling her breathy voice. "The turbine worked! Better than we could have expected. It produced far more RPMs than we could use, so if we built it to full scale, we'd probably have to use some kind of reduction gearing to get it to turn the sternwheel at the right speed...but it *is* possible, Jack!"

"Course it is," Jay butted in as the three of them approached the bar. Taylor straightened up and gave them a smile much more like the one she'd flashed from the stage. Jack kept wiping down the glass he'd been cleaning.

"Taylor Smith, meet a few friends of mine. Some new, one old. This is Jay, Chuck and Ariel," the big man said, nodding at each in turn.

"A pleasure to meet all of you," Taylor said. "Welcome aboard. I hope you enjoyed our set."

"*Enchanté*'" Jay said. He captured the singer's fingers with his own and brought her hand to his lips. He didn't quite kiss her but Chuck suspected that mostly had to do with the low growling sound coming from behind the bar.

Chuck opened his mouth to say something to break the tension but a new distraction saved him the trouble. Ariel, of all people, stepped in front of him to address the blonde singer.

"You're a beautiful singer," she said, "but what kind of turbine?"

"I beg your pardon?" Taylor asked, her smile chilling slightly.

"What kind of turbine?" Ariel repeated. "I've worked on them. Are you trying to use it to run this ship? Because you're right, you're going to need significant reduction gearing, even with a load on the system. And you might consider multiple stages for maximum efficiency."

Taylor's smile changed to something that looked more like a

gape. Chuck knew what it was, because he could feel the same expression on his own face. Jay merely looked amused. He also looked perfectly content to hold the singer's hand until someone noticed enough to tell him to stop.

"How do you...where did you learn about turbines?" Taylor asked. "No one around here in six territories has anything but theories. My father is the leading expert."

"You're the leading expert, Tay," Jack rumbled. "Your father would say the same. He's a solid mechanic but you're the one figuring out new things."

Taylor looked like she was about to wave her hand dismissively but realized that it was still attached to a smiling old man who smelled of whiskey. She tugged her fingers free and gave Jay a tight smile.

"I'm a singer," she said. "Daddy's the real genius."

Jack harrumphed but didn't bother arguing.

"Listen," Taylor said to Ariel. "I've got to go for the second set but I'd like to speak with you afterward. If you know how to make a turbine power the *Sally*, we could be the fastest ship on the river!" She glanced up at Jack as she said this.

Chuck caught the smile that passed between them. His parents would look at each other that way sometimes. It usually meant an in-joke, or maybe a shared dream.

Damn. Jack *was* in deep.

"I'm happy to talk to you but I don't know if I can do what you want," Ariel was saying. "Our turbines are much bigger, big as the sternwheel itself. I don't know how much output power you'd have from a scaled-down unit...but it's possible."

Taylor gaped yet again. Chuck had to give it to her, the singer had a pretty gape.

"Big as the...never mind. I don't have time. We'll talk later! So pleased to meet you, Ariel! And you gentlemen, too, of course!" She turned to go, hustling back toward the curtained side of the stage on her impossibly high heels. Chuck watched her for a moment, wondering how she could move so fast in those shoes. That was the only reason he caught the look that Taylor threw over her shoulder at Jack before she ducked behind the curtain.

Interesting. Maybe...did she love him, too? They seemed such an unlikely pair but Chuck had learned a few things on this journey and Jack and Taylor seemed a lot like a couple of star-crossed lovers in his book. Or rather, the book his ma cherished and read to him and Ellie when they were little. One of the books. She had several. Ma had liked her stories.

"She's probably going to be disappointed, though," Ariel said, drawing Chuck's attention back to her. "I doubt she's got the materials to build a turbine to power this ship. High-energy turbine metallurgy is complex. But it's possible. An interesting problem. I'm...looking forward to discussing it with her."

She sounded somewhat surprised. She wasn't the only one.

The band started in on an instrumental number, Taylor nowhere in sight. Behind the bar, Jack racked the glass he'd been cleaning and leaned forward.

"She's a great singer but her real love is engineering," he said. "I took her over to a place I know, not far down the river. Used to be an aircraft manufacturing plant. She picked up a few turbine blades there and was off and running, trying to adapt them for our steam boilers. I wish—"

"What's that?" Jay asked, facing the stage. "Whatcha wish, Bun-bun?"

"Nothing," Jack said softly as the blonde singer walked out onto the stage. "Never mind."

Once more, Taylor's breathy voice filled the dining room, stilling all conversation as she wove her spell of heartache and triumph. Chuck caught himself watching Ariel and thinking about their conversation earlier. Unless he missed his guess, she'd never known love. His throat ached at the thought.

"Your girl's got quite a range," Jay said, leaning back, elbows on the shiny bar top. "Emotionally, I mean. From ballads to this. Quite a range."

Jack harrumphed agreement. Jay raised his eyebrows at Chuck, who shrugged. It seemed the best answer to whatever was going on. He wasn't sure he was catching all of the byplay, so he figured he'd just keep his mouth shut. He looked over at Ariel, who seemed to be staring into space.

"Are you all right?"

"Hmm? Oh! Yes. I was just thinking about Taylor's turbine hypothesis. I wonder...could I go look at the sternwheel?"

"If you want," Jack said. "Keep your feet on the deck and don't get in my crew's way. There's a railing to keep you from much harm. If you want to wait until the set's over, I can take you up myself but I have to keep the bar open until then."

Chuck glanced over at the far end of the bar, where a woman quickly and efficiently served drinks. He began to feel certain that "keeping the bar open" was nothing but an excuse to watch Taylor perform.

"I'll go," he said instead. "We won't be any trouble."

Jack gave him a short nod and turned his eyes back to the stage.

Ariel was already heading for the door. Chuck jogged ahead to catch up with her.

The rhythmic beat of the music followed them out into the hatchway and halfway up the ladder. As they climbed to the open top deck, Chuck felt wetness chill his face. The thick fog that they'd encountered just outside of Old Kansas City seemed to be blanketing the whole river, even obscuring Quetzalith's bed on the top cargo deck. For one foolish moment, Chuck wondered if he'd ever feel sunlight again.

Unlike the dining room and passenger decks, the top deck of the *Long Tall Sally* was a utilitarian place. Oh, it had lovely hardwood and brass construction that gleamed wetly in the fog-scattered lantern light, but it was obviously a place where men did hard, sometimes backbreaking work. Chuck supposed that it took quite a bit to keep a ship of this size afloat.

Ariel made a beeline for the stern and the massive paddle-wheel that propelled the ship forward. Chuck followed, sidestepping quickly to avoid the sailors hustling here and there all over the deck.

"Best if you go back down belowdecks," one of the sailors said to Chuck as he passed. "We're headed into the Appalachians. You know, mountains? Dragon territory. They're still rare, but you can tell their population is on the rise. There's been a few attacks on boats already this season."

"We'll be quick," Chuck promised, only halfway paying attention as he tried to follow Ariel's winding path toward the stern. "Thank you."

"Oh, that's very interesting," Ariel said as he came up beside her. She stood against a chest-high railing at the very back of the boat, leaning out to peer at the sternwheel. Luckily, it was painted white, so even in the foggy gloom, it was visible.

"What's that?" Chuck asked, more because he felt obliged to say something than anything else. He figured she'd answer with some kinda technical stuff that would fly right over his head. But at least she was talking to him.

"The sternwheel. Look there, see how the individual paddles are hinged? As they drop toward the water, they hang vertical, so that they slice *down*, rather than slapping the surface. Very smart. Reduces splashing and is far more hydrodynamic, so it minimizes the power required to turn the wheel. Which must be significant...I wonder if Taylor's father would show me the steam engine below?"

Chuck's answer died on his lips as a fireball streaked down out of the foggy night toward them.

"Get down!" he shouted as he launched himself toward Ariel. He wrapped his arms around her waist and dragged her to the deck, hitting his knee and shoulder rather hard in the process. The fireball streaked past them, hitting the water and exploding.

All around them, the river sailors shouted. Someone racked a shotgun nearby, firing into the night. Chuck kept his head tucked down with his arms around Ariel. And hoped that the sailors had good aim.

Beneath him, Ariel started to struggle.

"Let me up!" she gasped, jamming her elbow into his gut.

"What? No!" Chuck croaked. "It's not safe!"

"That is not Quetzalith!" Ariel hissed. "Let me up! I have to get Jasmine!"

"Seriously? Oh shit!" Chuck said, letting her go.

Chuck watched her run, slipping in her fancy boots, toward the hatchway. Somewhere, a rifle cracked in the darkness. The scent of gunpowder drifted through the chill.

Another fireball streaked toward the front of the ship. This one hit the deck, splashing into a sheet of oily flame. Chuck took off in that direction, feeling his feet slip on the deck just as Ariel's had done.

"If that's yours, tell it to stop attacking!" someone yelled.

"It's not!" Chuck shouted. A scream issued from the sternwheel area, where Quetzalith had been sleeping. Another blue-white streak of fire blasted forth from that area, searing up through the night toward the attacker.

"SAND!" someone else called. "Get the sand!"

"You!" a whipcord-thin sailor grabbed Chuck by the shoulder, spinning him around. "Get that barrel over!"

Chuck fought to stay upright and did as he was told. "That barrel" turned out to be full of sand, heavy as sin itself. He was able to get it onto its side and roll it toward the fire. One of the sailors took it from him and bashed the end in with some wicked-looking metal hook-ended tool. Sand spilled onto the deck. A horde of men descended, scooping it up in buckets and throwing on the thin sheen of flame.

A shadow swooped low, wings spread wide, before wheeling back up into the fog. Chuck saw a flash of a red-tinged hide disappearing beyond the reach of the ship's lantern light.

Red?

Jasmine exploded up onto the deck. She still wore her gown but her feet were bare and her hair loose and wild as she whipped her head around, searching. Garman and Ariel both followed her, the latter looking out of breath.

"Quetzalith!" Jasmine shouted, her voice nearly lost in the chaos of the sailors' firefighting efforts.

Another scream like the cry of a hunting raptor drifted through the fog, followed by one more, a little louder. Overhead, a shadowy figure dropped into view, wings spread wide and banking to the left as the dragon circled.

This dragon opened its mouth and Chuck braced himself to dive out of the way of another fireball when a third scream pierced the sound of panicked chaos all around.

Another dragon dropped out of the foggy sky like a knife thrown from above, impacting the red dragon before it could flame. Jasmine's inarticulate scream confirmed Chuck's gut: *This* one was Quetzalith! His magnificent crest flashed in the lantern light as he struck the other dragon with his long, daggerlike beak.

The pair of dragons fell to the deck with a thud that reverberated through the boards. Jasmine bolted toward them, her bare feet allowing her much better purchase. Chuck tried to run after but his boots slipped out from under him. He went down hard on his knees. Wetness soaked through his trousers.

"Get up!" Garman yelled, grabbing Chuck's collar. While the Windfist hauled him to his feet, Chuck fought to try and see where Jasmine had gone.

Quetzalith—or perhaps the other dragon—screamed again. It seemed impossible to tell, because the two of them rolled, wings and necks tangling. One of them made an angry, rasping sound, causing the gathered sailors to back up a step.

The pair rolled again, knocking over a pile of barrels and putting Quetzalith back on top. Chuck could see Jasmine scrambling, pushing through sailors and climbing over loose barrels in her haste. Quetzalith screamed, arched his neck and stabbed down with his beak, catching hold of the other dragon's neck just below the head. The other dragon let out a garbled cry and tried to cough once more. Quetzalith answered by viciously whipping his head from side to side. The crack of the other dragon's neck breaking echoed out over the water. For half a heartbeat, everyone on the deck seemed to freeze in stunned silence.

"Shoot it!" one of the sailors shouted. He raised his rifle to his shoulder.

Jasmine leapt through the air, tackling him. The rifle clattered to the deck.

"Bloody woman!" Garman swore, running to pull the dragon tamer off of the hapless sailor.

"Cease fire!" Chuck yelled again. "This one is ours! He saved us from that other one!"

"How d'ya know he won't attack? These parts are lousy with wild dragons!" someone shouted back.

"Look at him!" Chuck shouted, turning. He fought to see who'd spoken in the fog. "He ain't attacking no one!"

It was the sad truth. For all his valiant and dramatic rescue, the dragon looked sorely the worse for wear. His left wing's trailing edge fluttered in ragged tatters, while some kind of wound seeped nastily low on his neck. He looked exhausted, letting his head droop above the corpse of his prey.

He let out a pathetic-sounding *cheep.*

Jasmine, busy hitting the would-be rifleman about the head and shoulders, looked up at the sound. Her face blanched in the uncertain light and she scrambled to her feet once more.

"Baby?" she said softly. Quetzalith lifted his head again and gave her another cheeping sound. Jasmine reached out toward him, then burst into tears.

Garman looked helplessly over to Chuck but all he could do was shrug.

"What do we do?" Ariel asked softly from behind his shoulder. Chuck shook his head.

"I haven't got the faintest," he said. "He's hurt but I don't know how to..."

"I do, I do!" Jasmine said wetly. "I'm just so...relieved he wasn't hurt worse!"

More tears followed, until Garman wrapped her into a tight embrace.

"Well, can we get the dead dragon off my deck, at least?"

Jack emerged from the hatchway, his frown thunderous. Jay followed, his long-fingered hands already reaching into his jacket for a flask.

"Wait," Jasmine said, stirring in Garman's arms. "Quetzalith needs her. Please don't discard her body. He's opened up his wounds and her meat has nutrients that he needs."

Jack looked at the dragon tamer for a moment. Swiping at her eyes, she brushed her wild hair back and straightened her shoulders.

Jack snorted, then his beard split in a grin.

"You've got moxie, girl, you know that? All right. He can keep the corpse. Just get him back up to the aft deck above the sternwheel so he's out of my crew's way." He raised his voice. "You lot hear me? *This* dragon is a paying customer, so don't shoot it!"

"Him," Jasmine said quietly.

"Don't shoot *him*," Jack said. Then he looked over at Quetzalith and squinted. "He looks a mite beat up. You want the vet?"

"No, thank you. I can do what needs to be done. He mostly needs rest and to be near me. I'll stay with him. I promise that we won't be in the way."

Jack sighed, lifting his hands in surrender. Jasmine's expression made it clear that she didn't intend to be separated from Quetzalith again any time soon. He turned, muttering and walked toward the fire-damaged part of the deck.

Jasmine let out a breath and seemed to sag slightly. Garman reached for her again but she shook her head, straightening up and walking toward Quetzalith. The Windfist dropped his arms, frowning.

"C'mon," Chuck said. "Let's go see if she needs help getting Quetzalith up to his deck."

It turned out that the live dragon didn't need help but the

dead dragon did. It—or she, as Jasmine corrected them—wasn't heavy but she was awkward to move, her wings and neck gone slack in death.

"I expected she'd be heavier," Garman said to Jay. "You planning on helping?"

"Me? I'm old and creaky..." the drunk said, grasping at his back. He took a drink from a bottle he'd "acquired." "The fog has the old war wound acting up!"

"Just pick up your end," Chuck said.

Ariel had gone up to the top of the deck and was busy swinging the cargo pulley system into place.

"Hollow bones, like a bird," Jay said, following the two younger men. "Helps 'em fly. Watch that wingtip there, kid!"

Chuck looked down; he'd let one of the wings droop to drag on the deck. He struggled to get his arms around the mass of wingsail, trying to get all the bones bundled together without tripping over his feet. He was mostly successful. Eventually, they came to a stop at the base of the ladder.

"Here!" Ariel's voice came from above. Chuck looked up to see a net and hook descending toward them. He stepped aside and let it collapse next to his feet. "Put her in there, then I will winch her up."

"Perfect," Jay said. "You boys hold the dragon; I'll get the net wrapped 'round 'er."

It worked approximately like that, with Jay stopping to take multiple swig-breaks, usually while Chuck and Garman awkwardly held parts of the corpse up so that the net could be placed underneath. Eventually, they got the dragon's body cradled in the net. Chuck stepped back.

"Take it away, girlie!" Jay saluted with his bottle. The former cultist began turning the crank-handled mechanism. It didn't rise particularly quickly but the dead dragon did rise.

"That's high enough!" Ariel called. "Now we just need to get this swing arm to rotate inward—"

She let out a startled squeak as Quetzalith's head snaked beside her before whipping out to butt the corpse-laden net. The bundle swung ponderously out and away, then rebounded back toward the dragon's waiting open mouth. Powerful jaws snapped shut on a protruding wing and dragged the bundle back onto the deck with him.

Ariel let out a nervous laugh and walked carefully to the base of the lift's swing arm. She reached up and disconnected the hook, releasing the net. The wild dragon's slack body sagged free.

Quetzalith set to, tearing hungrily at the flesh of his former opponent. Chuck noticed that Ariel carefully averted her eyes and made her way down the ladder. He stepped up to greet her but didn't get the chance.

"What in Gant-ridden hell is that?" Jack bellowed, his booted feet stomping back across the deck. "Who said you could touch the equipment on my cargo deck, girl?"

Chuck took a step in front of Ariel, intending to take the brunt of the big man's irritation but Jack suddenly stopped. His eyes went wide as he got a look at the savagery with which Quetzalith consumed his meal.

"We needed the lift assist," Ariel said quietly, peering around Chuck's shoulder. "I'm sorry if I wasn't allowed to use it, but I couldn't think of how else to get the dragon corpse up to Quetzalith."

"Hot damn," Jack breathed. "He really is tame?"

"She raised him from an egg, Bun. As long as Jasmine's all right, Q won't bother anyone," Jay said, clapping the big man on the back. Jack frowned down at him and found himself holding one of Jay's flasks, which Jay then nudged up toward Jack's face. The big man shrugged and took a long drink.

"Fair enough," Jack said. "Now, the sun's about to come up, so if you lot want to get any sleep tonight, I suggest you go below."

"I'll stay here with Quetzalith," Jasmine called down. "I want to get his wounds clean and make sure he is otherwise all right."

Chuck glanced at Garman. The monk didn't look happy with this arrangement but didn't say anything. Ariel, at least, seemed pleased to go below and Chuck himself felt more than ready to get out of the wet.

"Guess I'll stay, too," Garman muttered to Chuck. "In case she needs something."

"Damn, Junior, you do have it bad," Jay said. "Suit yourself! I'm for the bar!"

The old drunk made an elaborate bow toward the cargo deck, then tumbled forward onto his face as his feet slid out from under him. Jack snorted a laugh, then went below himself. Despite his size, the big man once again proved nimble and sure-footed. No slipping for him. Chuck smiled and held out a hand to help Jay up.

"Did he laugh?" Jay asked.

"Who?"

"Jack."

"A little, yeah."

"Good. You're a mooncalf and Garman's got it bad but I ain't never seen anyone as lovesick as Bun-bun right now. I'm startin' to think we need to do ourselves some matchmaking."

"Jay, I don't think that's a good idea."

"Don't worry, kid, you never do."

Jay rolled backwards over his head onto his feet and scampered below.

With the endless blue sky of Ironhelm stretching above him, Baron Schilling brushed the roan's pelt, smiling at the young girl perched on the saddle. A breeze, redolent of sage and coming rain, teased at the girl's hair.

"Do you like her, Keelie?"

Keelie nodded, quietly running her hands through the mare's black mane.

"Now, what have we discussed about manners?"

"Answer when spoken to, milord."

"That's correct. Now, I'll ask again. Do you like her?"

"Yes, Milord Baron, she's lovely."

"Much better, my dear. Now, let me see a smile." The girl obliged, tight-lipped, the corners of her mouth barely turning upwards. "That's better. You're so pretty when you smile."

"Thank you, milord."

Schilling turned to his photographer, signaling that they were ready. Several quick clicks and the woman let him know she was finished. He waved her off.

Lieutenant Sampsei entered the stable, saluting.

"Milord, you have a visitor."

"Thank you, Lieutenant, I'll be along shortly." Schilling turned back to Keelie. "Now, enjoy your lesson. Pay attention to your instructor and you will be an expert rider in no time."

"Yes, milord."

"Good girl." He handed the reins to the riding tutor. "I will see you for dinner."

He watched them walk away, a slight smile playing across his lips. She still resented him but she would come to love him. Jasmine had been much the same when he'd found her—distant, stubborn and defiant.

He frowned at the thought of the former Lady Moore. The report from Kansas City had been...disappointing. Several crystal decanters had become no more than scattered shards before he'd come to grips on his ire.

Some brief introspection, however, showed him that the signs had been there. Not one to overlook his own mistakes, he vowed to learn from them and make sure he didn't commit them again with Keelie.

His generosity had been too liberally applied with Jasmine. He'd allowed her entirely too much power and freedom before she had truly come to appreciate him. Also, she'd been older when he'd started—a younger ward could be convinced of his benevolence far more easily.

Lieutenant Sampsei coughed, reminding him of his appointment. Best not to keep the Gant leader waiting.

He strode into the great hall, pausing briefly to allow his eyes to adjust to the dimmer, cooler interior. His visitor stood next to his dais, a tall woman clad in the silk robes of a Gant cultist. He approached, a smile spreading across his face.

"Ah, Mariah! How lovely to see you again. I trust you are well?"

"Baron Schilling," the woman said, bowing her head slightly. "I am as well as I can be. May the Queens bless you this day."

"Please, have a seat," he said, waving a hand toward a chair nearby as he took his throne. "Please forgive my directness but time is of the essence."

"I prefer to keep meetings short and to the point, Baron. My hive needs my guidance."

Schilling knew for a fact there wasn't an actual Gant enclave within fifty miles of Ironhelm. Bug-loving freaks labeled any dwelling a "hive," no matter how many Gants were there. In Mariah's case, he had good intel on the exact number of scouts and acolytes she commanded. Still, diplomacy was needed. He kept his smile firmly in place.

"Of course, my dear, I understand. It has come to my attention that an item of importance to your"—he stopped himself before he said "cult"—"order has been stolen. I have a possible lead as to its whereabouts."

That got her attention.

"That information would be useful, Baron," she said, her usually cold, clinical exterior becoming more animated than he'd ever seen. "What payment would you require to share it?"

"My good Mariah," he said, pouring a tumbler of water from the jug next to his elbow, "I require no payment at all! I consider this an opportunity to strengthen our alliance, no more. In fact, as I have interests in the area in question, I will be more than happy to help you or your followers on their journey."

"That is very generous, Baron," Mariah said, her face resuming its blank expression. "How do you propose to assist?"

"I will provide my fastest train, as well as thirty of my men to escort you and yours. The information I have indicates the item is traveling east, by river. Most likely destination is Pittsburgh. I understand that you have a facility in the area?"

"Yes, we do, as well as a minor hive nearby."

"Excellent!" he said, standing to bow with a flourish. "I will see that you may depart first thing tomorrow. My men will meet you at the depot by first light."

The cult leader stood as well, inclined her head and took her leave. As the door closed behind her, Schilling summoned Lieutenant Sampsei.

By the time he arrived, Schilling had orders penned and sealed.

"These are to be delivered to Ronen. Assign your best men to this, Lieutenant, and ensure they understand that Jasmine is to be returned to me unharmed. Any other members of her party are considered expendable. Dismissed."

When alone again, he pulled the recently acquired chain from under his shirt. Dog tags, like his father's, spun slowly in the gaslight. He focused on the object hanging with them, a red plastic card, not much larger than the credit cards from his youth. Something about it seemed familiar.

Important items, indeed. Important enough for Master Munn to keep on his person. He made a mental note to do some research in his archives, and replaced the chain.

Schilling considered his good fortune. The cultists were useful, especially their fervor at recovering their artifact. Pittsburgh had a reputation as a tough nut to crack. However, with both Gants and Windfist on his side, it was possible to do so. At least, with enough disruption, he could perhaps forge an alliance with the Burghers.

He reached into his vest pocket, removing a small folding frame. The photograph inside showed Jasmine sitting primly in the garden, a young Quetzalith perched carefully on her raised forearm. He slowly traced her features with an index finger, as though brushing hair back from her face.

And if the cultists were repelled successfully?

Well then, it was perfectly acceptable to sacrifice a bishop to capture a queen.

Chuck watched the riverbanks sliding by on either side. He knew the same trip would likely take twice as long on horseback... but still. It didn't *feel* like he was going anywhere. It made him edgy.

"You okay?" Jasmine asked him at one point about midway through the trip. He'd gone up onto the deck for the third time before noon and had settled for leaning against one of the passenger railings in lieu of something useful to do.

"Yeah," Chuck replied. "Restless. Being up here helps, a little. Reminds me that we're not standing still."

"I know what you mean," she said, pulling the fingers of both hands through her long, dark hair before leaning her elbows on the railing next to him. "After running for so long, it feels wrong to just be sitting still, even if we're moving. It's good for Quetzalith, though."

"How's he feeling?"

"Better. Stronger every day. That fight with the wild dragon took it out of him. And he was already hurt when... when we boarded."

"Jasmine... about that. I... I really am sorry we..."

She looked at him for a long moment. Then closed her eyes and nodded.

"Me too," she said. "I didn't mean to hurt you, or Garman. That is, I *did*, but I realize you were just trying to take care of me. It's just that, well... I don't like having my arms pinned like that, like how Garman held me. The Baron did that a time or two, so..."

"Shit, Jasmine," Chuck breathed, so rattled he didn't even notice his own profanity. "I'm so sorry. We didn't know."

"I know," she said. "It's not your fault. You should have just listened to me, but I probably wouldn't have been willing to leave any of *you* behind either. I'm glad you said something. I need to go talk to Garman about it, too. Like it or not, we're a team."

"Yeah, we are. Quetzalith, too. Which reminds me, how did he find us?" Chuck asked, turning his head to look up at the sleeping dragon. "It was awful foggy. And you were so certain that he would. Why?"

Jasmine looked at him for a long moment, then shrugged one shoulder and looked down at the water below.

"Instinct, I think," she said. "I always told the Baron it was my training but I think it's more than that. I hatched Quetzalith. I'm the closest thing he has to a mother. Dragons aren't terribly parental in the wild but something has formed a bond between Quetzalith and me. I don't truly understand it but my gut says that it's instinct and I always listen to my gut."

"Instinct?" Chuck asked. "Not love?"

A startled, delighted laugh rippled out from Jasmine.

"Well, of course it's love," she said. "What do you think instinct is made from?"

"I don't follow," Chuck said, shaking his head slightly. "What does one have to do with the other?"

"Everything!" Jasmine said, still chuckling. "Look, instinct is the gut feeling, right? The hunch? The feeling in the back of your mind that says 'You really want to go and do this thing'? Well, why?"

"Why what?"

"Why do you want to go and do the thing?"

"What 'thing'? I don't ..."

Jasmine shook her head and reached out to cup Chuck's face with one hand.

"Try to keep up," she said. "The reason you have a gut feeling at all is because you care about something. Even if it's only yourself. If you didn't care, the universe wouldn't bother telling you what to do to protect what you care about. Or you wouldn't bother to listen. But the fact that you have a gut instinct means that you care about—that you love—someone or something. Even if it's only yourself."

Chuck blinked several times, trying to wrap his head around Jasmine's incredibly circular logic. He was about to ask her to repeat that whole spiel, slowly, when something at the water's edge caught his eye. Behind him and to the right, Quetzalith lifted his head, letting out a low chittering sound.

"You still don't understand, do you?" Jasmine said. "See..."

"Wait, shhh," Chuck said, stilling her with a hand on her forearm. Then he pointed to the riverbank. "Look."

There, barely visible through the scrub that lined the water's edge, a scout Gant crouched. It may have been doing anything: drinking from the river, waiting for prey, searching for something for the Hive...but Chuck immediately had the strong feeling, the *instinct*, that its appearance there wasn't a good sign at all.

Hours later, Jasmine sat on the top deck of the *Sally* and stroked the leathery skin of Quetzalith's crest. He continued to heal quickly, thanks in large part to the dragon meat he'd consumed. Jasmine supposed she should be weirded out by Quetzalith's eager cannibalism, but the reality was she was just happy that her dragon was doing better.

"*Meep.*" She turned her head to see his nearest eye, as large as her head, staring at her with something like patient reproach.

"I know," she sighed. "I need to go talk to him. We're part of a team, and I can't let this become a problem between us. It's just...he's so infuriating!"

Quetzalith's huge eyelid swept down over the eye and then back up again, causing laughter to bubble up within her.

"Okay," Jasmine said. "Okay. I'm going."

"*Mrrrurrr,*" Quetzalith trilled, managing to make the soft, rolling sound salacious. Jasmine laughed again and smacked his crest lightly.

"Mind your own business, love," she said. "I'll be back after a little while."

"*Ruup,*" the dragon said, sounding disappointed. He closed his eyes again, ostentatiously. Jasmine, still laughing, shook her head and dropped a kiss on his crest.

"I love you too," she said. Then she stood up, stretched, squared her shoulders and climbed down from the top deck in search of music to face.

She found him in his quarters, cleaning his weapons. Naturally.

"Journeyman Garman," she said, hating the stiffness in her tone. He looked up to where she stood in the doorway of his berth, and a slow flush began to darken his neck just above his open collar.

"Ah, hello," he said, moving the barrel of his rifle off his lap and setting it beside him on the bunk. He brushed his hands together, then wiped them on the rag next to him before standing up. "Can I help you?"

"Yes," she said. Oddly enough, she was pleased to see his discomfiture. It made her own that much less irritating. "I think you can. Would you take a walk with me?"

"Walk?" he asked, the flush creeping higher on his neck. "Uh, sure. Where...ah...where did you want to go?"

"I don't know," she said. "Let's just explore the ship? I don't think Jack will mind, as long as we don't get in his crew's way."

"All right," Garman said. He reached back onto the bed for his sheathed kukri, which he tucked into his belt before straightening his tunic and stepping toward her. She walked back out into the passageway and gestured for him to come along. He fell in beside her as they headed toward the ladder leading down another deck level.

"I wanted to talk to you," she said after a few moments of really uncomfortable silence. "I kind of want to apologize to you, but I kind of don't want to do so."

He laughed, which caused her eyebrows to shoot up. She hadn't expected that reaction from him.

"I beg your pardon," he said, still chuckling. "But the truth is, that's pretty much how you make me feel all the time."

"Yes, well," she said, allowing her mouth to turn up in a little grin. "I suppose that's fair. The thing is, you really shouldn't have tried to force me onto the boat before Quetzalith came back."

"Yes but—"

Jasmine held up a hand. "I know *why* you did it, and like I told Chuck, I don't really blame you too much for that. I probably wouldn't have been willing to leave any of you behind. So it's not so much that you didn't listen to me, although you should have...it's more..." She broke off, took a deep breath and came to a stop. She turned and forced herself to meet his eyes.

"When you pinned my arms like that, in the bear hug? The Baron used to do that, when I was first with him. Or he would have his men do it. In any case, I can't stand it. That's why I bit you and said...what I said."

"Oh... oh bloody saints, Jasmine," Garman said, his eyes going wide and the flush fading as his face went horribly pale. "Oh gods above and below, I'm so sorry. I didn't know—"

She cut him off with a slashing motion of her hand.

"There's no reason you should have known. You should have listened to me when I said I wasn't coming, but we agreed that there were extenuating circumstances. I just wanted to say that I'm... mostly sorry. And I don't want it to be a big thing between us. That weakens the team."

"But Jasmine..."

"Stop," she said, and her voice cracking like a whip. "Please don't. I don't need you to feel sorry for me, or to pity me or to look at me like I'm spun glass. I'm not. I'm fine. You just... hit an old injury, that's all. But you didn't know, and it's fine."

She took another deep breath and reached up to the open collar of his shirt. His skin felt warm under her fingertips as she moved the cloth to the side to see the bruised half-circle she'd caused with her bite. She heard him inhale through his nose as she touched the wound, but he didn't flinch or otherwise move.

"Damn," she said. "Okay, I guess I *am* sorry about this."

"I'm sorry too," he said, his voice softer and a bit deeper. "I know, I'm not pitying you, but I *am* regretful that we tried to force you on board. But I would never have left you behind."

"Oh?" she asked, tracing around the circle of her bite mark. "Because we're a team?"

"Yeah," he said, "and—Saint Baddis forgive me—but it's not just that. What you screamed... well, it rattled me because... I like you."

"You like me?"

"I... yeah."

"What are we, eight?" she asked, and humor threaded through her tone. "Are you trying to say you're attracted to me, Windfist? The way a man is attracted to a woman he wants to sleep with?"

"Well," Garman said, "yes. That and... more, maybe?"

"Are you asking me or telling me?"

"Hell if I know."

That got another laugh out of her. She flattened her palm against the swell of his chest muscle and tilted her head to the side as she chuckled and considered her next move.

When in doubt, go with your gut.

She rose up on her tiptoes and brushed her lips against his, then dropped down and repeated the process just below the hard angle of his jaw.

"I like you too," she breathed across his skin. "The way a woman likes a man she wants to sleep with. But please understand, we have to do this at my pace, or not at all. Can you agree to that?"

"Wholeheartedly," he said, his chest rumbling under her hand.

"Good answer," she replied, and kissed him again.

CHAPTER THIRTEEN

EVENTUALLY, CHUCK'S DAYS ON THE *SALLY* SETTLED INTO A KIND of pattern. He'd wake at a leisurely hour—shortly after dawn—and head down to groom Millie. The mare seemed to be holding up to the travel fairly well, though she clearly disliked being cooped up. Toward the end of their journey, she was greeting him with reproachful looks and restive stamps.

"I know, Millie, I'm sorry. We should get there today or tomorrow, I think," Chuck told the mare on day ten as he scooped grain into her feed bucket. "And then we'll get you out and you can walk around. I bet you'll be glad to travel on your own four hooves again, won't you, pretty girl?"

Millie gave a snort, stamped and nipped at his sleeve to show that she wasn't mollified by these promises. But she submitted to his curry combing well enough, even pressing back against him in affection.

Chuck finished his ministrations and got cleaned up. True to routine, he went above to see what progress they'd made, both in navigation and in the ongoing process of nursing Quetzalith. The dragon had improved at an astonishingly quick rate but Jasmine said it was normal for his "fizzy-ollo-gee." He'd had to ask Jay what that meant.

She was fanatic about keeping him fed, though. Quetzalith subsisted on the corpse of the wild dragon for those first few days and that seemed to have kickstarted the healing process. No sooner had he picked the bones clean than Jasmine pronounced him able to hunt for himself and she shooed him off daily to do so.

When Chuck emerged from the ladderway, in fact, the dragon was nowhere in sight. Chuck wondered if Quetzalith would find more Gants like the one Chuck had seen a few days ago. He rather hoped the dragon would.

He took a turn about the decks, nodding friendly if silent greetings to the sailors. They returned his courtesy in kind, which was nice enough but didn't cure his restlessness one whit. With a sigh, Chuck headed back down the ladder.

After the cool upper deck, the dining room was almost uncomfortably warm. Chuck walked in to see the tables configured in what he thought of as "saloon style"—spread throughout the room, rather than being clustered around the stage.

Across the room, Jay looked up from his hand of cards and waved wildly. Chuck didn't recognize the men who'd joined Jay at the table, though the woman was familiar. The other two were probably new fares taken on when they'd stopped earlier in the day. Poker, it seemed, was yet another one of Jay's myriad set of skills, and he loved to play with anyone who'd sit a few hands. Chuck felt himself smile and started in that direction.

"Pay attention, old man!" the player at Jay's left snapped. "We don't wanna wait all night for you to be sociable!"

"Now, what kind of thing is that to say," Jay said, leaning back in his chair. "I thought this was a friendly game!"

"Just play your hand, you old coot."

"Cav, you're such a spoilsport," Jay said. "This, here, is my very good friend Chuck. Chuck, this impatient fella is Cavett Stepanek. You already know Lady Green, our stunning redhead in blue, and this fine kilted gentleman is Shannon Gafney. We're having us a friendly game of cards."

Jay grinned up at Chuck, who nodded at each of the men and touched his forehead in the direction of the lady with the suspiciously derringer-shaped bulge in her handbag. Lady Green smiled at him in a way that made his cheeks heat up.

"Why don't you go get us some drinks, kid? Tell Bun I want my usual Old Fashioned, all right?" Jay said, giving Chuck a wink.

"Oooh, a drink sounds lovely. I'll have champagne," Lady Green said, her voice low and smooth. She leaned forward over the table and Jay's eyes widened as he took in her bountiful assets.

Stepanek cleared his throat menacingly and scowled up at Chuck.

"Whiskey," he growled. "And be quick about it so we can get on with the damn game."

"Oh, now don't be a boor, Cavett," Lady Green said. "The boy's being a dear to get drinks for us. It isn't his fault Jay is stalling."

Jay let out a laugh and pushed one of his coins (which Chuck strongly suspected had started the day as part of his own luggage) toward the center of the table.

"I'll have a beer," Gafney said quietly to Chuck. "And thanks."

Chuck nodded and turned for the bar, feeling like a child who had just been dismissed from the adults' table.

Jack was, as usual, wiping down the surface of the bar. He looked up as Chuck approached.

"What's up, kid?" he asked. "Jay send you over?"

"Yessir," Chuck said. "He wants a drink but I think it's a code or something, because he's asking for something I've never heard him order. An 'Old Fashioned'?"

Jack snorted and turned to retrieve one of the short glasses from the wall behind him.

"You're a smart kid," Jack said, pouring liquor into the glass. "He's telling me that he thinks one of his fellow players is cheating, so he's going to start cheating in order to find out who."

"Really?"

"Yep. It's a code we worked out a long time ago. 'Old Fashioned' means that he's going to start some shenanigans. 'Tom Collins' means that things are already interesting and I should be ready to save his skinny ass, and 'Sloe Gin Fizz' means come quick and hot and bring a lawyer."

"How long have you known Jay, sir?" Chuck asked. The big man behind the bar just chuckled.

"Long enough, kid. Now, what else for those cheaters at the table? Because if I know Jay, he's never one to let pass an opportunity to butter up the competition."

"Whiskey, neat, I guess. A beer, and a glass of champagne for the lady."

"Ah, Lady Green. Yeah, she came aboard right before your lot did. I'll send you with an extra drink for her, compliments of the house. That'll tell Jay that she's working for me and not to fleece her too badly."

"You guys have done this a time or two," Chuck said, smiling.

"Once or twice," Jack said. "Nice job being laconic, by the way. But next time, you want to tone down your smile and make your voice just a bit drier. It ruins the effect when you grin like a puppy."

Chuck puzzled over what exactly "laconic" meant while Jack poured the rest of the drinks, including a second Old Fashioned for Lady Green, and put them onto a tray. Chuck then took the tray and, feeling slightly ridiculous, did his ever-loving best not to spill the drinks as he carried them to the foursome.

"Mr. Jack said this one is on the house for you, Lady Green," Chuck said as he put the small glass in front of her. "And here's your champagne."

The lady smiled up at him again and raised the champagne glass toward the bar. Jack returned her salute with a slight wave and a smile and cut his eyes to Jay.

Jay didn't appear to be paying attention at all, frowning comically at his cards.

"Thanks, kid," Gafney said as Chuck set the pint glass in front of him. He shifted in his seat and Chuck saw the butt end of a revolver peek out from the waistband of his kilt.

That made two of Jay's opponents armed, with the good possibility of a third. Stepanek hadn't acknowledged him at all when he'd set the whiskey down in front of him, simply glowering at Jay.

All in all, it seemed that it might be best to stay nearby, just in case. He wished he could call Garman, too. He hadn't seen the Windfist that day, which meant that he was probably hidden away doing Windfist meditations. Or exercises. Which was what he did when he wasn't watching Jasmine.

Chuck took the tray back to the bar. Jack was busy talking with one of his uniformed ladies, so Chuck put the tray down and waited. He figured he'd have to pay for the drinks, and sooner was better than later.

Not that Jay wouldn't just put things on his tab. Or start a tab in Chuck's name. That was the way of things with Jay, it seemed.

"Hi," Ariel said, popping up to her feet behind the bar.

"Shi—Hi," Chuck said, startled. "What are you doing back there?"

"Looking at the refrigeration system on the *Sally*," Ariel said, her eyes as bright as her voice. Chuck didn't think he'd ever seen her so animated. "It is really brilliant; you have to come see."

"Um, I don't think Jack wants me behind his bar," Chuck said, glancing up at the big man. "Can you just tell me about it?"

"Do you think you would understand?"

Ouch.

"I can try."

Ariel's face lit up.

"See here? Inside is the piping that conducts the compressed fluid throughout the ship." Chuck leaned over the bar as she pointed to what looked like a thick wool sock underneath. "There are copper lines that run below to the compressor. I will have to ask what they use for coolant. I am certain I can improve the design if I knew more about the components. The compressor system is very well built, using steam power from the paddlewheel to turn the fans as well as create a low-pressure vacuum pump that forces the coolant mix through the system."

Chuck blinked, his head spinning.

"Wow, okay. That sounds really...uh...cool."

"Well, of course it is, that is the whole point." Ariel narrowed her eyes, tilting her head at him. "Or...wait. Were you telling a joke? Because it is both a really ingenious design and a refrigeration system?"

He felt his face heat up as he nodded.

"I see," Ariel said. "That's interesting."

Chuck didn't know what to say. He felt his face heating up as an awkward silence stretched between them.

"Well...uh..."

"You cheating bastard!"

Chuck whirled to face Jay's table. For the first time since meeting the old man, Chuck actually felt glad that he was so prone to getting into trouble. Fights and trouble he understood. Talking to Ariel was beyond his capabilities.

Over at the card game, the angry-faced whiskey drinker had come to his feet and stood, fists clenched, looming over Jay. Jay was drawing the small pot toward himself.

"Ain't no way you got dealt that hand, old man. You've been keepin' cards in your sleeve!"

"Now, Cavett, you know I wouldn't stoop so low," Jay said with an easy grin. "Sit back down, you're makin' a fool of yourself."

"Hell with that. I'm done playin'," Cavett said, and turned to stomp away from the table. Lady Green pouted after him for a moment, before shrugging and gathering up the scattered cards. The other man, Gafney, sipped at his beer.

Chuck turned to excuse himself from Ariel, only to find that she had ducked back down behind the bar to continue tinkering with the refrigeration system. He shrugged and headed back over to the table.

"Everything okay?" he asked.

"Right as rain, kid," Jay replied.

At that moment, the world exploded. At least, that's what it seemed like. The polished deck of the dining room heaved under Chuck, causing him to lose his footing and slam down on his shoulder and hip. A deafening *boom* deadened all sound, save for a high-pitched ringing in his ears.

Chuck pushed himself up to his knees, coughing through the sudden smoke pouring in through the high porthole windows and from the corridor outside.

"Jay?" he shouted, his voice sounding flat and far away. "Ariel?"

"Here, kid," the old man said. "Where's Jack?"

"I'm here," Jack replied. Chuck's hearing was starting to return, because he could hear the deadly emptiness in the big man's voice. "Your girl's here, kid. She's cut up some from the glass but she's okay. Ladies and gentlemen, please remain calm and either come join the fight, or stay here where it's safe."

"What the fuck is happening?" It was Lady Green. Chuck pushed to his feet to see her holding her derringer. He offered her a hand and pulled her to her feet. Jay bounced up not far away. For once, he was missing his usual wide grin.

"Check the girl, kid," Jay said. "Jack and I will go see what's going on. You get her and find your way down to the stables. Get our horses out. If someone's going to sink us, they may be able to swim for safety. If I find Garman or Jasmine, I'll send them to you."

"Got it," Chuck said. He started moving toward the bar, careful to keep out of Jack's path. The big man stood behind the counter, strapped and loaded for bear.

He had put on a set of old-style body armor—really just plates that covered front and back—over his usual swanky suit. His wide leather belt now sported pouches for ammunition, a holstered handgun and several large knives. As Chuck watched, Jack chambered a short-barreled black rifle and lifted it to check the optic. With a grunt of satisfaction, he bent back down behind the bar and emerged wearing a helmet painted with a white skull and crossbones. He tossed a shotgun to Jay.

"You don't run a riverboat without dealing with the occasional problem," Jack said dryly. "Unruly guests, misplaced cargo, nosey customs... and sometimes pirates. But if this river trash thinks they're going to take my *Sally*, they got another thing coming. I'm a damn pirate king."

Jay laughed and racked the shotgun as Jack sauntered out from behind the bar. He stopped in front of Lady Green.

"You coming?"

She shrugged. "You're paying me, I might as well."

"I'll go, too," Gafney said. He got up from where he'd fallen and opened his vest a few inches. Chuck caught the gleam of a metal star.

"Never told me you're a lawman, Gafney," Jack said.

"Never asked."

"Fine, there's more equipment behind the bar. You two grab some and come on. I suspect we're about to repel boarders."

"Chuck?" Ariel called, coughing. Chuck snapped his attention back to her and ducked under the passthrough.

"You okay?" he asked. He could see a few cuts and scrapes from where one of the glassware racks had crashed down on top of her in the explosion. He reached out a hand to try and help her brush the glass out of her hair.

"I think so. I am cut but nothing bad."

He pulled her from the glass over to an open compartment in the floor. This must have been where Jack had stashed his equipment. Gafney was there, handing another short-barreled rifle to Lady Green and taking another shotgun for himself. He also pulled out a long, slightly curving sheathed knife and tucked that in his belt.

"You want another shotgun, kid? Big man's got several."

"Uh, sure, Sheriff," Chuck said. His own weapons were in his quarters and he decided they'd stop there on the way to get the horses. If the boat sank, he wasn't about to let Fat Lady end up on the bottom of the river. He grabbed a twelve gauge and a pouch that held shells. He slung the pouch over his shoulder as Gafney stood up.

"It's marshal, actually," the lawman said with a grin and a wink. "Good luck. Shall we, Lady?"

"Let's," Lady Green said, slapping a magazine into her rifle with practiced skill.

Those two followed Jack and Jay out into the corridor and turned right to go up the ladder to the top deck. Chuck grabbed the shotgun and Ariel's hand and followed them, cutting to the left for the ladder leading down to the berths.

Another explosion, not as big, rocked the boat. Chuck stumbled, missed his footing on the last rung of the ladder and came down hard. His ankle rolled under him and a ripping pain lanced up his lower leg.

"Fu—udge!" he swore through gritted teeth.

"Chuck?" Ariel sounded scared.

"I'm okay. Just rolled my ankle. Watch your step coming down here..."

A telltale *whizz-crack* of a bullet snapped by his ear, causing Chuck to flinch. He reached up to grab Ariel, pulled her to the floor and rolled on top of her. The shotgun came up and he fired, hoping to keep their attacker's head down for long enough to get set.

"I'm okay," Ariel whispered, before he could ask. He patted her with his free hand, easing into a crouch. His ankle sent shooting pains up his leg but he did his best to ignore it for the time being. He motioned to Ariel to stay down as he moved forward along the corridor, staying low.

Chuck reached the doorway that led to the girls' room and gently nudged it open with the barrel of the shotgun. Clear. He ducked inside, sweeping around the fancy, yet compact space, again finding nothing. Good enough. Back out to the corridor, he caught Ariel's eye and motioned to her to come forward and into her room.

She'd just cleared the threshold of the door when Chuck caught sight of someone peering around the entrance of another room across the hall and farther down. Twin impulses warred within his brain. Part of him wanted to shoot first, ask questions later. Another part didn't think Jack would appreciate him killing a paying customer.

Fortunately (or unfortunately), the individual turned out to be a hostile. Gunfire filled the corridor, sending Ariel to crouch behind the small bureau. Chuck quickly reloaded and chambered another round.

"Be right back," Chuck whispered. He stepped out into the corridor and blasted the wall beside the occupied door. Jack's shells were loaded with heavy buckshot, which put a very pretty pattern in the thin wooden walls on this boat. Someone on the other side screamed in pain.

Chuck pumped another round into the chamber and dove across the door, firing through it. He had no idea whether or not he hit anything but that wasn't the point. The point was to keep his assailant off guard long enough for him to get a kill shot. He racked the slide again.

He crouched next to the door and peered in. A large, spreading pool of dark red covered the floor. Slumped next to the doorway, a figure lay face down, its back a pulpy ruin. The scent of scorched meat joined the stench of gunpowder in the air. Chuck swallowed hard and bent to retrieve the fallen rifle. It looked similar to the ones Jack had had stashed away, with a thirty-round magazine that, when checked, proved to be about two-thirds full.

He waited just a moment longer to be sure that there weren't any other pirates busy ransacking the guest berths but he figured that if the gunfire hadn't brought them out, then they must be busy elsewhere.

"Ariel," he called softly. "It's safe for the moment. Let's go."

Ariel emerged carrying two bags, Jasmine's and hers. He took one and threw it over his shoulder. Then took her hand in his.

"Come on," he said. "Don't look."

"I have seen death before," she said softly.

"I know." He led her to the far end of the corridor to where another ladder led down to the rooms he, Garman and Jay used. "But still, be careful going down the ladder. There might be more of them below."

The lower deck clear, Chuck sent a heartfelt mental "thank you" to whoever might be listening. Apparently only one enterprising soul in the boarding party had skipped the battle above to get right to the looting. Probably Jack's crew of sailors had had something to do with that, not to mention Jack himself.

They made their way to Chuck's room without further incident. It took him a minute to gather up his belongings, then move to Garman's and do the same. Jay, naturally, didn't have anything but what he was carrying, so that made things a mite easier. Chuck fumbled for a minute with all of the various weapons, finally settling on handing the shotgun to Ariel. He carried Fat Lady and the rest down one more ladder to the stable hold.

The horses knew something was wrong, stamping and snorting in their stalls. Without saying a word to him, Ariel moved from stall to stall, petting noses and murmuring comforting words. She also unlatched each half-door.

"I don't think that will do much good," Chuck said. "The ladder opening is too small for any of them to swim through if this deck starts to flood because the boat is sinking."

"I know," Ariel said. "That did not make sense to me when Jay said it. But then I thought that if it comes to that, we can open the ramp door and swim for the shore."

Chuck gaped, kicking himself mentally. Why hadn't he thought of that?

"That's . . . a really good idea."

"Yes," she said, nodding. "Just don't open it right now. Because we don't know if the pirates are winning and we don't want to let a bunch of water in. We are just above the waterline."

"How'd you know that?"

She gave him a long look and then pointed at the round porthole windows at head height around the bulkhead of the compartment.

"Oh," he said, feeling his face heat up as his confidence plunged to his feet. "Right."

Tense minutes passed, punctuated with bouts of gunfire, and occasional explosions. Chuck was torn—he desperately wanted to find his companions, but knew he couldn't leave Ariel alone. He forced himself to stay vigilant, keeping an eye on the entrances.

"Chuck!" Garman's voice drifted down to them from the deck above. Chuck jumped and moved to the base of the ladder.

"Down here!" he shouted up, trying not to sound too relieved. "I've got Ariel!"

"I've got Jasmine and Taylor. Give us a hand, she's hurt!"

Chuck swore. He slung Fat Lady over his chest and climbed halfway up the ladder—enough to poke his head up and see Jasmine and a bare-chested Garman holding the blonde singer between them. Her middle looked like a red ruin. Her head lolled, her eyes betraying her semiconsciousness.

"What happened?" He hooked an arm and leg through the ladder so that he could help lower her down. He managed to get his arms around her hips, though he was afraid he made her pain worse as he took her weight.

"I'm here," Ariel said from below. "Lower her down; I'll help her to the deck."

"She said the pirates got into the dining room," Garman said. "Came in through the stage, started slaughtering the staff."

"No!" Ariel gasped. Chuck felt a shudder go through Taylor as he strained to lower her gently. His arms and shoulders started to burn.

"Yeah," Garman said. "Taylor and her band started fighting back. She's the only one who made it. She found Jasmine and I found them in the boiler room. She'd apparently crawled through an accessway under the bar."

"Why were you in the boiler room?" Ariel asked. Chuck wasn't entirely sure, since he was primarily focused on the injured singer but he thought he heard Garman give an uncomfortable cough.

"We were exploring," Jasmine said, bitter laughter in her tone. "I was able to get a bandage on her but most of my medical kit is here with the horses."

"I have her," Ariel said, then gently lowered the singer to lie on the deck.

Chuck swiped his forearm across his head and then jumped down, helping Ariel move Taylor closer to the horses. Jasmine followed after, then headed for her saddlebags hanging on the rear wall. She came back with a roll of bandage material and a few other items she'd gotten from the Windfist compound.

After tossing Garman's rifle up to him, Chuck took a closer look at the injured girl. He could see Jasmine's hasty attempt at a bandage, using what looked like Garman's shirt. He glanced up at his companion, and noticed he sported several red marks around his throat and shoulders. Chuck started to ask, then thought better of it.

When Jasmine started to peel the makeshift bandage away, Chuck hauled in a breath. The sweet, pretty singer had been gut-shot, leaving a wound that looked a lot like Journeyman Stephens's had, only worse. Her left side looked like it had been caved in or carved out and Chuck could see the white flash of her lowest rib bone in the dim light.

"Jas..." he said softly, "I don't think she's gonna make it."

"What are you, a doctor all of a sudden?" Jasmine rounded on him, anger boiling in her eyes.

"He's right," Taylor gasped. With a little cry, Jasmine turned back to her patient.

"Taylor!" the dragon tamer turned medic said. "Still with us."

"For the moment," the singer replied, her beautiful voice breathier than usual. "But Chuck's right. Not for long. I gotta get back to the boiler room."

"What? Why?"

"We gotta blow it up." A spasm of pain crossed her face, causing her to bite down on her lower lip. "Jack said if the ship was ever taken, we're to trigger the boiler overload and blow the thing."

"But how do we know?" Chuck asked. "Jack and the others could be winning, or at least still fighting."

As if in answer, gunfire came from above, followed by Garman's shout.

"That's getting closer! Clear the way!" He dropped to the deck heavily, rifle slung.

Taylor's face creased in pain once again.

"Got anything for lots of pain?" she asked. "Just enough to get me there?"

Jasmine pressed her lips together tightly, then nodded.

"I have a little morphine. It will . . . you'll be very sleepy though. And then . . ."

"I won't wake up. Got it. That's fine. I can fight through it long enough to do what needs to be done."

"Wait!" Chuck cried out, panic pushing in at him. "What are we doing? They're still fighting up there! Why are we talking like we lost?"

"Listen to me," Taylor said. "There were scores of them. If Jack were alive, there wouldn't be."

"But Jay . . . Lady Green . . . the marshal!" Taylor turned to smile at him and just shook her head.

"Get me to the boiler room. There's a passage from this compartment. I'll give you guys enough time to get out with your horses and then I'll blow the *Long Tall Sally* sky high."

Taylor was young and achingly pretty. She was fine-boned and delicate and her light, breathy voice reminded Chuck of birds in the morning. But right then, looking at her lying in her own blood, Chuck thought he'd never seen anyone so hard and fierce.

"Okay? Now stop staring at me. Let's get this shit done," Taylor said. That seemed to galvanize everyone into action. Jasmine pulled a small vial and a syringe out of a pouch and injected the vial's contents into Taylor's arm. Seconds later, the singer's pinched look eased and the ghost of a smile curved her lips.

"Well," she said. "That's rather nice. It still hurts but I don't care at all!"

Ariel gave her a sharp look as Taylor let out a breathy laugh but didn't say anything. Instead, she moved to help Jasmine wrap a proper bandage around the injured girl's middle.

"I've got the horses ready to go," Garman said. Chuck looked up to see that the Windfist had pulled a coat on over his bare chest and had been busy putting the horses' tack on them. Garman had grabbed Jay's nag, too.

Just in case, Chuck thought, worry lancing through him.

"Let me take them." Ariel moved toward Garman and took the leading rein from his hand. "You go help carry Taylor."

"Third stall, on the starboard side," Taylor said. The morphine made her voice slur just a bit and she let out a girlish giggle. "The passage is behind the back panel. You'll have to kick the bottom to get it to open."

"You go," Jasmine said, looking at Chuck while Garman gently lifted Taylor. "I'll stay with Ariel and help her get the horses out." She flicked her eyes toward the ladderway and Chuck understood. If anyone came down those steps, Jasmine would give them a fighting chance.

With that, Chuck found himself crouched in the third stall on the starboard side, looking for something that shouldn't be there. And he found it. A small seam that ran along the grain of the wood, nearly invisible.

"Kick it, at the very bottom," Taylor said again, her head lolling back against Garman's shoulder. Chuck shrugged and did as she suggested. Sure enough, the panel popped out a fraction of an inch, as if it had been on some kind of spring release.

"That would be inconvenient if the horse kicked it," Garman muttered.

"It's too low," Chuck said. "Horses kick up and out. They wouldn't get the force needed down here by the deck. Plus, didn't you notice? The stall door latch is broken. Probably so they never have to put a horse in here. Jack's clever like that."

As he spoke, the young man did his best to get his fingers around the edges of the panel and pulled it off. A low, wide passageway yawned open beyond it. Chuck ducked inside. To his relief, he found that the low part was only a couple of inches wide and he was able to stand fully erect once past.

"Hand her through to me," he said, turning back to the opening. Garman grunted and Chuck crouched to receive the nearly limp dying girl. He tried to keep her head from jostling too much but in truth, she didn't seem to mind. That morphine must have been powerful stuff.

Once he got Taylor in his arms, Chuck stood aside to let Garman follow him through. He took a look around and realized, with a start, that they must already be in the boiler room. It was nearly pitch dark but the high, wet-sounding whistle of the boilers was unmistakable.

"Wish I woulda known about that passageway earlier," Garman muttered as he straightened up to stand beside Chuck. "We had to fight our way up and over to get down to the stables."

"We didn't see any pirates on our deck when we came down," Chuck said. "One on the girls' level but that was it."

"We found some." Garman's tone told Chuck that whoever they'd found no longer breathed. A savage gladness shot through him at the thought.

"Take me over there," Taylor said, waving a hand vaguely ahead of them. "I gotta get to the main boiler control."

"This way," Garman said and started forward. "I think I know where it is."

"Because of your 'exploring' earlier?" Chuck couldn't help but ask.

"Something like that," Garman replied, stiffly. Chuck wished he could see the Windfist's face. He'd have bet every coin he had that the man was beet red. Jay would be chortling himself sick.

Jay.

"Do you think . . . is there a chance that Jack or the others might still be alive?" Chuck kept his voice to a whisper.

"I don't know," Garman answered, when it became clear that Taylor wasn't going to. Chuck gave her a little bounce and she mumbled something, so he knew she still lived.

For the moment. Bloody hells, what a mess this was.

Gunfire from the direction they'd come made him whip his head around.

"We're good!" Jasmine's said. Relief flooded through him.

After several minutes of navigating the area, they found the main boiler . . . mostly because of the sound. To Chuck, it looked like a mess of pipes, valves and levers. Several gauges and dials dotted the contraption, bouncing and hissing in time to the moving parts. Small glass tubes here and there showed water levels in various tanks. He blinked in confusion at the sheer complexity of it all.

Chuck got Taylor situated as best he could in front of the controls and slapped her face lightly to get her to wake up.

"Mmm? Oh! Good work," she said, sleepily. He slapped her again, slightly harder, until her eyes focused. "Okay, so I need you to jam the safety valve shut. Use something heavy to bend the pipe. Then, stoke the fire as big as you can. Just throw all the fuel on it. After that, I'll close the valves and let the pressure build. You'll have maybe five minutes to get out before it blows."

She smiled, sadly, as she placed her hands on the controls.

"Be quick, my friends. And . . . thank you. I couldn't have made it this far without you guys."

"Taylor, are you sure?" Chuck had to ask one more time. "There could still be survivors, and maybe we can get you to a doctor?"

"Nope. Don't be silly, Chuck. There's too many of them. Go build my fire so you can save your girl. Oh! She likes mechanical things. Give her my turbine model over there, and the goggles next to it," Taylor said, pointing to a small hunk of metal against the bulkhead not far away. "Remember, even smart girls like cool presents. Now get to work, boys. I ain't got all day."

Chuck felt sick but he grabbed a heavy wrench and hammered on the valve. At Taylor's nod, he and Garman set to work shoveling coal into the firebox. Before long, their face and arms were black with coal dust, streaked with rivulets of sweat. The heat in the compartment built and built, until it seemed to be a living thing crushing the life out of the three of them.

"Good enough," Taylor said, her voice nearly inaudible over the shrieking whistle of the boiler. "Now go. And promise . . ."

"Taylor."

Jack's voice, ragged with pain. Despite the morphine, the blonde girl's head shot up as the captain's giant silhouette detached itself from the shadows behind the main boiler.

He wasn't moving well. He kept one hand on the safety railing around the boiler, and leaned heavily that direction as he walked. When he emerged fully from the darkness, Chuck could see his clothes were streaked with black that shone wetly in the flickering light from the boiler.

"Jack," Taylor breathed. "You're alive."

"Not really, baby girl," he said. He fell heavily to one knee beside her, then reached out to run his hand over her hair. He left a streak of red behind. "Knew you'd be here."

"You always said, don't let them take the ship. If they take it, they don't get to keep it."

"That's right. That's how I knew. But I didn't . . . want you to be alone."

Taylor let out a sob and reached for him. The big man groaned and fought to move toward her, his arms outstretched.

Garman swore and dropped his shovel, then he picked Taylor up and handed her to Jack, laying her broken body in his arms.

"Thank you," Taylor said, as she leaned her head against Jack's blood-soaked chest. "You should go. And promise me something."

"What?" Garman asked. Chuck found that he couldn't speak.

"Say you'll remember me . . . us. And don't make our mistake. Love your ladies, boys. Don't be cowards about it. Now run."

With that, she pulled the levers down, holding them in place. Chuck could hear the metal straining as all of the valves squealed shut. Garman grabbed his arm and started to haul him back toward the passageway into the stables. Chuck barely managed to reach out and grab the model and goggles.

By the time they stumbled back into the stables, Ariel had the door almost open. Jasmine stood at the base of the ladder, firing her Mare's Leg up at someone trying to come down.

"Go! Ariel! Go!" Garman yelled, shoving Chuck toward her. Chuck reached out and slapped Millie's rump and the mare leapt forward, throwing her weight against the door. It released from its catch, slamming down into the water, drenching all of them with a splash that left Chuck coughing. Millie obediently jumped into the river, the other horses following suit. He waited long enough to see Millie's surface and watch her start to swim for the bank. He grabbed hold of Ariel with one hand, the gifts in the other, and took a wild leap of faith.

The water was a shock. After the inferno of the boiler room, the air itself would have been pleasant, but the river water was so cold it *hurt*. Chuck felt it close over his head and forced himself not to gasp at the pain. He kicked his legs, driving himself and the girl he still held toward the surface of the thankfully slow-moving current.

His head broke out into sweet, blessed air. Chuck dragged in a breath. Next to him, he heard Ariel coughing and spitting, so he knew she was alive. He turned to try to orient himself, looking for Millie and the other horses, or Garman and Jasmine, when the world exploded.

The *Sally* had been moving at quite a clip, but it wasn't so far away that the sight and the sound didn't hit him like a two-by-four to the face. Chuck felt himself driven back down under the surface, air knocked from his lungs. The need for air clawed at him, pounding his brain and chest. He couldn't see, he couldn't hear but for the roaring of the water in his ears...

Something grabbed at his hair and yanked. Pain like a million needles stabbed into his scalp and he kicked out, involuntarily, in response. Something wrapped around his chest and he felt himself moving. He couldn't tell the direction but a moment later his face broke the surface again. He dragged in a breath that was at least half water. He choked, coughed, spat and sucked in another lungful of sweet, delicious, pine-scented air.

"You okay?" Ariel asked, sounding sorta gaspy herself. She had her arm around his chest and one hand buried in his hair. He found himself floating with his head on her breasts. He was absolutely certain that it wasn't an appropriate place for him to be and equally certain that he never, ever wanted to move. Ariel had saved him from drowning.

Ariel.

"Thanks...to you," he said. His throat felt torn to ribbons, probably from trying to breathe so much water. "How did you...?"

"I just grabbed you," she said with a shrug that made his head bob in the water. "Like you were one of the kids at the dam back home. Sometimes they would fall in the water before they could swim and if no one was paying attention...well. I tried to keep an eye out. I managed to grab a couple of them before it was too late."

He wanted to ask about their parents and why a girl like Ariel should have to be looking out for other people's children. He wanted to say something to erase the very obvious old sadness in her voice. He wanted to kiss her and thank her for his life.

He was too exhausted to do any of those things. So he just laid back on her chest and let her kick them to the shore.

As they got close, he heard Jasmine shout. He opened his eyes to see Quetzalith's great wings circling overhead.

"You can stand up now," Ariel said, exhaustion in her voice. "We're nearly at the bank."

With a start, Chuck put his feet down and felt his boots sink into the muddy bottom. He straightened, the water coming to a level just below his chest. He turned to see Jasmine and Garman coming toward them, reaching out to pull him and Ariel securely up onto the riverbank.

"Come on," Jasmine said. "Let's get you warmed up, then we'll see where we're at."

"Where we're at" turned out to be a hillside that had once held a suburban neighborhood. The river made a hairpin turn to the south—they and some of the wreckage of the *Sally* had washed up on the north bank. The vegetation in this hilly area seemed to be quite aggressive but within a few steps, Chuck realized that he was walking on a surface that had once been leveled and paved.

"Quetzalith saw me get out of the water and herded our horses toward us," Jasmine said. "And there was this pile of driftwood right there, so I had him light it up. Go on, get warm and let's get your clothes dried out. It'll be dark soon."

"What about the pirates?" Chuck forced the words through chattering teeth. "Or other wildlife?"

"I haven't seen any other survivors. When that boiler blew, it really blew," Jasmine said, soberly. "And if there are other boats or whatever, they're either long gone, or they went when the *Sally* did. As for wildlife... I think Quetzalith's presence should be enough to keep us safe tonight."

"But we'll post a watch anyway," Garman said, walking up to them with an armful of wood. "After we eat and take inventory of what we have."

Thanks to the ladies' foresight in saddling the horses, they at least had access to the trail rations they'd kept in their saddlebags. As Chuck crunched down on a slightly waterlogged bar of pressed nuts and dried fruit, he felt a pang for the delicious meals from the *Sally*'s galley.

"I see you got your rifle," Garman said, nodding to where Fat

Lady lay next to Chuck. "I got mine, plus my pistol. Jasmine's got her Mare's Leg. We're gonna be short on ammo until we get to Pittsburgh but there should be resupply there."

"A Windfist outpost?" Ariel asked. Garman's face pinched and he shook his head.

"There is one, of course, but I don't think it's wise to check in there. After what happened in KC, I can't risk it. I have to get my information to the Bunker...shit! How are we going to get there without Jay? He was the only one who knew the way."

"I know it," Chuck said, keeping his head down. Something huge and heavy settled into his chest as he thought of the laughing, teasing, comfortably uncomfortable old man. "My pa told me."

"You do?" Garman asked. "But...I thought Jay was guiding you there."

"He was," Chuck said. "But I always knew the route. Jay was just making sure I made it alive."

"An' a good thing, too!"

Chuck spun at the sound of the slightly hoarse, slurred words coming from the foliage behind him. Across the fire, Quetzalith lifted his head and let out a chittering sound that seemed less like a warning and more like some kind of welcome.

Wet, bedraggled, dirty and very clearly drunk, Jay staggered from the brush into the circle of light cast by the fire.

"Jay!" Jasmine cried out. While Chuck gaped, stunned, at the reappearance of the man they'd all thought dead, she leaped up to help him fall next to where the tack lay spread out to dry.

"Hey kids. Miss me?" Jay asked. He let out a hoarse cackle and reached into his leather jacket for a flask. He opened it, took a swig and made a face. "Gah. River water."

"Are you hurt?" Jasmine asked.

"Just muh pride, darlin'," he said. "I'm getting a bit old to be blown up."

"Is anyone else with you?" Ariel asked. Jay shook his head.

"Jack...well. It's how he wanted to go. Killin' river trash as though they was pirates. Whole damn boat went boom and next thing I know I'm wakin' up underwater."

"Taylor and Jack blew the boiler," Chuck found himself saying.

"Sounds right. Damn shame. Right pretty girl, that one. Brave and brilliant," Jay said, closing his eyes for a moment. He lifted his flask again in a toast to the courage of the lost singer.

"She made it so we could get out," Garman said, his voice low and soft. "She had the courage of a Windfist, even while she bled her life away."

Jasmine looked up from checking Jay over and scowled at Garman.

"Windfists don't have a monopoly on courage, you know," she said. "You don't have to sound so damn patronizing. Taylor was a warrior in her own right. *She* killed all those pirates. Not you. Not Jack. Not any man. *She* did it. That's all you have to say about it."

Chuck felt his own eyes go wide at her tone. He bit his lips together. Garman's face creased in confusion.

"That's what I said..."

"No, it isn't. You said she had courage enough to be a Windfist. As if that's the best anyone could ever aspire to be. Would *you* have been brave enough, tough enough to crawl through the refrigeration duct to get to the boiler room just so that you could blow the ship up and kill everyone on it? Including yourself? Taylor was *braver* than a Windfist. Braver than any man I've ever met! So don't you dare sit there all sanctimonious and expound upon her virtues. She had more virtue in her little finger than you could ever hope to have!"

"What does 'sanctimonious' mean?" Chuck whispered to Jay.

"Don't talk now, kid. It ain't a good idea to draw her attention."

Jasmine stared at Garman in white-faced fury, then spat out a curse and surged to her feet. She stalked over toward Quetzalith, who mantled his wings protectively. Ariel cast one quick look at the rest of them, then rose slowly to her feet and went after the other woman.

Jay let out an explosive sigh and started to laugh.

"Hell. I guess it's good to be back home."

CHAPTER FOURTEEN

ASIDE FROM A LOT OF BRUISING, JAY CHECKED OUT ALL RIGHT. They made what camp they could there, sheltering under tree boughs cut from the surrounding foliage. The temperature dropped quickly, enough that those who weren't on watch huddled together under smoke-scented saddle blankets for warmth. Chuck spent most of his watch walking around, chafing his hands together and keeping the fire lit.

His was the last watch, so when dawn started to turn the eastern sky pink, he stretched and started to gather up their food stores. He figured the least he could do was start breakfast before waking everyone up.

Quetzalith chittered at him, then dipped his head and opened his long jaw. Chuck was no dragon tamer but it looked like a smile and so he smiled back and flipped a piece of jerky at the dragon. Quetzalith snapped it up and chittered again. Chuck didn't know if that meant "thanks" or not but it sure as hell seemed like it.

"He likes you," Jasmine said, sitting up from where she'd slept curled between Garman and Ariel. Apparently Garman's "sanctimoniousness" (whatever that was) didn't overshadow his usefulness as a sleep warmer.

"Does he?" Chuck asked quietly.

"Sure. He likes all of you. You're my friends now, so he likes you."

"Well, I guess I like him, too."

"You can tell him. He'll understand."

"He understands language?"

"Some. A little more than a horse or a dog. Mostly, though, he seems to respond to people's emotions. You've seen how he reacts to mine."

"Yeah. He does do that. Instinct again?"

"Something like that," she said with a smile. "Is that breakfast? Let me help you."

Together, the two of them boiled some jerky and dried vegetables to make a thin soup. One by one, the other members of their group woke up, stretching sore muscles and easing into the motion of another day. By the movements of his fellows, Chuck figured that he clearly wasn't the only one who felt like he'd been...well...blown up.

Or near enough as to make no difference.

Eventually, they got organized enough to break camp and start moving toward Pittsburgh. As they traveled, Jay gave them some history about the city.

"The bugs had all but cleaned it out in the initial invasion," he said, swaying in his saddle and pausing frequently to take a pull from his flask. "But in the years that followed, our boys and girls fought like hell to recover the Steel Town. Thousands died but when it was all over, we held the refineries and steel mills. A few minor hives fought on for some years but they eventually died out or went to ground."

"Why?" Ariel asked, Taylor's goggles perched on her forehead. She'd fallen into position next to Jay as they rode, her face rapt at his storytelling. She was sitting her horse much better than she had before, too.

"Well, darlin', the only people in the area were the industrial workers and the military. And they were all armed to the teeth and veterans of the war. Not easy targets for the Gants, so they'd starved. Eventually, the workers and the fighters became one force, fanatically loyal to one another and dedicated to keeping the steel mills and the city of Pittsburgh, alive."

Even growing up in the far west, Chuck had heard of Pittsburgh. His pa had told him once that Pittsburgh was one reason they still had as much as they did. Without Pitt steel, Pa'd said, they'd have been stuck back in the Stone Age. Which was why

Pittsburgh had evolved into a city-state of its own. You wanted Pitt steel? You dealt with the Burghers of Pitt, on their terms.

The group entered the outskirts late afternoon on the second day. The terrain was hilly—steep, with thick, tenacious vegetation lurking everywhere. It choked what appeared to have been broad streets and well-to-do neighborhoods.

"Appalachian Red Pine," Jay said at one point, as the horses picked their way through the forest of dry boughs. Sharp brown and green needles sloughed to the ground with every touch, muffling their hoofbeats and creating an eerie hush. A sharp wind cut through the trees every so often and dark, foreboding clouds crouched low overhead. Chuck could feel the bite of early winter in the air as they climbed higher up into the foothills toward the Steel City.

They stayed close enough to the river to use it as a guide into the city. As they approached, Chuck caught the scent of hot metal and coal smoke heavy on the breeze. They topped a rise next to the river and came to a halt. The hill beneath them fell away in a sheer cliff that overlooked the joining of three rivers. Chuck counted at least five bridges, surprisingly elegant in the noonday sun, arching over the glittering water.

"Why are so many bridges still standing?" he asked.

"Pittsburghers," Jay said, taking his prelunch swig. "They're rabid about their steel. Those bridges keep the supply lines into and out of the city running...along with the rivers, of course."

"And why are they painted that way?" Ariel squinted, shielding her eyes against the glare. "Yellow and black?"

"Gold," Jay corrected her. "Black and gold. Again, it's a Pitt thing. Back in the World That Was, the city's pro sports teams all wore those colors. So they became the city's colors. The Burghers' city guards all wear black and gold. They don't like it when you call it yellow. Keep that in mind when we get to the bridge."

They didn't have to wait quite that long.

Out of nowhere, a band of armed and similarly dressed men stepped out of the underbrush and surrounded them at very close quarters, weapons drawn and pointed right at them. True to Jay's description, the squad wore black trousers with a yellow stripe down the leg, white shirts and yellow gloves. On the breast of each jacket, Chuck could see a patch—a white circle with three diamonds colored red, yellow and blue, surrounding the word

"Steel" in black lettering. Their helmets followed the pattern, for the most part, black with yellow stripe.

"What yinz want in The Burgh?" the guy holding the gun on Garman demanded. His helmet colors were reversed, yellow with black stripe. Chuck assumed he was in charge. Overhead, Quetzalith gave a warning scream. Jasmine threw up an arm to tell him to hold off, which made the guards twitchy.

"Move easy, lady," the spokesman said.

"Unless you'd like to be barbequed, I really shouldn't," Jasmine retorted. Chuck gave an inward sigh as the eight guardsmen got visibly more tense.

"Look," he said, nudging Millie slowly forward toward Garman. The Windfist sat relaxed and apparently at ease but Chuck knew that his fingers would be a hair's breadth away from his own weapons. "We don't mean no harm. The lady is just taking precautions. She's a dragon tamer and we've come to find her uncle here."

The guard narrowed his eyes, looked at Chuck, then Jasmine and back to Garman.

"And this is Journeyman Garman," Chuck filled in.

"Hmph. Windfist," the guard growled. "I heard things. Not all of them Windfists keeping neutral, these days. I hear they's causing trouble, riling folks up. That your plan, Windfist? Because we Steel Curtain Boys ain't having none of that."

"I am no traitor," Garman said stiffly. "I follow the precepts of my order."

"Right," Chuck said, jumping in. "We're just escorting the lady to her uncle's house and then we'll be moving on out of your city."

"Yinz lookin' a bit rough," the guard said, still suspicious. "Banged up. How'd I know you didn't just take that cloak from a dead Windfist to sneak in my city?"

"We were on a riverboat, had some trouble with pirates..." Chuck felt as if the situation was slipping through his fingers. He broke off when an unexpected scream split the air from above.

Chuck looked up to see the streamlined figure of a diving dragon. Before he could do so much as duck, another dark shape arrowed in from above on an intercept path. Quetzalith let out a scream of warning and the first dragon whipped out its wings and came to a hover above the group, buffeting them all with her downdrafts. She—judging by the smaller crest, Chuck guessed it was female—landed on one of the branches nearby, chittering at them as she settled. That and the way she tossed her head, made him think she was flirting. Quetzalith's wingbeats faltered once and he climbed back up to circle above the scene below.

"Ease up, willya, Petey? I don't think these ragamuffins are going to attack your precious city," a new voice said. A man pushed through the vegetation and black-clad guards to stand, hip-cocked and arms folded, in front of Garman's horse. Chuck heard Jasmine's quick intake of breath.

"They've got a dragon, Rickman."

"Mmm hmm," Rickman said, his eyes running over Garman's chest. He grinned, winking at the Windfist. "Among other assets, I see. If I weren't a married man ... Aw hell, Petey, give it a rest. I've got one too, in case you hadn't noticed."

"Uncle Mark?" Jasmine breathed, nudging her horse forward with her knees. Chuck moved Millie to the side slightly to let her through, keeping his eyes on the newcomer the whole time.

The man was tall and lean, maybe slightly younger than Pa but still handsome enough, with a chiseled jaw and bright green eyes. Like the guards, he was dressed mostly in black, though he lacked the yellow accessories or the "Steel" patch. While Chuck watched, he took a step toward Jasmine, his eyes first narrowing, then going wide with surprise.

"It can't possibly be ..."

"It's me, Uncle," Jasmine said, her voice thick.

"Jasmine ... but how?"

Jasmine threw her leg over the side of her mount, slid to the ground and threw herself into her uncle's embrace. Rickman's green eyes filled with tears as he held his niece close to him.

Petey, too, watched this scene. He cleared his throat and Chuck glanced his way to see the tiniest glint of moisture in the guard's eyes. Chuck swallowed, clearing the lump in his own throat.

"Well, hell, Eggs," Petey said. "Guess you know this lady?"

Rickman gave a mighty sniff and let go of Jasmine with a watery laugh.

"You got it, Petey," he said. "This is my brother's girl, Jasmine. I thought she was dead these last six years. But she survived and found me ... and brought me a breeding male?"

"Yes," she said, excitement showing through her tears. She laughed, then swiped at her eyes before lifting her hand to signal Quetzalith. He winged in, alighting on another of the pine branches overhead, keeping one eye on Jasmine. The other was focused on the female dragon.

"Uncle, this is Quetzalith. He's the last of Dad's breeding stock," Jasmine said. "He was an egg when . . . I raised him from a flapling, using what I could remember from Dad. Figured the rest out on my own."

"Quetzalith. Your father did love his Pern references," Rickman said, shaking his head. "Lovely to meet you, fine sir. He's a beauty, Jazz. You trained him? Someday, I think you'll have to tell me the whole story."

"Probably not," she said and before her uncle could react, Jasmine turned and pointed. "This young man is Chuck Gordon. I hired him and his friends to escort me and now they're my friends too. These are Jay and Ariel and the Windfist is Garman."

"Yes, I noticed him earlier," Rickman said, with another wink. To his credit, Garman remained stone-faced. "Mr. Gordon, thank you and your friends for bringing Jasmine here. I can't . . . I thought she was dead so long ago. If I had any notion she'd lived, I'd never have stopped looking for her."

From the fine tremor in Rickman's hands and the thickness in his voice, Chuck could tell that the man was close to the edge. Hell, *he* was close to the edge. Having an honest to God friendly on their side was a nice change. Relief washed over him.

"She's a fine gal, Rickman," Jay said. Chuck felt a surge of gratitude to the old man for speaking up, as he found himself tonguetied. "Tough as nails and rescued herself. Don't s'pose you got any whiskey, do ya? Feels like we should drink to y'all's reunion."

Petey let out a snort and Rickman threw back his head and laughed long and loud.

"So we should, Mr. Jay, so we should. Preferably before this sky opens up and dumps on us. Petey, thank you for not shooting my niece and her friends."

"Anytime, Eggs," Petey said. "Yinz be good in my city." He stepped to the side and waved them forward along a narrow path through the overgrown forest. Jasmine hugged her uncle one more time before remounting. The two dragons launched and the rest of them picked their way through the brush on horseback. Rickman led the way on foot.

Chuck looked back over his shoulder to see where Petey and his men had gone but they'd disappeared into the forest as if they'd never existed. He found himself wondering just how many black- and gold-clad warriors roamed this area.

The forest itself ran right up to and into the city itself. So much so that Chuck didn't realize they were actually in Pittsburgh until after Millie's hooves clattered on paved surfaces again. Even then, trees and vegetation crowded close to the streets, rearing up along half-tumbled buildings and crumbling ruins.

Rickman led them back closer to the river, then followed it until it intersected with two others to form a Y. Damage was more visible here, mainly because it looked like the area had mostly been paved over before the war.

"My Weyr's in the old stadium," he said, then laughed and shook his head. "My brother insisted on calling it that, you know. A 'Weyr.' He said that no other name would work for a place where dragons lived."

"I remember," Jasmine murmured.

"Your dad was a big reader when we were kids. Science fiction, fantasy, you name it. His favorites, though, were a series of books by a lady named Anne McCaffrey. About people who lived with and rode on the backs of dragons. The dragons' names always ended with a 'th' and they lived in a 'Weyr.' He always swore he was going to be a pilot, because it was close to being a dragonrider. But then the bugs came."

"And the dragons," Jasmine put in.

"And the dragons." Rickman nodded. "I was in my mid-twenties when it all went to shit and we evacuated. But your dad was always super excited about the dragons. He'd sneak out of the refugee camp and try to find eggs up in the mountains. Took him ten years but he did it. Hatched his first flapling and the rest was history. We were going to be rich, selling trained dragons to those that wanted them for protection from Gants."

"But?" Jasmine asked when he fell silent.

"But I got restless and fell in . . . well . . . I thought it was love. Anyway, I told Richard I wanted to see more of the world, I wanted to go to sea, find some more clients and I'd come back and then we'd grow our business. He agreed and I left. And when I came back . . ."

"He was dead," Jasmine said, her voice gentle. Rickman dropped his head down and stopped, causing Chuck to rein Millie in quickly to avoid running him down.

"Yeah," Rickman said, so softly that Chuck could barely hear. "Story was that you all were. That someone had come and killed you all, killed the dragons. So I changed my name. Stayed near the Islands, biding my time, hiring out to various ships. Dragons are damned useful at sea, you know. And then I heard about the wild population up here and thought, well, hell, maybe I can go to Pittsburgh. Maybe I can make my big brother's dream come true after all..."

Tears were streaming down the man's face. They'd come to some kind of plaza facing a large ruin. Though vegetation choked the area, Chuck could see the skeletal remains of metal poles poking up out of the ground at intervals, marching toward the curved building in front of them.

"What is this place?" He hoped he could change the subject and let Rickman get himself together.

"It was called Heinz Field. It used to be the stadium where the Steelers played but it got damaged in the war," Rickman said, sniffing. He turned to gesture expansively at the broken curve of the oblong building.

Though the north end was nothing but a piled mass of rubble and twisted steel, Chuck could see that the stadium had once had a distinctive shape, with rows of seats extending up like dragons' wings from either long side of the oval. As they got closer, it became clear that the exterior of the building was actually a series of ramps that wound around the central area. Judging by the width, hundreds of people must have come there once, watching whatever a "Steeler" did.

"I thought it would be a good place to breed Pearl," Rickman was saying. "It's the right shape for a Weyr. Turns out, though, that we weren't the only ones that think so. There's several wild dragons that have made their nests here over time.

"I've got some of their eggs," he said, with a note of smugness. "They stay toward the north end and don't bother us on the south. Pearl's made it plain that that's *her* territory,"

"She doesn't seem to be objecting to Quetzalith's presence," Jasmine said dryly.

"Oh no," Rickman said, smiling. "Pretty sure she likes him. She's about to go into season and I imagine she's decided he's her type."

"Interesting."

Chuck shot her a look. She threw him a wink but said nothing else. Only then did he remember that she'd once spoken of stud fees. Thinking about Rickman's surprise—once he realized that his beloved long-lost niece was likely to haggle worse than any merchant—made Chuck choke on a laugh.

Rickman gave him a curious glance before continuing.

"Anyway, I've got a nice area fixed up in the owner's box up top. Comfortable and secure. You're all welcome to stay with me for a few days...as long as you need, really. It's the least I can do for you, after you safely brought Jasmine here."

"Hell, man," Jay said, "she brought herself. We just came along for the ride. But we appreciate the hospitality just the same."

The "owner's box" was a level all its own, with great wide windows looking down onto the center of the stadium. Chuck fought off a sudden wave of dizziness as he stared out the window.

"Not much to look at, is it?" Garman said, joining him. "Maybe it was nice, once, but now it's just a bunch of dirt and rubble."

Whether from whatever strike that had taken out the north end of the stadium, or the years of wind and weather that had followed, the interior of Heinz Field had seen better days. Piles of dirt and dragon soil littered the grounds, along with more pieces of Gant armor than Chuck wanted to count. In some places, the seats had been completely torn away and piled haphazardly, so that the sloping interior bowl resembled a maze of carnage. Scorch marks gave mute testimony to the territorial squabbles of the dragons who had nested here over time, as did the occasional whiff of rotting meat carried in by the breeze.

"Yeah," Chuck said, turning back to look at the apartment Rickman had fashioned for himself. "It's much nicer in here."

Indeed, the owner's box, it turned out, was nearly as high class as the *Long Tall Sally* had been. Thick carpet stretched from wall to wall and long, low-slung chairs and sofas stood in groups that seemed to invite long, comfortable conversations. A polished bar stretched along the far wall, perpendicular to the windows and judging by the quantity of bottles, it was well stocked. There was even a wood stove in the corner, which both warmed the spacious interior and apparently cooked Rickman's food.

The man himself bustled around the stove now, stoking the fire and checking the flue to ensure that the smoke ran out through what had once been the corner pane of the window wall.

"I've got some meat for stew," Rickman was saying. "And help yourself to whatever you find behind the bar."

"Don't mind if I do," Jay said and hustled over there so comically that Chuck could hear Garman's snort of laughter next to him.

"So how did you end up here, Uncle?" Jasmine dropped herself into one of the chairs facing the window. Outside, Quetzalith and his new friend perched nearby, tucking into their own meal of some unidentifiable carcass.

"Wait," Chuck said, "you didn't *know* he was here?"

"I'd heard rumors, grapevine talk really, about a tamer in this area," Jasmine said. "Nothing concrete but solid enough to chance it."

"You *played* us?"

"Like a fiddle, son," Jay said, chuckling. "Told ya that gal was savvy when we met her!"

Chuck couldn't keep his shock from showing. He stood there, flushing as laughter filled the room.

"You were saying, Uncle?"

"Well . . ." Rickman dropped some chunks of meat into a pan, causing a sizzle and a delicious scent to rise through the room. "When I heard rumor about what happened, I was out in the Bahamas. Pearl and I'd hired on with an organization of ships' captains. They liked having a trained dragon around. Liked it even more when she'd clutch an egg and I could teach one of their sailors how to be a handler.

"Anyway, word got back to me and I took the first ship for New Orleans I could find. When I got there, I checked in with some friends. They confirmed that Richard had been attacked. Said everyone was killed."

"All except for us," Jasmine murmured. It didn't sound like a correction, more like she was lost in her own thoughts or memories.

"Yeah but I didn't know that. And I was scared that whoever had gone after your father would come after me, next. So, like I said, I changed my name and fled back to my friends in the Caribbean. Someone wanted to come for me there, they'd have a helluva fight on their hands."

"Sure," Jay said, as he lifted a short glass full of amber liquid. "But how'd you get *here*?"

"Worked myself out of a job, mostly," Rickman said. "Mostly, the captains who wanted dragon support have all got it now and unless they're a mated pair, it isn't a good idea to have two dragons on a ship. Not enough room for their territorial instincts. Since all the dragons I trained were Pearl's offspring, I had to find something else to do. That was last spring."

He hesitated, started to speak, then stopped. After a moment of looking at them all, Rickman shrugged.

"I knew that Pitt had a large wild dragon population, so I talked my husband into agreeing that I come up here for the season, gather some new eggs, and then we'd retire. There's this nice little spot down in the Keys where we can breed dragons together."

"Your husband?" Jasmine asked. Rickman ducked his head slightly, smiling shyly.

"Yeah, well, I call him my husband. Nobody cares about paperwork or whatever anymore. Anyway, his name is Dave. One of the captains I mentioned. He's... well. He's who put me back together after I heard about your family, Jazz. You're going to really like him. He's... I don't know how to describe it. I couldn't imagine spending my life with anyone else."

Jasmine got up out of her seat and threw her arms around her uncle.

"Uncle, I'm so happy for you. Congratulations! I can't wait to meet him. I assume he's not in Pittsburgh?"

"Nah, Dave isn't happy unless he's on the water. He'll be in New Orleans in three weeks to pick me up. You can come with us, of course. Quetzalith will be a perfect asset as we set up our Weyr in the Keys."

"I'll certainly come with you to meet your husband," Jasmine said. "But we'll need to talk about the rest of it later. I wouldn't want our business discussions colored by the emotions of finding one another after all this time."

Rickman threw his head back and laughed, then hugged his niece a bit harder.

"You're Richard's girl, all right! Smart as a whip! As you like, then. We'll eat and catch up and then talk business tomorrow."

"Eat and drink!" Jay lifted his—now mostly empty—glass. Rickman laughed harder, throwing his hands wide. Chuck figured he had no idea what Jay was about to do to his bar. Garman gave Chuck a small grin and began to walk that way. Chuck glanced toward Ariel but she seemed absorbed in watching the dragons out the window. He shrugged and followed the monk.

"Do we trust this guy?" Chuck asked Jay as they approached.

"Hell no, kid," Jay said. "But we don't trust nobody, remember?"

He laughed, shaking his head as he handed over a beer bottle. It wasn't cold, like on the *Sally*, but Chuck figured it might taste good all the same. He popped the top off and took a swig.

Yep. Tasted just fine.

"Do you think Jasmine is safe with him?" Garman straightened up a little and looked back toward where uncle and niece sat deep in conversation.

"I think she's as safe as she ever is," Jay said. "Trust me, Junior. That girl can take care of herself. She don't need you."

Pain crossed the Windfist's face before it went carefully blank. Jay laughed and poured more whiskey into his little glass.

"Gotcha," he said with a wink. "Just cause she don't need you, don't mean she don't want you. Remember that, both of you."

"Something is burning," Ariel said. Everyone looked over at the stew but it was just starting to bubble and no smoke came from the stove itself.

"No," she said, pointing out the window. "Out there, to the north. Something big."

Chuck grabbed his beer and walked over. He shivered, a sudden chill coming over him as he joined her. He tried to tell himself that it was just the proximity to the colder outside air but somewhere in the back of his mind, he knew better. Something was happening.

"What's going on?" Garman asked, walking up to stand next to them. Chuck shrugged, squinting, trying to see past the reflection cast by Rickman's oil lamps. It was growing dark outside and a dirty smudge of orange light illuminated the underbelly of the cloud layers above.

"Don't know," Chuck replied, "but Ariel's right. Something big is on fire up north."

"Could be the old city," Rickman said. "Lots of ruins up there. Could be someone squatting in the maze, lost control of their cookfire?"

"Too sudden for that," Ariel said. "I think..."

Quetzalith and Pearl lifted their heads and screamed, nearly in unison. Jasmine shot to her feet.

"Gants," she said, her tone flat. "Lots of them, coming here."

"What?" Rickman said. "How can you tell?"

"Nothing else makes him that angry," Jasmine replied. "Have you got a horse?"

"Yeah but..."

"Get your stuff, Uncle. We need to leave. Now."

"Now wait just a moment, Jasmine," Rickman said, stress ratcheting his voice up in pitch. Chuck and the others began to move, gathering up their weapons and gear. "There's no way you can know that. It's just a fire! And dragons will scream at any provocation."

"Not Quetzalith, and not like that. You can stay here if you want but I really think you should come with us. We've covered a lot of ground in the last few weeks and everything we've seen has pointed to the idea that things are about to get worse before they get better." She pushed past him and began shoving dried meat and fruit from his shelves into her bag. "I always listen to my instincts and it's kept me alive when nothing else could. Right now my instincts say to run."

She stopped, turning to look him in the eyes. Hers were hard but pleading.

"You're welcome to run with us but I won't make you. I will, however, suggest you look at what the wild dragons are doing right now."

Chuck looked toward the north end of the stadium. Sure enough, streaks of flame arced through the twilight. And not just one or two but closer to twenty, in rapid succession.

"Gods above," Rickman breathed. "They must be overrunning the city! The steel mills..."

"Not our problem right now," Jasmine said, voice crisp. "We need a way out of here."

"They're all coming from the north," Ariel said. "We can slip south and cross the river, then run up into the hills. They'll likely come this way eventually, but the dragons will keep them away for a few minutes."

"Can I...the eggs in the wild nests—"

"No time," Jasmine said. "A few minutes, nothing more. Enough to get us and our two out. Let's go."

Finally, something clicked and Rickman jumped into action. He produced a bag from somewhere and was throwing supplies into it when Chuck and Garman went to saddle the horses. Because of the dragons, Rickman had fashioned the neighboring stadium box into a stable with blacked-out windows. Millie and the others had greeted Rickman's chestnut gelding with friendly whickers when they'd arrived—Chuck hoped that meant that they'd work well together now.

"This way," Rickman said as he and the others emerged from the apartment. Chuck spared a thought of regret for the delicious beer stash that the man was abandoning but then he caught sight of Jay throwing him a wink. For some reason, that lifted his spirits. Clearly the old man had "rescued" some things.

They mounted up and followed Rickman and his gelding down the long, sloping ramps of the stadium. Sounds of chaos mixed with the rumble of thunder drifted toward them as they exited the building. They picked their way through the rubble and overgrowth toward the river.

"We'll take the Fort Duquesne bridge to cross the Allegheny," Rickman said, over increasing thunder. "The water should hopefully provide a bit of a barrier. Then after that...I don't know."

"We got you," Jay said. "The boy knows our route from here. Might as well come with us, Uncle Mark. I got a notion that the people where we're going might be happy to meet a man of your talents."

"I...all right," Rickman said. "Once we get outside the city, I'll send Pearl to Dave and tell him what's going on. Will Quetzalith follow her? They'll have to fly above the clouds, with this storm coming in, but it's a good a plan as any, I suppose."

"I'm not sure," Jasmine said. "I don't think Quetzalith would go so far without me, but he's never been near a female in season."

"I believe we need to go, soon," Ariel said. "The Holy Warriors are not behaving quite the way they should."

"What?" Chuck asked, shifting his attention to her. "What do you mean?"

"I am not certain...it is just that...when a nest swarms, they do so in all directions at once. This does not look like that. You can see out toward the east, along the river? Nothing. It makes no sense that they would be staying contained and driving in a single wedge. That is not how Holy Warriors act. This is more..." Ariel shrugged, as if she couldn't quite find the right word. "T...tactical?"

"Tactical?" Garman looked surprised. Chuck couldn't tell if it was from the situation, Ariel using the word correctly, or both. "Like...what? Like someone's leading them?"

He paused and turned toward the east, as if to verify what Ariel said. Chuck looked too. Seemed the former cultist was right. There wasn't much anything moving in that direction. Nor, for that matter, from the west as far as he could see. What was happening?

"Whatever it means, we don't have time to figure it out!" Jasmine said. "We know they're heading toward the stadium. We need to get moving!"

She threw her arms up, and with another scream, Quetzalith took off, followed closely by Pearl. The two dragons made one flaming dive back toward the north end of the stadium, then climbed up into the boiling mass of clouds above.

A look of longing passed over Garman's face—Chuck wondered if they were going to have to force the Windfist not to go looking for a warrior Gant to try and kill with his bare hands. But apparently Jay's constant reminders of their mission had had some effect, because Garman straightened in his saddle and kicked his horse into motion toward the golden arc of the Fort Duquesne Bridge.

The rest of them followed, hooves clattering over the broken concrete. Within a few minutes, fat drops of rain pattered down all around them. It started slowly but before long, they were soaked to the skin as the skies opened. The wind picked up too—soon they were dodging thrashing tree boughs while trying to stay together as they rode as quickly as they could for the bridge.

The storm winds kept at them, driving the rain sideways. More than once, Chuck had to wipe water out of his eyes just so that he could continue to see Garman's cloak in front of him.

Thunder exploded overhead as they clattered up the approach to the bridge. A jagged bolt of lightning split the sky, the flash of blinding light revealing a line of men midway across the bridge, blocking their escape.

"It's okay!" Rickman shouted over his shoulder. "It's gotta be the Steel Curtain Boys. They're just..."

He trailed off as another bolt of lightning lit the night. These men weren't wearing black and gold.

Instead, they wore uniforms of heavy velvet, pointing their rifles at the group.

"I'd suggest you stop, dragon tamer," one of the men called. "Someone wants to talk to you."

"Who?" Rickman asked, reining in.

"Me," a voice came from behind them.

In his head, Chuck heard the sound of a steel trap snapping shut. He reined Millie around to see another line of men blocking the way back. Two men, one wearing robes like Ariel's, then another in uniform, stepped forward.

"Hello, brother. Been awhile, hasn't it?" A third man advanced wearing a Windfist cloak.

"Ronen." Garman sounded strangled.

Chuck wanted to wipe the smug smile from the newcomer's face. With a stout piece of hickory.

"What are you doing?" Garman asked, his voice thick. "Why are you doing this?"

"I told you before, Garman. Times are changing. We need to change with them."

"But going back on our teaching, our training? Our Masters?"

"That was always your problem, you know," Ronen said. "You're stronger than me, faster than me, you learn tactics faster and better than I do...but you always followed the rules, Garman. Even when you know that fighting dirty is the only way to win, you still play by the rules. And that is why you continue to lose."

The other Windfist spread his arms, his cloak billowing out behind him. Chuck felt Millie shift.

"It's a brave new world, Brother. The Windfist masters are nothing but a bunch of short-sighted old men, too paralyzed by age and indecision to be an effective force of any kind. *We* are the future, Garman." He brought his hands out in front him. "You can still join me, you know. With Ironhelm as our ally, we'll take back the Territories!"

The zeal in his voice, the look in his eyes—it reminded Chuck of the cultists at the farm.

"Think of it! No more petty disputes to settle every time we travel anywhere. No more tiresome focus on what we once had... The Baron is far more interested in focusing on the future...on what we *can* have!"

"On what *he* can have, you mean," Jasmine said.

Ronen's smile stayed in place as he turned to look at her. The velvet-clad behemoth standing next to him inclined his head to her in a small bow.

"Hello, Captain Conason," Jasmine said. The captain stayed silent.

"Ah! You must be the infamous Lady Moore." Ronen's smile grew slightly. "Yes, Baron Schilling is *extremely* interested in speaking to you. And, I imagine, this gentleman riding beside you. A lover perhaps? You should know, sir, that the Baron does not seem the type to share."

"Ew, gross," Rickman said. "No, I'm her uncle."

"The dragon tamer! Even better. I imagine it's really frustrating to know that the weather is preventing your abominations from blasting us all off of this bridge right now, isn't it?"

"Pearl don't mind the rain," Rickman said. "She's just got somewhere else to be."

"Hm, pity. I should like the opportunity to defend myself against an abomination."

"Keep it up," Jasmine said darkly. "You'll get it."

Another blast of lightning split the sky overhead, followed by the crack of thunder. Chuck tried to blink away the resulting flash-blindness, as the sounds of terror clawed through the ringing in his ears.

Millie reared under him, screaming her own panic. He fought to stay in the saddle, trying to see what in the hell was going on. Slowly, as the white blobs faded from his sight, he could see shapes moving in the darkness. Shapes that looked a hell of a lot like warrior Gants.

"What's happening?" he heard Ronen yell. "You said your people had them under control!"

"It...must be the storm, sir!" an unfamiliar voice answered. Probably the cultist. "Our scent markers can only do so much to fight instinct, especially in this heavy rain. The Holy Warriors are in a frenzy for all of this electricity!"

"Well, for the love of artillery, keep them from attacking us!"

"We've got to get off the bridge, sir! The steel is attracting the lightning! They can sense the ionic buildup!"

At that moment, one of the warrior Gants crashed through the line of men blocking the entrance to the bridge. It was followed by three others. All immediately set to destroying everyone in their path.

Conason shot at the closest one, the insect rearing up as his fire shredded one of its eyes. More gunfire immediately brought it down but not before the man caught in its mandibles was torn in half. His screams faded into the sounds of chaos.

Behind Chuck, Ariel shouted. He looked back over his shoulder to see her horse plunging again. He reached for her reins but missed in the darkness and the confusion. Garman had better luck, though, leaning in from the other side to make a spectacular one-handed grab. Muscles bulging in his arm, he held the gelding steady.

"Mine!" Chuck heard behind him, along with an accompanying hail of gunfire. He ducked as Millie turned again, reacting to this new source of fear.

Ronen fired several rounds, from a handgun that Chuck hadn't even seen him draw. The rogue Windfist leapt into the air and somersaulted, landing on the back of a Gant in the melee. More lightning cracked overhead, glinting off the Windfist's knife as he plunged it elbow-deep into the Gant's left eye.

The warrior, predictably, didn't like that. She thrashed, massive saw-toothed jaws crashing together again and again. The vinegar stink of fear and pain hit Chuck like an acid sledgehammer as the warrior released the chemical equivalent of a scream.

Millie reared up once again in panic and from the sounds of things, she wasn't alone. Horses cried out, their whinnies punctuating the sounds of humans shouting, all joining thunder and gunfire. Chuck quickly looked around, attempting to find his friends.

Garman was trying to control Ariel's horse and keep Ronen in sight. He couldn't see Jay anywhere. Jasmine and Rickman had their hands full with their own mounts, as well as avoiding gunfire from the line of men blocking their path.

The line of men who looked terrified, ready to break and white-faced in the sudden light.

Another bolt of blue-white fire danced overhead and struck the steel arch of the bridge. Every hair on Chuck's body stood on end and the stink of burnt ozone joined the acid stench of the Gant warriors' pain.

But all Chuck could see was the other end of the bridge.

"Go! Now!" he shouted, kicking Millie for all he was worth. She leapt forward, smashing into the withers of Ariel's horse, taking the gelding's attention off of the battle. Together, the two horses started to charge toward the line of terrified velvet-clad men. A few raised their weapons but in the uncertain light, none of them fired. Chuck became aware of Rickman and Jasmine falling into line with them, just as he heard a shout of triumph from behind.

"You see, Brother!" Ronen shouted. "Now I earn my mastery! Join me and no one will stand against—FUCK!"

Chuck risked a look over his shoulder and caught a confused scene. Ronen stood atop the dead Gant, the carapace riddled through with bullet holes. The rogue Windfist clutched at his shoulder, as if he'd been shot. He glared at Garman with a look of complete betrayal.

Garman wasn't looking back. After shooting his fellow Windfist he'd spun his horse and was riding hell-for-leather after them, Jay right beside him. But he did hear, apparently.

"A PISTOL DOESN'T COUNT, RONEN!" Garman shouted over his shoulder. "HAND OR KNIVES ONLY! YOU WILL NEVER BE A MASTER!"

Chuck turned just in time to see the first man go down under Millie's hooves. He forced himself not to think too deeply about the sickening wet *crunch* or the disturbingly warm liquid splashing up over his legs.

Just ride on, he told himself grimly, kicking Millie again. *Just keep going, as fast as you can.*

They clattered over the bridge as the storm raged overhead, lightning striking the span. Blue flames sang down the steel beams but left their party untouched. Rain continued to hammer at them, coming from above and both sides as the wind whipped and gusted.

"Keep low!" Chuck shouted. He reached out one more time to catch Ariel's reins and wrap them around his fist. Not the smartest move, he knew, but better than losing Ariel if her horse bolted.

They raced off the bridge, plunging into low scrub. In between the lightning strikes, it got very dark. But Chuck didn't want to slow more than they had to. Who knew how long it would take their enemies to regroup and come after them?

Without warning, they broke through the brush, into an open area. The grass stretched up to the horses' bellies.

"This is Fort Duquesne!" Jay shouted from the back of their group. "You know where to go from here?"

"Pa said to find Liberty Bridge, then stay on that path." Chuck slowed Millie to a walk.

As he said it, he realized that for the first time, he was talking openly about his destination with the group. Somewhere along the line, they'd become people he could trust, despite his dad's warnings.

"Liberty Bridge?" Rickman perked up. "It's east of here, but it's just a shell. There's not much 'bridge' left to speak of."

"Can it get us across this river?" Chuck thought he saw Rickman shrug in the darkness.

"Us? Maybe. Horses? Probably not."

"Figure it out when we get there," Jay said. "Probl'y better if we keep moving."

"This way, then. There's sort of a path but we can't go quickly," Rickman said and kicked his horse toward the front of the group. Jasmine followed, Garman right beside her. Chuck tossed Ariel her reins and nodded for her to go next, figuring that her skittish mount might be calmest in the center of their little herd. He let Millie fall into step beside Jay's gelding.

Rickman was right, they couldn't go fast. The undergrowth on the narrow spit of land was incredibly dense. The overarching boughs choking the path sheltered them from the rain a little but the wind continued to toss the branches in a wild, chaotic dance, forcing them to lie flat against their horses' necks. Chuck felt the excitement of the battle drain away, leaving him feeling wet, cold, tired and worst of all, hungry.

"Ain't adventures fun?" the old man said behind him. Chuck swore Jay was reading his mind. He looked over his shoulder to see the white flash of the old drunk's teeth as he grinned in the darkness.

"You got a strange definition of 'fun' Jay," Chuck said. That made the old man laugh out loud.

"We used to have a saying, back in the day," Jay said. "'Embrace the Suck.' It means when things get real shitty, like you're getting rained on and the wind is like the breath of frozen hell itself, the only thing to do is to flip that switch in your brain that says 'Yes! I love this! Gimme more!'"

"Why on Earth would I want more?"

"'Cause pain is weakness leaving the body, kid. What doesn't kill you makes you stronger. Additional motivational quotes as required! Pay attention, you put these pearls on a T-shirt, you'll make a mint one day."

"Pearls? Jay, I'm sorry but I don't know what the hell you're talking about."

Jay laughed, fishing his flask out of his jacket.

"Kids. Never mind. Have a drink. It won't make it suck any less but at least you'll be buzzed." The old man tipped the flask to his own lips and then held it forward.

Unable to argue with Jay's logic there, Chuck shrugged and took the drink. For once, he welcomed the burn of the liquor as it savaged its way down to his belly. At least it was something else to think about.

Pretty soon, Chuck could see that the path cut a relatively straight line toward the east. The remains of buildings hulked on either side, shrouded by the choking vegetation. He wondered what it would have been like to have lived in a city like this one, or Kansas City, before the Gants invaded and everything got turned on its head.

"Bridge is up there," Rickman said after a while. They came to an upsloping ramp that peeled off their path to the right. "But like I said, it's a shell."

"That is a cantilever bridge," Ariel said. She'd gone about halfway up the curving ramp and peered through the darkness at the structure itself. "See the arches, though? They are intact all the way across. It should be solid for the whole length."

"Sure and it would be," Rickman said, with a bit of sarcasm. "Except that the asphalt cracked hard down the length of the whole bridge, right down the middle. There're holes as big as a house in the center section. The only way across is to hug the right side...and if one of the horses slips, it's dead. And so's the rider."

"Is there another way across? A place to ford? Another bridge?" Chuck asked.

"Not really," Rickman shrugged. "Birmingham might work but it's miles away. And you can't ford the Mon, not on horses. The banks are too crumbly. That's what *Monongahela* means: falling banks."

"How under the sky do you know that?" Jasmine turned toward her uncle. Rickman shrugged.

"You pick things up, living in the Burgh."

"Right," Chuck said. "Well, shit. I say we try the Liberty Bridge. Pa said this was the one to take. I suppose we could dismount and walk the horses over."

"Might have to blindfold 'em," Rickman said.

"Might." Chuck nodded. "But we can do that if we gotta. And we ain't accomplishing anything standing here. So let's go see what we've got."

With that, he nudged Millie into a walk up toward Ariel's position, studiously ignoring the looks from his various companions. Jay seemed amused and slightly approving. Jasmine, surprised. Ariel, merely curious, while Rickman looked discontented and pessimistic. Only Garman said anything as Chuck approached.

"Decisive leadership is a good thing," the Windfist murmured. "Well done. That's how you'll earn their respect."

"The hell with their respect," Chuck said. "I'm just trying to keep everybody *alive*."

"That's how you'll earn their respect, too," Garman said. He gave Chuck one of his rare grins—though it didn't quite reach his eyes—and dismounted. Chuck followed suit and the two men led the way onto the span of the Liberty Bridge.

Unlike the Fort Duquesne Bridge, Liberty lacked the soaring suspension towers and lines. It was, instead, rather a plain-Jane affair, though it was easily five times as long as the other. In the flashing lightning, Chuck could see the glitter of water through the gaping holes marring the surface of the bridge.

"Rickman's right," he said. "We're going to have to blind the horses."

Millie tossed her head in protest but eventually, Chuck got one of his bandannas tied in her bridle and over her eyes. Then he and Garman helped the others, taking extra care with Ariel's horse.

"Just remember," Chuck told the wide-eyed girl, "if he starts to fall, you let go of his reins, got it? Either he'll scramble himself up or he won't but you won't be able to stop him from falling."

"I understand," Ariel said, her voice soft and miserable. Her wet hair was plastered to her face, which looked pinched and cold in the faint light. He wanted to tell her everything was going to be all right. He wanted to promise her that they'd be warm and safe, soon. But as he didn't truly believe either of those things, Chuck elected to say nothing.

"Single file," Garman was instructing everyone. Rather needlessly, in Chuck's opinion but it seemed to make the Windfist feel useful. "And don't bunch up too close."

The wind continued to whip at them, howling down the channel of the Monongahela and making it hard to keep a steady pace. It didn't help matters that rain made the crumbling asphalt slick and treacherous.

The bridge was a little over a mile long. Not quite two-thirds of the way there, another thunderclap shattered the air around them. Millie started, then stumbled into one of the larger cracks.

Chuck forgot his advice and reached out to grab Millie's bridle. She whinnied at him in fear and he could see that her back-left hoof was wedged in the crack itself.

"Hold up!" he called out over the lashing rain. He swiped at his face to try and see more clearly but the dark and the deluge made it difficult.

"Easy, girl, easy," Chuck murmured to the horse as he bent down to inspect her predicament. He left one hand on her withers—he could feel her trembling with cold and fear.

"How bad is it?" Garman asked, crouching next to Chuck.

"Can't tell. She might be cut; she might just be stuck. I don't want to just yank her hoof free, though. Do you think we could crumble some of the asphalt away?"

"Worth a shot," Garman said. "Long as she doesn't panic."

"She's steady," Chuck said, patting the mare and hoping he wasn't lying. She'd been through a lot in the last few days. They all had. "She'll be fine."

"All right," Garman said and pulled out his big utility knife. Chuck kept one hand on Millie's ankle and one up on her withers, trying to steady her while Garman dug at the crumbling blacktop, trying to get it to loosen enough that the mare could pull free. Millie whinnied and Chuck tried to keep talking, keeping up a stream of loving nonsense to hopefully help keep her calm.

"Almost...got it!" Garman said, a big chunk of the asphalt coming free in his hand.

Chuck barely had time to let go of Millie's ankle before she jerked it up to her body. But, she didn't kick them, or more importantly, didn't step back into the hole.

"Good," Chuck said. "I don't think she's badly hurt but I can't tell in all this rain. We've got to get across this bridge and out of this weather."

"Yep," Garman said, straightening. He sheathed his knife. "I agree. Especially with the lightning still going on,"

"She's fine!" Chuck called. "Let's keep moving. Slow it down and be careful but keep going," he said. From the front of the line, Jasmine acknowledged with a wave and she and her uncle started forward again. Garman retook his place behind them, leading Ariel and her horse, then Chuck, then Jay, who appeared to have fallen asleep while they were working with Millie.

"Jay!" Chuck said, kicking at the old man's crossed boots. Jay let out a strangled snore, then lifted his hat to squint up at Chuck.

"Your mare's good?" he asked.

"Yeah," Chuck said, smiling despite himself. Jay never changed. "We're moving."

"Damn skippy," Jay said and bounded up to his feet with an energy that Chuck wished he felt.

It's a little bit obscene, how much energy he has as an old man. Why can't I feel that way? Maybe I should become a drunk. Too bad I don't have any liquor on me. Must be why he always carries those flasks. I'm going to have to get one of my own.

Oddly, the thought cheered him and turned his mind to picking their way across the rest of the bridge. It seemed to take forever but it couldn't have been more than an hour or so. The storm still raged, though it showed signs of slowing as the group stumbled, one by one, off of the bridge and toward the rising terrain ahead.

"The closest trail that continues south is a ways to the east, following the Mon," Rickman said.

"We're not following the river," Chuck said as he untied Millie's blindfold and stroked her nose. "That's exactly where they'll be looking for us."

"You don't want to try and go cross-country around here."

Chuck ignored Rickman's protests, nudging Millie into a slow walk. She didn't seem to be favoring her hoof, at least.

"This ain't settled territory," the dragon tamer said. "Plus, the horses will never make it over Mount Washington here. It's too steep."

"Not planning to go over it," Chuck said absently, as he continued to follow the rapidly dwindling path straight ahead, toward what looked like an old rock fall.

"What is he talking about?" Rickman's voice jumped up a notch, sounding tight with strain.

"Hush, Uncle," Jasmine said. "Chuck's a smart guy. My gut says he's on the right track."

"Look at the road." Chuck pointed. "Where does it go? It just continues straight for the rock, inside that cut. It doesn't make any sense, unless..."

"A tunnel," Ariel breathed.

"Baddis's Knife Hand, I think you're right!" Garman said. "And if the rocks have been there for a while, then it's probably clear inside."

"Unless it's not!" Rickman protested. "Who's to say that the other side isn't wide open? Or worse, totally caved in like this one?"

"My pa," Chuck said. "He told me to find Liberty Bridge and the path. That's the way we have to go to get to safety."

He turned to look at Jasmine's uncle.

"Sir," Chuck said. "I'm sorry for the trouble we've brought to you. If you want to keep your dragon alive and get down to New Orleans to your husband, I think you should continue to come with us."

"Kid's right." Jay sat up his saddle as everyone turned to look at him. "This is an old comm runner route. Man and a horse could get through single file."

And how exactly does he know that? Chuck wondered. *One of these days, I'm going to have myself a long talk with that drunk old man.* It wasn't the first time he'd made that promise to himself and he doubted it would be the last.

Light-colored rocks had fallen onto the broken-up roadway, peeking out from the darker vegetation that covered everything. They were also crumbly, Chuck noticed, as Millie crushed one with her hoof. In fact, he realized abruptly, it wasn't rock at all—they were pieces of concrete that once marked the entrance to the tunnel. He glanced up, and sure enough, he could just make out the overhang deep in the cut in the hillside.

"Help me find the entrance," he said. His companions joined him as he did his best to peer into the darkness, trying to see what was plant, what was dirt and what was something else.

Jay walked past him, raising his hands.

"*Mellon!*"

Nothing happened. The old man shrugged.

"Worth a shot."

"I think I found it," Ariel said, as another jagged streak of lightning raced overhead. "Or something, anyway."

"Why?" Garman stopped searching to look at her. "What did you find?"

"Wind." She pointed. "Look."

Though it was difficult to make out in the darkness, when Chuck moved closer, he could see that she was right. Thanks to the cut in the hillside, they were shielded from the storm winds but the vegetation in front of Ariel moved slowly back and forth. He also thought he heard a faint whistling, low and very far away.

"Pull it aside," he said, grabbing a handful. Ariel joined in and before long, all six of them were digging and pulling, trying to clear the rubble and leaves that masked the entrance to the tunnel.

The driving rain slowed its intensity to a steady downpour by the time they had it cleared enough for a horse to pass through.

"Jasmine, go first," he said. "You're smallest and you've got those lights from the chapterhouse. We'll be right behind you."

"Got it," Jasmine said crisply, and though Rickman looked like he might have wanted to protest, he wisely said nothing.

The lithe dragon tamer pulled out one of the chemlights Stephens had given them and pushed her way through into the gloom of the tunnel. Chuck heard a faint *crack* and an eerie green light spilled from her hands.

"Ohh," she said, lifting the light high. "It's plenty big enough in here. There's some rusted old cars in here, but Jay's right. The floor's wet but it's not standing water. I think the horses will be fine coming through here."

"Good," Chuck said. "Keep a watch. Rickman, you're next, then Ariel. Let's get in out of the rain and we'll figure out our next move."

It took a bit of persuading but eventually they got all of the horses inside the tunnel. Chemlights distributed among the group made an eerie cloud of light surrounding them. Chuck wasn't convinced that it helped them see any better but it beat peering into the inky darkness. The entire place smelled dank and cold, but it was better than being out in the rain, he supposed.

After putting brush and other debris in front of the entrance, they moved deeper into the tunnel. It was slow going—at times they needed to clear rubble or move vehicles. Eventually, Chuck lost track of time and distance. He could tell the floor gently sloped upwards but only because the water seemed to be running down at them.

"Hold up a bit," Jay called out at one point. Chuck blinked, realizing that he'd been staring at his chemlight for the last several minutes. He reined Millie in, feeling her fatigue as she plodded to a stop. She wasn't usually a plodder.

"It's gonna be a bit damp but I think this is a good place to camp," Jay said.

"*Camp*?" Jasmine asked. "In *here*?"

"Better than out there," Jay said. He gestured to one of the spills of water coming from the ventilation tubes high above. Clearly, it was still raining up top.

"No," Chuck said. "Jay's right. We could all use the rest and I've been staring at this damn light for I don't know how long. Better if we stop awhile. I ain't seen anyone or anything else in here, so we should be safe enough if we keep a watch."

Unfortunately, necessary good idea or not, there was really no place to make a camp and no way for them to make a fire.

"Probably not a good idea, anyway," Garman said when Ariel brought it up. "Fire in a confined space can have bad effects. We could suffocate in our sleep and no one would find us down here."

"Enough," Chuck said, not wanting to scare the girl. "We'll be alright without a fire. We'll sleep close and hobble the horses together so they can bunch up for warmth."

It sounded good but in practice was hard to carry out. Everyone was soaked through to the skin, of course. Without a fire or even any dry clothes, it was very difficult for them to stay warm.

Eventually, Jasmine cursed and beckoned Ariel with her chemlight.

"Come share your blankets with me," she said. "We'll strip down and conserve our body heat that way. You men should pair up and do the same. It's the only way we're not going to die of hypothermia."

"Die of what?" Chuck asked.

"Freeze to death."

"B-But wh-who will w-watch?" Ariel asked, unable to hide her shivers. She still had less body fat than the rest of them and the cold seemed to be affecting her the worst.

"Chuck and I," Garman said, his voice gentle. It seemed that the Windfist had lost his distrust for the one-time cultist over the past weeks. "We'll watch in pairs, keep each other awake and move around. You guys get warm and sleep."

Ariel nodded, then took her small bundle of blankets and joined Jasmine next to the curving wall. The two girls hid their chemlights, so they were in near-darkness. Chuck forced himself to turn and avert his eyes. Averting his mind wasn't nearly as easy.

"How about it, Rickman?" Jay was asking. "You wanna be bed-buddies?"

"Why Jay, I thought you'd never ask," the dragon breeder said, flirtatiously. "Of course, you do know that I'm a married man."

"Yeah, it's alright though. Dave's an old friend. He knows I wouldn't poach...plus, you ain't got tits."

"You know my husband?"

"Used to. A long time ago. Crawl in." Jay held open the blankets that he'd wrapped around himself.

From the way the shadows fell, Chuck couldn't see if Jay was truly naked but he looked like he might be. The young man blinked and turned quickly away, blushing.

"Come on, Chuck," Garman said. "Let's get the horses settled."

Not that there was much they could do for the poor beasts. They were worn out, scared, uneasy at being underground, and hungry. While the water continued to trickle miserably all around, Chuck leaned his head against Millie's neck, hoping against hope that he was doing the right thing.

"I'm sorry, girl," he whispered. "I don't have any grain for you right now. But you did really good today. Really good. Not just today, either. This whole trip..."

Where were his folks now, Chuck wondered suddenly. Had they gotten away safely, or had more cultists tracked them down? Or...anyone else?

A spike of fear went through him as Chuck thought about what they'd learned on the bridge earlier. The Baron was in league with the cultists and Ronen.

What if they went after his family?

No, he told himself, *impossible. No one knows who I am, let alone where I live. And Pa's smart. He's not going to let anyone track him, let alone hurt him or Ma or Ellie. Right?*

He didn't know.

The fatigue, the damp, the fighting—nothing bothered him more than that simple statement.

It was easily the most miserable night of his life. The watch he shared with Garman seemed to last forever and though they both tried, neither of them wanted to talk much. That made it even more awkward when it came time to strip down and crawl into a nest of shared saddle blankets together but Chuck found himself intensely grateful for the warmth of the other man's body.

Before he could think of something to say to relieve the tension, he fell fast asleep.

CHAPTER FIFTEEN

"CHUCK."

He woke with a start, feeling a small hand settle over his mouth with a surprising amount of strength. His whole body ached and he felt like he'd slept for maybe ten minutes. Though if Ariel or Jasmine was waking him, it had to be at least several hours. The girls had been assigned the third watch.

"Shhh," Ariel whispered in his ear. "Listen."

He nodded and her fingers fell away from his mouth. Judging by the absence of water pouring down the vent shafts, it had stopped raining. However, he could hear something else. Distant but still there...

Voices. Voices that sounded like they were barking orders. He couldn't make out the words but he could certainly recognize the tone. Someone was looking for something. Or someone.

"Wake the others," he whispered. He thought he saw her nod and move away while he sat up. Next to him, Garman stirred. Chuck elbowed his friend in the side. The Windfist sat up silently, alert and ready, even naked in the dark.

"We have company up top," Chuck said. He kept his voice low, so it wouldn't carry.

Garman cursed softly before pulling himself out of their blankets. Chuck did the same, hurrying to put his still-clammy clothes back on. They didn't do much to help keep the chill down but it was better than nothing.

"I don't know if they heard us but let's keep it down anyway," he said, once everyone had gotten up and gathered around. "We'll continue on, at least until we get close to the exit, so we can see where the situation stands. Anyone got any idea what time it is?"

"About four in the afternoon," Jay said. He pointed to an antique wristwatch that Chuck hadn't even realized he wore. The hands glowed faintly in the darkness. Not enough for Chuck to read them but he'd take Jay's word for it.

"Okay," he said. "That could be good for us. We'll make our way closer to the end of the tunnel, then try to slip out under cover of darkness. If we're lucky, they'll miss us entirely."

"Mount Washington is a big place," Rickman said, nodding. "If they don't know about this tunnel, they might never see the exit point."

"And if they do know?" Jasmine asked. She and her uncle seemed to have swapped personalities, or at least attitudes. Rickman seemed rested and positive, while Jasmine was clearly tired and grumpy. In all their time on the road, she'd never liked waking up.

"We'll hit them hard, blow through before they know we're there," Garman said, his voice steely. "Any chance of air support from the dragons, if it comes to that?"

"Depends on the weather," Jasmine said. "If they can't see through it, they won't fly through it."

"Right. Well, we'll hope for the best then," Chuck said. "But let's get moving and at least get to the end of the tunnel. I'd much rather fight them near the exit than stuck here in the middle with nowhere to run."

"If we have to fight at all," Rickman said. He seemed determined to be cheerful.

"Right. If." In his mind there was no question. Their enemies were going to find them. It was just a matter of when. Garman met his eyes and nodded. He too, it seemed, was convinced. There would be a fight.

Hard to know for sure but Chuck rather thought Jay agreed. The old man seemed as sloppy drunk and jovial as ever but Chuck noticed that he very carefully checked his ammo load and made sure his knife was ready to go. Generally speaking, Jay didn't do much fighting, but Chuck had no doubt that the old man knew how.

As for the girls, Jasmine was grumpy and Ariel quiet...which when he thought about it wasn't much different from their usual. He didn't have any idea what that might mean for their chances, but then he rarely had any ideas at all when it came to women. So, again, nothing new there.

It didn't take them long to pack up their miserable, wet camp. It took slightly longer to wrap the horses' hooves with whatever clothing they could. Jasmine passed out new chemlights, as the ones they'd been using had faded into uselessness. Chuck resisted the urge to crack his open and just followed the green glow of Jasmine's as she continued to lead the way down the endless-seeming dark of the tunnel.

Or up the endless dark, he thought, as his boots squeaked and slipped on the damp asphalt of the tunnel's floor. His calves and thighs burned slightly, so even if he couldn't see it, he knew they were still climbing up the deceptive slope.

When a pine-scented breeze sliced across his face, Chuck called a whispered halt.

"I think we're getting close," he said, once everyone had huddled around him. His breath puffed in the light of the chemsticks. "Do you feel that? The temperature has dropped."

"It's late enough to be dark out," Jay said. "We could send someone to scout the exit, see what's waiting for us."

"But what if they get caught out alone, with no backup?" He shook his head. "No, we stick together and just be very, very quiet from here on out. I'll take point."

Jasmine nodded in the sickly green glow and stepped back, gesturing for him to take the lead.

"Okay, weapons out and hide your lights. Be quiet as you can, stay close to me and the wall so we don't run into any cars," Chuck started moving toward the icy tendrils of air that seeped in from ahead.

Within about five steps, he regretted not opening his own chemlight. The darkness was absolute. He could feel his eyes straining to penetrate it but all they found was more darkness. Opening it now wasn't the best option, however, because what if the sudden addition of light caught someone's attention?

Still...he groped forward, one hand outstretched while the other held to the tunnel wall. It felt ridiculous. He was about to give in and crack the light open when another sharp wind blasted through the tunnel. This time, it was strong enough to create a whistling, howling kind of sound and up ahead, something shifted, just a little bit.

Just enough. Chuck saw stars. He blinked, hoping it wasn't his eyes playing tricks. Nope.

They'd found the exit.

He handed Millie's reins back to Jay, who followed close behind him. With a whisper of metal against leather, he pulled Fat Lady from her saddle holster and crept forward. He crouched, a plan forming in his mind. One hand on the wall, he reached out to touch more of the creeping vines and vegetation that had grown over the exit point of the tunnel.

Chuck got down on his belly and flipped Fat Lady's bipod out. He put his eye to the scope, trying not to make any more noise than necessary. With excruciating slowness, he used her barrel to move one flat hanging leaf to the side.

The sky had cleared enough that moonlight shone down, bathing the hillslope in front of him. The air, and the clearing in front of the exit, looked crystalline, flash frozen and diamond-hard, like the frost that glittered on the ground. Nothing moved. Silence and stillness reigned. He drew in a deep breath, tasting the edge of snow on his tongue.

He lifted his head and turned back, motioning with his hand for them to move forward. Jay answered his call.

"It's clear," he breathed into the other man's ear. "You've just got to cross this open area and get into the trees yonder. I think we can make it if we go quickly, one at a time."

Jay nodded and gave him a thumb's up. Then, moving like a much younger man, he smoothly, slowly slid out from the hanging greenery and darted across the open slope.

Chuck lowered his eye to the scope, looking for Jay in the treeline. For a long moment, he saw nothing and then the wizened, dark face of the old man appeared next to the trunk of a very large tree. He raised his hands and flashed a hand sign that he'd last seen from his pa, during the shootout at the farmhouse.

Two men, armed, top of the ridge, Chuck mentally translated. *I'll wave when clear.*

He lifted his barrel and lowered it slightly, hoping that the movement was large enough for Jay to understand his acknowledgement but small enough to remain unseen by anyone else.

Across the way, Jay gave another thumbs-up and melted back into the shadows.

Chuck looked back over his shoulder and found Jasmine waiting there. He waved her forward and put his mouth next to her ear, just as he'd done with Jay.

"There's an open area before you get to the treeline where Jay is waiting. He says there are two armed men at the top of the ridge. There may be more he can't see. He's going to give me the signal and when I tap you, run like hell for the trees. Got it? Don't speak, just nod."

She nodded and then shuffled forward to crouch behind the curtain of greenery. Chuck lowered his eye back to the rifle scope and waited.

A shadow passed over the ground and the moonlight dimmed. Cloud cover! He looked and sure enough, Jay materialized out of the darkness again, waving in a "come on" gesture. Chuck reached up and tapped Jasmine . . . right on her butt. Blood flooded his cheeks but he told himself firmly that he could be embarrassed about it later. She certainly seemed to pay him no mind, for she slid out from under the vines and took off like a shot for the treeline.

Chuck watched her disappear into the gloom. Jay reappeared and waved on another runner. Cursing himself for not having Jasmine pass the instructions back, Chuck reached back and grabbed hold of someone by some part of clothing.

It was Rickman, and the dragon breeder came willingly to the front. He even seemed to be wearing a grin. Strange man.

Chuck repeated his whispered instructions and half-pushed the man out himself. Ariel came next, but by the time she got to the trees, the cloud passed. Jay cut a hand across his throat. *Stop.*

Behind him, Millie stamped and Chuck cursed out loud. He'd forgotten all about the horses. The two men on the ridge might not notice a single person slipping across the open space. They could hardly miss half a dozen horses doing the same. But if there were only two of them . . .

Chuck looked back over his shoulder to find Garman at the ready. He slid backwards until he could whisper in the Windfist's ear.

"Jay's in the trees but there's a clear area we gotta cross. And I forgot about the horses."

"We can leave them," Garman said. "They'll be able to forage for food and there's plenty of water hereabouts."

"No," Chuck said. "We can't. We're going to need them if we have to run. I think . . . I think we've got to make a break for it. If there's only two of them, maybe they won't react fast enough to be able to do anything."

"I don't like it."

"Me neither but I don't see as we have much of a choice."

Garman hesitated, then leaned forward just enough to look through the hanging curtain of vines.

"There's some crumbled rock and stuff around," the Windfist said. "What if you got out in that cover with the big gun?"

"Don't know if I'll have a clear line of sight . . ."

"Well, if not, you hop on that mare of yours and go with Plan A."

Chuck pursed his lips and considered for a moment but had nothing better.

"Okay," he whispered. "I'll give it a shot. Get their hooves free, leave Millie, and string the other horses together. Let me know when ready to ride. Go hell-for-leather, man, because the minute Fat Lady sings, we're definitely going to draw their attention."

"You got it," Garman said. In the dimness, Chuck saw a flash of white that might have been the Windfist grinning. The sight of it both thrilled and terrified him.

No more time to think about it, though. Chuck reached out, clapped him on what he hoped was a shoulder and eased back up to take Fat Lady. Minutes later, he heard the other man pull himself into the saddle, as well as the horses shifting as they readied to move.

Chuck didn't look toward Jay as he slid through the vines. He stayed low in a crouch, trying to keep close to the broken pieces of concrete that obscured the tunnel's exit. There was a rough slope, like a rockfall, down to the open area that his friends had crossed. Maybe if he worked his way to the bottom of it, he could get enough of a look at the ridgeline to be able to take out the two men up there.

He very deliberately didn't think about the fact that there could be more men in the trees around him. A lot of men. Men who would hear Fat Lady and come running. He couldn't do anything about it, so he forced it out of his head.

Once again, wisps of cloud moved over the moon, diffusing

the light. The edges of the stones underfoot bled away into shadow and Chuck had a harder time stepping carefully so as not to slide down the hill.

At the bottom, he crouched behind a half-buried boulder and turned to look up at the ridge behind him. It was hard to see in the darkness but maybe... Yes. A shape moved slowly along the ridge, silhouetting itself against the sky.

Chuck moved carefully, bringing Fat Lady into place and bracing her against the top of his dubious cover. He bent to look through the scope and saw that the shape was, indeed, manlike. Good enough.

He took a deep breath, exhaling evenly, feeling the tension drain from him as he emptied his mind. Only the shape in the scope and the metal curve of the trigger mattered. One more breath in, hold it briefly, let it out. As it trickled past his lips, Chuck squeezed.

Fat Lady sang. The figure up on the ridge fell.

Above him, the exit of the tunnel exploded with noise as Garman and the horses thundered out. The second man came into view, rushing to check on his buddy.

Once again, breathe, hold, trickle, squeeze. A heavy thump against his shoulder, another song ringing in his ears and he was up, whistling for Millie.

He didn't look for the mare. She'd be there, he knew it. He grabbed Fat Lady, slung her over his back and sprinted after Garman and the rest of the horses. Sure enough, one of them turned back, running flat out toward him, coming so close that he thought she was trying to run him down. With a turn that nearly put her flank on the ground, Millie pivoted and came up beside him. Chuck reached out and grabbed her saddle horn. She picked up the pace, hooves pounding on the turf. It was either get into the saddle or get dragged. With effort, he got a foot in the stirrup and pulled himself up.

The sky cleared again and Chuck found himself riding through the silver light of the moon. He looked up to see the last flash of one of the horses' tails disappearing into the trees. Garman and the others were safe. He leaned forward and touched his heels to Millie's sides, willing the brave mare to go faster. Exultation zinged through his body as they got closer and closer to the treeline. Twenty yards, ten...

Something hammered into him, just below his right shoulder. Chuck felt himself lurch forward, off balance, slipping from Millie's saddle. He hit the ground hard, breath exploding from his lungs as pain lanced through his right side. He heard Millie scream but he couldn't move. Agony held him pinned, gasping, unable to pull air into his stunned lungs. Something yanked at his left arm, and he realized that it was tangled in Millie's reins.

Finally, he dragged in a gasp of air. His starved lungs rejoiced but the pain that engulfed him doubled in intensity. It didn't help that Millie pulled on him again, trying to drag him along the ground.

A *snap* echoed off the rocks around him and all of a sudden, realization hit. He'd been shot. There *were* more men in the area and he was just lying in the open, drowning in moonlight. He had to do something.

Okay, what?

He yanked at Millie's reins so she'd stop trying to drag him. Flashes of brightness swam before his eyes as he fought to get his right hand under him. He clung doggedly to consciousness, gritting his teeth and forcing the agony to the back of his mind.

Somehow, he made it to his knees, just in time to see Jasmine and Rickman darting out of the treeline. Garman followed, firing at something behind Chuck and to the left. Jasmine and Rickman ran to Chuck, reaching under his shoulders to help him to his feet.

He heard someone screaming. Once the fire of excruciating pain receded, he realized it was him. He might have blacked out for a moment, because the next thing he knew, Garman was shouting, Rickman was hauling him into Millie's saddle and Jasmine stood with her hands held high, face lifted to the starry sky.

Flames bloomed in the darkness, illuminating the treeline, Millie's coat, the individual blades of grass beneath her hooves. In between the bits of blessed darkness, Chuck caught impressions like photographs. Men screaming. Millie running. Throbbing, piercing, burning, hateful pain pulling him down into oblivion.

"Chuck, Chuck! Wake up!"

He blinked his eyes, or tried, anyway. His eyelashes felt like they weighed far too much for such wispy little things. Though the girls back in town near home had always seemed to like them...

Something cool and delicious dribbled across his lips, seconds before something white-hot stabbed through him. He screamed, only to have a hand clamped over his lips hard enough to smash them against his teeth.

"It looks like it went straight through," someone said. Jasmine. Instantly, his mind brought back the memory of her calling down dragonflame. To save him.

"I'm sorry," he said, or tried to say. It came out as a weak moan that turned into a cough. And if his shoulder hadn't hurt enough before, it certainly did now.

"Still with us, then?" she asked and he finally got his eyes open to see her looking at him with a worried expression. Scared of coughing again, he settled for a small nod.

"Good deal. You're a lucky guy, you know that? It looks like the bullet went right through your upper arm, just missing your shoulder. I'm going to bind it up but then we gotta go. Quetza-lith and Pearl got most of them but I saw at least one run. They know where we are and they'll be after us with reinforcements. So we have to ride."

"I'm . . . okay . . ." he croaked. "Let's . . . go."

It soon became clear to Chuck that he was not, in fact, okay. His vision grayed out twice while Jasmine worked but she revived him with water and the whiskey that she'd poured from Jay's flask into the wound. When she was done, his arm lay wrapped from shoulder to elbow, bound tightly against his ribs. Another swig of Jay's flask and he felt as ready as he was going to get.

As they piled into the saddles, he overheard Garman telling the others about why, exactly, they'd abandoned stealth and started shooting. He could have joined in, but shame kept his head low and his eyes hooded. He couldn't believe he'd miscalculated so badly. He slumped in the saddle, pretending to be in and out of consciousness, just so that he wouldn't have to talk to any of the people he'd let down.

He hadn't reckoned on Jay.

The old man sidled his horse up next to Millie and kicked Chuck's boot in the stirrup. Chuck turned to glare at the man, only to meet his wide grin.

"Nice job getting them horses out," Jay said. "Little flashier than I woulda done but you did the job. Now what?"

"What?"

"Now what? You're the one in charge, kid, remember?"

"I can't be in charge," Chuck spat. "I screwed the pooch at the tunnel, Jay, no use pretendin' otherwise."

"Oh, I wasn't pretending," Jay said. "I was just being diplomatic. Doesn't change the fact that you're the boss, boss. You're the one who knows where we're going. So where we going?"

Chuck continued glaring at the obnoxious old man. Jay's grin only grew and he reached inside his jacket to pull out a flask. He uncapped it, lifted it in Chuck's direction and took a swig. All the while, his expression said very clearly that he would wait forever, if need be.

Hell with it.

"That way," Chuck said, pointing down the path. "Follow that road south until it crosses the river again."

"Sounds good," Jay said. "You want Jasmine on point again?"

Dammit. "Yes."

"Good move. Especially now that Q and his lady friend are back. When d'ya wanna go?"

"Right now," Chuck said, forcing the words through gritted teeth.

"Then I guess you'd better tell 'em to move out, then," Jay said, winking as he lifted his flask again.

"Jay..."

"What's that, boss?"

"Nothing, dammit. Let's move out."

Within ten minutes after hitting the trail, in the first clearing they met, Quetzalith swooped over them in an intricate dance. Jasmine swore.

"What?" Garman asked.

"Riders, behind us. Close," Jasmine said. "We might want to pick this up a bit. I know it's going to hurt, Chuck, but..."

"It's all right," he said. "I'll tie in to my saddle. If I pass out, Garman's in charge. Jay knows where we're going...for the next day or so anyway."

Before he realized it, Ariel had ridden up next to him and had her arms around his waist. He was too startled to realize what was going on at first but then he realized that she'd come to help secure him into the saddle. She had some long strips of something—he didn't know what. She tied them around his waist and to the saddle horn. He snuck a look at her and she gave him a shy smile before nudging her horse forward. He followed.

They crossed the clearing, kicking their horses into a run as the road disappeared into the trees. Almost immediately, Chuck began wishing he had one of Jay's flasks. Millie was a smooth runner but even her gentle gait stabbed into his wounded shoulder with every step. He ducked low in the saddle, laid his head against her neck and closed his eyes. The pain made him want to throw up. Or pass out. Or both.

He must have passed out. The next thing he knew, they were stopping to water the horses at a small stream, the sun peeking over the mountain's summit to their left.

"How long has it been?" Chuck asked Ariel. She'd come up to assist him again. Her hands were strong, he noticed, as she helped him to sit up and drink some water. Dark shadows smudged under her beautiful eyes.

"A few hours," she said. "We can't linger long. Just enough to water the horses and see to our personal needs. Jasmine says they are still right behind us. I will untie you..."

"Don't bother," he said, weakly. "I don't have to go. Not enough water, I'm guessing, lost too much blood. I hope they have good medical care at the Bunker."

"They must," she said. "I'm certain that they do."

He nodded, kicking Millie forward after she'd drunk her fill. Ariel was a rotten liar but it wasn't the time to bring it up.

The group took off again. Though not at a full gallop, they moved quite quickly, trotting and cantering where the trees and the trail would allow.

Chuck changed his mind about the night in the tunnel. *This* was the most miserable he'd ever been. Once again, he drifted in and out of consciousness, borne on a sea of agony. As if that weren't enough, fever set in around noon and he could feel sweat soaking through his clothes. His nerves felt raw: every sound, every touch, magnified by a power of ten.

As the sun started to set over the western horizon, the constant icy breeze that had kept them company since the tunnel died down. Chuck had a moment to feel grateful, before the first fat, wet flake drifted down from the darkening sky.

The temperature plummeted. As the trail started to slope down again, Garman called another quick halt, allowing everyone to get out any heavy clothing they had. Chuck found himself wrapped in a spare saddle blanket that reeked of horse. His entire body shook with cold but his face felt like a glowing, red coal.

"He can't keep going," he heard Jasmine say at one point.

"We can't stop," Garman said, voice grim. "His only hope now is that we make it to the Bunker."

Chuck didn't know what happened next but when he became aware again, Millie was splashing through a creek up to her belly and his boots were wet. His feet stung, then went numb in the icy cold.

"Which way?" someone asked. He didn't know who.

"South," he whispered. Details from his map broke through the fog in his head. "Along the ridge, follow Nineteen to the lost creek."

"Nineteen?"

"The road." That was Jay. "Highway Nineteen. We need to find a marker. Pray that there's one still standing."

No, that couldn't be right. That wasn't Jay. Jay didn't sound serious and grim like that. Jay sounded...gleeful. Mischievous. Like a kid contemplating breaking into a candy store.

Later, though he didn't know how much later, someone patted his face rapidly, with an intensity that stung through his fever-dream.

"Chuck! Come on, Chuck, wake up!"

He remembered this dream. He was going to open his eyes and Jasmine would wrap his shoulder and it would hurt and Jay would make him keep leading and...

Whizz-crack!

"Chuck!" the someone said, sobbing. "Wake up! They are right behind us! We have to run but I cannot keep you in the saddle by myself. I need your help!"

His eyes felt puffy and sore, like the rest of him, but he got them open. Ariel stared at him, her face white and pinched with cold and fear. He could see her breath puffing between them like a cloud.

Did he still have toes? He couldn't feel his toes. He wished he couldn't feel the rest of him.

"Can you ride?" Ariel asked, her voice intense.

He blinked, then nodded as another bullet pierced the air

nearby, causing snow to come cascading down from the branches above. It was still falling from the sky, he saw, piled several inches deep on the ground in front of them.

Like a blanket. Or a pillow. I like pillows.

Someone smacked Millie on the rump and she jumped forward, nearly toppling him out of the seat. Ariel cried out but Chuck stayed where he was and forced himself to lean down to talk to his old friend, his faithful mare.

"I've got a fever, Millie," he said. A sudden crystal clarity gelled his thoughts. "And some bad men are after us. I'm not going to make it through this without you, though I guess that's been true the whole time. You're a good mare, Millie. The best. I promise, if I live through this, I'll see that you're treated right, given a good brushing, lots of hay... all the things you deserve. Treats, though. I'll find you some treats if I have to search the whole damn Bunker for them. Someone's got some tasty horse treats for you and I'm going to find them. I promise, pretty girl. Just get me there and you'll see."

Time seemed to slow to a crawl. Chuck wasn't sure if that was the fever or knowing that if they faltered, they were dead. He looked back once and could see the dark shapes of men and horses following after them. With the snow, it didn't look like the dragons had been able to hang around. They were on their own.

The world narrowed down to the trail, the trees and the ever-falling snow. Chuck didn't notice the way the trail suddenly sloped upward, nor the way it started switching back and forth as they climbed. As they passed their pursuers, more bullets whizzed out toward them. He wanted to stop and fire back but he couldn't seem to make himself move.

Millie's hooves slipped and she nearly went off over the edge. Ariel screamed and another *crack!* came from below. Their trail made an abrupt turn to stop at a sheer face. The rest of the trail disappeared under debris from an apparent rockslide. They weren't going to make it.

Sound shattered the stillness of the growing twilight, refusing to be muffled by the falling snow.

Ka-chunk. Ka-chunk, Ka-chunk.

Someone cried out behind them. Chuck risked a look back and saw men falling as the deep, throaty coughs continued.

Fifty cal, he realized, the shots sounding much like Fat Lady's but faster. Pa had described it, long ago, the first time they'd shot the rifle. What had he called it?

"Woo hoo!" Jay's voice came from somewhere ahead of him. "Ma Deuce, you sexy thing!"

"Get in!"

Chuck turned at the shout to see a yawning entrance.

Was that there before? He could've sworn there had been stone. Someone grabbed his slack rein. As they rode forward, darkness closed over his fevered mind.

CHAPTER SIXTEEN

VOICES DRIFTED IN AND OUT OF THE FOG. CHUCK DIDN'T REC-
ognize the female, but the male sounded familiar.

"...And you think this bunch is the answer?" The woman's
harsh whisper carried over the odd sounds nearby.

"Not the heroes we wanted," the male said.

"Oh, for Christ's sake, now is not the time."

"Okay, how about this: I've been setting things up for over
twenty-five years, and find my hand forced," the man said. His
voice, even in a whisper, was firm and confident. "So, here's the
question: Do we wait for what we want, or work with what we
have?"

Silence hung thickly for a few moments.

"You're right, dammit," the women said, eventually. "So what
do you need from me?"

"The Windfist is to report to the President, in person. Same
with the kid. He won't talk to anyone else."

More silence. Finally, the female spoke again.

"Fine. I'll brief the President."

Any reply faded into the background as Chuck lost consciousness.

It smelled strange.

That was the first thing Chuck noticed, when awareness came
creeping back. It smelled like someone had spilled a load of really

harsh moonshine. There was also a strange low hum that seemed to linger at the edge of his hearing.

He slowly opened his eyes. A blinding, crystalline white light stabbed into his brain and he flinched, which made him realize that his whole body felt battered from head to toe. His arm was a knot of aching misery and he felt weak as a half-drowned kitten.

But he was lucid. The fever was gone. He carefully squinted his eyes open again.

The room he lay in was also white, which might have had something to do with the startling clarity of the light that shone down from the ceiling. Or rather, it came from a pair of skinny tubes laid side by side on the ceiling. He'd never seen anything like it and, though it made his eyes water, he couldn't help but stare.

"Awake, then, are we?" a male voice asked. It wasn't Jay or Garman, or even Rickman. Chuck felt tension rising through him as he allowed his head to fall slowly in that direction.

Where am I?

"Seems so," Chuck answered. Or tried to. What came out was something closer to a bullfrog's croak than actual words. He swallowed, cleared his throat and repeated himself.

The man wore an unusual getup: a soft shirt and loose pants of a thin, green material. He was older than Chuck by a few years, with salt-and-pepper hair and very pale skin.

"Good. Let's get your vitals." The man produced a thin stick and shoved it under Chuck's tongue.

"I'm Dr. Holmes. Russel, not H. H." he added with a small grin as he strapped some kind of cuff to Chuck's arm. He punched a button on the squarish contraption next to the bed, which beeped. The cuff began to grow tighter around Chuck's bicep. "Don't get the reference, huh? Not your fault. You probably never learned about early American serial killers in school."

"Can't say that we did," Chuck mumbled around the stick, wondering what on earth this doctor was talking about. "Are my friends all right?"

"Hmm? Oh, yes! They're outside, constantly bugging me to see if you're awake yet. I'll send them in as soon as I finish checking you out."

He removed the stick from Chuck's mouth, nodding as he

looked at the contraption. It glowed and beeped, seeming to tell him information of some kind. The cuff, too, reached its tightest point, and just as Chuck thought his fingers might burst, it began to deflate.

"Welp," Dr. Holmes said. "Temperature and blood pressure look good. I'd say you beat the infection. One of the small silver linings of the Bug War... antibiotics work wonders on you kids who've never had them. Anyway, you're likely to be weak for a few days, so don't overdo anything yet. But I'll let your friends in to see you now if you want."

"Yes, please, sir...I mean, Doc," Chuck said, remembering his manners. He pushed himself up to a sitting position as the doctor gave him one more nod and went out the door.

"Chuck!" Jasmine damn near knocked the doctor over in her haste to get into the room. Ariel, Garman, Jay and Rickman shoved in after her, all wearing big smiles. Chuck grinned back at them and endured Jasmine's fussing about, plumping pillows and shoving them behind his back so he could sit up more comfortably.

"Gave us a bit of a scare, brother," Garman said, clasping Chuck's good hand. Chuck squeezed his friend's hand in a tight grip and started to give him a hug. Only then did he realize that his right arm was still in a sling across his chest. "Thought we might have lost you there for a bit."

"Did we make it?" Chuck dropped Garman's hand and leaned back. "This... this has to be the Bunker, right?"

"We made it, kid," Jay said, pulling out a flask. "You did good, real good. Your dad'll be proud."

He took a nip, then offered it to the others. He looked at Chuck for a long moment, then shook his head and put it away.

"Maybe when you're not on so many drugs," he said. With a wink, he stepped back.

Chuck felt small fingers intertwine with his and he turned his head.

"Hi," she said softly, warm brown eyes locking onto his. "Please be careful. I was really worried about you."

"Okay." His fever returned. But only in his face.

"Okay," she said, squeezing his hand. She gave him a little smile and let go, but slowly, her fingers sliding out of his gasp. Chuck's hand twitched, a heartbeat too late to hold her.

"Okay," Jay said slowly, his grin growing. "So. Now that you're not mostly dead, let me tell you what's happened. No, there is too much. Let me sum up..."

He looked around expectantly and then sighed.

"Kids." A female voice came from the doorway.

Chuck leaned to look around Garman's bulk and saw a formidable woman march inside. Not walk—march. As if she were about to face down an enemy or a rebellious child. Her silver-streaked blonde hair was pulled back away from her face and her sharp, intelligent eyes glittered behind the glasses. Even Jay backed up a step as she charged up to him.

"They're kids, Jay," she repeated herself. "They don't get your prewar references. Hello, everyone, I'm Shirley Kunz."

"Ms. Shirley runs the place here," Jay said.

"Don't be telling them lies," she said sharply. When she'd come closer, Chuck could see that her face held the fine lines of laughter and sorrow of an older woman. Perhaps even Jay's age. The two of them certainly seemed to know each other well. But then, Jay seemed to know everyone.

"I ain't lyin', Shirley! You do run the place!"

"The President is in charge here, Jay and don't you forget it."

"I didn't say 'in charge,' I said you run things," Jay said. "And you do. How's Himself doing?"

"Just fine, Jay, just fine." This time, the voice was male, deep and resonant. Shirley turned quickly to the door in response.

"Ladies and gentlemen, The President of the United States of America," she said as a man in a wheeled chair rolled across the threshold.

Jay snapped to attention and saluted. Garman followed suit shortly after.

Chuck was shocked—he would've never guessed Jay saluted *anyone*. He moved to stand, but Ariel reached out and put her hand lightly on his chest. That stopped him cold.

"Oh, for Pete's sake, Shirley, do you have to do that every damned time?" The President continued to roll forward, coming close to the side of the bed.

Chuck could see his face, etched with the bone-deep lines, yet still friendly and smiling. His hair was a pristine white, still thick and full atop his head, but his hands shook as he toggled the switch that seemed to control his chair.

"Yes, Mr. President, I do." Shirley's tone said she answered that question on a daily basis. "May I present Mr. Chuck Gordon, Windfist Journeyman Garman, Lady Jasmine Moore, Mr. Mark Rickman and Ms. Ariel. Jay...you already know."

"We're going with just 'Jay' this time, are we?" The President asked, returning the salutes.

"What else would we be going with, sir?" Jay asked, then hiccupped. Garman dropped his hand, but remained at attention.

"It's good to see you again, Jay. It's been too long," the President said and held out his hand for Jay to shake. Once again, Chuck noticed the fine tremors that raced along the older man's hand. "Who have you brought me?"

"It's the young man in the bed there that's brought us here," Jay said. "He's Bullet Gordon's son."

"I had wondered. It's a pleasure to meet you, son. How is your old man?"

Chuck blinked. *Pa knows the President?*

"He's, uh, fine, sir. Or was, when I saw him last."

"Excellent. Give him my best. Now, what brings you here?"

"With respect, sir," Garman cut in, "I have orders to report to the National Command Authority."

"Well, you found it, Journeyman," the President said. "What do you have for me?"

"My orders were to deliver this, sir," Garman said, producing a sealed pouch. The President took it, broke the seal, and read the contents.

Several moments of silence passed as he scanned the documents. Finally, he began reciting.

"'Red code packet stolen recently by deserter. Whereabouts unknown.'"

Garman scowled, but remained still.

"'Recent intel indicates that the Grand Coulee activation key has been recovered,'" the President continued. "'Current location also unknown, but likely in Deseret. Recommend Journeyman Garman to locate and deliver key to Bunker.'"

The President frowned at Jay's snort. Chuck couldn't help himself, and began to laugh. Garman stayed at attention, but shot them an annoyed glance.

"Go'wan, kid," Jay said. "Show him."

"Show me what, exactly?" the President asked.

Chuck fumbled inside the crinkly paper gown tied closed over his chest.

"Uh, this, sir," he said, as his fingers finally closed over the ball chain. He drew the jingling necklace over his head. "It was brought to us by a man named Gunslinger. Those are his dog tags, there. Pa said it was the key for the device at Coulee."

Garman stared wide-eyed for a second, regained his composure, and turned back to the President.

"Journeyman Garman reporting: Mission accomplished, sir."

After that, they had a little party around Chuck's bed.

Jay found a couple of bottles of liquor somewhere, while Ariel and Jasmine rounded up some food. They gathered back in Chuck's room, shared a meal and had a cheerful couple of hours filling each other in.

Apparently, shortly after their dramatic entrance, the guards had chewed up the rest of their pursuers with that fifty-...caliber machine gun. The following night, Jasmine and Rickman had been taken up "topside"—the summit of the mountain—to look for Pearl and Quetzalith.

"Though truth be told, it's early yet for them to be back," Rickman said around a mouthful of something that tasted like heavily sauced chicken. It wasn't bad, exactly, but it didn't taste as fresh as the food Chuck was used to eating at home...or anywhere else.

"Yeah, I'd honestly expect them late tonight or early tomorrow at the soonest," Jasmine said, nodding. "But it's good to know that there will be a place for them to land up there that we can easily access."

"And we can just go wherever we want?" Chuck asked. "No one's going to mind?"

"There are restricted areas but that's not one of them," Garman answered for them. "Ms. Shirley took me on a tour the first day we were here. We're free to go anywhere but into the command center and the President's private quarters. Of course, there are armed guards everywhere, so even if you wanted to do something, you'd have a rough time of it."

"So we might as well have a drink!" Jay said, lifting one of the purloined bottles of booze to his lips.

And so they did. And another. Truth be told, Chuck was

feeling pretty good himself an hour later. The doc had reduced his meds and told him he could have a single drink, so he'd been nursing a beer while the others went ahead and tied one on.

Well, everyone except Ariel. She just sipped her water. But she seemed happy enough and engaged in the conversation readily. Chuck found his eyes drawn more and more to her as the evening progressed. He wondered...

"She was really worried about you, you know," Jasmine said. She leaned forward from her position lounging against Garman's chest and spoke low enough that the others' conversation didn't falter. "She kept asking for updates, didn't know what to do with herself."

"I'm sure sorry I scared her," Chuck said. Jasmine snorted and lightly smacked the back of his head.

"You scared *all* of us, but that's not the point," she said. "The point is that *she* was the most scared. I think she likes you, kid. You should do something about that."

"What'm I gonna do?" he asked. "I'm no charmer."

"That's a lie," Jasmine said with a grin. "You're charming as hell when you're earnest. You should just tell her how you feel, see where it goes."

"Begging your pardon, ma'am," Chuck said, "I'm afraid I'd be bearing my heart to a brick wall."

"Don't be so judgmental, Chuck," Jasmine said. "Ariel's got a good heart. Not a lot of experience with love, perhaps, but then, neither have you, am I right? Your choice, but I think you should give it a shot."

"I'll think about it," he said, trying to shut the conversation down before it got any more uncomfortable.

"I bet you will," Jasmine said, leaning back against Garman's chest once more, her lips firmly curved in a knowing smirk. Garman wrapped his arm around her waist and said something in her ear, but she only shook her head and kept eye contact with Chuck until he was the one who looked away.

Damn it all, anyway.

Chuck looked at the faces of his companions around the oval table, wondering if they had an idea why they'd been called here. Everyone else looked as confused as he felt, except Jay. Jay was asleep.

No, that ain't right, he thought. *Not just companions, friends.*

The room itself was plain, containing only the table, chairs, two flags, and a strange black window. Chuck had learned the solid blue flag with the eagle was the President's personal sigil. The other—red and white stripes, with a starred blue field—was the country's. He had no idea what the window was for.

Shirley strode in, taking a seat under the window. She made eye contact with each of his friends in turn, and smiled when she got to him.

"How are you feeling, Chuck?" Shirley asked.

"Much better, ma'am," Chuck replied.

Two weeks in the hospital had done him a world of good. He wasn't quite up to fighting Gantists and rogue Windfists—yet—but he could probably sit a horse again.

"That is fortunate," Shirley said, looking dyspeptic. "We need to discuss what's next."

"Problems in paradise?" Jay asked.

"You could say that," Shirley replied. She picked up a rectangular device and pushed a button. "Word just came back that Kansas City has declared itself part of the Barony of Ironhelm."

Chuck felt his jaw drop as the window lit up, showing a map similar to the one he had. A quick glance at the others showed similar reactions, with the exception of Rickman and Jay.

"Here's what we're getting from our people," Shirley continued. Another button press and the area around Old Kansas City filled the glass, colored a deep red. "The Baron, it seems, has been busy over the last few years, seeding the area with his people and weapons. It fell shortly after you left."

"His reach is growing," Jasmine said darkly. "He wants to own it all, eventually. That's one reason he had me and Quetzalith around. Intimidation."

"Yes, well, as lovely as your two winged friends topside have been, I can see where he'd get that idea," Shirley said tartly. "He seems to have found a bigger stick to swing, though."

"My people," Ariel said, quietly. She had been staring at the map in fascination, but now focused on Shirley. The older woman nodded. Ariel continued in a louder voice. "My former people. I will not return to them as an acolyte."

Shirley pressed another button. Pittsburgh moved into view. It too was mostly red.

"The Baron's forces now control half of Pitt and have the steel mills under siege. They have the situation under control but... well, there's very little we can do from here to help them."

"Can the Steel Curtain Boys last?" Jay asked, his tone serious and devoid of any intoxication.

"They can. They've been fighting off bugs and dragons since the war ended." She let out a sigh and sagged a little bit. For the first time since meeting her, Chuck realized that this formidable woman was tired way down deep in her bones. "I wish Pitt were our only problem, but there's a bigger issue."

"Windfist," Garman said. All eyes turned toward him. "Ronen is out there, recruiting them to the Baron's cause."

"Got it in one, Journeyman," Shirley said. "With your report, we at least know Ronen is able to sway some of your brethren to his side."

"And has enough support to eliminate those that refuse," Garman said, nodding.

"Yes. And that's why it's a problem. Your order has focused on the Gant threat since its inception. You are our first line of defense. Add to that what you've come to symbolize to the people—fair, non-biased, arbiters of justice—and the Baron has a powerful propaganda tool at his disposal."

"Excuse me, ma'am," Chuck said. "How exactly do we fit into all of this?"

"We need a win. A big one," the President said, rolling into the room. Jay, Garman, and Chuck stood, saluting. The President waved a hand. "Oh, knock that off."

"How can I help—" Chuck started to say, before Garman interrupted.

"How can we help, you mean."

The others nodded their agreement. Chuck looked at his friends and grinned.

"How can we help, sir?"

"Glad you asked, my boy. We need you to fulfill your father's mission: Destroy the Grand Coulee Dam."

Ariel gasped. Jasmine sat silently. Rickman whistled softly. Jay burped.

"That's a tall order, sir," Chuck said, after a moment.

"It is, son, and there's more. Shirley?"

"Each device requires three things," Shirley said. "A key and two separate codes. One code to access the keyhole, the other to arm the device. The renegade Windfist stole one."

"Any chance your boy knows what the codes are?" Jay asked, glancing over at Garman, who shrugged.

"Even if he doesn't, Ironhelm likely will," Shirley said. "That's why I need you to go get it. He's been spotted moving south and west, likely trying to get back to the so-called-Baron's stronghold. Intercept him, capture him if you can, kill him if you must. But above all else, we must recover those codes."

"What about the other one, ma'am?" Chuck asked.

"Right here." The President pulled a chain from under his shirt. A gold plastic card swung gently at the end of it. He held it out toward Garman. "Journeyman Garman, you have a new mission: Find the red codes, secure them, and escort Mr. Gordon to the Grand Coulee. Do you understand and accept this mission?"

Garman stood, eyes ahead, and saluted.

"I do, and accept, sir. Only death will stop me."

"This is a no-fail mission, son. Death is no excuse."

"I know how the Baron thinks," Jasmine put in before Garman could reply. "You'll have my help."

"That was where I came from," Chuck whipped his head around at Ariel's words. She met his eyes, soberly. "The Grand Coulee. It is the only remaining Great Nest."

"You're from there," the President said. "Interesting."

"It's true, sir," Ariel said. "In fact, I'm the only one that could get you in, really. Anyone who isn't familiar with the Hive would get lost and captured in a very short amount of time. No other members of my Family would do it. They'd rather die than betray the Queen. They would have let me die. You will have my assistance, as well."

"Pearl seems quite taken with Quetzalith," Rickman said, thoughtfully. "There's nothing for me in Pittsburgh, and I'll be damned if I'll let her get captured or killed there. I'm in."

"And my flask!" Jay stood, posing dramatically. He grinned at Shirley's groan. "Ain't had this much fun outside of Bangkok in forty years."

"Everyone is sure about this?" Chuck looked at each of his friends in turn. Each nodded. He faced the President.

"We're on it, sir."

"Excellent. Begin as soon as possible. The Bunker's stores are at your disposal. Please relax and enjoy the little hospitality I have left to offer while you prepare. The United States of America is grateful to you all."

"Our pleasure, Mr. President," Jay said. "And drinks are on the house, right?"

That startled a laugh out of the somber leader and Shirley simply shook her head as they turned for the door.

Once they left, Jay let out a gusty sigh.

"What's wrong, Jay?" Chuck asked.

"I didn't get a chance to ask Himself if he'd pardon my bar tab. Do you have any idea how expensive thirty years of interest can be?"

EPILOGUE

"KEELIE, MY DARLING GIRL," THE BARON CALLED OUT.

Keelie kept her head lowered but peeked up through her eyelashes at the group of men entering her chamber. As she'd been taught, she lowered herself into a curtsey and held it until she felt his hated hand stroke her hair.

"Your lessons in deportment are paying off, child," he said. She knew that tone in his voice—he was trying to sound kind. "You look like a proper young lady."

"Thank you, my lord," Keelie said, straightening. She folded her hands in front of her velvet skirt and waited, eyes still cast down.

"Poor girl, I am afraid it has been very lonely for you lately."

His voice carried an edge of steel. He must be thinking of Lady Moore, then. Keelie was both fiercely glad that the lady hadn't been captured yet and intensely disappointed that she hadn't found a way to come back to free her. Not that she'd ever promised such a thing...but still...

"As my lord says."

It was usually a safe answer. The Baron seemed to enjoy her docility. Lady Moore had been pert with him from time to time, she'd learned, but she didn't think he'd tolerate such cheek from someone he wished to raise as a daughter.

"Indeed. Well, never fear, my child. For I have brought you a gift," the Baron said, snapping his fingers toward the door. Two of his velvet-clad guardsmen brought in a young woman.

She was filthy, skirts torn and muddy, hair a scraggly mess

that hung down into her face. A dirty rag tied over her mouth functioned as a gag and her wrists were bound with a wire that cut into her bruised, dirty flesh.

The Baron pointed and the guards shoved the woman forward, onto her knees. One of them grabbed her roughly by the hair and pulled her head back, forcing her to look at Keelie. For just a second, there was a flash of defiance in the woman's eyes. Keelie blinked and it was gone, replaced by a blank, dead stare.

"Keelie, this is Ellie. Ellie, this is your new mistress, Lady Keelie," the Baron said. "Lady Keelie is my daughter and will be treated as such. You will be her companion and chaperone. Obey her implicitly. Make her happy, or I shall have you given back to my men."

Keelie felt a surge of horrified pity jolt through her as naked fear crossed the woman's face and the tremor that suddenly appeared in her bound hands.

"My darling, do be kind to Ellie. She has had a hard few weeks. But should she offer you any hurt, or displease you in any way, you are to tell one of your guards at once. They will be *most* eager to correct the situation."

Keelie felt all over again the burning hatred that she held for the man.

"Thank you, my lord," she said, careful to keep her voice steady and meek.

He leaned forward and dropped a kiss on her forehead.

"You are welcome, my dear. You are most welcome. We will leave you two to get acquainted. Do remember what I've said."

He gestured and the men began to file out of her tower room. The Baron blew her a kiss, and followed the men, closing the door behind himself.

Keelie kept the tremulous smile in place for a good thirty count, just in case he should come back. Ellie, too, didn't move, save for her quick, harsh breaths. When she was certain that they were alone, Keelie looked at the older woman.

"Would you like a bath?" she asked softly. Ellie glanced quickly at her, then nodded. Keelie tried to give her a smile but the older woman wouldn't meet her eyes.

"I'm lucky; my room has a steam boiler, so I always have hot water when I want it," Keelie said.

She walked over to the alcove that held her personal bathing tub and pulled the brass ring that opened the flow. Steam curled up from the cascade of water into the shiny copper tub, fogging the expensive mirror that sat on the shelf nearby. She tested the bathwater with her elbow, the way her mother used to do when she was little, and then reached for the little cake of lavender-scented soap she used.

"Here," she said, turning to hand the soap to the silent Ellie. The woman had followed Ellie into the bathing room but seemed disinclined to do anything else.

"It's not the softest lather but it will get you clean," Keelie said. Then, mindful of Lady Moore's warnings, she bit her lip and stroked her finger over the foggy mirror.

"I HATE HIM," she wrote.

She smiled and shoved the mirror into Ellie's hands. She watched the older woman's dark eyes pass over the letters, then look up sharply. For the first time since that first flash of spirit, Ellie's eyes looked like those of a living woman.

"So much," Keelie whispered, under the roar of the water into the tub. "He killed my mother and destroyed my father. He sent my big brother to the mines...I hate him and I want him to die."

"Me too," Ellie whispered back. Her raspy, broken voice seemed as rough as the rest of her. "He killed my parents, too. My brother...I don't know where he is."

Keelie nodded, then turned off the water before anyone could come investigate why she was running it so long.

"Into the tub with you, then," she said in her normal voice, taking the mirror back and wiping it clean. It immediately began to fog again from the cloud of steam in the room. "I'll give you some privacy."

"Th-thank you, my lady," Ellie said. She glanced toward the door and Keelie nodded. It wasn't safe to talk openly. She mouthed the word "later" and Ellie nodded back.

"You're most welcome, Ellie," Keelie said. She wrote another message on the hand mirror. "I'm so very glad you're here."

She turned the mirror so that Ellie could see the words.

HELP ME KILL HIM

"Yes!" Ellie breathed, with such ferocity that Keelie shot an alarmed look at the door. "That is...me too. My lady."

"Good," Keelie said and wiped the mirror one more time.

Her heart pounded in her chest but for the first time since Lady Moore had left, she felt a fierce hope. She didn't know how they would make it happen but between the two of them, the Baron's fate was all but sealed.

"It's getting cold in here," she called as she left the bathing alcove and pulled the curtain closed. "When you're clean, we can build up the fire together."

The End, For Now.

Chuck, Garman, Ariel, Jasmine and Jay
will return in *Smoke and the Water.*